Quick Reference Editing Shortcut Keystrokes

To:	Press:
Cut	Ctrl+X
Copy	Ctrl+C
Paste	Ctrl+V
Create a new document	Ctrl+N
Save	Ctrl+S
Print	Ctrl+P
Undo	Ctrl+Z
Select All	Ctrl+A
Edit the active cell	F2
Paste a cell name into a formula	F3
Change the reference type of a selected cell reference in a formula	F4
Complete an entry in the cell or formula bar	Enter
Cancel an entry in the cell or formula bar	Esc
Insert blank cells	Ctrl+Shift+plus (+)
Delete cells	Ctrl+minus (-)
Copy the value from the cell above the active cell	Ctrl+Shift+ " (quotation mark)
Alternate between displaying cell values and formulas	Ctrl+ ` (grave accent)
Display the AutoComplete list	Alt+↓
Copy an entry down	Ctrl+D
Copy an entry to the right	Ctrl+R
Start a new line in a text-wrapped cell	Alt+Enter
Repeat the last action	F4 or Ctrl+Y
Insert an AutoSum formula	Alt+ = (equals sign)
Enter the current date	Ctrl+ ; (semicolon)
Enter the current time	Ctrl+Shift+ : (colon)
Insert a hyperlink	Ctrl+K

Quick Reference Navigation

To Move:	Press:
Down one screen	Page Down
Up one screen	Page Up
One screen to the right	Alt+Page Down
One screen to the left	Alt+Page Up
Top to bottom within a selection	Enter
Bottom to top within a selection	Shift+Enter
Left to right within a selection	Tab
Right to left within a selection	Shift+Tab
To the end of a row or column of data	Ctrl+Arrow key
To the beginning of the row	Home
To the beginning of the worksheet	Ctrl+Home
To the lower-right corner of the worksheet	Ctrl+End
To the next sheet in the workbook	Ctrl+Page Down
To the previous sheet in the workbook	Ctrl+Page Up
Scroll to display the active cell	Ctrl+Backspace

Using
Microsoft®
Excel® 97
Third Edition

Julia Kelly

A Division of Macmillan Computer Publishing, USA
201 W. 103rd Street
Indianapolis, Indiana 46290

Contents at a Glance

Using Microsoft® Excel® 97, Third Edition

Library of Congress Catalog No.: 97-80901

ISBN: 0-7897-1571-6

01 00 99 98   6 5 4 3 2 1

Interpretation of the printing code: the rightmost double-digit number is the year of the book's printing; the rightmost single-digit number, the number of the book's printing. For example, a printing code of 98-1 shows that the first printing of the book occurred in 1998.

Composed in *Formata* and *Janson* by Que Corporation.

Credits

Executive Editor
Lisa Wagner

Acquisitions Editor
Jamie Milazzo

Development Editors
Robin Drake
Joyce Nielsen

Technical Editor
Kurt Hampe

Managing Editor
Thomas F. Hayes

Production Editor
Heather E. Butler

Copy Editors
Tom Stevens
Marilyn J. Stone

Indexer
Craig Small

Production Team
Michael Henry
Linda Knose
Tim Osborn
Staci Somers
Mark Walchle

Contents

About the Author

Julia Kelly, cybergirl in cowspace, ex-jet jockey, and former mad scientist, has also done time as a stable cleaner, hardware-store cashier/barrista, theme park candy girl, veterinary cat-holder, Caribbean pilot, and teacher of diverse topics.

She currently lives on her farm in north Idaho, where she writes books, teaches classes, builds databases, chops wood, and shovels snow.

Dedication

To God, who always answers my prayers, usually in the most unexpected ways.

And to all of my family and friends, for being there.

And to my dogs and horses, because they are hourly providers of joy and delight.

Acknowledgments

As with all computer books, this one was a team effort, and I want to thank all the team members who made the process smooth and successful. My terrific agent, Margot Maley at Waterside Productions, my delightful acquisitions editor, Jamie Milazzo, and technical editor Kurt Hampe were all wonderful to work with.

We'd Like to Hear from You!

Que Corporation has a long-standing reputation for high-quality books and products. To ensure your continued satisfaction, we also understand the importance of customer service and support.

Tech Support

If you need assistance with the information in this book or with a CD/disk accompanying the book, please access Macmillan Computer Publishing's online Knowledge Base at **http://www.superlibrary.com/general/support**.

Also be sure to visit Que's Web resource center for all the latest information, enhancements, errata, downloads, and more. It's located at **http://www.quecorp.com/**.

Orders, Catalogs, and Customer Service

To order other Que or Macmillan Computer Publishing books, catalogs, or products, please contact our Customer Service Department at **800/428-5331** or fax us at **800/882-8583** (International Fax: 317/228-4400). Or visit our online bookstore at **http://www.mcp.com/**.

Comments and Suggestions

We want you to let us know what you like or dislike most about this book or other Que products. Your comments will help us to continue publishing the best books available on computer topics in today's market.

Que Corporation
201 West 103rd Street, 4B
Indianapolis, Indiana 46290 USA
Fax: 317/581-4663

Please be sure to include the book's title and author as well as your name and phone or fax number. We will carefully review your comments and share them with the author. Please note that due to the high volume of mail we receive, we might not be able to reply to every message.

Thank you for choosing Que!

Introduction

So, you have Excel 97. Or perhaps your workplace is upgrading its computers and software and acquiring Office 97, and you're wondering how to make sense of the new software. Well, you've come to the right place; my goal with *Using Microsoft Excel 97, Third Edition* is to get you comfortable with Excel 97.

I'll be honest with you: I won't gush over Excel or Microsoft software or computers in general, or tell you I love them or that I think they're the greatest thing since sliced bread, because for me they're just tools. They're useful, multifunctional tools, and for many businesses they've become very important tools, but the sun doesn't rise and set according to a computer program. Most of us only need to know how to use our software tools efficiently, as an aid to our work, and then get back to our real jobs (which might be teaching, designing ad campaigns, training horses, selling real estate, running a department store, creating pottery, or whatever).

With that in mind, I'll teach you how to carry out various business tasks as easily and efficiently as possible; I'll show you which of Excel's features are most efficient for a given task, and when you'd want to use one technique instead of another.

All the Office 97 programs give you several ways to accomplish nearly everything (I can think of six ways to copy the contents of one cell to another), but I'm not going to inundate you with every possible way to do everything. Instead, I'll show you the most efficient ways to do things. I'll teach you how to use Excel as if I were sitting next to you at your computer (which is how I usually teach), and I won't bend your ear or waste your time with theory or extraneous details; I'll just show you how to do what you need to do.

The changes between Excel 97 and Excel 95 are not spectacular, and for most people there's no need to upgrade from Excel 95 to Excel 97; but if you've just bought a new computer, you'll have Excel 97 and its new goodies. Some of the new features are pretty cool, like hyperlinks, AutoReturn, and the new Chart object, but perhaps not essential enough to be worth upgrading. Other new features in Excel 97 are simply new ways to do old tasks. The new ways are supposed to be easier, but in some cases they're not; in those cases I'll teach you the old way and the new way, and let you decide which is easier. My aim is to make Excel 97 easy, comfortable, and efficient for you, and to that end I'll share my honest opinions with you throughout the book.

Why This Book?

Using Microsoft Excel 97, Third Edition is a fresh approach in a popular and long-lived series of computer books, designed to reflect the changing needs of today's computer users. This book's streamlined, conversational approach to painless productivity includes these features:

- **An Improved Index:** To help you find information the first time you look. If you're new to Excel, you can't be expected to know intuitively which words or feature names to look up; for example, if you wanted to find information about *built-in equations*, would you think to look up *functions*? So, in addition to the official Excel terms, the index contains all the other words and names that the Que team thought you might look up.

- **Real-life Solutions:** Throughout the book I've used real-life examples to demonstrate how to accomplish a task or solve a problem. My examples are drawn from my own work, my clients' problems, and my students' questions. I'll tell you when using a wizard is easier than doing something yourself, and when doing it yourself is faster and less confusing; and I'll tell you when the best way is a combination of the wizard's work and your own tweaking. And I'll tell you when I think something is silly (which I couldn't do if Microsoft was publishing this book).

- **Relevant Information Written Just for You:** This book is not a "doorstop" book (those encyclopedic tomes that tell you every esoteric detail about a software program). I've focused on the tasks that normal folks with real jobs need to do on a computer, and on the most efficient means of accomplishing those tasks.

  I realize that most folks will not use most of Excel, but everyone will use different parts of it; the one-size-fits-all approach to modern software design means that each one of you will find some, but not all, of this book's information useful. My goal is for each of you to find all the information you *do* need, without having to waste time on information you *don't* need.

- **A Reference Orientation:** Every task and procedure is self-contained, so if you need to learn a new task or just need a quick reminder about a task you haven't performed in several months, you can find the instructions you need quickly. General procedures are written out step by step, and illustrated with real-life examples for clarity. Cross-references point you to related information that you might need to look up.

- **A Wise Investment:** Pay the right price for the right book. I won't waste your bookshelf space or budget on redundant or irrelevant material or assume that you want or need to know everything there is to know about Excel. This book is the meat (or soyburger) without the parsley or the pickle slices or the fancy toothpicks.

- **Easy-to-Find Procedures:** Every step-by-step procedure in the book begins with a short title explaining exactly what the procedure does (no clever titles that make you guess what's in the procedure). This saves you time by making it easier to find the procedure you need right away.

- **Cross-Referencing to Additional Related Information:** I've tried to cross-reference all the topics and tasks related to each procedure. So, if you need to look up information that leads up to what you're working on, or if you want to build further on your skills, you have the references to quickly guide you to related information.

- **Sidenote Elements with Quick-Read Headlines:** Extra information and helpful tips are in the margins, with titles that help you locate a specific Sidenote that you read last month and want to find again quickly.

Who Should Use This Book

Anyone who uses Excel and needs to accomplish a specific task or solve a problem, or wants to learn a better technique for something he needs to do. Basically, anyone who

- Has basic Windows 95 skills but is new to Excel
- Uses Excel, but wants to become more proficient
- Uses Excel at work
- Uses Excel at home
- Needs to create special spreadsheet files, such as invoices or expenses lists
- Wants to learn more efficient ways to manage flat-file databases such as contact lists or mailing lists
- Wants to learn how to use Excel's mathematical capabilities more efficiently
- Wants to learn how to combine data in Excel files with other Office programs such as Word and Access

This book is *not* for you if you have never used a Windows-based computer program. This book is also not for you if your goal is to learn everything there is to know about Excel 97; in that case, I recommend you read *Special Edition Using Excel 97*.

How This Book Is Organized

Using Microsoft Excel 97, Third Edition has task-oriented, easy-to-navigate reference information presented in a logical progression from simple to complex tasks, with related tasks grouped together. It covers features of the program you use in your daily work, and examples are real-life, drawn from real client, student, and personal situations, questions, and problems. You can work through the book chapter by chapter if you're just learning Excel, or you can look up specific procedures when you need to perform a task quickly.

Using Microsoft Excel 97, Third Edition is divided into nine parts.

Part I: Workbook Basics

Stuff you absolutely must know to work in Excel includes how to start and quit Excel, how to find what you need in Excel's help files, and what all the gadgets and doo-dads in the Excel environment are. You'll find that information in this section, along with how to open, save, and close files, how to search for specific files, how to move around in a worksheet and in a workbook, and how to change the Excel windows to see data in different worksheets and in different workbooks at the same time. You'll also learn how to connect different files with hyperlinks to make them instantly, easily accessible.

Part II: Building Worksheets

Excel's *raison d'etre* is to hold data so you can calculate it and arrange it until it's meaningful. This section contains procedures for getting data into a worksheet, and then editing, rearranging, and calculating that data.

Part III: Formatting

Formatting is a worksheet frill—you don't *have to* format the data in a worksheet, but it's sure a lot easier to read and understand if you do. This section covers procedures for formatting the worksheet cells with colors, borders, and so forth, and for formatting the data you enter into those cells. You'll also find procedures for working with styles, which are packages of formatting characteristics that make formatting repeatedly or on a large scale much faster.

Part IV: Sorting, Filtering, and Summarizing Data

To make a sea of numbers meaningful to most readers, you'll need to organize it. Organization includes sorting lists into a useful order so you can find individual items quickly, filtering lists to hide data you're not interested in so you can focus attention on the specific data you *are* interested in, and summarizing detailed data so you can see the big picture.

Part V: Charts

Charts are an effective means of communicating an idea, because they present data visually and allow instantly understandable comparisons between quantities. This part presents basic procedures for creating charts, and then formatting charts to achieve a custom look. You'll also find procedures for using Microsoft Map to create geographical maps that display geographically related data.

Part VI: Printing

Everything in a worksheet is printable, and you have a lot of control over what your printed pages look like. Moreover, formatting printed pages is important if you want to create a professional, highly readable printed presentation. In this part you'll find procedures for controlling what gets printed and how it looks on the page.

Part VII: Sharing Data with Other Users and Other Applications

Sharing data might mean sharing a workbook with other users, *at the same time*, so that nobody has to wait their turn to open and use a workbook; it might also mean sharing data between programs, such as using a picture of an Excel chart in a Word report, or using Access to create a professional report from an Excel table. All these procedures are covered in this part.

Part VIII: Customizing and Automating

Here you'll learn how to make your Excel screen efficient for *you*, and how to create macros, your own personal bits of VBA programming, to make your repetitive work go faster. None of this is absolutely necessary to know, but all of it contributes to a more efficient work environment for you (and it's fun!).

Part IX: Creative Excel

This part is about being creative in Excel. You'll find real-life examples of inventive solutions to business problems, all of which combine different Excel features in original ways. I don't expect that many of you will need these specific sample projects, but I want to light a fire in your imagination so you can figure out imaginative, ingenious solutions to your own real-life business problems. You'll also find procedures for using Excel's graphical arts tools, which you can use to liven up your worksheets and charts while you vent your artistic inclinations.

Conventions Used in This Book

This book defines various conventions to make it easier to use.

- *Menu and dialog box commands and options.* You can easily find the onscreen menu and dialog box commands by looking for bold text like you see in this direction: Open the **File** menu and click **Save**.

- *Hotkeys for commands.* The underlined keys onscreen that activate commands and options are also underlined in the book as shown in the preceding example.

- *Graphical icons with the commands they execute.* Look for icons like this ⬚ in text and steps. These indicate buttons onscreen that you can click to accomplish the procedure.

- *Cross references.* If there's a related topic that is requisite to the section or steps you are reading, or a topic that builds further on what you are reading, you'll find the cross reference to it after the steps or at the end of the section like this:

SEE ALSO

➤ *To see how to format cells, see page 195.*

- *Glossary terms.* For all the terms that appear in the glossary, you'll find the first appearance of that term in the text in *italic*, followed by its definition.

Your screen might look slightly different from some of the examples in this book. This is due to various options during installation and because of hardware setup.

Workbook Basics

Starting, Quitting, and Getting Help

Starting and Quitting Excel

If you're a new Excel user, check out this chapter for details about starting, exiting, and getting onscreen help when you're using Excel.

Starting Excel is the same as starting any other program in Windows 95—you click the Start button and go looking for Excel in the Start button's nested menus. Perhaps a faster or more efficient way to start Excel, if you use Excel often, is to put a shortcut icon for Excel on your Windows 95 desktop; or, if the Office shortcut bar is installed, you might find a button for Excel there. The following three sections show you how to start Excel with these three handy methods.

Starting Excel from the Windows 95 Start Menu

Start Excel from the Start menu

1. Click the Windows 95 **Start** button.

2. Point to **Programs**.

3. Click **Microsoft Excel**.

Your copy of Excel might be stored with other Office programs in a Microsoft Office folder, in which case you need to point to **Microsoft Office** and then click **Microsoft Excel**.

When Excel starts, a new, blank *workbook* (an Excel file) opens.

Starting Excel from a Shortcut Icon

Follow this procedure to create a shortcut icon on your desktop.

Start Excel from a shortcut on the Windows 95 desktop

1. Minimize or resize any open program windows so that you can see the Windows 95 desktop.

2. Right-click the desktop.

3. On the shortcut menu, point to **New**, and click **Shortcut**.

   A new icon appears on the desktop, and the Create Shortcut dialog box appears (as shown in Figure 1.1).

Can't find the desktop?

If your desktop is currently cluttered with open windows, it might be hard to get to the desktop itself. Right-click the taskbar and then click **Minimize All Windows** to minimize all open programs at once.

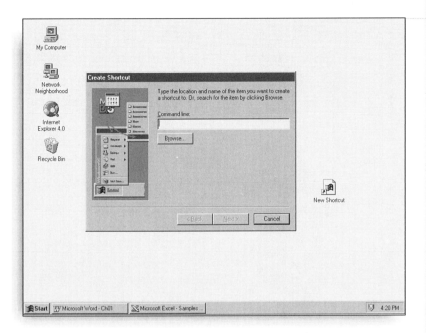

FIGURE 1.1

Browsing for the file is the easiest way to enter a path in the **Command line** box.

Where's the icon?

When you create a new shortcut on the desktop, the Create Shortcut dialog box may hide the New Shortcut icon. Drag the dialog box by its title bar to move it out of the way.

Your Windows 95 settings may differ

If you see the filename `Excel.exe`, it means Windows 95 is set up to display file **extensions**, which identify the **file type** (`.exe` identifies an executable file, which starts a program). If you find a file called Microsoft Excel (or Microsoft Excel.lnk) in your Microsoft Office folder, that's a shortcut to Excel, and you can create your desktop shortcut from that shortcut, if you like, rather than from the executable Excel icon in the Office folder. Either way, the result is the same.

Don't like the icon name?

Click the name twice (not a double-click), type a new name and press Enter.

4. In the dialog box, click the **Browse** button.

The Browse dialog box appears, and the **Files of type** box reads **Programs** (which means you only see folders and executable program files, like Excel, listed).

5. In the Browse dialog box, navigate to the folder that contains a file called Excel. This usually appears in the folder `C:\Program Files\Microsoft Office\Office`, but you may need to look elsewhere (in my computer, this file is in the Office folder, in the path `C:\MSOffice97\Office\Excel`).

6. Double-click the Excel filename (shown in Figure 1.2).

The entire path to the file appears in the Create Shortcut dialog box.

7. Click **Next**.

8. Rename the shortcut icon, if you want. (The name Excel is fine, but if your system is set up to show the file extension, `.exe`, you can delete the extension.)

9. Click **Finish**. A new shortcut icon, like the one in Figure 1.3, is created on your desktop.

FIGURE 1.2

Double-click the filename, or click it once and then click **Open**.

 Look for this icon

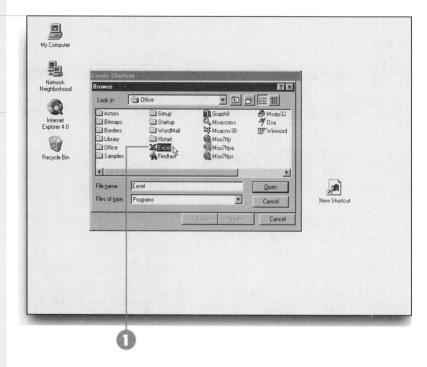

To start Excel, double-click the new icon.

FIGURE 1.3

Create a shortcut on your desktop to open Excel rapidly.

1 Double-click the shortcut icon to start Excel

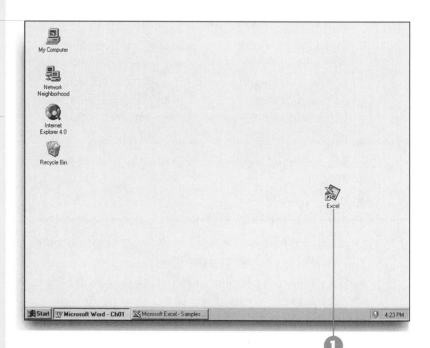

Starting Excel from the Office Shortcut Bar

Follow this procedure to start Excel from the Office shortcut bar.

Start Excel from the Office shortcut bar

1. If the Office shortcut bar is displayed, click the Excel button (shown in Figure 1.4).

2. If you don't see an Excel button:

   • Add one (see the sidenote).

   • Click the New Office Document button and then double-click the Blank Workbook icon (the icon shows the Excel logo over a worksheet).

Quitting Excel

When you've finished using Excel, you may want to exit the program to free up your system resources for other programs. Follow this procedure to *exit* (*quit*) Excel.

Exit Excel

1. Click the Close button in the upper-right corner of the Excel window (shown in Figure 1.5).

   Be sure you click the Close button in the Excel window, not the one in the workbook window.

2. If any open workbooks need saving before you close them, Excel asks you with a message box. Click **Yes** to save the workbook, or **No** if you don't want to save the changes.

FIGURE 1.4

If you don't have an Office shortcut bar on your desktop, you can reinstall Office 97 to install the shortcut bar, and then customize it to suit yourself.

1 Excel button

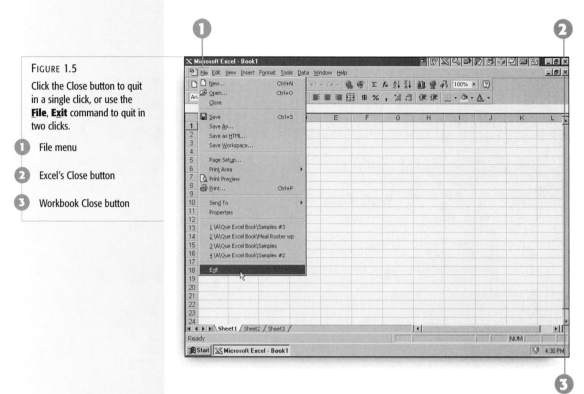

Click the Close button to quit in a single click, or use the **File**, **Exit** command to quit in two clicks.

① File menu

② Excel's Close button

③ Workbook Close button

Which is the button I want?

All those buttons are a bit mysterious until you get to know them, but if you place your mouse pointer over a button, after a moment, a **ScreenTip** (the name of the button—sometimes called a **ToolTip**) appears.

The Excel Environment

If you're new to Excel, you find a lot of unfamiliar terms and objects in the Excel landscape. Figure 1.6 shows many of the terms and objects I refer to in procedures throughout the book.

The two toolbars that appear when you first start Excel are the Standard and Formatting toolbars. You use these two toolbars more than any others.

FIGURE 1.6
Part names and terms in the Excel environment.

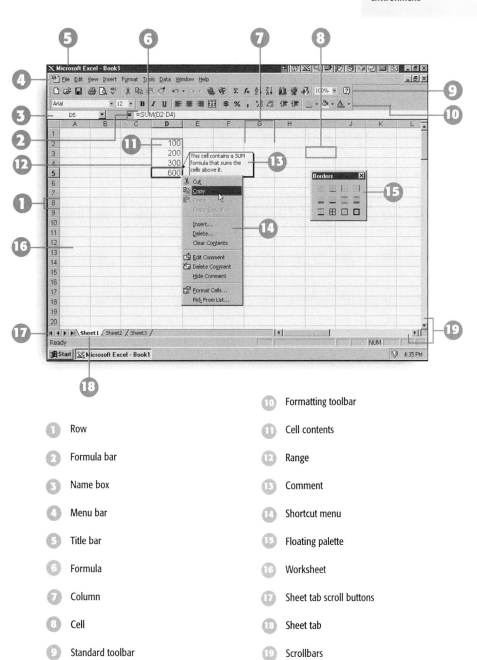

10	Formatting toolbar
1	Row
11	Cell contents
2	Formula bar
12	Range
3	Name box
13	Comment
4	Menu bar
14	Shortcut menu
5	Title bar
15	Floating palette
6	Formula
16	Worksheet
7	Column
17	Sheet tab scroll buttons
8	Cell
18	Sheet tab
9	Standard toolbar
19	Scrollbars

The following two tables help you sort out the buttons on these two toolbars, and in Chapter 26, "Customizing Your Excel Screen," you find procedures for customizing your toolbars to get rid of button clutter.

TABLE 1.1   **Standard toolbar buttons**

Button Face	Button Name	Function
	New	Opens a new workbook
	Open	Opens an existing workbook
	Save	Saves the active workbook
	Print	Prints the active worksheet
	Print Preview	Previews the printed page
	Spelling	Opens the spell-checker
	Cut	Cuts selected data for pasting
	Copy	Copies selected data for pasting
	Paste	Pastes cut or copied data
	Format Painter	Copies formatting from one area to another
	Undo	Undoes previous actions
	Redo	Reverses Undo actions
	Insert Hyperlink	Inserts a hyperlink
	Web Toolbar	Displays the Web toolbar
	AutoSum	Writes a SUM formula

Button Face	Button Name	Function
f_x	Paste Function	Opens the Function dialog boxes
	Sort Ascending	Sorts table in ascending order
	Sort Descending	Sorts table in descending order
	Chart Wizard	Starts the Chart Wizard
	Map	Creates a map based on the selected cells
	Drawing	Displays the Drawing toolbar
100%	Zoom	Changes worksheet magnification
	Office Assistant	Calls up the Office Assistant for help

TABLE 1.2   Formatting toolbar buttons

Button Face	Button Name	Function
Arial	Font	Displays list of available font typefaces
10	Font Size	Displays list of font sizes
B	Bold	Boldfaces selected data
I	Italic	Italicizes selected data
U	Underline	Underlines selected data
	Align Left	Aligns data to left in selected cells
	Center	Centers data in selected cells
	Align Right	Aligns data to right in selected cells

continues…

TABLE 1.2   **Continued**

Button Face	Button Name	Function
	Merge and Center	Combines adjacent cells into a single cell
	Currency Style	Formats numbers in Currency style
	Percent Style	Formats numbers in Percent style
	Comma Style	Formats numbers in Comma style
	Increase Decimal	Increases number of decimals displayed
	Decrease Decimal	Decreases number of decimals displayed
	Decrease Indent	Decreases indent (moves entry left)
	Increase Indent	Increases indent (moves entry right)
	Borders	Applies borders or displays a palette of border options
	Fill Color	Applies cell color or displays color palette
	Font Color	Applies font color or displays color palette

Getting Help

The best way to get help is to look it up in a good book (like this one); but if someone else is using the book, or you want the answer to an obscure question that's not covered in your book, you can look up a topic in Excel's help files.

Several ways to get onscreen help from Excel are

- Contents and Index: access to all Excel's help files
- Office Assistant: an animated helper
- What's This?: context-sensitive help in dialog boxes
- The ? button: context-sensitive help in dialog boxes

Using the Contents and Index

Contents and Index is the old Microsoft help workhorse. It's not context-sensitive like the other help features; instead, it's a general Table of Contents and Index to all Excel's help files.

Use the Contents and Index help files

1. On the **Help** menu, click **Contents and Index**.

The Help Topics dialog box appears, as shown in Figure 1.7.

2. Click the appropriate tab at the top of the dialog box for the way you want to search.

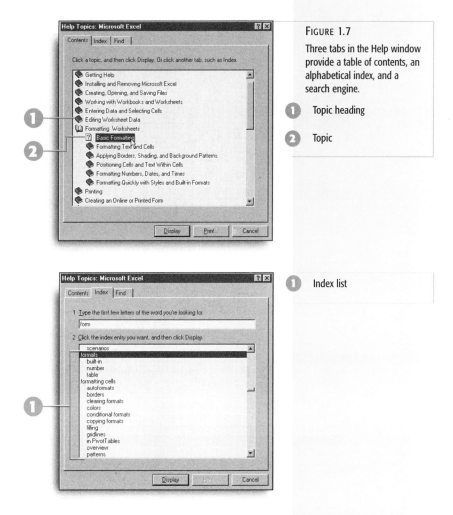

FIGURE 1.7

Three tabs in the Help window provide a table of contents, an alphabetical index, and a search engine.

1 Topic heading

2 Topic

1 Index list

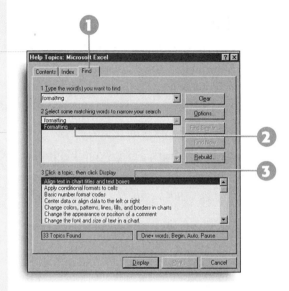

❶ Find

❷ Select

❸ Topic

- On the **Contents** tab, double-click topic headings until you locate a topic that might be useful; then double-click that topic to open the help file.

- On the **Index** tab, type a word that you'd look up in an index. The index scrolls to that point in the alphabetical list. Double-click a likely topic (if you see one).

- On the **Find** tab, in the box for step 1, type a search word. In the box for step 2, select various words and see whether one of them locates a list in the step 3 box that has a useful topic. Double-click the useful topic to read the help file (or select it and click **Display**, as indicated in the dialog box).

  The first time you try to use the **Find** tab, Excel needs a few moments to build its search index. Click the **Next** and **Finish** buttons, as appropriate, and then drum your fingers while Excel builds its word list. Next, give the **Find** tab a spin (I find it the most helpful source of help in Excel).

Some help files are more graphically helpful than others; for example, in the help file shown in Figure 1.8, you click topics to get more details about that topic.

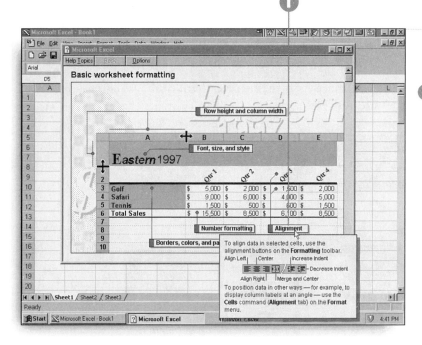

❶

FIGURE 1.8

A picture is worth a thousand words.

❶ Click here for details

Return to a Previous Help File

To return to a previous help file, click the **Back** button or the **Help Topics** button; you might or might not be returned to your previous help file, but it's worth a try.

Help on Top, or Not

The help files try to stay on top of your work, right in your way, but you can change that. In any help file:

Change the Help window's position

1. Click the **Options** button.
2. Point to **Keep Help on Top**.
3. Click **Not On Top**.

The help file stays open, but moves underneath the active file when you click your worksheet. To see the help file again, click its button on the taskbar.

Help bookmarks

You can bookmark a specific help file so that you don't have to search for it next time you need it. Right-click the help file screen and then click **Define Bookmarks**. Change the bookmark name if you want to, and then click **OK**. To find the bookmarked help file later, right-click any help file and click **Bookmarks**. Click the bookmark name, and click **OK**.

Using the Office Assistant

Some people love the Office Assistant, and some hate it. If you like it, I tell you how to use it; and if you hate it, I tell you how to get rid of it.

The Office Assistant has several evil twins, as shown in Figure 1.9.

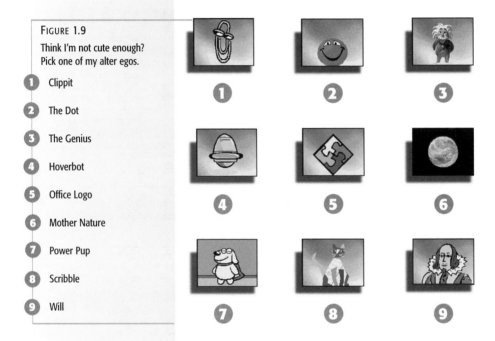

FIGURE 1.9

Think I'm not cute enough? Pick one of my alter egos.

1. Clippit

2. The Dot

3. The Genius

4. Hoverbot

5. Office Logo

6. Mother Nature

7. Power Pup

8. Scribble

9. Will

Get Help from the Office Assistant

Use the Office Assistant

1. On the Standard toolbar, click the Office Assistant button 📇.

The Office Assistant appears on your screen, as shown in Figure 1.10.

2. In the **Type your question here** text box, type a word, a phrase, or an entire question.

Keep it short

A few well-chosen words yield better results than complete sentences or questions.

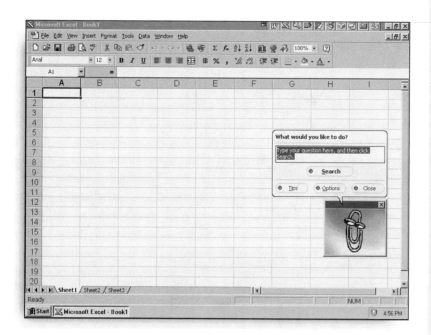

FIGURE 1.10
Ask me anything; I know everything.

3. Click **Search**.

The Office Assistant attempts to sort out what you really want to know and gives you a list of possible topics. (If it clearly doesn't understand what you're looking for, type a new word or phrase.)

4. Click an option button for a topic that looks useful.

After you've opened a help file, click the icons, buttons, or underlined words in the help file to open more related help files; eventually you may find what you need.

Change the Office Assistant's Behavior (a Bit)

If you click **Options** in the Office Assistant's initial dialog box, you can activate or deactivate other behaviors, such as making sounds, responding to the F1 key, and displaying keyboard shortcuts.

Get a New Office Assistant

Switch Office Assistants

1. Right-click the Office Assistant's title bar, and then click **Choose Assistant**.

2. On the Gallery tab (shown in Figure 1.11), scroll through the various assistants by clicking the **Next** and **Back** buttons.

FIGURE 1.11

Trade an old assistant for a new one on the Gallery tab.

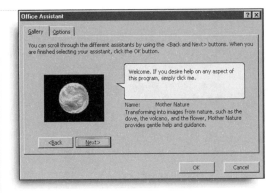

3. When you find an assistant you like, click **OK**.

Get Rid of the Office Assistant Temporarily

Hide the Office Assistant

1. Right-click the Office Assistant's title bar.

2. Click **Hide Assistant**.

You can recall the Assistant by clicking the Office Assistant button wherever you see it (it sometimes appears on dialog boxes).

You can also drag it out of your way by dragging its title bar.

Get Rid of the Office Assistant Permanently

To remove the Office Assistant completely, uninstall it with the Add/Remove Programs feature in the Windows 95 Control Panel.

Remove the Office Assistant from your computer

Are you sure you want the thing removed?

If you uninstall the Office Assistant, it disappears from all Office 97 programs.

1. Put your Office 97 CD-ROM in your computer's CD drive. (If your CD drive window opens, click its **Close** button to close it.)

2. Click **Start**, point to **Settings**, and then click **Control Panel**.

3. In the Control Panel window, double-click **Add/Remove Programs**.

4. Select **Microsoft Office 97** (or **Excel 97**, if you installed it separately) and then click **Add/Remove**. If instructed to insert the Office 97 CD, click **OK**. If Setup advises you to close open applications, do so and then click **OK**.

5. In the next dialog box, click **Add/Remove** again.

6. In the next dialog box, under **Options**, select **Office Tools** and click the **Change Option** button.

7. Clear the **Office Assistant** check box and click **OK**.

8. Click **Continue** (when asked if you're sure, click **Yes**).

9. The next dialog box indicates how many components you will be uninstalling. Press Enter. If asked about removing shared Windows components, click **Remove None**.

10. Click **OK** to acknowledge that the Setup procedure is complete.

11. Click **Cancel** to close the Add/Remove Programs/Properties dialog box.

To reinstall the Office Assistant, repeat these steps, but mark the check box in step 7.

Asking What's This?

What's This? help is context-sensitive help for those occasions when an item in a dialog box is a mystery.

What's This?

Get "What's This?" help in a dialog box

1. Click the small button with the question mark in the upper-right corner of the dialog box, next to the Close button (as shown in Figure 1.12).

2. Click the mysterious item.

   A quick answer appears (shown in Figure 1.13).

Don't see the What's This button?

Right-click the mysterious item, and click the **What's This** button that appears.

FIGURE 1.12

Most dialog boxes have a What's This? button.

1 Right-click

2 What's This?

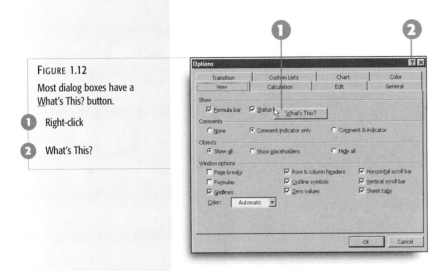

FIGURE 1.13

Quick solutions to the mysteries of dialog boxes.

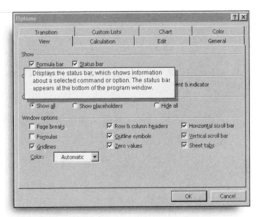

What's This Other Thing?

To inquire about items that aren't in dialog boxes, use the **What's This?** command on the **Help** menu. For example, toolbar buttons are sometimes mysterious, and the button names that show up in ScreenTips may not help; however, the **What's This?** command can explain what the button does. (It works on most parts of the Excel screen, not just toolbar buttons.)

Get What's This? help in the Excel window

1. On the **Help** menu, click **What's This?**

The mouse pointer becomes a question-mark pointer (shown in Figure 1.14.)

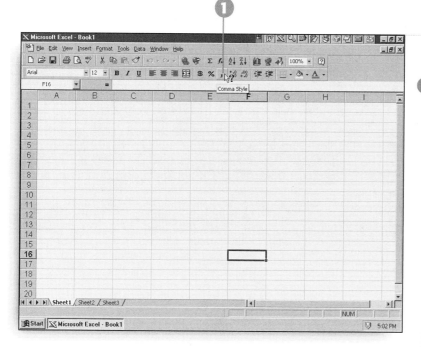

FIGURE 1.14

What does this button do?

1 Click a workbook item

2. Click the mysterious item.

An explanation of the item appears in a ScreenTip (see Figure 1.15).

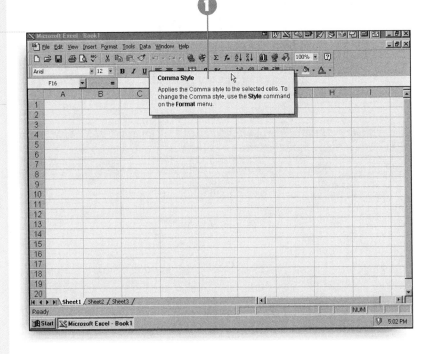

FIGURE 1.15

Oh, yeah, now I remember.

1 Get an explanation

Opening, Searching For, and Closing Files

Opening Files

More than one workbook

You can have as many workbooks open simultaneously as you like, until you run out of system resources. All workbooks that you open remain open until you close them.

This chapter is all about different techniques for opening, finding, and closing files.

Opening a single Excel workbook file is a common, straightforward procedure; but we look at other useful procedures and efficiency tricks that fall under the topic of opening files, such as opening several files at once, opening a non-Excel file in Excel, finding a file you've lost, and opening other files by clicking a hyperlink in your workbook.

You can open a new default workbook, a copy of a custom template, or an existing workbook in which you want to make changes.

Open a new, blank *default* workbook (the same as the workbook that opens when you start Excel)

1. On the Standard toolbar, click the New button 🗋.

A new, blank workbook opens, as shown in Figure 2.1.

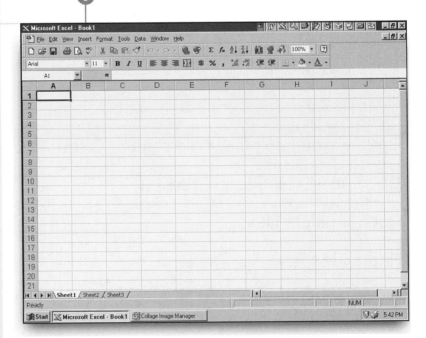

FIGURE 2.1

The New button opens a copy of Excel's default workbook template.

1 Unsaved workbook name

A *template* is like a printed pad of invoices or sales receipts: each copy is preprinted with standard labels and formatting, and you tear off copies. A template, like a stationery pad, saves you work because you don't have to re-create the same labels, formatting, and formulas over and over again; you just open a copy of the workbook template, and all the labels, formatting, and formulas are already in place.

Open a new workbook from a template

1. Open the **File** menu, and choose **New**.

The New dialog box appears (shown in Figure 2.2). In the New dialog box you find Excel's default workbook template, named Workbook, and any custom workbook templates that are saved in the Templates folder.

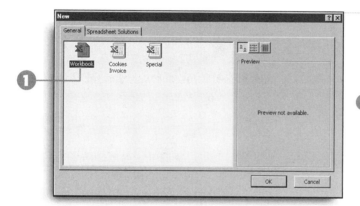

FIGURE 2.2

The **New** command on the **File** menu enables you to select from any custom templates in your Templates folder.

❶ Excel's default workbook

2. Double-click the icon for the workbook you want to open.

A copy of the template that you double-clicked opens.

SEE ALSO

➤ *To learn how to save a workbook as a template, see page 45.*

Open an existing workbook file (a file you saved previously)

1. On the Standard toolbar, click the Open button 🖻 .

The Open dialog box appears, as shown in Figure 2.3.

Recently used files

If the file you want is one of the last few Excel files you've opened, you'll probably find its name at the bottom of Excel's **File** menu (which saves time spent navigating to the folder where it's stored). Click **File**, and then click the name of the file.

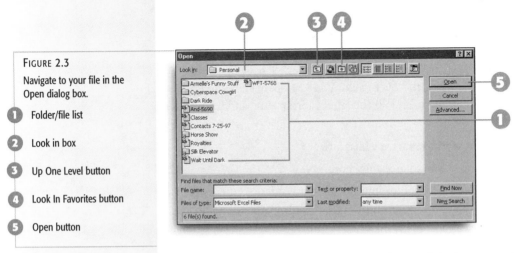

FIGURE 2.3

Navigate to your file in the
Open dialog box.

1 Folder/file list

2 Look in box

3 Up One Level button

4 Look In Favorites button

5 Open button

I'm tired of all this clicking

To make Excel's Open dialog box
always open to a specific folder (not
the default Personal or My
Documents folders), open the
Tools menu and choose **Options.**
In the Options dialog box, click the
General tab. In the **Default file
location** box, type the path to your
folder and click **OK**.

2. In the Open dialog box, use the **Look in** box to navigate to
the folder where your file is saved.

- Click the Up One Level button to navigate backward
through folders.

- Double-click folder names in the folder/file list to navigate forward through folders.

- Click the down-arrow button on the **Look in** box to
drop a file-tree list (shown in Figure 2.4); then you can
select a folder or hard drive several levels back up the
file tree.

- To navigate to a network drive, click the down-arrow
button on the **Look in** box to drop a file-tree list; then
click **Network Neighborhood** and navigate to the
drive and folder that you want.

FIGURE 2.4

Drop the **Look in** box list to
jump backward several levels.

1 Click here to go to the hard
drive level

3. When you see the filename you want in the folder/file list, click the filename, and then click **Open** (or just double-click the filename). The file opens, and the Open dialog box closes.

Start Excel and open a file at the same time

1. In the My Computer or Windows Explorer window, locate the folder where your file is stored (as shown in Figure 2.5). Excel files display an Excel icon, which makes the file easier to find.

2. Double-click the filename.

Excel starts, and your file opens in Excel.

Opening Non-Excel Files in Excel

Sometimes the data you need is not in an Excel file; it is saved in a file of a different type (for example, a text file, or a Lotus 1-2-3, Quattro Pro, Works, or dBASE file). You can open many of these file types in Excel—sometimes directly, and sometimes with the help of the Text Import Wizard.

Open a non-Excel file in Excel

1. On the Standard toolbar, click the Open button 📂.

The Open dialog box appears (shown in Figure 2.6).

2. In the Open dialog box, use the **Look in** box to navigate to the folder where your file is saved.

3. In the **Files of type** box, click the file type (if you know it) or click All Files to display all the files in the folder.

Take a shortcut to the file

To create a desktop shortcut icon that opens your file and starts Excel for you, use the right mouse button to drag the filename out of the My Computer or Windows Explorer window and drop it on the desktop, and then click **Create Shortcut(s) Here**.

FIGURE 2.5
Double-click the filename to open both the program and the file.

You can always find a way to get the data

If the data is in a file format for which you don't have an Excel converter, you get a message indicating that Excel can't read the file format. To get around that problem, have whomever sent the data save it as a text file and send that to you.

FIGURE 2.6

Select non-Excel file types from the list in the **Files of type** box.

1 Click here to show a list of other file types

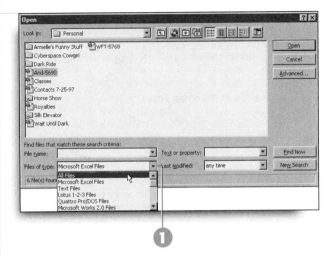

4. When you see the filename that you want listed in the dialog box, click the filename, and then click **Open**.

The file opens, and the Open dialog box closes.

If the Text Import Wizard starts, follow the procedure in Chapter 7, "Copying and Importing Data from Other Files," in the section "Importing a Text File," to bring the data into an Excel workbook.

SEE ALSO

➤ *To learn how to save files as a specific file format, see page 48.*

➤ *To learn how to import a text file, see page 113.*

Opening More Than One File at a Time

Often you may need to open several Excel files at the same time (for example, if you're copying data from one workbook to another, or comparing several workbooks to each other). Instead of opening the files one by one, you can save time and mouse clicks by opening them all at once.

Open multiple files at once

1. On the Standard toolbar, click the Open button .

2. Navigate to the folder where the files are located.

3. Click the first of the filenames you want to open.

4. For filenames that are located next to each other in the dialog box (*adjacent* filenames), press and hold down the Shift key and click the last file you want. All files between the first and last are selected.

For filenames that are *nonadjacent* (not next to each other), press and hold down the Ctrl key, and click to select each of the remaining filenames you want (see Figure 2.7).

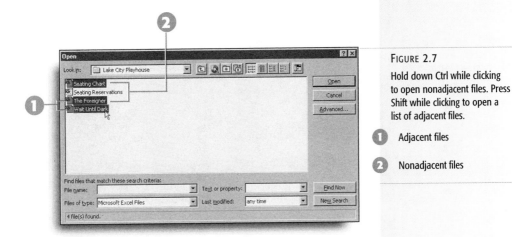

FIGURE 2.7

Hold down Ctrl while clicking to open nonadjacent files. Press Shift while clicking to open a list of adjacent files.

1 Adjacent files

2 Nonadjacent files

5. Click **Open**.

The Open dialog box closes, and all the files open.

Searching for a File

If you've forgotten where you saved a file or what you named it, you can search for it. When you've located a number of likely possibilities (for example, several invoices you sent last week), you can quick-view each file's contents to locate the one you want rapidly.

Finding a File by Searching for File Properties

If you've saved a file with specific file properties such as author name or keywords (which are explained later), you can search for those properties to find the file—even when you can't remember the filename or the folder where you saved it. Although you can try searching for a file using just the boxes in the Open dialog box, you won't often find what you're looking for, and you don't have much control over the search. You make a better search when you use the Advanced Find dialog box.

Search for a file with isolated details

1. On the Standard toolbar, click the Open button.

   The Open dialog box appears (shown in Figure 2.8).

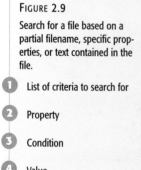

FIGURE 2.8

Search for files that have specific properties.

1 Advanced button

2. In the Open dialog box, click the **Advanced** button.

   The Advanced Find dialog box appears (shown in Figure 2.9).

FIGURE 2.9

Search for a file based on a partial filename, specific properties, or text contained in the file.

1 List of criteria to search for

2 Property

3 Condition

4 Value

5 Where to search

6 Start searching

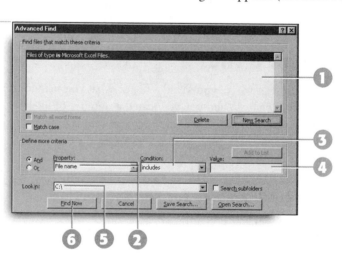

3. In the Advanced Find dialog box, click the down-arrow button in the **Property** box, and click a property for which you want to search (such as **Author**, **File names**, **Text**, or **Keywords**).

The **Text** property is any word or phrase contained anywhere in the file, such as a worksheet label or the word total. **Keywords** are properties you can set when you save a file.

4. In the **Condition** box, click the down arrow and click a phrase that describes what you're looking for.

For example, the **Keywords** condition **includes words** narrows the search to specific keywords that you saved. The **File names** condition **begins with** narrows the search to file names that have specific starting characters such as inv or cr.

5. In the **Value** box, type the words, characters, or dates for which to search the **Property** and **Condition**.

6. Click the **Add to List** button.

The criteria are added to the **Find files that match these criteria** list.

7. In the **Look in** box, set the path to the area that you want to search, and click the **Search subfolders** check box to search all subfolders in the path you set. (For example, to search every folder on your hard drive—which could take awhile—set the path to **C:** and check the **Search subfolders** check box.)

8. Check to see that the **Find files that match these criteria** list contains all your criteria and nothing extra that might unnecessarily limit your search (such as extra criteria that you didn't mean to set).

9. Click **Find Now** to start the search.

Be patient while Excel searches. If you start the search from your hard drive, the search can take a few seconds or longer.

Excel searches all folders in the path that you set and eventually returns a list of folders matching your criteria.

Reuse your searches

If you want to use the same search in the future, save the search. Click the **Advanced** button, and then click the **Save Search** button. Name the search and click **OK**. In the future you can open the Advanced Find dialog box, click the **Open Search** button, select your saved search, and click **Find Now** to run it.

Figure 2.10 shows the results of a search of my hard drive for Excel files I saved with the keyword *invoice*.

FIGURE 2.10

The results of a search include the path to each found file.

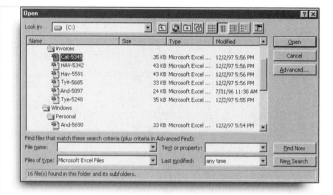

SEE ALSO

➤ *To learn how to save files with specific properties, see page 47.*

Locating the File You Want with Quick View

Quick View displays the contents of a file without opening the file, which can save you considerable time if you've just searched for files and you're not sure which of several files is the one you want.

Check the contents of files without opening them

1. On the Standard toolbar, click the Open button 🗁.

2. Conduct the search, or navigate to the folder where the files in question are stored.

3. Right-click a filename.

4. Click **Quick View**.

   A Quick View window opens displaying the contents of the first worksheet in the workbook (shown in Figure 2.11). You can't edit a workbook in the Quick View window, but you can open the file by clicking its **Open File for Editing** button.

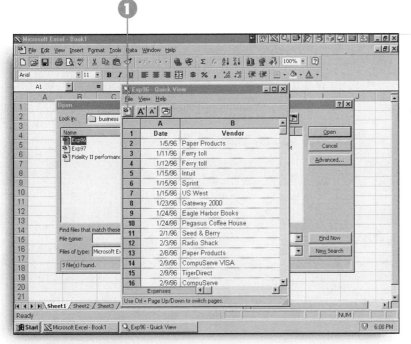

FIGURE 2.11
Use Quick View to check a file's contents without opening the file.

1 Click to open the file

Using Hyperlinks

One new thing of real value in Excel 97 is the capability to create *hyperlinks* to other files on your computer or network. Hyperlinks to other files work just like hyperlinks in Internet Web pages, but they open other files in your computer or network instead of Web sites on the Internet.

You're not limited to Excel files; for example, you can use a hyperlink in a worksheet to open background information that's in a Word document or open a splashy, motivational PowerPoint slide.

Connecting Files with a Hyperlink

You can create a hyperlink to another file on your computer and then use the hyperlink to open the hyperlinked document.

Add a hyperlink to a file

1. Click the cell where you want to place the hyperlink.

2. On the Standard toolbar, click the Insert Hyperlink button 🔲.

If Excel asks you to save your workbook, click **Yes**. The Insert Hyperlink dialog box appears (shown in Figure 2.12).

FIGURE 2.12

Using the Insert Hyperlink dialog box is the easy way to create a hyperlink to another file.

1 Click here to browse to the hyperlinked file

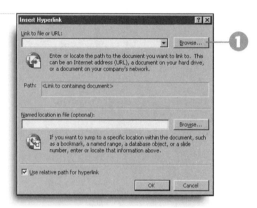

3. Click the **Browse** button next to the **Link to file or URL** box.

The Link to File dialog box appears.

4. In the Link to File dialog box, navigate to the file to which you want to hyperlink.

5. Click the filename, and then click **OK**.

The path to the hyperlinked file appears in the **Link to file or URL** box.

6. In the Insert Hyperlink dialog box, click **OK**.

The name of the hyperlinked file appears as a blue, under-lined hyperlink in the worksheet cell, as shown in Figure 2.13. (This is a hyperlink to a Word document on my hard drive. When I click it, Word opens, and the document opens in Word.)

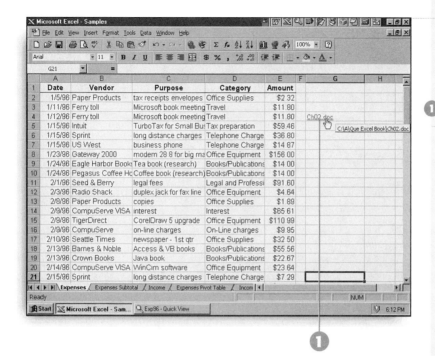

FIGURE 2.13

You can click the hyperlink to open the hyperlinked file without opening another program or searching for the file.

1 Hyperlink

Opening Files Using Hyperlinks

Using hyperlinks to open files enables you to open other files much more quickly. To open a hyperlinked file, click the hyperlink. After you've used the hyperlink to open the linked file, the hyperlink turns purple to indicate that you've used it.

Closing Workbook Files

When you're finished using a workbook but you want to continue working in Excel, close the open workbook to save system resources. You can close workbooks in a couple of ways.

To close a single workbook, use one of these techniques:

- Click the workbook window's Close button (in the upper-right corner of the workbook window, as shown in Figure 2.14)

- Open the **File** menu and choose **Close**.

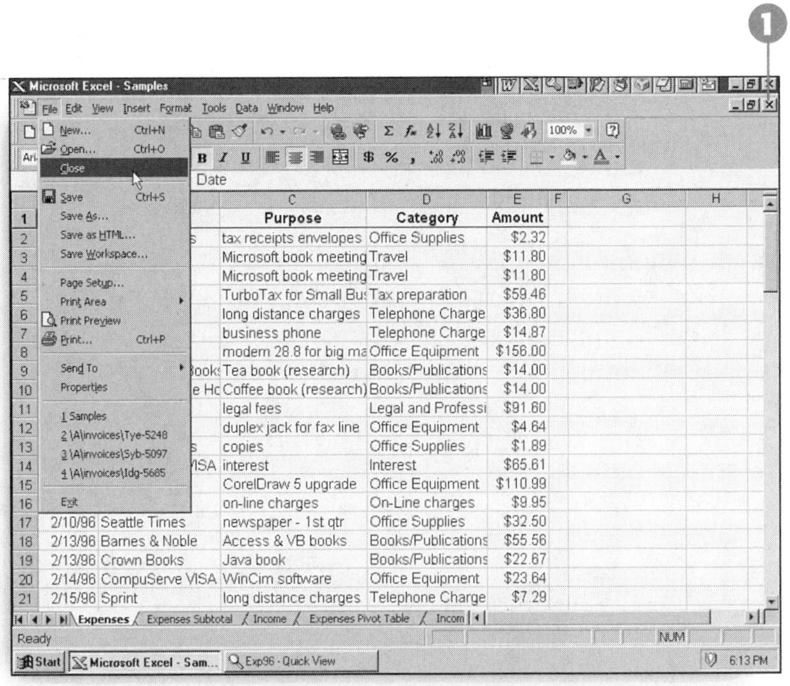

FIGURE 2.14

You can close a workbook with a single click, two clicks, or the keyboard (on the keyboard, press Alt+F and then C).

① Close button

Close all open workbooks with a single command

1. Press Shift as you click the **File** menu.

   When you press Shift, the **Close** command changes to a **Close All** command.

2. Click **Close All**.

   All open, saved workbooks are closed. You are asked whether you want to save any unsaved workbooks, and then they're closed, too.

Saving Files and Using Templates

Saving Files as Workbooks

This chapter is all about the many different and useful ways you can save Excel files. Saving an Excel 97 file can be as simple as clicking the Save button on the Standard toolbar; however, as with everything else in Excel, you can choose from many other useful and efficient ways to save your files. For example, you can save a file as an Excel 95 workbook so that someone who's using Excel 95 can open it, or you can save it as a text file so that you can send the unformatted data to someone working in an incompatible program.

Saving a File

When you save a file for the first time (first time for the file, not the first time for you), you give the file a name and indicate to Excel where to store the file. After the file has been saved initially, one click of the Save button on the Standard toolbar saves any changes you make.

Save a new file

1. On the Standard toolbar, click the Save button 🔲.

The Save As dialog box appears (shown in Figure 3.1).

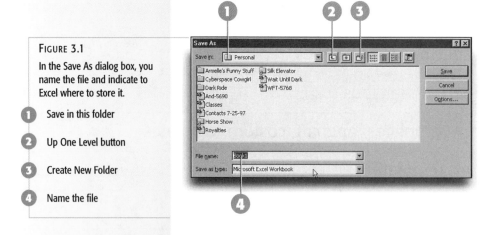

FIGURE 3.1

In the Save As dialog box, you name the file and indicate to Excel where to store it.

1 Save in this folder

2 Up One Level button

3 Create New Folder

4 Name the file

2. In the **Save in** box, navigate to the folder where you want to store the file.

3. In the **File name** box, select the default filename (to highlight it) and type your own filename.

4. Click **Save**.

The file is named and saved in your designated folder, and the Save As dialog box disappears.

Saving File Properties

Searching for a file that you can't find is easier if you've saved it with specific file properties, such as category, subject, or keywords. For example, if you save all invoices with the keyword *invoice*, you can find all your invoices, no matter where you saved them, when you search for the keyword.

SEE ALSO

➤ *To learn how to search for files with specific properties, see page 37.*

To give a file specific properties

1. Open the file in which you want to save file properties.

2. Open the **File** menu and choose **Properties**.

The File Properties dialog box appears (shown in Figure 3.2.)

3. On the Summary tab, enter any file properties that might be useful in a later search.

Author and **Company name** are usually filled in automatically with information that you provide when you install Excel; however, you can change them (for example, if your accountant sent a file for you to use).

4. Click **OK**.

Can't I go straight to my own folder?

To make Excel's Save dialog box always open to a specific folder (not the default Personal or My Documents folders), open the **Tools** menu and choose **Options**. In the Options dialog box, click the **General** tab. In the **Default file location** box, type the path to your folder and click **OK**.

Save effort with templates

File properties saved in a workbook template are included in all copies of the template.

Use multiple keywords

If you save a file with more than one keyword, you can use any of those keywords to find the file in a search, so save a file with all the keywords you might think of years from now, when you can't remember much about the file any more.

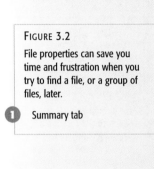

FIGURE 3.2

File properties can save you time and frustration when you try to find a file, or a group of files, later.

1 Summary tab

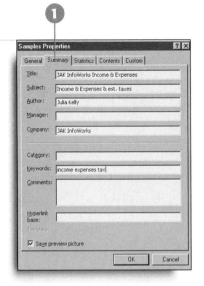

Everyone gets what they want

Some features in Excel 97 aren't supported in other file types or in earlier Excel versions; if you save a file as a different type, you lose those features. If you don't want to mess with your Excel file, but need to send it to someone as a different file type, save the file with a new name as well as a different file type.

Saving a File in a Different Format

If you need to send a file to a colleague who doesn't have Excel 97, you can save the file in a format they do have (such as an earlier version of Excel, or as a Works, Quattro Pro, or dBASE file). You can also save a workbook as a text file, which can be opened by virtually any program, including DOS programs; and text files are much smaller than formatted files, so they move through the email system faster.

Save a file as a different file type

1. Open the **File** menu and choose **Save As**.

2. Click the down-arrow button in the **Save as type** box, and click the file type you want (see Figure 3.3).

3. Click **Save**.

4. You probably see a message box indicating that some formatting or features in your workbook will be lost because the file type you're saving to doesn't support certain Excel 97 features. Because you can do nothing except be aware of it, click **OK**.

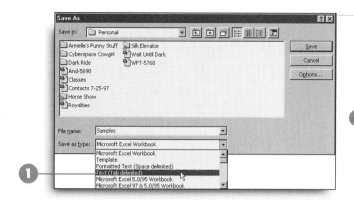

When you close the file, you get another message box about
losing changes—it's your last chance to think about what
you're doing before you lose features in your workbook.

Save an Identical Copy of a Workbook

Sometimes you may want to create an identical copy of a workbook so that you can make changes to the workbook without
affecting the original file.

Save a copy of the workbook

1. Open the **File** menu and choose **Save As**.

2. Give the workbook a new name, and click **Save**.

    An identical copy of the workbook, with a different name, is
    saved in the same folder as the original file.

Copy a workbook without opening the workbook or Excel

1. Open a My Computer window and navigate to the folder
    where the file is stored.

2. Right-click the filename, and click **Copy**.

3. To paste the copy, right-click a blank spot in the window
    and click **Paste**.

4. Click the new filename to highlight it (see Figure 3.4), type
    a new name, and press Enter.

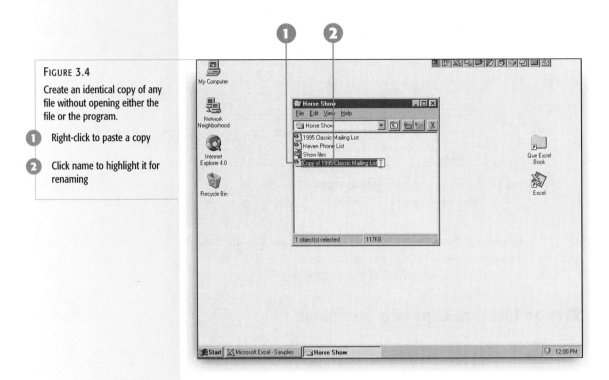

FIGURE 3.4

Create an identical copy of any file without opening either the file or the program.

1 Right-click to paste a copy

2 Click name to highlight it for renaming

Creating and Using Templates

A *template* is like a pad of preprinted paper: every time you open a copy of the template, it's like tearing off a new sheet of paper from the pad. You can save a lot of time by using templates, and you can either use templates that Microsoft has built for you or build your own (which is probably a lot more useful).

Templates are an efficiency tool. If you repeatedly set up workbooks with identical formatting, labels, formulas, and so forth, you can save a lot of work by setting up the workbook one time and saving it as a template. When you open a copy of that template, all your formatting, formulas, labels, and such are already in place.

Save a workbook as a template

1. Set up your workbook the way you want new copies to be set up.

You can include text, numbers, cell names, formulas, formatting, file properties, worksheet names, number of worksheets, hyperlinks, print areas, worksheet headers and footers—anything you want to have in place when you open a new copy of the workbook.

2. Open the **File** menu and choose **Save As**.

   The Save As dialog box appears.

3. In the **Save As Type** box, click **Template** (see Figure 3.5).

   The folder in the **Save in** box changes to show your computer's Templates location. Later, when you open the **File** menu and choose **New** to open a copy of the template, Excel automatically looks for it in the Templates folder.

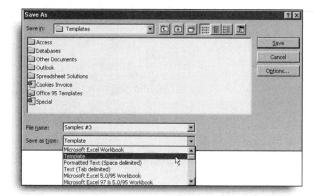

4. Give the template a filename.

5. Click **Save**.

   The template is saved in the Templates folder.

Opening a Copy of a Custom Template

Assuming that you had Excel save your template in the Templates folder, after you've created a custom template, you've saved yourself a lot of time.

Use the default Templates folder to save time

You can save the template elsewhere, but Excel won't remember where to look for it.

FIGURE 3.5

Select Template in the **Save As Type** box.

Replace Excel's default workbook with yours

To make a custom template replace Excel's default template (so that all new workbooks will be based on your custom template), give the template the name **Book.xlt** and save it in the XLStart folder (usually in `C:\Program Files\ Microsoft Office\ Office\XLStart`, or you can search for the XLStart folder).

To return to Excel's default workbook template, delete the Book.xlt template you created, or rename it and move it to the Templates folder. When you delete your Book.xlt template, Excel reverts to its built-in default template.

Fast template setup

A quick way to set up a template for a workbook that you use a lot is to copy an existing workbook that contains all the formatting and formulas you want in your template, instead of setting up a fresh copy of the workbook to create the template. In the copy, remove all the existing client-specific data and save the workbook as your template. (Even if the workbook formatting isn't exactly what you want, this method is faster than starting from scratch.)

FIGURE 3.6

The icon named Workbook is the default Excel workbook; custom workbook templates are displayed with the names you gave them.

You can't get there from here

The New button on the Standard toolbar won't take you to the Templates folder; you must use the menu command instead.

Open a custom template by default

Do you want Excel to open a copy of your custom template when you start Excel, instead of the default workbook template? Name your custom template Book.xlt and place it in Excel's XLStart folder. When you place a custom Book.xlt template in the XLStart folder, not only does your custom template open when you start Excel; it also opens every time you click the New button on the Standard toolbar.

Open a copy of a custom template

1. Open the **File** menu and choose **New**.

After you've saved a custom template, the **New** command on the **File** menu opens the New dialog box (shown in Figure 3.6.)

2. Double-click the icon for the template you want to open.

A new copy of your custom template opens. It's temporarily named with your template name and a copy number—you need to give it a new filename when you save it (see Figure 3.7).

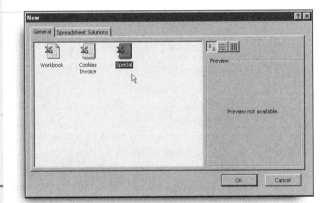

Editing a Template

Often a custom template needs to be tweaked—perhaps you need to add another column to a table, rewrite a formula, or change a few borders. To make these changes, you can open and edit the template itself.

Open and edit a template

1. On the Standard toolbar, click the Open button 📂.

2. Navigate to your Templates folder.

3. Double-click the name of the template you want to edit (see Figure 3.8).

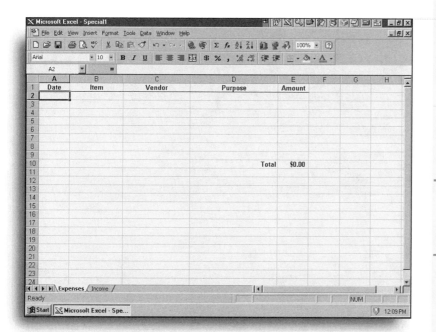

FIGURE 3.7

The title bar shows the template name and copy number until you save the new workbook with a new name.

No such folder?

If you can't find the Templates folder, try searching for the file name `*.xlt`.

What kind of file am I?

To find out what kind of file you have open in Excel, choose **File**, **Save As**. The type of file is displayed in the **Save as type** box.

The template opens, and if your system is set to show filename extensions, the title bar shows the name of the template with the extension `.xlt` appended. If your system is set to hide extensions, you see the filename without a number, as shown in Figure 3.9.

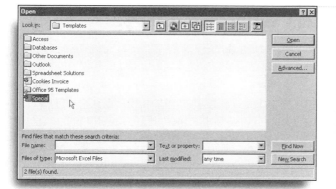

FIGURE 3.8

Opening a template in this way opens the template itself, rather than a copy of the workbook.

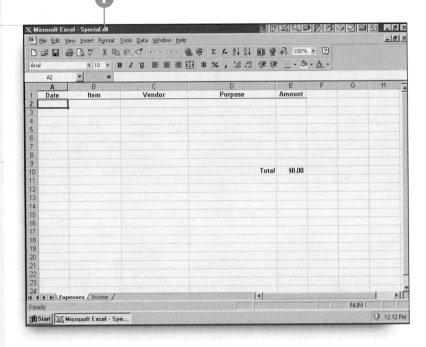

FIGURE 3.9

If the title bar shows the extension .xlt, you know you have the template open (but the title bar won't show the extension if your system is set to hide file extensions).

  Filename extension

4. Make the changes you want.

5. On the Standard toolbar, click the Save button 🖫.

6. Close the template.

Using Excel's Built-in Templates

How to get even more templates

You can find more Spreadsheet Solutions templates at the Microsoft Web site http://www.microsoft.com. The quickest way to get there is to open the **Help** menu, choose **Microsoft on the Web**, and click **Free Stuff**.

Excel comes with a few built-in templates, called *Spreadsheet Solutions templates*, that you might (or might not) find useful: Invoice, Purchase Order, and Expense Statement are included in a typical installation of Excel. These templates contain macros that automate the process of filling in data.

SEE ALSO
➤ *To learn more about templates, see page 45.*

Customize a Spreadsheet Solutions template

1. Open the **File** menu and choose **New**.

2. In the New dialog box (shown in Figure 3.10), click the **Spreadsheet Solutions** tab.

3. Double-click the icon for the workbook you want to open.

FIGURE 3.10

The Spreadsheet Solutions tab appears if you've installed any of the Spreadsheet Solutions templates.

A message warning you about viruses appears any time you open a file that contains macros, because some annoying viruses travel around in the form of Excel and Word macros. Excel doesn't know if a macro has a virus or not, so it warns you about every macro.

Because the Spreadsheet Solutions templates rely on macros for automation, click the **Enable Macros** button to open a fully functional workbook. If you don't want to be warned about macros in the future, clear the **Always ask before opening workbooks with macros** check box first.

4. Click the **Customize** button (see Figure 3.11).

The customizing worksheet appears (see Figure 3.12).

FIGURE 3.11

I'm going to customize an invoice template.

1. Customize button

2. Customize worksheet

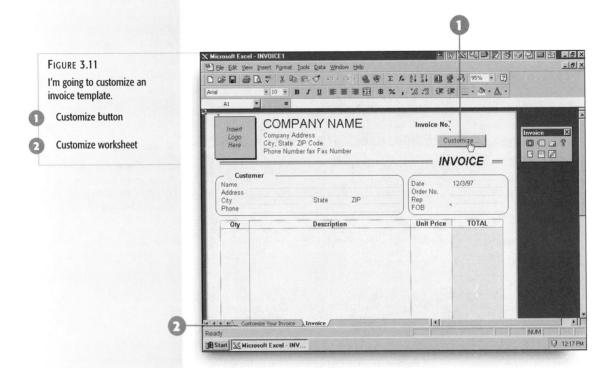

FIGURE 3.12

Data you fill in here appears on all copies of the template.

1. Lock/Save Sheet

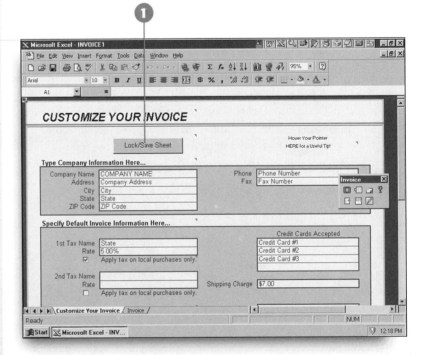

5. Fill in any company and other standard information that you want to appear in all copies of the workbook and then scroll to the bottom of the Customize worksheet to import a logo or format fonts.

6. Click the **Lock/Save Sheet** button.

7. In the Lock/Save Sheet dialog box, leave the **Lock and save Template** option selected, and click **OK**.

8. In the Save Template dialog box, give the template a name, and click **<u>S</u>ave**.

   Your Spreadsheet Solutions template is saved, and a copy of the workbook opens.

9. You may see a message indicating where your template is saved; if so, read the message and then click **OK**.

The workbook and its worksheet(s) work just like any other workbook/worksheet, the only difference is that they are preformatted and contain some macros for automation.

When you open a Spreadsheet Solutions workbook, a special toolbar for the template/workbook appears. Like all other toolbars, if you point to a button, the name of the button appears in a ScreenTip. But unlike other toolbar buttons, if you open the **Help** menu and choose **What's <u>T</u>his?** to find out what the button does, you get nothing useful or even correct. Table 3.1 explains what each button in the Invoice toolbar does, and the other Spreadsheet Solutions toolbars are similar.

Need to make more changes?

If you want to make further changes to either the workbook or the template, click the **Customize** button again, click the **Unlock This Sheet** button, click **OK**, and repeat steps 5 through 8. If not, your Spreadsheet Solutions workbook is ready to use.

TABLE 3.1 **Spreadsheet Solutions toolbar buttons**

Icon	This Button	Does This
	Size to Screen/Return to Size	Zooms the page magnification out so that you can see the whole page, and zooms it in again to 100%
	Hide Comments/Display Comments	Hides and shows the small red comment indicators
	New Comment	Adds a new comment to the selected cell (you can also add a comment in the normal way)

continues...

TABLE 3.1 **Continued**

Icon	This Button	Does This
	Template Help	Opens a help file for the specific Spreadsheet Solutions template
	Display Example/Remove Example	Enters sample data in the worksheet so that you can see what goes where, and removes the sample data
	Assign a Number	Assigns a nonrepeating, consecutive number to each worksheet you create from the template (you find the number in a cell labeled something like "Invoice Number")
	Capture Data in a Database	Saves the total from the worksheet in another workbook that's created to collect the totals from all worksheets based on the template

You can also

- Change the worksheet fonts
- Change worksheet shading
- Change or delete drawing objects (like the rounded boxes around the customer information)
- Fill in or delete the Fine Print and Farewell Statement at the bottom

SEE ALSO
➤ *For more on using the What's This? feature, see page 27.*

Saving a Worksheet as a Web (HTML) Page

If you want to post a worksheet as a Web page, you can save it as an HTML file that a Webmaster can include in a Web site.

Save worksheet data as a Web page

1. Click any cell within the table that you want to convert to a Web page (Excel includes the entire table in the Web page).

   Or, select the worksheet range you want to include in the Web page (as shown in Figure 3.13), and Excel includes only the range you select.

Watch those empty columns

If you want to include an empty column (as in this example), be sure you type a column heading so that the column has some width; otherwise, the column in the Web page is about 3 mm wide.

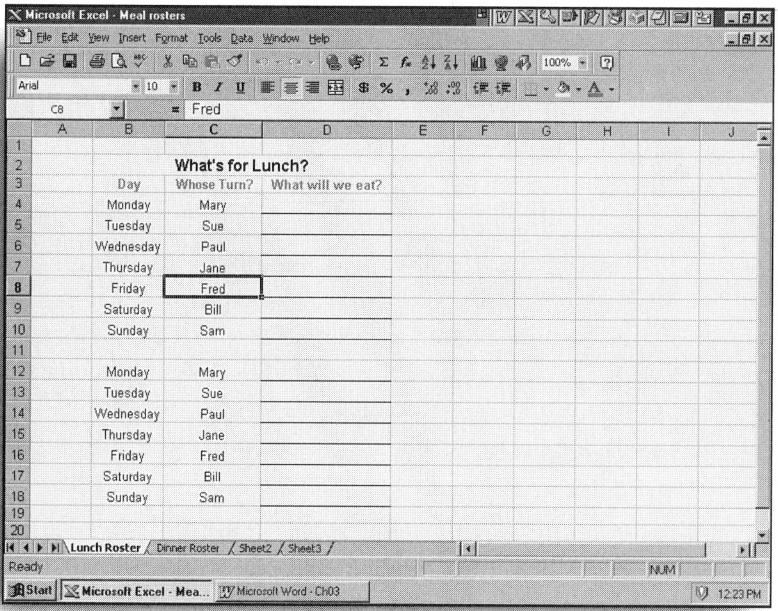

FIGURE 3.13

I'm posting a simple roster to the company intranet web, with instructions to print the page, fill it out, and return it via company mail.

2. On the **File** menu, click **Save as HTML**.

   The Internet Assistant Wizard starts (shown in Figure 3.14).

3. In the first wizard step, check the selected range.

   If the selected range isn't right, or you want to add another range, click the **Add** button; in the dialog box that appears, drag a different or additional range on the worksheet, and then click **OK**.

If you don't have an option to save as HTML

If the **Save As HTML** command doesn't appear on the **File** menu, you need to install the Internet Assistant add-in program. Open the **Tools** menu, choose **Add-Ins**, and then click the **Internet Assistant Wizard** check box. Click **OK** and wait a few moments while the Wizard is installed. If you cannot install the Wizard from the Add-Ins dialog box, you need to reinstall Excel's add-ins from your software CD-ROM.

FIGURE 3.14

Let the Internet Assistant Wizard turn your worksheet data into a Web page.

1 Change or add a range

2 Move a range up or down

3 Delete a range from the Web page

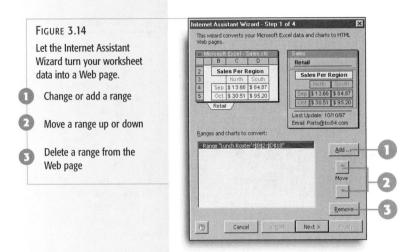

Adding on to an existing Web page

If you decide to add the selected worksheet range to an existing Web page, a different wizard step 3 appears. You must open your existing Web page and insert the characters <!--##Table##--> below the existing table so that the wizard knows where to put the new table. Placing the new data in the same workbook as the existing Web page data is a lot easier because the wizard adds the new table to the existing Web page, and you don't have to mess with HTML codes.

If you have two or more ranges selected but you want to rearrange their order on the Web page (that is, move a range from the bottom of the Web page to the top), click the range that you want to move in the **Ranges and charts to convert** box, and then click one of the **Move** buttons to reposition the range in the list.

4. Click **Next**.

5. In the second wizard step, decide whether you want to create a new Web page or add the selected worksheet range to an existing Web page, and then click **Next**.

6. In the third wizard page (see Figure 3.15), enter an appropriate title and header for the Web page (the default title is the workbook name, and the default header is the worksheet name).

7. If you want thin horizontal lines—*rules*—above and below the worksheet data, click the check boxes to add them and then click **Next**.

8. In the fourth wizard step (see Figure 3.16), decide whether you want the Web page to be a standalone HTML file or part of a FrontPage Web, and check the folder where Excel wants to save the file.

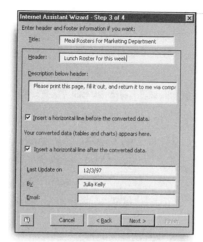

FIGURE 3.15

You probably want a better title and header for the Web page than the workbook and worksheet names.

If you don't have FrontPage, click the **Save the result as an HTML file** option.

If you want to save the file in a folder other than the one displayed, click the **Browse** button and navigate to the folder where you want to store the file.

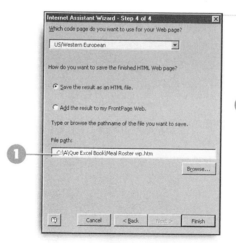

FIGURE 3.16

If you have FrontPage and are using it to build a Web site, you can add the file to that Web; if not, save it as an HTML file.

1   The file is saved here

9. Click **Finish**.

The wizard closes, and your HTML file is created and saved.

You won't be able to view the Web page in Excel (because it's an HTML file, not an Excel file), but you can view it in your browser.

Viewing the Web Page

To view the Web page quickly

1. Open a My Computer window and navigate to the folder where you saved the Web page.

   The Web page file icon looks similar to the one shown in Figure 3.17.

FIGURE 3.17

Double-click the HTML file to launch your browser and view the Web page. (By the way, my window shows a list view rather than the default icon view. You can choose a differ-ent view from the **View** menu.)

 HTML file

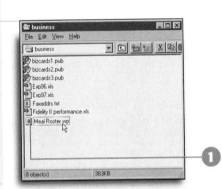

2. Double-click the HTML file.

   Your default browser launches, and the new Web page appears in the browser window (as shown in Figure 3.18).

   If you have an HTML editor (such as Microsoft FrontPage, Adobe PageMill, or Netscape Editor), or if you know a Webmaster who'll teach you, you can edit the Web page further.

Changing the Web page

The Web page is not linked to your Excel file, so if you want to make any changes to the data in the Web page, you must make the changes in the workbook and then create a new Web page.

Some Excel formats may not trans-late to HTML

Keep in mind that formatting such as wrapped text is not converted to HTML code.

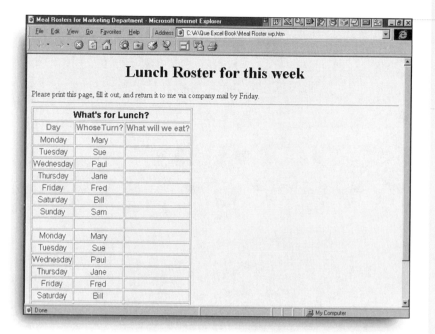

FIGURE 3.18

What Excel can do with HTML is somewhat limited, but with an HTML editing program you can jazz up the Web page.

Selecting and Navigating Worksheets

Naming and selecting worksheets

Moving among worksheets in a workbook

Moving from cell to cell within a worksheet

Adding and deleting worksheets in a workbook

Rearranging worksheets within a workbook

Moving and copying worksheets to other workbooks

Worksheets versus sheets

Worksheets are referred to as both "worksheets" and "sheets."

Naming Worksheets

In this chapter, you'll find procedures for finding your way around in workbooks and worksheets. In Excel, a workbook can contain one or more worksheets. The default worksheet names—Sheet1, Sheet2, and so forth—are decidedly unhelpful when you're looking for a specific sheet in a workbook; but you can name your worksheets anything you want and rename them whenever you need to.

Change the name of a worksheet

1. Double-click the sheet tab for the worksheet you want to name (or rename).

   The existing sheet tab name is highlighted, as shown in Figure 4.1.

FIGURE 4.1

Giving sheets descriptive names makes workbook navigation easier.

1 Highlighted sheet tab

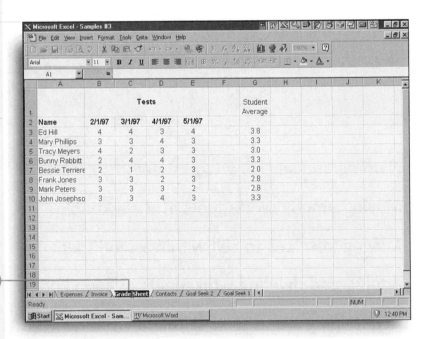

2. Type your new sheet name.

3. Press Enter.

Selecting Worksheets

Workbooks can contain a single worksheet or a huge number of worksheets, limited only by your system memory. Multiple worksheets make a workbook much more useful, because you can store related information together in a single workbook. You can use the sheet tabs at the bottom of the worksheet to select one or more sheets.

Selecting a Single Worksheet

Select a single worksheet in a workbook

1. Click the sheet tab for the worksheet you want, as shown in Figure 4.2.

   The sheet you clicked appears "on top" of the other sheets in the workbook.

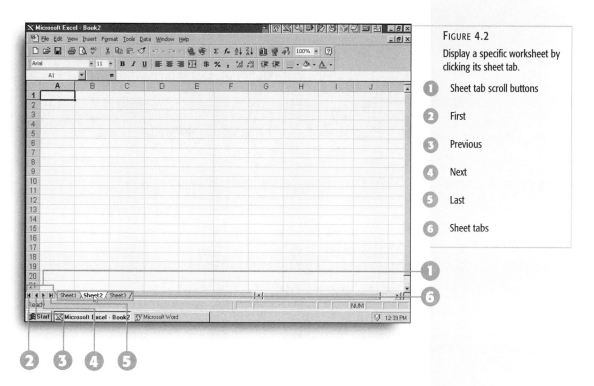

FIGURE 4.2

Display a specific worksheet by clicking its sheet tab.

1 Sheet tab scroll buttons

2 First

3 Previous

4 Next

5 Last

6 Sheet tabs

Where did that sheet go?

If a workbook has several worksheets, scrolling through sheet tabs can be time consuming. Instead, right-click the tab scroll buttons to see a list of all the sheet names; then click the name of the sheet you want.

Did you forget to group your worksheets?

If you forget to select a group of worksheets before you set up the worksheet, you can create identical copies of the finished worksheet by copying it (see "Copying Worksheets Within a Workbook," later in this chapter).

Another method for ungrouping sheets

You also can right-click one of the selected group of sheet tabs; then choose **Ungroup Sheets**.

2. If you can't see the sheet tab for the sheet you want, click the sheet tab scroll buttons to scroll more sheet tabs into view; then click the sheet tab you want.

Selecting Several Sheets at Once

There are occasions when it's helpful to be able to select a group of sheets instead of a single sheet: when you want to format a group of sheets in an identical manner, delete several sheets, or copy or move a group of sheets within a workbook or to another workbook.

When you've selected a group of worksheets, any entries you make on one sheet in the group are made on all the sheets in the group. This is one way to save yourself a lot of work: If you need to create several identical worksheets (for example, monthly expense worksheets, teachers' grade sheets for several classes), you can select a group of worksheets and do the worksheet setup just once.

Select a group of worksheets in a workbook

1. Click the sheet tab for the first of the worksheets you want to select.

2. For nonadjacent worksheets, press and hold down the Ctrl key; then click the remaining sheet tabs you want to include in the group, as shown in Figure 4.3.

   or

   If you want to select a group of adjacent sheets, press and hold down the Shift key; then click the last sheet you want to include in the group. All the sheets between the tabs you clicked are selected, as shown in Figure 4.4.

Deselecting a Group of Worksheets

To deselect a group of worksheets so that you can resume work on an individual worksheet, click another worksheet in the workbook—one that's not part of the selected group.

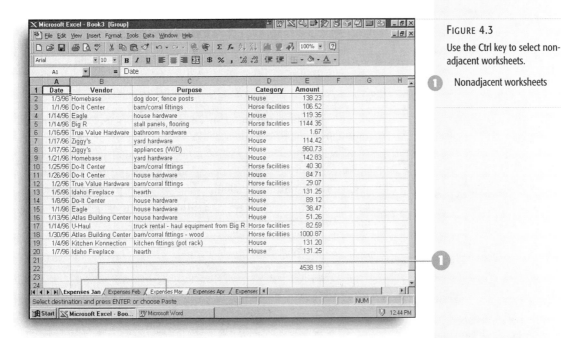

FIGURE 4.3

Use the Ctrl key to select non-adjacent worksheets.

① Nonadjacent worksheets

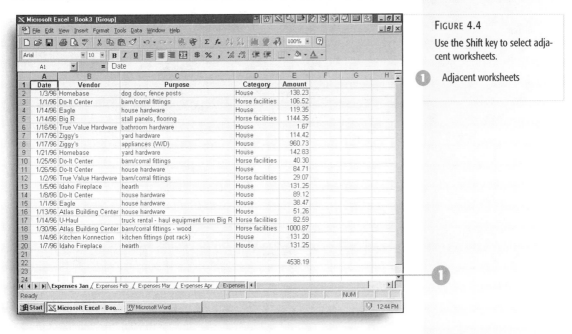

FIGURE 4.4

Use the Shift key to select adjacent worksheets.

① Adjacent worksheets

Moving Around in a Worksheet

When you've selected the worksheet (or group of sheets) you want to work in, you need to move around in that worksheet to get to the cells or ranges of cells you want to select.

A *cell* is the intersection of a row and a column in a worksheet. A rectangular block of two or more cells is also referred to as a *range* of cells. A *cell address* or *cell reference* is the position of a cell in the worksheet, in terms of its column letter and row number. (See Chapter 9, "Simple Calculations," to learn more about cell references.) Figure 4.5 shows the different methods you can use to move among worksheet cells.

FIGURE 4.5

Getting around in a worksheet means navigating to different cells or ranges.

①　Name box

②　Scroll bars

③　Scroll bar buttons

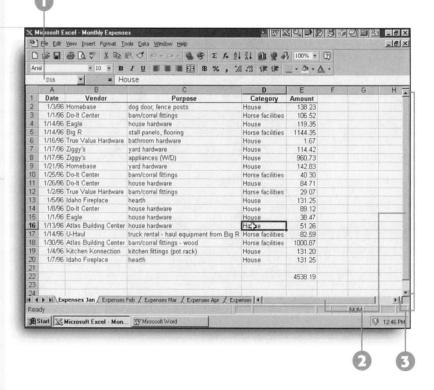

There are several ways to move from cell to cell in a worksheet. Table 4.1 lists the commonly used methods. Try different methods and use the ones that are most convenient for you.

TABLE 4.1   **Ways to move around in a worksheet**

To	Do This
Move down one cell	Press Enter
Move up one cell	Press Shift+Enter
Move right one cell	Press Tab
Move left one cell	Press Shift+Tab
Move one cell in arrow direction	Press arrow keys
Move to beginning of row	Press Home
Move to beginning or end of data range	Press End+arrow key
Move to upper-left corner of worksheet	Press Ctrl+Home
Move to lower-right corner of worksheet	Press Ctrl+End
Move view up or down by one row	Click vertical scroll bar buttons
Move view right or left by one column	Click horizontal scroll bar buttons
Move view by several rows or columns	Drag scroll bars up, down, right, or left
Move view back to selected cell	Press Ctrl+Backspace
Move to specific cell address	Type cell address in Name box

Selecting Cells in a Worksheet

When you're ready to enter data, you need to select a cell or range of cells. Figure 4.6 shows some different kinds of ranges you can select.

Table 4.2 shows some convenient ways to select cells and ranges of cells in a worksheet.

FIGURE 4.6

Select a cell or range in which you want to enter data.

1 Row

2 Name box

3 Column

4 Nonadjacent cells

5 Cell

6 Range

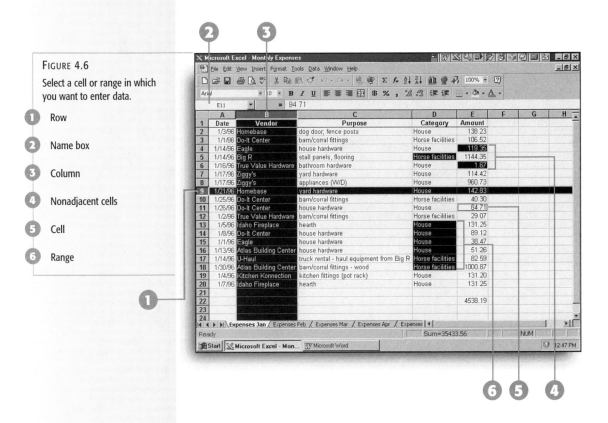

TABLE 4.2   **Ways to select a cell or range in a worksheet**

To	Do This
Select a cell	Click the cell
Select a range of cells	Click and drag over the cells
Increase selection one cell, row, or column in arrow direction	Hold down Shift and press arrow keys
Select an entire column	Click the column letter
Select an entire row	Click the row number
Select a nonadjacent range	Select one cell or range; then hold down Ctrl while you select more cells or ranges
Select a range of adjacent cells	Select the cell at the beginning of the range; then hold down Shift while you select the cell at the end of the range

Adding and Deleting Worksheets

New workbooks have 3 worksheets by default. They used to have 16, but Microsoft finally figured out that you and I found that annoying! You can delete worksheets you don't want or are finished using and insert new worksheets in a workbook.

Deleting Worksheets

If you don't need all three worksheets or if you've created a worksheet you want to throw away, you can delete the worksheet.

Delete a worksheet from a workbook

  1. Right-click the sheet tab for the sheet you want to delete, as shown in Figure 4.7.

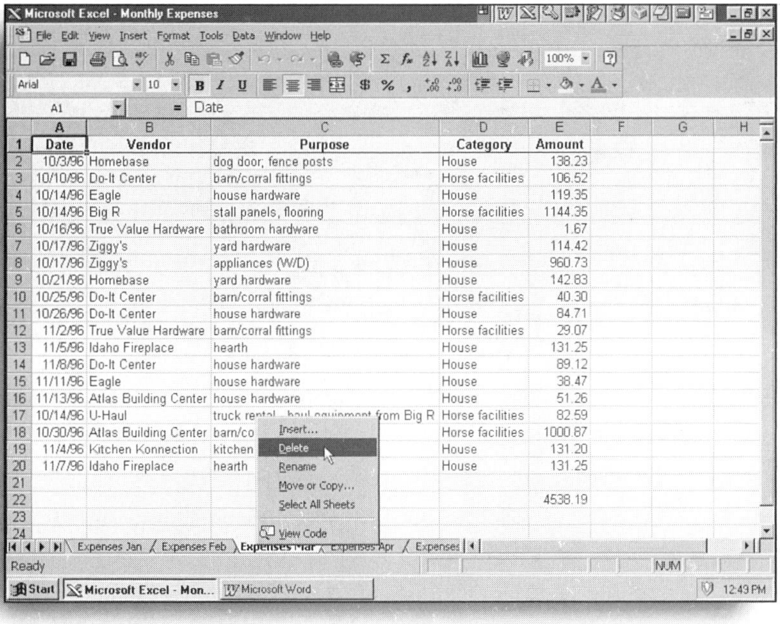

FIGURE 4.7
The sheet tab shortcut menu is the easiest way to delete a worksheet.

  2. Choose **Delete**.

  A message box confirms that you want to delete the worksheet (because when it's gone, it's gone—there's no Recycle Bin for worksheets).

  3. In the message box, choose **OK**.

Adding More Worksheets

If three worksheets are not enough for your project, you can add more. You can add as many worksheets as you want, limited only by your system resources.

Insert a blank worksheet in a workbook

1. Right-click any sheet tab in your workbook, as shown in Figure 4.8.

FIGURE 4.8

You can use the sheet tab shortcut menu to add more worksheets.

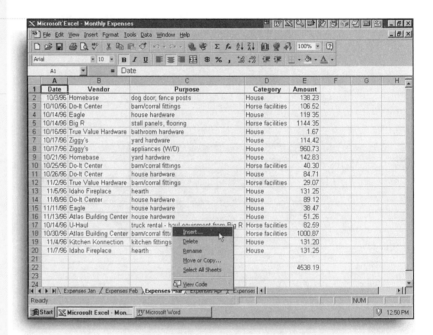

2. Choose **Insert**.

   The Insert dialog box appears, with a choice of worksheet types available (including any custom worksheet templates you've created).

3. Double-click the Worksheet icon to add a new default worksheet.

   The new worksheet is added to the left of the sheet tab you right-clicked. You can move and rename the new worksheet to make your workbook more efficient.

SEE ALSO

➤ *To learn more about creating custom worksheet templates, see page 50.*

Changing the Default Number of Sheets in a New Workbook

All new workbooks open with 3 worksheets, but if you routinely use just 2 worksheets or 23 worksheets, you can save a lot of effort by changing the default number of worksheets in new workbooks.

Change the default number of worksheets

1. Open the **Tools** menu, and choose **Options**.

2. Click the **General** tab.

3. Enter a different number in the **Sheets in new workbook** box.

4. Choose **OK**.

All new workbooks from here on out will contain the new default number of worksheets. The maximum number of default new worksheets you can set is 255; but you can add thousands (if you really want to) by adding them individually. I can't imagine why anyone would want to add this many worksheets to a single workbook, but some people like to know these things.

Rearranging Worksheets

Having lots of worksheets in a workbook is like having lots of files in a file drawer: A little organization makes the mess much more efficient. You can easily move worksheets around within a workbook to rearrange them, create copies of worksheets in a workbook to duplicate work you've already done once, and move or copy worksheets to other workbooks.

Moving Worksheets to Rearrange a Workbook

Like papers in a folder or files in a filing cabinet, worksheets in a workbook are easier to find if you arrange them in a logical order.

Rearrange worksheets in a workbook

1. Click the sheet tab for the sheet you want to move.

2. Drag the sheet tab right or left to its new position, and drop it (release the mouse button) when the position triangle is where you want to place the worksheet, as shown in Figure 4.9.

FIGURE 4.9

To reposition a worksheet, drag its sheet tab to a new location.

1 Moving-sheet mouse pointer

2 Position triangle

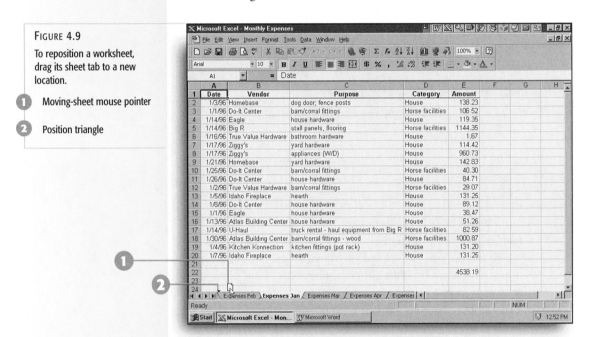

Copying Worksheets Within a Workbook

Copying a worksheet is one of several ways you can make identical copies of a worksheet. You can also select a group of worksheets to set up identical worksheets, and you can create workbook and worksheet templates to create identical new worksheets.

Create an identical copy of a worksheet

1. Click the sheet tab for the sheet you want to copy.

2. Drag the sheet tab right or left to where you want to position the copy; then press and hold down Ctrl.

Oops, I forgot to press Ctrl first

You don't have to hold down Ctrl while you drag, but you *do* have to be holding Ctrl down when you drop the sheet tab.

When you press Ctrl, the mouse pointer displays a tiny plus symbol on the tiny sheet symbol. The tiny plus symbol indicates that you're creating a copy.

3. Drop the sheet tab (release the mouse button) when the little triangle is where you want to place the copy, as shown in Figure 4.10; then release the Ctrl key.

A copy of the worksheet is created, with the same sheet name and the number (2) next to it. (You'll probably want to rename the new worksheet.)

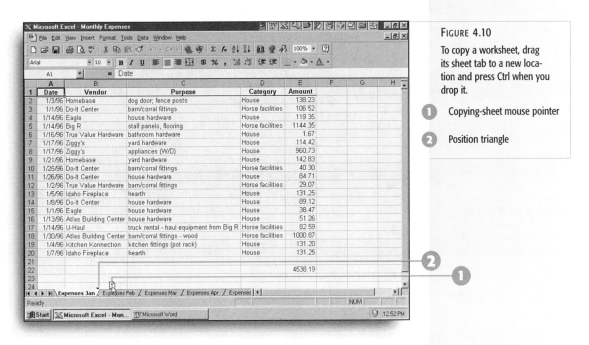

FIGURE 4.10

To copy a worksheet, drag its sheet tab to a new location and press Ctrl when you drop it.

1 Copying-sheet mouse pointer

2 Position triangle

SEE ALSO

➤ For information on using templates to create identical new worksheets, see page 50.

Moving and Copying Worksheets Between Workbooks

There are a couple of ways to move and copy worksheets between two workbooks. One way is to display both workbooks on your screen and drag sheet tabs from one workbook to the other in the same way that you move or copy a worksheet within the same workbook. Another way is to use the following procedure, which relies on the Move or Copy dialog box.

SEE ALSO

➤ *To learn more about arranging multiple windows so that you can see several workbooks or worksheets at once, see page 87.*

Moving or Copying a Worksheet to Another Workbook

Move or copy a worksheet out of one workbook and into another

1. Open both workbooks (the workbook that contains the worksheet and the workbook that you want to move or copy the worksheet into).

2. Right-click the sheet tab for the worksheet you want to move or copy.

3. Choose **Move or Copy**.

   The Move or Copy dialog box appears, as shown in Figure 4.11.

FIGURE 4.11

The Move or Copy dialog box lets you move or copy worksheets between workbooks when you're using a single window.

1 Select the workbook

2 Select a position in the new workbook

3 Copy instead of move

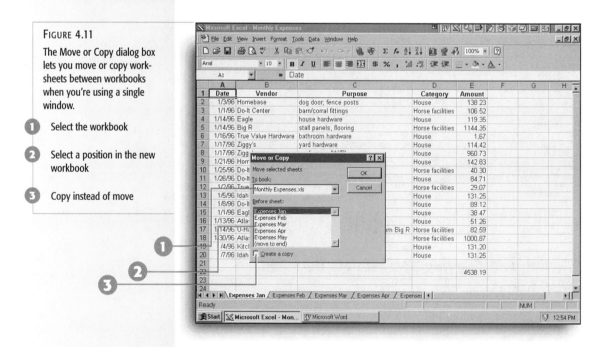

4. In the **To book** drop-down list, select the workbook you want to move or copy the worksheet into.

5. In the **Before sheet** list box, click the name of a worksheet where you want to position the moved or copied worksheet. (Don't worry if you pick the wrong worksheet—you can easily move the worksheet to reposition it later.)

6. If you want to copy the worksheet to the new workbook, click the **Create a copy** check box; if you want to move the worksheet without creating a copy, leave the check box blank.

7. Choose **OK**.

   The worksheet is moved or copied (depending on whether you checked the **Create a copy** check box) into the new workbook.

Moving or Copying a Worksheet to Another Workbook by Dragging It

The easiest way I know to move and copy worksheets from one workbook to another is to drag them.

Move or copy a worksheet by dragging it

1. Open both workbooks (the workbook that contains the worksheet and the workbook that you want to move or copy the worksheet into).

2. Arrange the two windows so you can see the sheet tabs in both workbooks, as shown in Figure 4.12.

3. To move a worksheet without copying it, drag the sheet tab from one workbook and drop it among the sheet tabs in the other workbook.

   To copy a worksheet to another workbook, drag the sheet tab as if you're moving the worksheet; then hold down Ctrl when you drop the sheet tab. A plus symbol appears with the mouse pointer to show that you're dropping a copy of the worksheet.

Start a new workbook with an existing worksheet

To create a new workbook from an existing worksheet quickly, reduce the window size of the active workbook so you can see part of the Excel desktop as well as the active workbook's sheet tabs; then drag the worksheet's sheet tab out of the workbook and drop it on the Excel desktop. A new workbook that contains the dragged worksheet is created.

FIGURE 4.12

Use multiple windows to drag
worksheets from one work-
book to another.

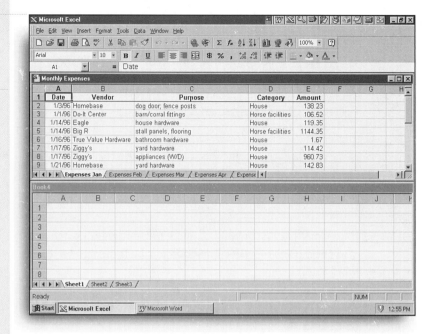

Changing Your View
of the Worksheet

Freezing and unfreezing worksheet panes

Splitting worksheet panes and removing split panes

Arranging multiple worksheet windows

Arranging multiple workbook windows

Closing extra windows

Arranging windows manually

Freezing Worksheet Panes to Keep Rows or Columns in View

You have a few different ways to change your view of your worksheet or workbook, and each different view is useful in specific circumstances. When adding items to the bottom of a long list or filling in a column on the far right side of a worksheet table, the important row and column headings in the top row(s) and leftmost column(s) are scrolled out of view. If you lose track of the row and column headings in your list, you may inadvertently enter data in the wrong row or column. To keep a row of headings in view at the top of your worksheet while you scroll down to the bottom of a long list, you can *freeze* the heading row in its own pane. To see two distant parts of a worksheet side by side, you can *split* the worksheet into panes and scroll around in each pane separately. If you want to see the contents of two or more worksheets or workbooks at the same time, which makes it easy to move and copy cells and worksheets by dragging them from one window to another, you can arrange them in *multiple windows*.

Freeze Panes

Which rows or columns do you want to freeze?

Select the row below the row(s) you want to freeze and the column to the right of the column(s) you want to freeze. To freeze both row 1 and column A, for example, click cell B2.

To keep the headings in view while you work in a distant part of your list, you can freeze the heading rows or columns using the following procedure. You can edit cells in frozen rows and columns just like other cells; freezing just keeps them in view while you scroll around.

Freeze worksheet panes

1. To freeze the top row of a worksheet, click the row selector for row 2 (shown in Figure 5.1).

   To freeze the leftmost column, click the column selector for column B.

2. On the **Window** menu, click **Freeze Panes**.

   The frozen panes remain in view no matter where you scroll in your worksheet (shown in Figure 5.2).

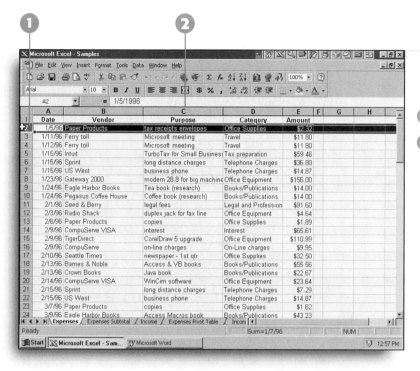

FIGURE 5.1

Select row 2 if you want to freeze row 1.

1 Row selector

2 Column selector

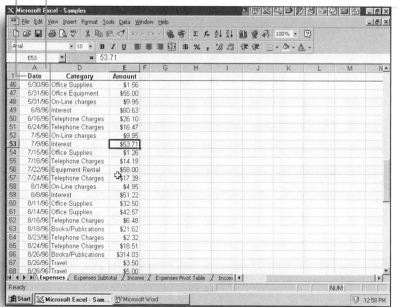

FIGURE 5.2

Even though the active cell is far to the right and bottom of the worksheet list, the top row and left column headings are still visible.

1 Frozen row

2 Frozen column

Unfreeze Panes

You can leave frozen panes in place for as long as you want, but if you need to split panes in a window, you have to unfreeze the panes first. To unfreeze the panes, open the **Window** menu, and click **Unfreeze Panes**.

Unfreeze panes before you split them

You cannot split panes in a worksheet with frozen panes. To unfreeze panes, open the **Window** menu and click **Unfreeze Panes**.

The panes are the wrong size

To adjust the sizes of split panes, drag the split bar with the mouse. To adjust the sizes of four panes at once, drag the intersection of the horizontal and vertical split bars.

Splitting Worksheet Panes to View Multiple Areas in a Worksheet

In a really long or wide table of data, visually comparing data from distant parts is difficult. If, however, you split the table into two or four panes, you can scroll in each pane separately and view the far right and left sides of the table, or the top and bottom of the table, at the same time. Splitting is different than freezing panes because frozen panes remain in view—you can't scroll around in them—but all split panes are scrollable.

Split panes in a worksheet

1. Position the mouse pointer over the vertical or horizontal split box (as shown in Figure 5.3).

FIGURE 5.3

Use the vertical or horizontal split box to quickly split worksheet panes using the mouse.

1 Horizontal split box

2 Vertical split box

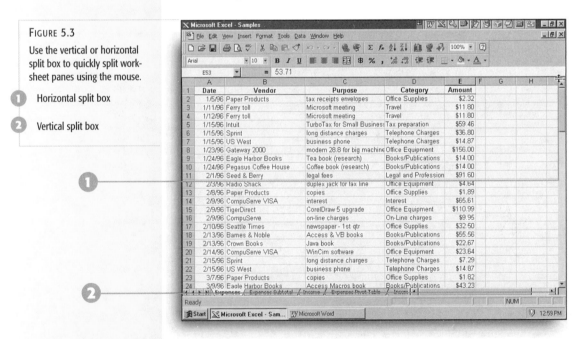

2. When your mouse pointer is a two-headed arrow, drag the split box into the worksheet.

A split bar appears in the worksheet where you drop the split box (as shown in Figure 5.4).

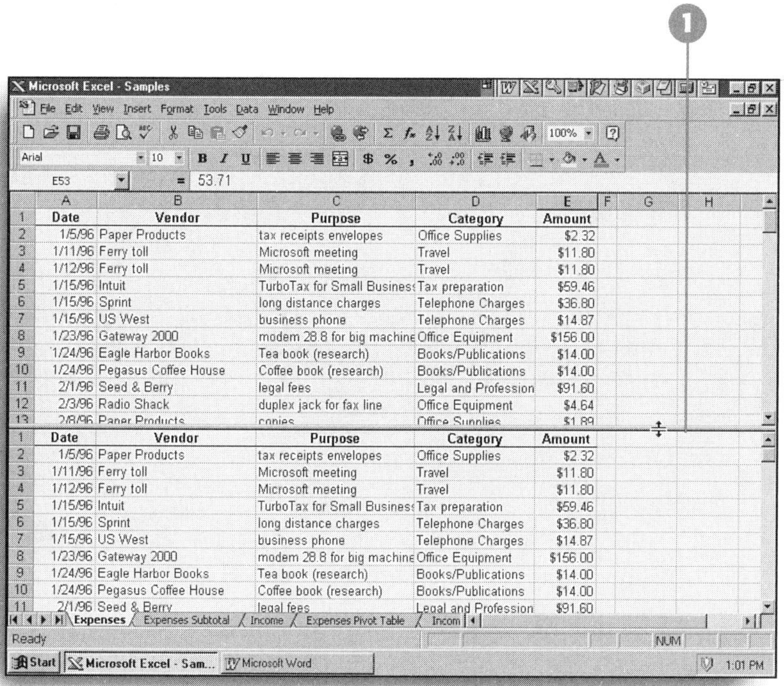

FIGURE 5.4
You can split the worksheet into two panes with one split bar.

1 Split bar

You can scroll in each pane separately with that pane's scroll bars. Scrolling to see what you want takes a little practice, though. Just keep in mind that split panes are just two (or four) different windows on the same worksheet. Changes you make in one worksheet pane are reflected in all worksheet panes. (Figure 5.5 shows four different panes.) When you select a cell, only the one cell is selected, although you may see it in all (or none) of your split-pane windows.

FIGURE 5.5

Four split panes provide four
different views of the same
selected cell.

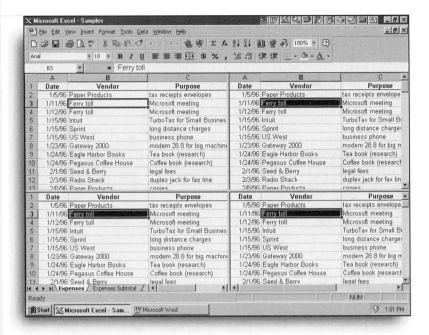

Remove split panes

1. Position the mouse pointer over the split bar (shown in
   Figure 5.6).

2. When the mouse pointer becomes a two-headed arrow,
   double-click the split bar.

   The split bar is removed.

Using Multiple Windows

If you're working in two or more worksheets (or workbooks) at
the same time, you often can switch must faster between them
by arranging them in multiple windows. The windows can be
arranged in a variety of layouts: vertical windows, side-by-side;
horizontal windows, top-to-bottom; tiled windows, laid out in a
grid; and cascading windows, like a deck of cards. Excel arranges
the windows neatly to fit within the Excel desktop; but I find
that after I've arranged my windows, I like to further arrange
them by dragging the window borders to change their sizes.

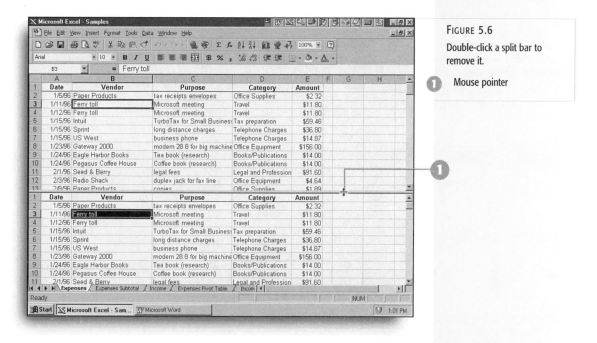

FIGURE 5.6
Double-click a split bar to
remove it.

1️⃣ Mouse pointer

Arranging Multiple Windows to See Several Worksheets at Once

If you want to move or copy cells to a different worksheet, the easiest way is to open multiple windows and drag the cells from one window to another.

Display worksheets from a single workbook in separate windows

1. On the **Window** menu, click **New Window**.

   A new window is created for the same worksheet, but you can't see it yet because both windows are full-sized.

2. On the **Window** menu, click **Arrange**.

   The Arrange Windows dialog box appears. (The arrangement options are shown in Figures 5.7 through 5.10.)

I want more windows

To open more windows, repeat step 1 for each additional window.

FIGURE 5.7

Vertical windows are good for comparing data on two or more different worksheets.

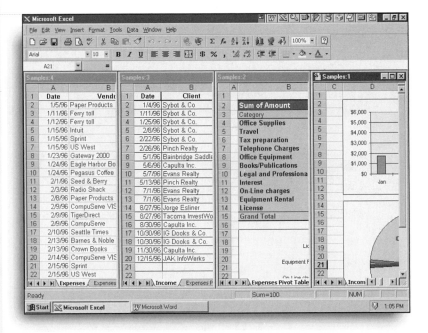

FIGURE 5.8

Horizontal windows are good for dragging sheet tabs between windows.

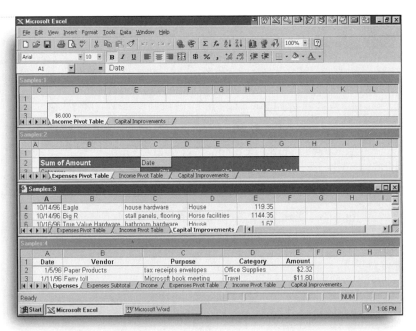

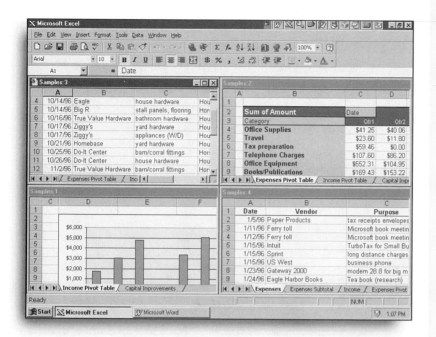

FIGURE 5.9

Tiled windows give you a view of all four worksheets at once.

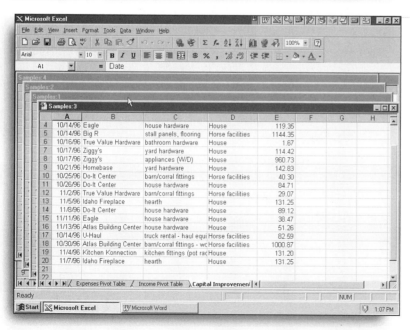

FIGURE 5.10

Cascaded windows enable you to see more data in each window, but also keep them all in easy reach.

3. Click the arrangement option you want—**T**iled, **H**orizontal, **V**ertical, or **C**ascade.

4. Click the **Windows of active workbook** check box.

   This check box limits the windows to the active workbook instead of opening windows on all the open workbooks.

5. Click **OK**.

   Your windows are arranged so that you can select a different worksheet in each window. You can then drag cells between windows to move or copy them from one worksheet to another.

SEE ALSO
> *For more information on moving and copying cell data between worksheets, see page 126.*

Arranging Multiple Windows to See Several Workbooks at the Same Time

If you want to move or copy worksheets to a different workbook, the easiest way is to open multiple windows and drag your worksheets from one window to another window.

Displaying multiple workbooks in separate windows

1. Open the workbooks with which you want to work.

2. On the **Window** menu, click **Arrange**.

3. Click a window arrangement—**T**iled, **H**orizontal, **V**ertical, or **C**ascade.

4. Clear the **Windows of active workbook** check box so that all the open workbooks are displayed in separate windows (shown in Figure 5.11).

5. Click **OK**.

SEE ALSO
> *To learn more about moving and copying worksheets between workbooks, see page 77.*

Two windows, same worksheet?

It may seem obvious, but be sure to select different sheets in each window (the sheet to copy or move *from* and the sheet to copy or move *to*) before you try to move or copy cells between windows.

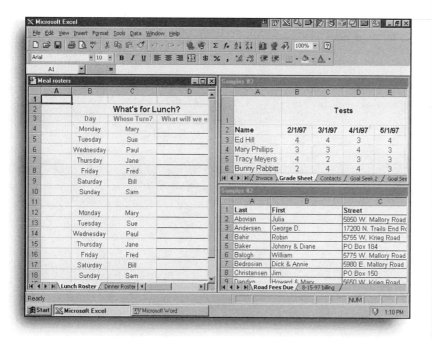

FIGURE 5.11

You can easily move or copy worksheets between workbooks if you drag sheet tabs from one window to another.

Closing Extra Windows

Close windows in the workbook

1. To close extra windows, click the Close button in the upper-right corner of each window.

2. To maximize the remaining window, click the Maximize button in the upper-right corner (shown in Figure 5.12).

Arranging Multiple Windows Manually

After Excel has arranged your windows so that you can see them all, you can further arrange them by dragging window borders to resize them or dragging title bars to move them.

Resize and move windows manually

1. To resize a window, point to a window border or corner until the mouse pointer becomes a two-headed arrow (as shown in Figure 5.13).

2. Drag a window border to resize or reshape a window.

3. To move an entire window, drag its title bar.

FIGURE 5.12

Close the extra windows and maximize the remaining window.

① Maximize button

② Close button

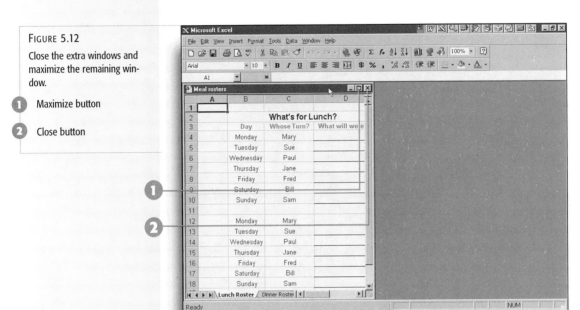

FIGURE 5.13

I like to tweak my multiple-window arrangement manually until it works well for me.

① Drag a border to resize

② Drag the title bar to move

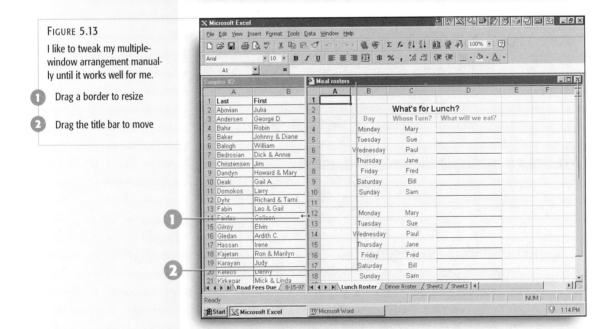

Building Worksheets

Entering Data

Entering data directly in a cell

Using AutoFill to quickly enter text and number series

Repeating cell entries

Entering data with a data entry form

Setting up and removing data validation

Raw data is what you type into a cell—in other words, values rather than formulas. Data might be text, as in a list of names or days of the week, or numbers, as in expense-account amounts or hours worked, dates, or column labels. In short, data is anything you type into a cell other than a *formula* (which performs mathematical calculations using the data you enter).

Excel has a number of tools that make data entry quicker—AutoComplete, AutoFill, and some old standby keystrokes are all very handy. You can also set up *data validation* for individual cells, to make sure accurate data is entered.

If the data you need to enter is already in electronic format (for example, in a text file, an Access database, or even a Word document), it's not necessary to retype it; instead, you can import the data straight into your worksheet.

SEE ALSO

➤ *To learn more about writing formulas in Excel, see pages 137 and 153.*

Entering Data Directly in a Worksheet

The basic procedure for entering data in Excel is straightforward: click a cell, type something, and press Enter.

But the magic of computers is that they make you do less work (usually) than a typewriter—and sure enough, Excel has easy tricks for making repetitive entries less work. In addition to entering data one cell at a time, you can

- Enter a series of numbers or repeated text entries into several cells by dragging the mouse across the worksheet (with AutoFill)
- Repeat the entry in the cell above with a keystroke
- Enter identical data in several cells after typing it once
- Repeat entries in a long list by typing the first one or two letters (with AutoComplete)

Entering Data in a Single Cell

The most common way to enter data is one cell at a time, because most data is not repetitive.

Enter data in a cell

1. Click a cell.

2. Type your data.

3. Press Enter.

   The active cell (the selected cell) moves to the next cell down when you press Enter.

AutoFill a Text Entry

To enter identical text entries or a built-in or custom list of different text entries, you can use AutoFill. If AutoFill recognizes your initial text entry as part of a built-in or custom list, it fills the list; but if AutoFill doesn't recognize your entry, it copies the entry to fill cells. For example, you can set up a table quickly by using AutoFill to enter month names across the top; or you can fill several cells with the word "North." The next procedure shows you how to use AutoFill to enter a list of day names.

Use AutoFill to enter text

1. Click a cell.

2. Type a day of the week (either the three-letter abbreviation or the full name).

3. Place your mouse pointer over the lower-right corner of the selected cell until it becomes a small black cross (see Figure 6.1), and drag to the right.

   The cells you drag over are filled with a series of day names, in correct order.

Creating Your Own Custom List

You can create your own custom lists (for example, a custom list of coworker or product names); then, when you enter any one of those names, you can use AutoFill to enter the rest of the list.

There's always another way

You can also press Tab, press an arrow key, or click another cell to complete the entry. If you press Tab to move across the bottom of a table and then press Enter, the active cell moves down one row and returns to the left side of the table.

Is it a number, or is it text?

To enter a number that's really text (like a ZIP code), type an apostrophe first. For example, the entry `'07623` is displayed as `07623` in the cell; it retains its leading zero and is not calculable. To learn how to format the cell to take care of this for you, see Chapter 11, "Formatting Cells."

AutoFill lists

Excel has built-in AutoFill lists for day names and month names, both full and abbreviated. If you start an AutoFill list with a day or month name, you'll fill cells with the built-in list instead of a repeated entry.

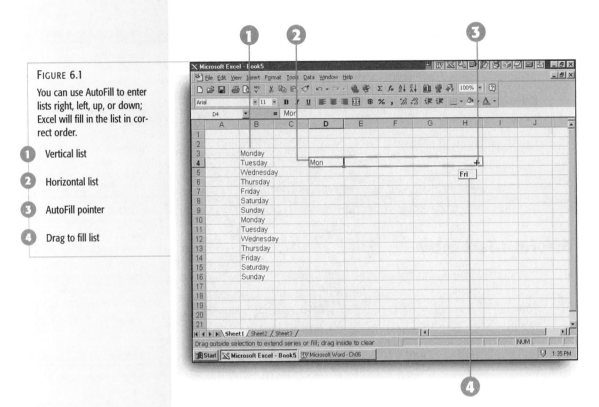

FIGURE 6.1

You can use AutoFill to enter lists right, left, up, or down; Excel will fill in the list in correct order.

❶ Vertical list

❷ Horizontal list

❸ AutoFill pointer

❹ Drag to fill list

The easiest way to create a custom list is to first enter the list in a worksheet.

Create a custom AutoFill list

1. Select the list in the worksheet.

2. On the **Tools** menu, click **Options**.

3. Click the **Custom Lists** tab.

The list range you selected is already entered in the **Import list from cells** box.

4. Click **Import**.

The list is added to Excel's AutoFill lists.

5. Click **OK** to save the new list and close the Options dialog box.

AutoFill a Number Series

You also can use AutoFill to enter a series of numbers that increases or decreases by a constant value (such as 1, 2, 3, 4; or 2, 4, 6, 8).

Use AutoFill to enter a series of numbers

1. Click a cell.

2. Type a number (for example, 1); then press Enter.

   The active cell moves to the next cell down.

3. Type the next number in the series (for example, 2); then press Enter.

4. Select both cells.

5. Drag the AutoFill handle (the small black box in the lower-right corner of the selected range) down to fill the series, as shown in Figure 6.2.

Change the active cell location

To change the direction in which the active cell moves when you press Enter, open the **Tools** menu and click **Options**. On the **Edit** tab, next to **Move selection after Enter**, select a direction from the **Direction** drop-down list. (You can also clear the **Move selection after Enter** check box to prevent the active cell from moving anywhere when you press Enter.)

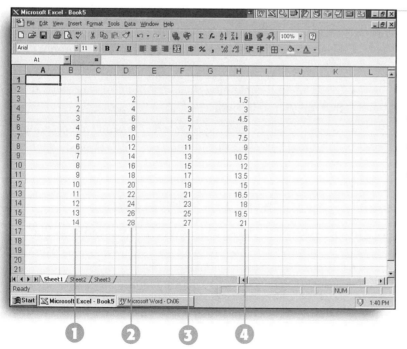

FIGURE 6.2

A number series is filled based on the cells you selected to begin the series.

1 Began with 1,2

2 Began with 2,4

3 Began with 1,3

4 Began with 1.5,3

AutoFill a Growth Series

Instead of a *linear* series (such as 1, 2, 3, 4), you might want to use AutoFill to enter a *growth* series (a series that grows by a multiplication factor, such as 2, 4, 8, 16, 32).

Use AutoFill to enter a growth series

1. Enter the first two numbers in the series.

2. Drag the AutoFill handle with the *right* mouse button.

   When you release the mouse button, a shortcut menu is displayed.

3. Click **Growth Trend**.

   Excel guesses the multiplication factor based on your initial entries and fills the list with the series.

Repeating the Entry in the Cell Above

To repeat an entry from the cell directly above the active cell, use any of these methods:

- Select the cell to be filled; then press Ctrl+' (apostrophe) and press Enter.

- Select the cell containing the entry you want to repeat; then drag the AutoFill handle.

- Select the cell containing the entry you want to repeat and the new cell(s) to be filled; then press Ctrl+D, as shown in Figure 6.3.

Entering the Same Data in Several Cells

To enter identical entries (text, numbers, dates, and so on) in several cells at one time, you can use an old standby keystroke, Ctrl+Enter.

Enter duplicate data in multiple cells

1. Select all the cells in which you want to enter the data (to select nonadjacent cells, click one cell; then hold down Ctrl and select the remaining cells).

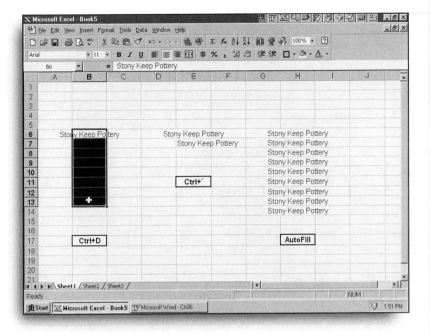

2. Type your entry.

3. Press Ctrl+Enter.

The identical entry is entered in all selected cells, as shown in Figure 6.4.

Repeating an Entry in a Text List with AutoComplete

To quickly enter an item in a list of repeated items (such as an expenses list), you can use AutoComplete.

Use AutoComplete to repeat entries in a list

1. Begin typing an entry at the bottom of a list.

2. If the characters you type are identical to an existing entry in the list, the rest of the entry is filled in for you (see Figure 6.5).

3. If your entry is different from the previous list entry, keep typing (the AutoComplete entry will disappear).

FIGURE 6.4

To enter the same data in several cells, use the Ctrl key to select nonadjacent cells; then type the entry and press Ctrl+Enter.

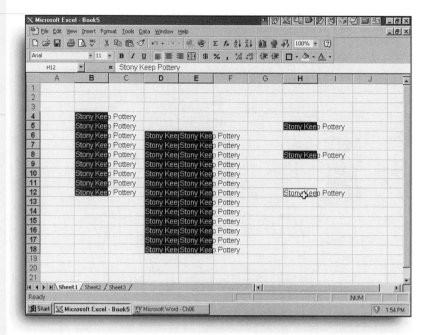

FIGURE 6.5

AutoComplete saves typing time by filling in the entry for you.

1   AutoComplete

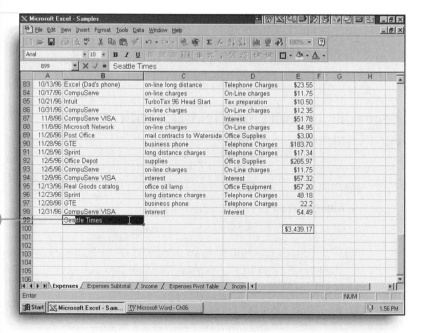

If there are two or more similar entries in the list, right-click the cell where you want to enter data; then click **Pick From List**. Click the entry you want from the list of existing entries (as shown in Figure 6.5).

AutoComplete bothers me

To turn off AutoComplete, open the **Tools** menu and click **Options**. On the **Edit** tab, clear the **Enable AutoComplete for cell values** check box.

Entering Data with a Data Entry Form

Some folks find entering data in a form to be less confusing than entering data in a big table. You can create a data entry form instantly, as long as you have entered column headings for your table.

Create a data entry form for a worksheet

1. Be sure your table has column headings and at least one row of data already entered.

2. Click any cell within the table.

3. On the **Data** menu, click **Form**.

    A data form is created for the table, as shown in Figure 6.6.

    - Click the **New** button to start a new record.

    - Press Tab and Shift+Tab to move from field to field in the displayed record.

    - Press Enter to move to the next record in the table or to start a new record if the last record in the table is displayed.

4. Click the **Close** button to close the data form. New record(s) are displayed at the end of the table.

Validating Data During Entry

It's all too easy to inadvertently enter inaccurate data, which renders the data worthless. Some inaccuracies can be prevented by setting up data validation, which displays an error message in response to data that doesn't meet standards you set, such as "text length equal to 16" or "date greater than =TODAY()."

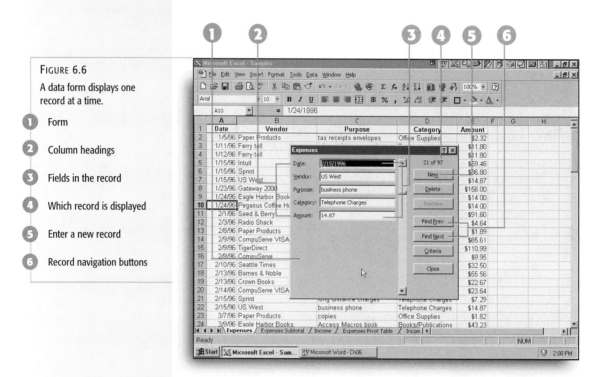

FIGURE 6.6

A data form displays one
record at a time.

1 Form

2 Column headings

3 Fields in the record

4 Which record is displayed

5 Enter a new record

6 Record navigation buttons

Set up data validation

1. Select the cell or range where you want to validate the entries.

2. On the **Data** menu, click **Validation**. The Data Validation dialog box is displayed, as shown in Figure 6.7.

3. On the **Settings** tab, select a type of data in the **Allow** drop-down list.

4. In the **Data** drop-down list (if it's available), select any value-limiting criteria you want, such as "between" or "greater than."

5. In the boxes that are displayed below the **Data** drop-down list, set criteria such as **Minimum** and **Maximum** allowable values (the criteria you can set are determined by the choices you make in the **Allow** and **Data** drop-down lists).

6. To require an entry in the cell, clear the **Ignore blank** check box.

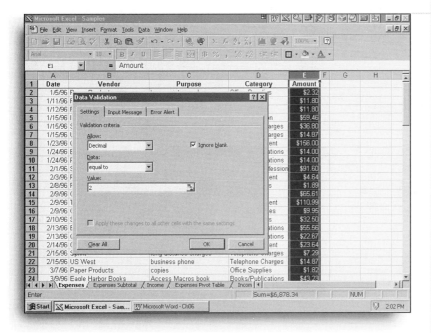

FIGURE 6.7

Use data validation to specify what type of data is allowable in selected cells and to display messages when data is entered.

7. On the **Input Message** tab, type a title and message that are displayed when one of the validated cells is selected (if you don't want a message when a cell is selected, clear the **Show input message when cell is selected** check box). An input message is shown in Figure 6.8.

8. On the **Error Alert** tab, choose an icon, type a title, and type an error message that displays when invalid data is entered (if you don't want a message but merely want invalid data entry refused, clear the **Show error alert after invalid data is entered** check box).

9. Click **OK**.

Invalid data that already exists on the worksheet won't show error messages, but you can locate it with Excel's Auditing tools.

SEE ALSO

➤ *To learn more about finding invalid data, see page 191.*

FIGURE 6.8

Your messages can be worded however you want.

1 Error message

2 Selection message

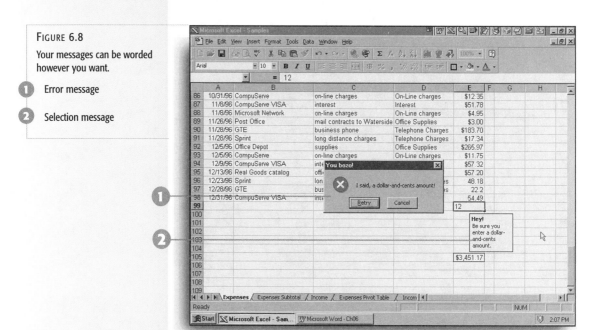

Which cells are validated?

To locate validated cells on a worksheet, open the **Edit** menu and click **Go To**. Click the **Special** button. In the Go To Special dialog box, click **Data validation** and **All**; then click **OK**. All cells with validation rules are highlighted.

Remove data validation

1. Select a cell where data validation is in place.

2. On the **Data** menu, click **Validation**.

3. Click the **Clear All** button.

4. To remove the same validation settings from all cells where they're enforced, click the **Settings** tab; then click the **Apply these changes to all other cells with the same settings** check box.

5. Click **OK**.

Copying and Importing Data from Other Files

Trading data between Excel and other programs

Copying data from Word to Excel

Sending data from Access to Excel

Sending data from Excel to Access

Importing a text file into Excel

Trading Data with Other Programs

Typing is not the only way to get data into a spreadsheet. If the data already exists in electronic form (for example, in a Word document, an Access table, a text file, or a dBASE table), don't reenter it. Instead, copy it or import it; you save time and you reduce typing errors. To copy data from another file, use the other file's copy procedures and Excel's paste procedures. To import data from another file type, open the file in Excel using the procedures outlined later in this chapter in the section "Importing a Text File."

As you can see from the following list, you can open or import data directly from most common file types:

- Earlier versions of Excel
- Lotus 1-2-3
- Quattro Pro
- Text
- DOS
- Microsoft Works 2.0
- dBASE II, III, IV
- SYLK (Symbolic Link)
- DIF (Data Interchange Format)

SEE ALSO

➤ *To learn more about sharing data between software programs, see page 457.*

Copying Data from Word

If the data you need is already in a Word file, it's easiest to copy and paste it into Excel. For example, if someone has kept a list of names and phone numbers in a Word document, you can start setting up a list of contacts in Excel quickly by copying and pasting the list from Word. To copy a list from Word to Excel, use the following procedure.

Copy data from Word to Excel

1. Open the Word document, and select the list of data (as shown in Figure 7.1).

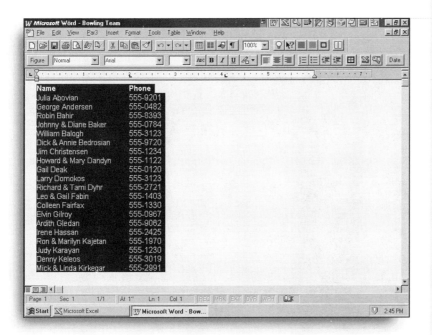

FIGURE 7.1

The two columns in Word are separated by tab characters.

2. Copy the data by clicking the Copy button (or use whatever copy method you prefer).

    Data you copy or cut is kept in a temporary file called the Windows 95 *Clipboard* until you cut or copy another bit of data. You can paste the copied or cut data repeatedly, but each time you cut or copy data, it replaces whatever data you previously cut or copied in the Clipboard.

3. Switch to the Excel worksheet.

4. Click the cell in which you want to paste the upper-left corner of the list.

5. Open the **Edit** menu, and click **Paste**.

    The list is pasted into your worksheet (as shown in Figure 7.2). The data is separated, or *parsed*, into columns according to how it was separated in the Word document (parsing

What files can I copy from?

You can also copy data from WordPerfect, Works, and other Windows-based word processing files.

means Excel uses tab characters in the Word text to separate the text into columns in the worksheet). As you can see in Figures 7.1 and 7.2, data that's copied and pasted by this method doesn't bring its formatting into the worksheet. You need to format the data and widen the worksheet columns to make it look nice again.

FIGURE 7.2

When you paste them into your worksheet, the columns are parsed with the tab characters that separated the columns in the Word document.

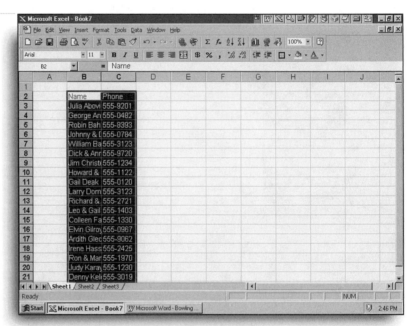

SEE ALSO

➤ *To learn more about formatting worksheet cells, see page 195.*

Sending Data over from Access

The biggest difference between an Excel worksheet and an Access table is that Excel is designed to maneuver, manipulate, calculate, and crunch numbers, whereas Access is designed to store and retrieve data. I don't mean that you can't do calculations in an Access database; I only mean that Excel is a far more flexible and easier program in which to crunch numbers.

That being said, if you have a table of data in Access in which you want to do some serious calculating, you can easily send the table of data to an Excel worksheet using the following procedure.

Send data from Access to Excel

1. Open the Access database.

2. Click the **Tables** tab, and then click the name of the table you want to send to Excel (but don't open the table).

3. Open the **Tools** menu, point to **Office Links**, and then click **Analyze It with MS Excel** (as shown in Figure 7.3).

    Excel starts (if it's not already started), and a new workbook opens. The new workbook contains a single sheet, and both the worksheet and the workbook are named with the name of the Access table (shown in Figure 7.4).

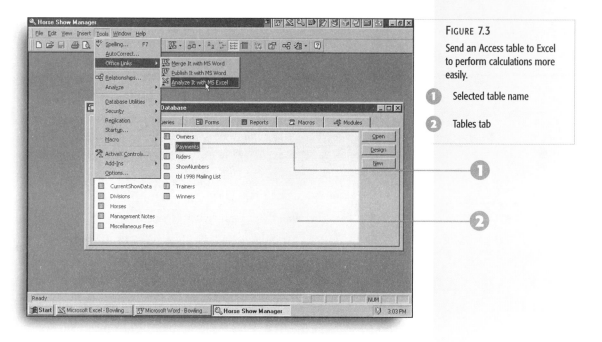

FIGURE 7.3

Send an Access table to Excel to perform calculations more easily.

① Selected table name

② Tables tab

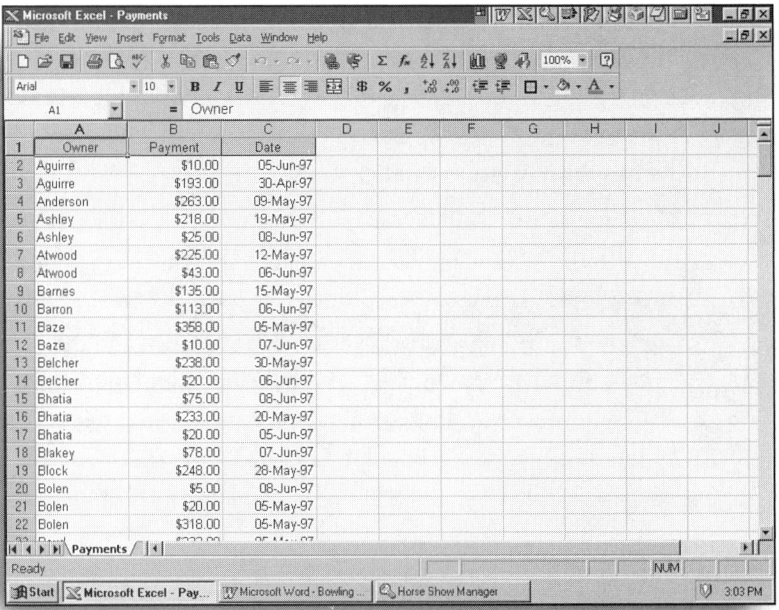

FIGURE 7.4

After you have Access data in Excel, the data becomes even more usable because you can calculate, chart, and analyze data more easily.

Sending Excel Data to Access

Do you have Access?

For this procedure to work—for the **Convert to MS Access** command to appear on the **Data** menu—you must have Microsoft Access installed and install Excel's AccessLinks add-in program. See the Help program in Excel for instructions.

Clean up the data first

To make this process easy, be sure there are no entries in the worksheet other than the table of data you want to convert to an Access table.

If you've been keeping a list in Excel, you can easily convert the Excel worksheet into an Access table, in either a new or existing Access database. From an Access database, you can create professional, easy-to-read reports from the data (which you can't do in Excel).

Send Excel data to an Access table

1. Open the worksheet you want to send to Access.

2. Open the **Data** menu, and click **Convert to MS Access**.

   Access starts, and the Import Spreadsheet Wizard (shown in Figure 7.5) guides you through the process of creating the Access table. Your worksheet column headings are the field names in the new Access table. If this part gets confusing, consult a good Access book or the Access help files for help.

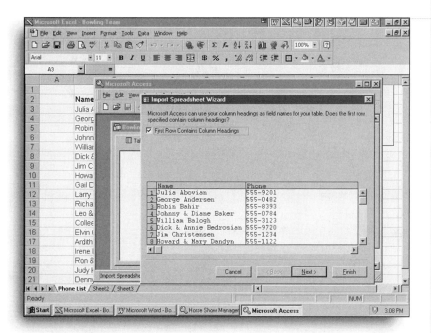

FIGURE 7.5

If you need to use Excel data in an Access database, converting the worksheet to an Access table is one of several ways to do it.

Importing a Text File

If a colleague has data you need but in an obscure file format you can't open in Excel, you can get around that obstacle by asking your colleague to save the data as a text file and then open the text file in Excel. To import a text file to Excel, use the following procedure.

Import a text file

1. On the Standard toolbar in Excel, click Open. 🖻

2. In the **Files of _type_** box, select **All Files (*.*)**.

3. Double-click the name of the text file.

   The Text Import Wizard starts (shown in Figure 7.6).

4. In step 1 of the Text Import Wizard, be sure the **Delimited** option button is selected and then click **Next**.

5. In step 2 of the wizard (Figure 7.7), mark the **_T_ab** check box. If the data isn't parsed into neat columns in the **Data preview** window, try marking other delimiters until you get good column separation. Then click **Next**.

Delimiters are just column separators

A _delimited_ file contains tabs, spaces, commas, semicolons, or some other consistent method of separating the data into columns of information. The Text Import Wizard is pretty good at guessing where the data should be divided, but you may need to do some adjusting to put everything into the right columns after the import process is finished.

FIGURE 7.6

The Text Import Wizard guides you through the process of setting up the text data as a workbook.

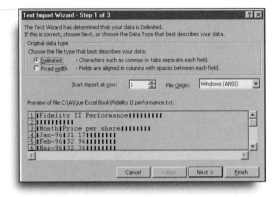

FIGURE 7.7

Text files are often delimited, or separated into columns, by tabs.

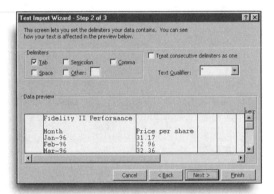

6. In step 3 (see Figure 7.8), you can set preliminary data formatting. Click the heading in the **Data preview** window for the column you want to format. If the column contains numbers, leave the formatting in the **Column data format** section set to **General**; if the column contains dates, select the **Date** option instead, and so on.

7. Click **Finish**.

The text file data is imported into your worksheet and properly separated into columns (as in Figure 7.9).

When you save the workbook, the Save As dialog box appears and tries to save the data as a text file. If you just click **Save**, the file is saved as a text file, and every time you open the file you have to use the Text Import Wizard again. To stop the endless Text Import Wizard cycle, you need to save the file as a workbook instead of a text file.

FIGURE 7.8

Leave columns of numbers as **General**, but set columns of dates to a **Date** format.

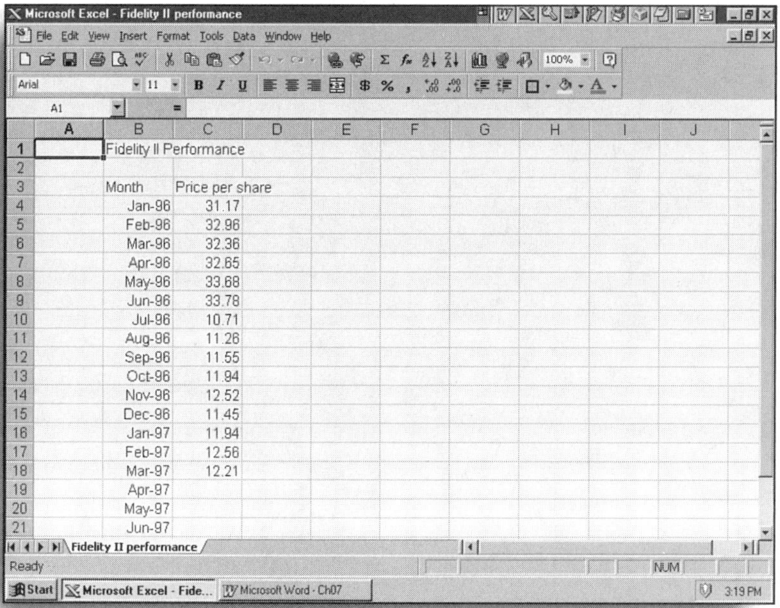

FIGURE 7.9

Now you can use the data in Excel.

To save the data as a workbook, select **Microsoft Excel Workbook** in the **Save as type** box, in the Save As dialog box.

Editing Data

Editing Cell Entries

No matter how you decide to get data into your worksheet, you can't get away from errors. Whether it's a typo or data that changed later, or a file you imported that had someone else's errors in it, inevitably something requires changing.

You can open a cell and edit data directly in the cell, or you can select a cell and edit its contents in the Formula bar.

Edit data directly in the cell

1. Double-click the cell.

2. Edit the contents of the cell:

    * Use the Backspace key to erase characters to the left.

    * Use the Delete key to erase characters to the right.

    * Use the mouse to select characters and replace, delete, or format them individually (see Figure 8.1).

3. Press Enter.

Can't open the cell?

If you cannot open a cell for editing, the *in-cell editing* feature is probably not activated. Open **Tools**, select **Options**, and click the **Edit** tab, click the check box for **Edit directly in cell**, and click **OK**.

Replacing cell contents is quick

To completely replace the contents of a cell, select the cell and type the new contents, and then press Enter.

FIGURE 8.1

You can edit a cell's contents directly in the cell.

1 Select characters with the mouse

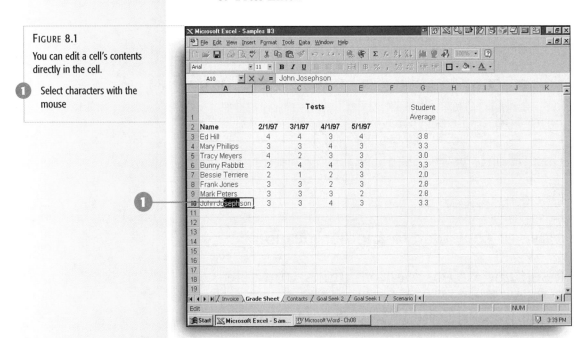

Edit data in the Formula bar

1. Select the cell you want to edit.

   The cell's contents appear in the Formula bar (see Figure 8.2).

2. Click the Formula bar.

3. Use the following to edit the contents of the Formula bar:

   • Use the Backspace key to erase characters to the left.

   • Use the Delete key to erase characters to the right.

   • Use the mouse to select characters and replace, delete, or format them individually.

4. Press Enter.

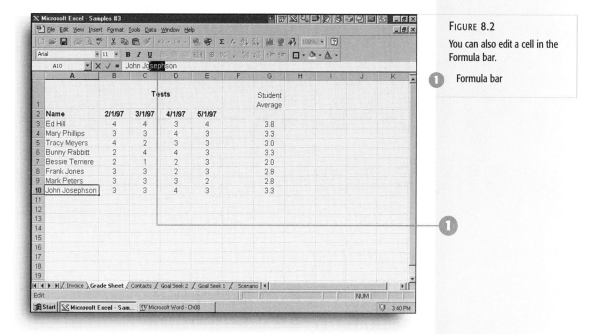

FIGURE 8.2

You can also edit a cell in the Formula bar.

1 Formula bar

Sometimes menu and keyboard methods are faster than mouse methods. If you've been using Windows a while, for example, you may be used to pressing Ctrl+X to cut text to the Clipboard, and that may be faster for you than grabbing the mouse and finding the right button to click. Table 8.1 shows a quick list of editing methods you can use in Excel to edit and rearrange your

Changed your mind?

If you discover that you're changing the data in the wrong cell(s) or the correction is turning into a hopeless mess, press Esc to return to the original cell contents and just start over with your changes.

data. These methods work in addition to those described throughout this chapter.

TABLE 8.1   **Quick methods for editing data**

Task	Shortcut Method	Menu Method
Cut the selection	Ctrl+X	Open the **Edit** menu and select **Cut**.
Copy the selection	Ctrl+C	Open the **Edit** menu and select **Copy**.
Paste the selection	Ctrl+V	Open the **Edit** menu and select **Paste**.
Remove cell contents		Right-click the cell or selected range, and click **Clear Contents**.
Delete selected rows/columns		Open the **Edit** menu and select **Delete**.
Undo the last change	Ctrl+Z	Open the **Edit** menu and select **Undo**. Note that the **Undo** option on the menu changes to show the last action you took that can be undone.
Redo your last undo	Ctrl+Y	Open the **Edit** menu and select **Redo**. Note that the **Redo** option on the menu changes to show the last undone action that can be redone.

Finding and Replacing Data

If you've entered a worksheet full of data correctly, but later learn that a word (perhaps someone's name) was misspelled, you can have Excel search out and replace every instance of the misspelling.

You can also find or replace data (for example, cell references or names) in formulas. You can find, but *not* replace, data in comments. (See the later section "Adding Worksheet Comments" for details on using comments.)

Find specific data, such as a word or number

1. From **Edit**, choose **Find**.

   The Find dialog box appears (shown in Figure 8.3).

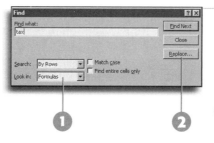

FIGURE 8.3

Use the Find dialog box to locate text strings, such as words, cell references, or values that are the results of formulas.

1 Select Formulas, Values, or Comments

2 Switch to the Replace dialog box

2. In the **Find what** box, type the text string you want to locate.

3. In the **Look in** box, select **Formulas**, **Values**, or **Comments**.

   • *Formulas*. Finds text strings entered in cells (such as the word tax) and formulas (such as =subtotal+tax).

   • *Values*. Finds text strings entered in cells and those displayed as the results of formulas.

   • *Comments*. Finds text strings in worksheet comments.

4. If capitalization counts (such as when you want to find Tax but not tax), click the **Match case** check box. To locate complete matches (such as tax but not taxable), click the **Find entire cells only** check box.

5. Click **Find Next**.

   Excel searches the worksheet and stops at the first instance of your text string. To find the next instance, click **Find Next** again.

If you want to replace the text string you've found, click the **Replace** button and follow the next procedure. If, on the other hand, you want to replace entries without finding each one first, follow the next procedure.

Replace one text string with another (for example, replace _expenses_ with _expenditures_)

1. Open **E̲dit** and select **Replace**.

The Replace dialog box appears, as shown in Figure 8.4. (The Replace dialog box also appears if you click the **Replace** button in the Find dialog box.)

FIGURE 8.4

To replace every instance of one text string with a different text string, click **Replace All**.

1 Replace text strings one at a time

2 Replace all text strings at once

2. In the **Fi̲nd what** box, type the characters you want to change.

3. In the **Replace with** box, type the new characters.

If you don't want to replace all instances of the text string, you can find and replace individual occurrences, or you can replace all occurrences at once.

- To find and replace individual occurrences, click **Fi̲nd Next** until you locate an occurrence that you want to replace and then click **Replace**.

- To replace all occurrences, click **Replace A̲ll**.

Deleting Data

When you need to remove data from a worksheet (for example, if you've been practicing entering data or typing formulas, or you change your mind about a table you entered), you can quickly delete the contents of cells. Deleting cell contents doesn't remove formatting, however, so you find your cell shading and borders still in place after the cell contents are gone.

Completely remove the contents of a cell or range

1. Select the cell or select the range.

2. Press Delete.

SEE ALSO

➤ _To learn about inserting and deleting cells, see page 130._

Undoing Mistakes

Undo and Redo are frustration solvers. Sometimes I do specific things in a worksheet, and then want to undo everything I just did. Sometimes I click the wrong spot on a worksheet, something completely unintended happens, and I don't know how I did it or how to fix it. The easy way out is to have Excel *undo* what you did, by clicking the Undo button. If, moreover, you undo something and then change your mind about having undone it, you can *redo* what you undid by click the Redo button.

Undo what you did

1. To undo the last single thing you did, click the Undo button on the Standard toolbar.

2. To undo the last several things you did, click the down arrow on the side of the Undo button and then select the number of actions you want to undo (see Figure 8.5).

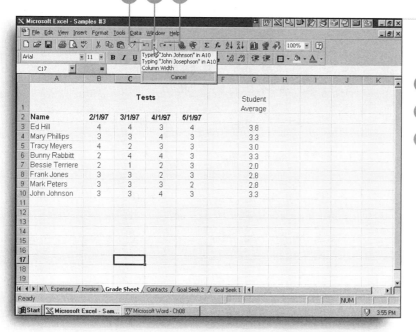

Clean it all off

To erase everything in a cell or range, including data, formatting, and comments, select the range you want to erase, and open **Edit** and select **Clear, All**.

FIGURE 8.5

You can undo up to 16 consecutive actions.

1 Undo

2 Down arrow for list

3 Redo

Redo what you undid

1. To redo the last single thing you undid, click the Redo button on the Standard toolbar. ⟳▾

2. To redo the last several things you undid, click the down arrow on the side of the Redo button, and select the number of undone actions you want to redo.

   Only actions you've undone appear on the Redo list.

Moving and Copying Cells on the Same Worksheet

The easiest way to move or copy cell contents to new locations on a worksheet is to drag the cells and drop them where you want them.

Move cells by dragging them to another location

1. Select the cell or range of cells you want to move.

2. Position the mouse pointer on one of the cell or range borders (see Figure 8.6).

   When the mouse pointer is over a border, it becomes an arrow.

3. Drag the border to a new location.

4. When the cell or range border is positioned (see Figure 8.7), drop the cell(s) by releasing the mouse button.

Copy cells by dragging them to another location

1. Select the cell or range of cells you want to copy.

2. Position the mouse pointer on one of the cell or range borders (see Figure 8.8).

   When the mouse pointer is over a border, it becomes an arrow.

Can't drag and drop?

If you cannot drag and drop cells, *drag-and-drop cell editing* is probably turned off. Open **Tools**, select **Options**, click the **Edit** tab, click the check box for **Allow cell drag and drop**, and click **OK**.

Do the cells really move?

Although you often hear or read the phrase "move or copy cells," what you're really doing is moving or copying the contents of the cells, not the cells themselves.

Where do these cells drop?

When you drag cells, a *range tip* indicates exactly where you have positioned them.

Try the right mouse button for more options

If you drag a range with the right mouse button, you can select a **Move** or **Copy** command from a shortcut menu after you drop the range.

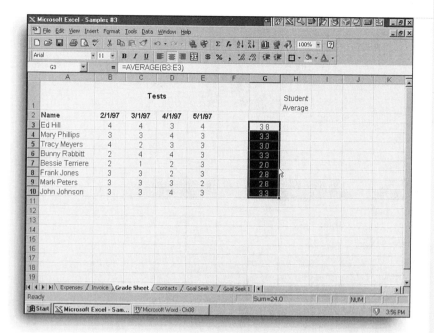

FIGURE 8.6

Position the mouse pointer on a border so that it becomes an arrow.

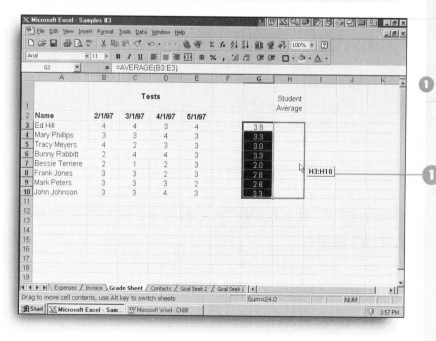

FIGURE 8.7

A border shadow shows where you're moving the range.

1   Range tip

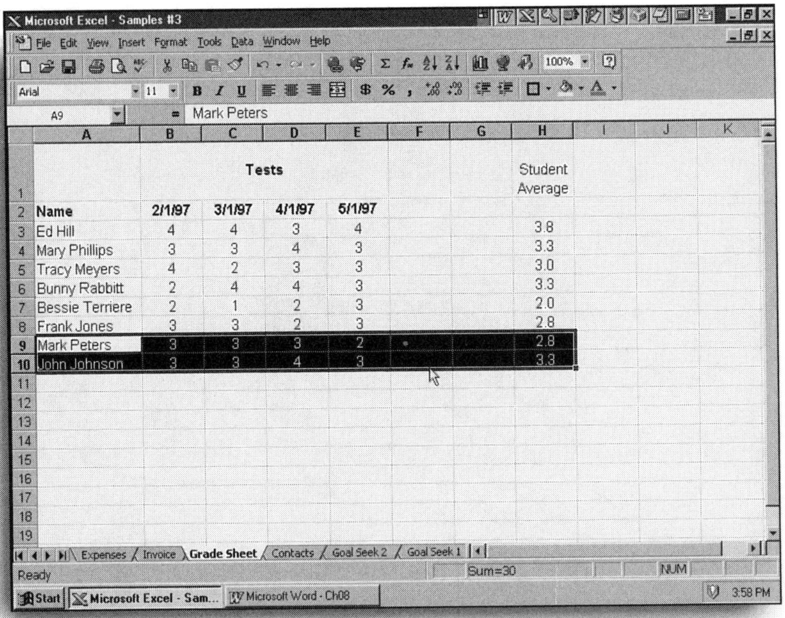

FIGURE 8.8

Position the mouse pointer on a border so that it becomes an arrow.

3. Drag the border to a new location.

4. When the cell or range border is positioned, press and hold the Ctrl key and then drop the cell(s) by releasing the mouse button.

When you press Ctrl while dragging cells to copy them, a small plus symbol next to the mouse pointer indicates that you're dragging a copy (see Figure 8.9).

5. After you drop a copy of the range, release the Ctrl key.

Special drag-and-drop techniques

Want to drop selected cell(s) *between* existing cells on the worksheet? If you're copying the selection, hold down Shift+Ctrl as you drag the cell(s). Moving the cell(s)? Hold down Shift as you drag. The edges of the existing cells are shaded, indicating where the new cell(s) are to be inserted. Going to a different worksheet? Hold down the Alt key and drag the selection over the sheet tab.

Moving and Copying Cells to a Different Worksheet

Cutting-and-pasting cells (or copying-and-pasting) is an alternative to dragging-and-dropping, and is the easier method if you're moving or copying the cells to another worksheet (or another workbook).

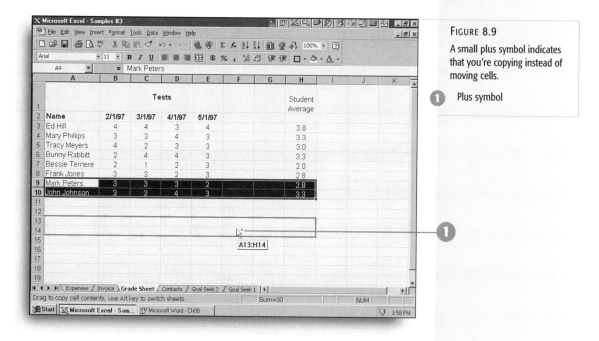

FIGURE 8.9

A small plus symbol indicates that you're copying instead of moving cells.

1 Plus symbol

Move cells to a different worksheet

1. Select the cell(s) you want to move.

2. On the toolbar, click Cut.

The cell(s) you cut are surrounded by a moving border.

3. On the worksheet on which you want to paste the cell(s), select the cell on which you want to paste the upper-left corner of the range.

4. On the toolbar, click Paste.

The cells move from their previous location to wherever you pasted them.

Copy cells to a different worksheet

1. Select the cell(s) you want to copy.

2. On the toolbar, click Copy.

3. On the worksheet on which you want to paste the cell(s), select the cell on which you want to paste the upper-left corner of the range.

The Status bar tells me to press Enter

If you press Enter to paste the selection, you get only one paste, and the Windows Clipboard is cleared. If, therefore, you want to paste repeatedly, use a method other than pressing Enter.

The shrinking worksheet

Deleting rows and columns won't reduce the size of your worksheet; you always have 256 columns and 65,536 rows. When you delete a row or column, Excel adds a new row at the bottom or a new column at the right side of the worksheet and changes the row numbers and column letters so that they remain consecutive.

All formulas that rely on cell references are updated with their new row and column references within the workbook. If, however, you have linked formulas in another workbook and that workbook is closed when you delete the rows or columns, those linked formulas need to be relinked to their new cell references the next time you open that other workbook.

Sometimes this is faster

Alternatively, click a cell, and then open the **Insert** menu and choose either **Rows** or **Columns**.

4. On the toolbar, click Paste. 📋

You can paste the copied cells as often as you like, until you cut or copy another selection (then the new cut or copied selection replaces the earlier selection on the Windows Clipboard).

Inserting and Deleting Rows and Columns

Sometimes you have entire rows or columns of information in a worksheet that you want to remove, but if you only delete the contents of the cells, you have blank rows or columns in the middle of a table. What you really need to do is delete the entire row or column from the worksheet and leave no empty spaces. At other times, you need to insert new rows or columns into a table because new data needs to be added into the middle of an existing layout. Use the following procedures to delete or insert rows and columns.

Delete rows or columns

1. Click the *row header* (the row number) or the *column header* (the column letter) to select the entire row or column, as shown in Figure 8.10.

2. Right-click in the selection, and then click **Delete** on the shortcut menu.

   The selected rows or columns disappear, and the remaining rows or columns are renumbered (or re-lettered).

Insert rows or columns

1. Click the row header below or the column header to the right of where you want to insert rows or columns.

2. Right-click in the selection and then open **Insert** on the shortcut menu.

   Row(s) or column(s) are inserted (see Figure 8.11), and the original rows or columns are renumbered (or re-lettered).

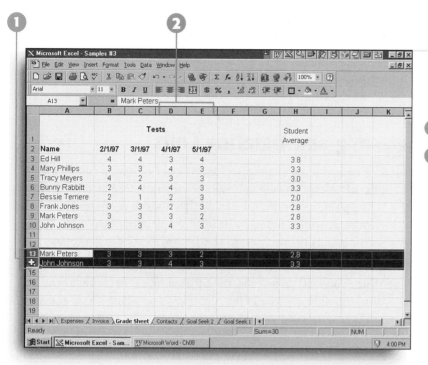

FIGURE 8.10

Select multiple columns or rows by dragging over their headers.

1 Row headers

2 Column headers

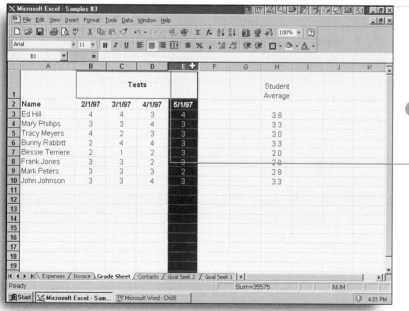

FIGURE 8.11

To insert more than one row or column, select a number of rows or columns equal to the number of rows or columns you want to insert.

1 Columns are inserted here

If you find that a formula gives incorrect results after you insert or delete rows or columns, you may need to correct the formula's cell reference types.

SEE ALSO

➤ *To learn more about cell reference types, see page 181.*

Inserting and Deleting Cells

If you need to delete or insert individual cells into a table, you can delete existing cells or insert new ones. (If the table of data is large, this method can be faster than moving a range of data to make room for new data or fill in for deleted data.) The surrounding cells in the worksheet move in the direction you specify to make room or fill in for cells you insert or delete.

When you insert new cells, the surrounding cells move down or to the right to make room, depending on what you choose in the Insert dialog box. When you delete cells, the surrounding cells move up or left, depending on what you choose in the Delete dialog box. This makes sense after you've tried it on a worksheet.

Insert cells

1. Select the cell(s) that are to be moved below or right of the cell(s) you insert.

    The cells you select will be moved to make room for an equal number of new cells.

2. Right-click the selected cells and then click **Insert**.

    The Insert dialog box appears.

3. Click the **Shift cells right** option to move your selected cells to the right to make room for the new cells. Click the **Shift cells down** option to move your selected cells down to make room for the new cells.

4. Click **OK**.

Delete cells

1. Select the cell(s) that you want to delete.

2. Right-click the selected cells and then click **Delete**.

   The Delete dialog box appears.

3. Click the **Shift cells left** option to fill in the space by moving existing cells to the left. Click the **Shift cells up** option to fill in the space by moving existing cells up.

4. Click **OK**.

If you find that a formula gives incorrect results after you insert or delete cells, you may need to correct the formula's cell reference types.

SEE ALSO

➤ *To learn more about cell reference types, see page 181.*

Separating a Single Column into Multiple Columns

Often I've entered a list of names in a worksheet and typed both first and last names in the same cell. Later, I realize that I need to separate the full-name column into a column for first names and a column for last names.

Instead of deleting and retyping all the last names, cell by cell, Excel can separate, or *parse*, each full-name cell into two separate-name cells for me. If you need to do something similar, use the following procedure.

Parse cell contents

1. Select the cells you want to parse (see Figure 8.12).

   Leave an empty column on the right of the column you're parsing so that the new column you're going to create has somewhere to be pasted.

2. Open **Data** and select **Text to Columns**.

   The Convert Text to Columns Wizard starts.

3. In step 1 of 3, be sure the **Delimited** option is selected and click **Next**.

In step 2 of 3, you choose a delimiter. In a case like this, the names are separated by a space character, so the delimiter is a space.

FIGURE 8.12

Let the Convert Text to Columns Wizard separate your column into separate columns.

1 **Delimited** option

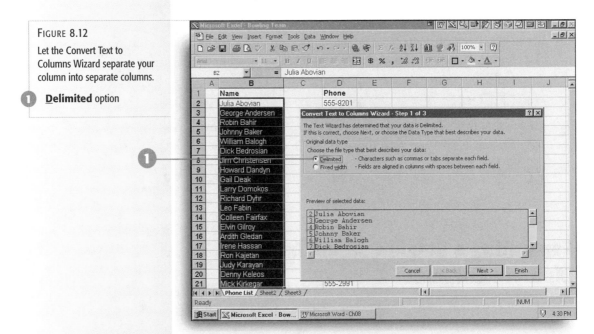

4. Click the **Space** check box (see Figure 8.13) and click **Next**.

5. In step 3 of 3, you don't need to set any particular data format, so click **Finish**.

Your list is separated into two neat columns (like the one in Figure 8.14) with a new column started at each space character.

Do I need to clear the Tab check box?

You can clear the **Tab** check box if you want to, but it won't matter if you have no tab characters in your list.

I got three columns instead of two

A cell that has two spaces in it (for example, Mary A. Jones) is separated into three columns. You can fix those cells with individual cell editing.

Adding Worksheet Comments

Information in a worksheet is not always intuitively obvious to someone who didn't create the worksheet or to the worksheet's creator a year or three later. If you want to add extra information about data in the worksheet (perhaps an explanation of the formula or the name of the contact who gave you the information), you can add a *comment* that floats on top of the worksheet rather than taking up a cell in the worksheet. Comments also help to prevent inaccurate data entry by adding extra on-the-spot instructions for data entry.

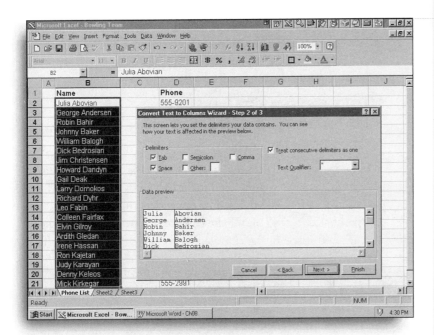

FIGURE 8.13

You know you've selected the correct delimiter when the Data preview window shows your list separated into columns.

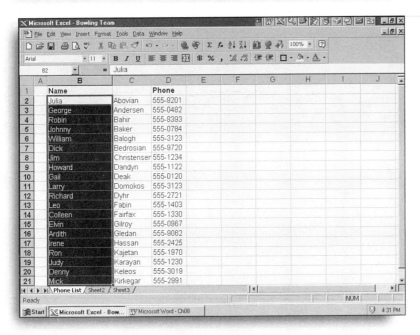

FIGURE 8.14

The wizard pastes the newly separated column of data into the column that you left empty.

A small red triangle in the upper-right corner of the cell indicates a comment. When you point to a cell that has a comment indicator, its comment appears. Use the following procedures to add, edit, and delete comments.

Add extra information with a comment

1. Right-click the cell to which you want to add the comment.

2. Click **Insert Comment**.

   A new comment frame appears on the worksheet, with your computer's user name filled in (as shown in Figure 8.15). You can select and delete the user name; format the font, point size, and so on for the comment text; and change the size and shape of the comment by dragging resizing handles.

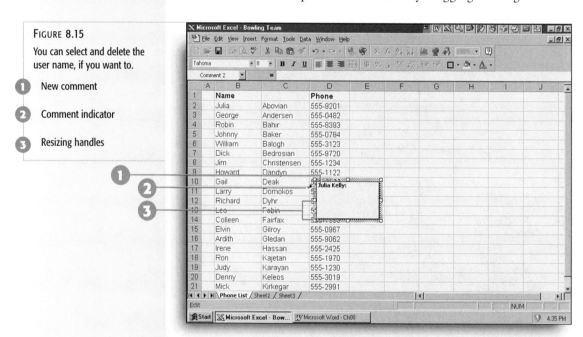

FIGURE 8.15

You can select and delete the user name, if you want to.

1 New comment

2 Comment indicator

3 Resizing handles

3. Type your comment.

4. Click another cell on the worksheet.

   Your finished comment closes. To see the comment, position the mouse pointer over the cell, as in Figure 8.16.

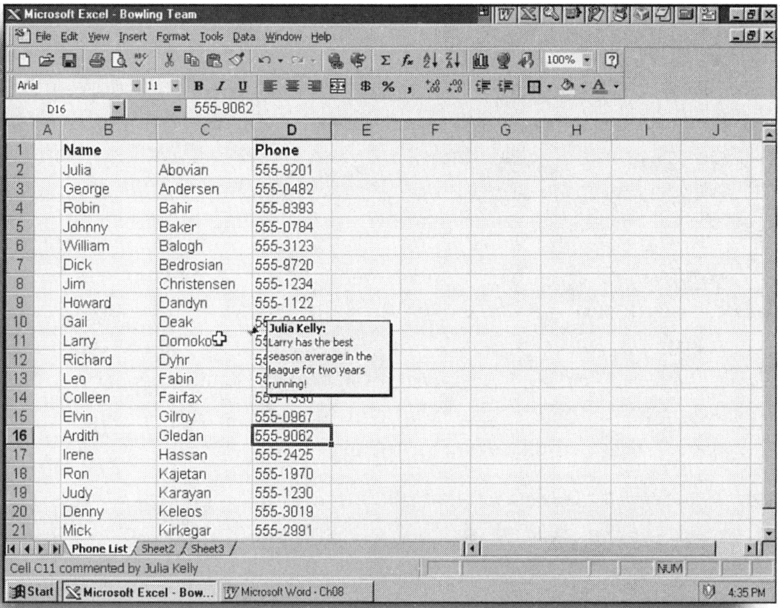

FIGURE 8.16

Comments are a good way to add extra information to a table without interfering with the table layout.

Edit a comment

1. Right-click the cell with the comment.

2. Click **Edit Comment**.

The comment opens with a hatched border and resizing handles, like a new comment.

3. Edit the comment. If desired, drag resizing handles to change the shape or size of the comment.

4. When the comment is complete, click another cell in the worksheet.

Your finished comment closes.

Delete a comment

1. Right-click the cell with the comment.

2. Click **Delete Comment**.

The comment is deleted.

Using AutoCorrect

AutoCorrect corrects your spelling as you type, which prevents a great many errors before anyone catches them. It recognizes many common misspellings, such as *teh* (*the*) and *adn* (*and*), and corrects them before you notice the misspelling.

You can personalize AutoCorrect by adding your own personal common misspellings to AutoCorrect's list (I tend to type *tabel* for *table*), and you can make AutoCorrect do a lot of repetitive typing for you. For example, if your job requires you to type *Lake City High School Alumni* often, you can make this an AutoCorrect task so that when you type the acronym **lch**, AutoCorrect replaces it with the entire five words.

To make AutoCorrect help do your work

1. Open **Tools** and select **AutoCorrect**.

    The AutoCorrect dialog box appears (shown in Figure 8.17).

2. In the **Replace** box, type what you'll type in the worksheet (either a misspelling or an acronym you want replaced).

3. In the **With** box, type what AutoCorrect is to enter in place of your misspelling or acronym.

4. Click **OK**.

Delete an AutoCorrect entry

To delete an AutoCorrect entry, select the entry in the AutoCorrect dialog box, click **Delete**, and then click **OK**.

Undo an AutoCorrect

If occasionally you don't want AutoCorrect to correct a word or acronym you've typed, press Ctrl+Z immediately after AutoCorrect corrects the spelling. The AutoCorrect action is undone and your original typing remains unchanged. This works when you are still typing in the cell and AutoCorrect corrects your spelling when you type a space; however, if you've pressed Enter before pressing Ctrl+Z, the whole cell entry is undone and erased.

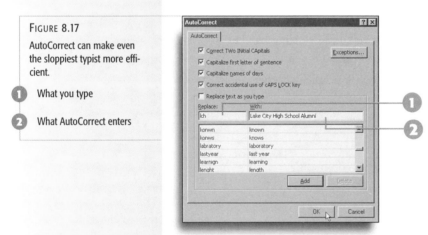

FIGURE 8.17

AutoCorrect can make even the sloppiest typist more efficient.

1 What you type

2 What AutoCorrect enters

Simple Calculations

Simple Calculations, Quick Answers

Calculations are why Excel exists. To perform calculations in a worksheet, you write formulas; to perform complex calculations, you use functions in your formulas (*functions* are built-in mathematical equations that save you time and effort).

This section contains lots of procedures that make simple calculations easier and more useful, and you don't have to write any formulas yourself.

To get really quick answers without writing a formula yourself, you have two options: AutoCalculate, which calculates cells you select but doesn't write a formula in the worksheet, and AutoSum, which writes a SUM formula for you in the worksheet.

Quickly Calculating Numbers Without a Formula

To calculate selected cells "on the fly," without writing a formula, you can use AutoCalculate.

Use AutoCalculate to perform quick calculations

1. Select the cells you want to add up (or average, or count).

Look at the AutoCalculate box in the status bar of Figure 9.1.

2. To change the calculation function, right-click the AutoCalculate box; then click a different function.

You can select from six functions (Sum, Average, Count Entries, Count Numbers, Minimum, Maximum), or you can select **None** to turn the feature off.

Using AutoSum to Enter a Formula

To enter a formula that sums a group of numbers, without actually writing the formula yourself, use the AutoSum button on the Standard toolbar.

Can't find the status bar?

If your status bar is missing, open the **Tools** menu, and click **Options**. On the **View** tab, click the **Status bar** check box; then click **OK**.

I don't see my AutoCalculate box

AutoCalculate appears in the status bar only when a function is selected *and* calculable cells are selected. (For example, if the selected function is Sum but no cells with numbers are selected, AutoCalculate is hidden.)

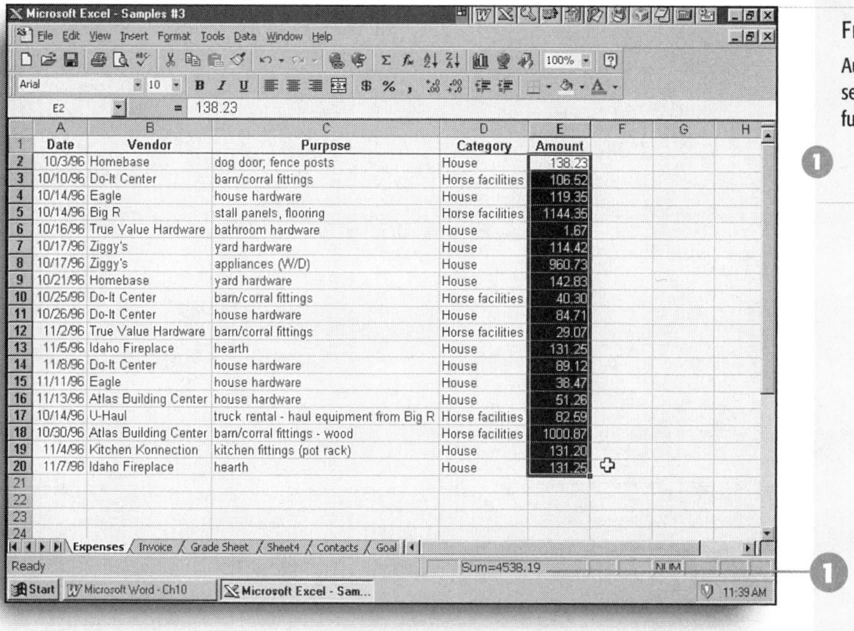

FIGURE 9.1
AutoCalculate calculates all selected cells, according to the function you select.

❶ AutoCalculate

Use the AutoSum button to enter a SUM formula

1. Click a cell at the bottom of a column of numbers you want to sum, as shown in Figure 9.2.

2. On the Standard toolbar, click the AutoSum button Σ.

   A SUM formula is written, and the cells Excel thinks you want to sum are surrounded by a moving border. If you want to sum different cells, drag to select them on the worksheet.

3. Press Enter.

AutoSum is versatile

You can sum a row of numbers by placing the AutoSum formula at the end of the row; or you can place the AutoSum formula anywhere on the worksheet, and then drag to select the cells you want to sum.

About Cell References

A *cell reference* is the cell's address on the worksheet, in terms of its column letter and row number. You can tell what a cell's reference is by either looking at the row and column that intersect at the cell or selecting the cell and looking at the Name box (see Figure 9.3).

FIGURE 9.2

AutoSum writes the formula
and guesses which cells; but
you can drag to select different
cells.

❶ Moving border

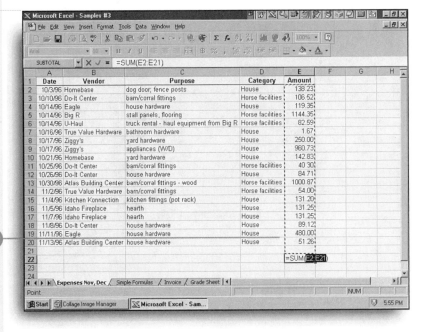

FIGURE 9.3

Cells are identified and located
by their cell references, or
addresses. This cell's reference
is A1: It's at the intersection of
column A and row 1.

❶ Name box

❷ Cell A1 selected

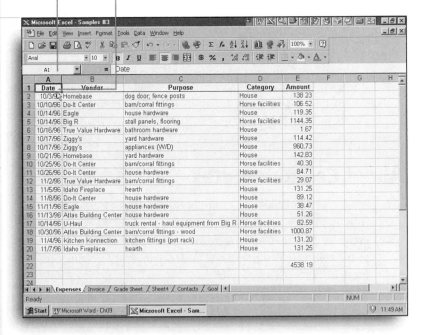

If you click in the upper-left corner of a worksheet, the Name box reads A1, which is that cell's reference: a combination of the column letter, A, and the row number, 1.

When you write formulas that include cells, the cells in the formula are identified by their references; for example, the formula =A1+B1 adds together the values stored in cells A1 and B1.

About Cell Reference Types

Cells can have different types of references, depending on how you want to use them in a formula. First I'll explain the terminology and how to create the different types; then I'll show you how they work with actual examples (at which point they'll make more sense).

For any cell there is only one reference but four reference types: relative, absolute, and two mixed types. Dollar signs ($) in the reference determine the type.

For example:

- A1 is called *relative*
- A1 is called *absolute*
- $A1 and A$1 are called *mixed*

A *relative* cell reference is like a relative location, as in "one block west and two blocks south."

An *absolute* cell reference is a fixed geographical point, like a street address, such as "123 Cherry Street."

A *mixed* cell reference is a mixture of absolute and relative locations, as in "three blocks east on Hampton Avenue." A mixed cell reference can have an absolute column and relative row, as in $A1, or a relative column and absolute row, as in A$1.

The dollar signs designate the row and/or column as absolute, or unchanging, within a reference. When you write formulas, the meanings of absolute, relative, and mixed become more clear.

Changing References to Relative, Absolute, or Mixed

If you need to change a cell reference type in a formula, there's a much faster way than typing in the dollar signs ($).

Cycle through the cell reference types

1. Double-click the cell containing the formula.

2. Within the formula, click in the cell reference you want to change (see Figure 9.4).

3. Press F4 until the reference changes to the type you want.

    Pressing F4 repeatedly cycles through all the possible reference types.

4. Press Enter to complete the change.

FIGURE 9.4

To change the reference type, click in the cell reference; then press F4.

1 Click in the cell reference

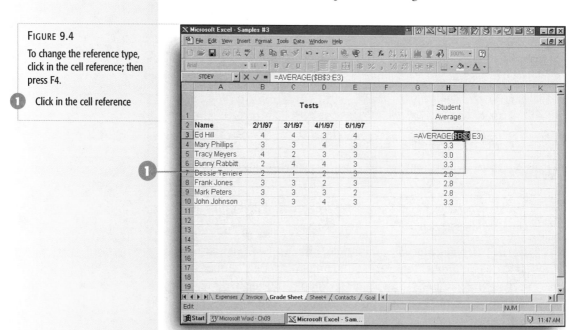

Writing Your Own Formulas

You'll probably need to do more calculations in your workbooks than AutoSum can do for you, which means learning how to write formulas.

A simple formula might consist of adding, subtracting, multiplying, and dividing cells. Excel's arithmetic operators are detailed in Table 9.1.

TABLE 9.1   **Arithmetic operators**

Operator	Description
+ (plus sign)	Addition
− (minus sign)	Subtraction
* (asterisk)	Multiplication
/ (forward slash)	Division
^ (caret)	Exponentiation

All formulas can calculate cells in the same worksheet, on different worksheets, and even in different workbooks (which links the workbooks and worksheets together).

Writing a Simple Formula

You can write a simple formula that adds the values of two cells; to write a simple formula with other arithmetic operators, type another operator in place of the plus sign.

Write a formula that sums the values in two cells

1. Click a cell where you want to display the results of the formula.

2. Type an equal sign (=).

3. Click one of the cells you want to add.

4. Type a plus sign (+).

5. Click the other cell you want to add (as shown in Figure 9.5).

Starting a formula in Excel

All Excel formulas begin with an equal sign (=).

6. Press Enter.

The formula is complete.

When you build a formula by clicking cells and ranges (as in the previous exercise), the cells have relative references. What the formula in Figure 9.5 really does is add the cell *two cells left* and the cell *one cell left* of the current cell, because the references are relative. The advantage of using relative references will become clear in the next exercise, when you use AutoFill to copy the formula.

Using AutoFill to Copy a Formula

When you write a formula that uses relative references, the references adjust themselves when you copy the formula. They do this because the formula is calculating cells that are located relative to the formula on the worksheet.

Understand the concept of relative references

1. Write a formula that adds the cell left of the formula and the cell left of that cell (as in Figure 9.6, the formula in F4 adds cells D4 and E4).

2. Position the mouse pointer over the AutoFill handle (the small black box in the lower-right corner of the selected cell). Then drag down to fill the formula down the right side of the table.

Sideways, too

AutoFill also works horizontally to copy formulas across a row.

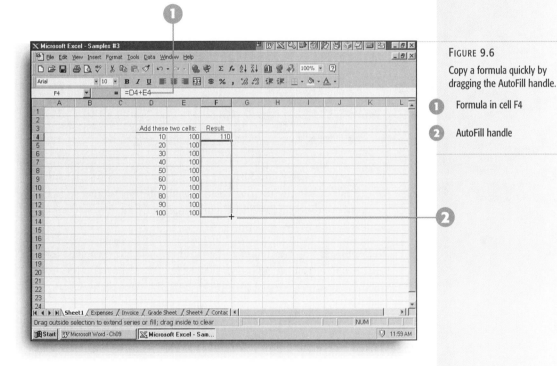

FIGURE 9.6

Copy a formula quickly by dragging the AutoFill handle.

1. Formula in cell F4

2. AutoFill handle

3. Release the mouse button after you've dragged to AutoFill all the cells down the side of the table.

   The formula is copied to all the cells you dragged, as shown in Figure 9.7.

The formulas you copied using AutoFill have adjusted themselves, so that every formula adds the two cells left of it. The formulas are self-adjusting because they contain relative references.

FIGURE 9.7

Relative references are self-adjusting when you use AutoFill to copy a formula.

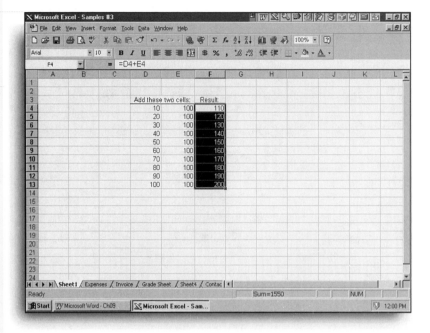

In Figure 9.8, the same formula has been copied down the side of the table, but the formula contains absolute references. The references add cells D4 and E4 all the way down the column—which in this example is quite useless.

But suppose you wanted every formula to add the two cells left of it (relative references) to the value in cell A1 (an absolute reference). In this case (see Figure 9.9), an absolute reference for cell A1 ensures that the correct values are calculated in every copy of the formula.

Mixed references allow a formula to refer to cells that have relative row references within an absolute, or unchanging, column (as in $A1), or relative column references within an absolute row (as in A$1).

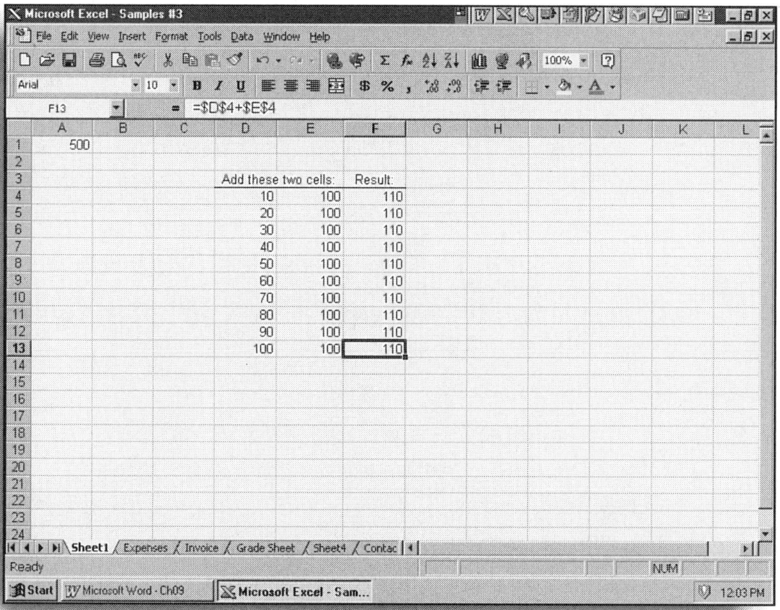

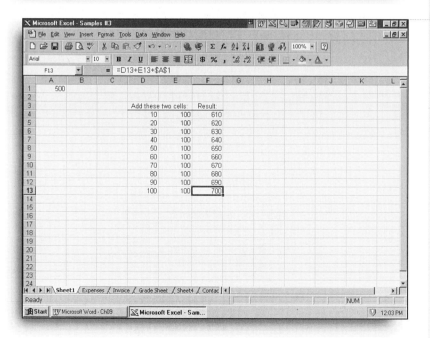

FIGURE **9.8**

Absolute references do not adjust when you copy a formula; they always calculate the same cells.

FIGURE **9.9**

In these formulas, the relative references adjust, and the absolute reference always refers to the same cell.

Writing a Formula that Links Workbooks

A formula that *links* workbooks is a formula that refers to cells in more than one workbook. (You can also link worksheets in the same workbook.) For example, if you have two workbooks that represent sales from two districts, you can write a formula that sums values from both workbooks.

Write a formula that adds the values of cells in two workbooks

1. Open both workbooks (and a third workbook, if that's where you want to write the formula).

2. Begin the formula by typing =.

3. Click in one of the source workbooks (the workbooks with values you want to sum), and click the cell you want to include in the formula.

   The cell reference is added to the formula, but because it's in another workbook, the reference includes the workbook name and worksheet name, too (see Figure 9.10). The workbook name is in square brackets and is followed by the worksheet name; the worksheet name is separated from the cell reference by an exclamation point, like this:

   `[workbook name]worksheet name!cell reference`

4. Type a plus sign (+).

5. Click in the other source workbook, and click the cell you want to include in the formula.

6. Press Enter.

   The formula calculates the sum of the cells in the two source workbooks, and all three workbooks are linked by the formula (refer to Figure 9.10).

The next time you open the workbook containing the formula, called the *dependent* workbook, you'll be asked if you want to update all linked information.

- If you click **Yes**, the formula is updated with current values in the source workbooks, even if those values have changed.

- If you click **No**, the formula won't be updated with current values but will retain its previous values, which saves you time spent waiting for a large workbook to recalculate.

How can I break this link?

If you don't want the formula to recalculate, ever, you can save the current formula result as a value; see the procedure in Chapter 10, "Complex Calculations," in the section titled "Converting Formula Results to Values."

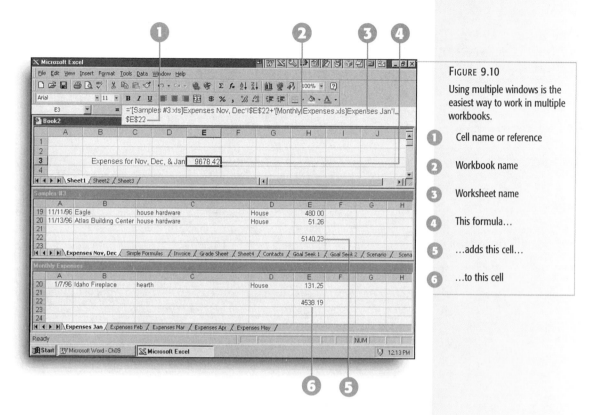

FIGURE 9.10

Using multiple windows is the easiest way to work in multiple workbooks.

1. Cell name or reference

2. Workbook name

3. Worksheet name

4. This formula…

5. …adds this cell…

6. …to this cell

- If you open one of the source workbooks, the formula will automatically recalculate with the values in the open source workbook.

Editing a Formula

You can easily change an existing formula in any way (change the function, arithmetic operators, cells, or constant values).

Edit an existing formula in the worksheet

1. Double-click the cell to open it for editing.

As shown in Figure 9.11, the cell references and names are colored, and the colors correspond to colored cell borders on the worksheet (which makes it easy to see at a glance which cells the formula refers to).

Another way

You might find it easier to click the cell and edit it in the Formula bar.

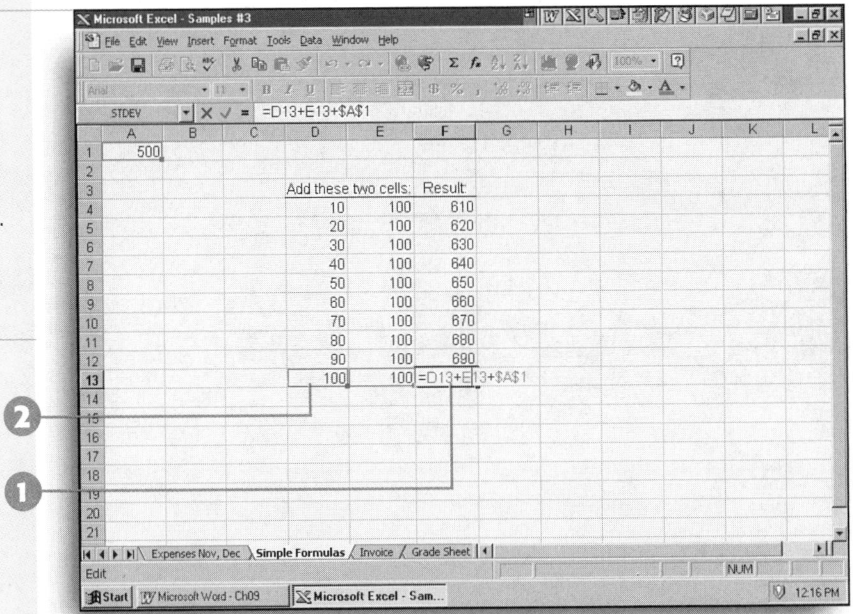

FIGURE 9.11

To replace one cell reference with another, double-click the reference in the formula; then click the replacement cell on the worksheet.

1 The color of this reference...

2 ...matches the color of its cell border

2. Select and replace whatever you want to change:

- To replace a referenced or named cell, double-click to select it; then, in the worksheet, click the replacement cell.

- To replace a range, double-click and drag over both references (to select them). Then, in the worksheet, drag the replacement range.

- To replace a constant value or an arithmetic operator, select it and type the replacement characters.

3. Press Enter.

Auditing a Formula

I want to see all my formulas

To show all the formulas in a worksheet, press Ctrl+` (the grave accent, left of the 1 on your keyboard). To hide the formulas again, press Ctrl+` again.

If you've created a worksheet with formulas before, you might want some help tracing how you built your formulas (especially if the worksheet is a complicated one).

Auditing, or tracing, a formula is a way to see at a glance where the referenced cells (the *precedent* cells) are in the worksheet; you can also trace a formula's *dependent* cells—those cells where other formulas use the results of the formula you're tracing.

Find a formula's precedent (or source) cells

1. Click the cell containing the formula.

2. On the **Tools** menu, point to **Auditing**; then click **Trace Precedents**.

   Lines are displayed on the worksheet that trace source cells to the formula cell, as shown in Figure 9.12.

   If the precedent cells are on another worksheet or in another workbook, you'll see a dashed line and an other-workbook symbol (see Figure 9.12).

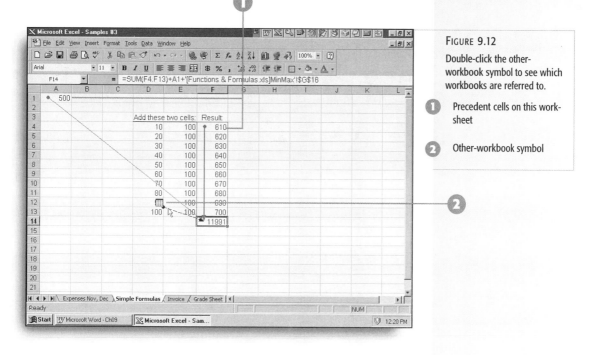

Are there toolbar buttons for auditing?

To trace precedent and dependent cells with toolbar buttons, you can use the Auditing toolbar. On the **Tools** menu, point to **Auditing**; then click **Show Auditing Toolbar**.

FIGURE 9.12

Double-click the other-workbook symbol to see which workbooks are referred to.

1. Precedent cells on this worksheet

2. Other-workbook symbol

3. To remove all trace lines from the worksheet, open the **Tools** menu, point to **Auditing**, and then click **Remove All Arrows**.

Find a formula's dependent cells

1. Click the cell containing the formula.

2. On the **Tools** menu, point to **Auditing**; then click **Trace Dependents**.

Lines are displayed on the worksheet that trace the formula to its dependent cells, as shown in Figure 9.13.

If the dependent cells are on another worksheet or in another workbook, you'll see a dashed line and an other-workbook symbol (see Figure 9.13).

FIGURE 9.13

Dependent trace lines point away from the formula cell, whereas precedent trace lines point toward the formula cell.

1 Other-workbook symbol

2 Dependent cells on this worksheet

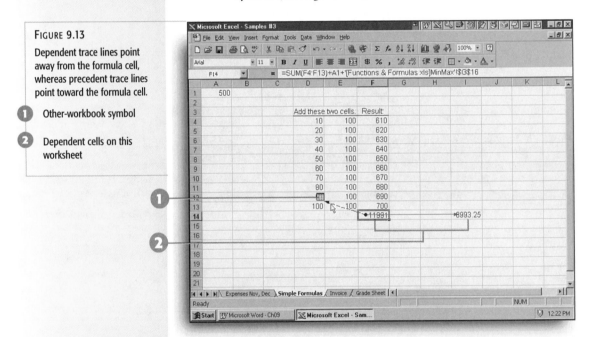

3. To remove all trace lines from the worksheet, open the **Tools** menu, point to **Auditing**, and then click **Remove All Arrows**.

Complex Calculations

Understanding functions

Writing formulas that use functions

Using cell names and labels

Converting formula results to values

Finding errors in worksheets

Understanding Functions

Not all calculations are simple. Fortunately, Excel can handle tremendously complex calculations for you.

Functions are built-in formulas that perform complex math for you. You enter the function name and any *arguments* (extra information) the function requires, and Excel performs the calculations. SUM and AVERAGE are examples of simple, straightforward functions, and PMT and VLOOKUP are examples of common but more complex functions that I show you how to use.

Any formula is easier to read and understand if you use cell *names* and *labels* in place of cell references (for example, the formula =tax+subtotal is easier to understand than =H32+H33). After you create cell names or labels, Excel automatically uses the cell name instead of the reference when you use the cell in a formula. A cell name can be anything you create. A cell label is similar to a cell name, but is a row or column label that Excel automatically uses to identify cells in a formula. In this chapter I show you how to create and use cell names and labels to make your formulas easier to understand.

Errors and invalid data always seem to find their way into worksheets, especially when you're working with complex calculations; however, they're easier to locate and correct when you have the proper tools. In this chapter I show you some helpful tools for ferreting out problems.

Using Functions

Where are the advanced functions?

The more advanced (and less commonly used) functions are found in the Analysis Toolpak add-in. If you don't see the Analysis Toolpak add-in listed in the Add-Ins dialog box (open the **Tools** menu and select **Add-Ins**), you need to install the add-in from your Office 97 or Excel 97 CD-ROM.

Excel comes with a slew of functions, some you use all the time, and some you're only be interested in if you're an electrical engineer or nuclear physicist. Functions have specific names, such as SUM, AVERAGE, and BETADIST, and function names must be spelled correctly or Excel won't recognize them; however, Excel provides dialog boxes that do the spelling for you and help you fill in the arguments each function requires.

Write a Formula Using Functions

Use the Paste Function dialog box to write a formula

1. Click the cell in which you want the results of the formula to appear.

2. On the toolbar, click the Paste Function button f_* .

The Paste Function dialog box appears (shown in Figure 10.1).

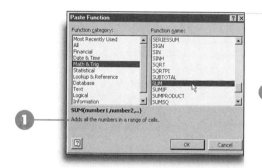

FIGURE 10.1

The Paste Function dialog box briefly explains the selected function.

① Function explanation

3. Click a category of functions and double-click the function you want.

The Formula Palette opens to help you complete the function (shown in Figure 10.2).

4. Click the argument box and read the description of the argument to figure out what information is needed.

This formula thing is in my way

You can drag the *Formula Palette*—the dialog box in which you supply arguments for the formula—elsewhere on the worksheet to move it out of your way.

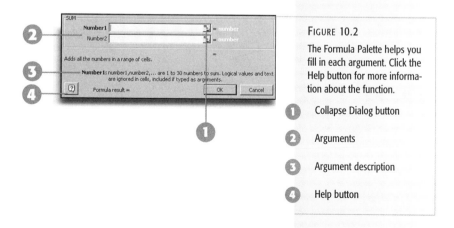

FIGURE 10.2

The Formula Palette helps you fill in each argument. Click the Help button for more information about the function.

① Collapse Dialog button

② Arguments

③ Argument description

④ Help button

5. Click or drag worksheet cells to fill in arguments (if the arguments call for cell references).

To shrink the Formula Palette so that it doesn't cover worksheet cells you want to select, click the Collapse Dialog button at the right end of the argument, select the worksheet cells, and click the Expand Dialog button (at the right end of the collapsed argument box) to display the Formula Palette again and continue building your function.

6. Click **OK**.

The function is built and the formula is completed.

This is the basic procedure. Now I show you how to use it to write the specific, common, and useful worksheet formulas (shown in Table 10.1).

Writing your own formulas

After you get comfortable with formulas, you can often write them faster yourself, but you must spell the function name correctly. Try this tip: type the function name in lower case letters. If it's spelled correctly, Excel converts it to upper case after you press Enter (for example, **sum** is converted to **SUM**); but if it's spelled incorrectly, Excel won't convert it to upper case—that's your clue that it's misspelled.

TABLE 10.1 **Common and useful worksheet functions**

Function	Purpose
SUM	Add together the values in a selected range
MIN	Find the minimum value in a selected range
MAX	Find the maximum value in a selected range
AVERAGE	Average the values in a selected range
COUNTIF	Count all values that meet specific criteria
SUMIF	Add together all values that meet specific criteria
VLOOKUP and HLOOKUP	Find a value in a table
IF	Display a value that depends on criteria you set
PMT	Calculate the payment for specific loan terms
NOW	Returns current date or time, as a serial number
TODAY	Returns the current date
CONCATENATE	Joins cell values together in a single cell
LEFT and RIGHT	Returns a specific number of characters from the left (or right) end of a cell's value

Some Common and Useful Functions

In this section I show you examples of the functions in Table 10.1, with suggestions about where they're useful in real life. This short list of functions is just a few of the hundreds of functions available in Excel. If you explore the list of functions in the Paste Function dialog box, you find functions that calculate sine, cosine, tangent, the actual value of Pi, functions for a lot of accounting and engineering equations, logarithms, and binomials. It's nearly endless, but I'm only showing you the functions that you most likely want to use.

SUM

The SUM function is universally useful: it adds up all the numbers in a selected range. A good place for the SUM function is at the end of a list of numbers, like the list in Figure 10.3.

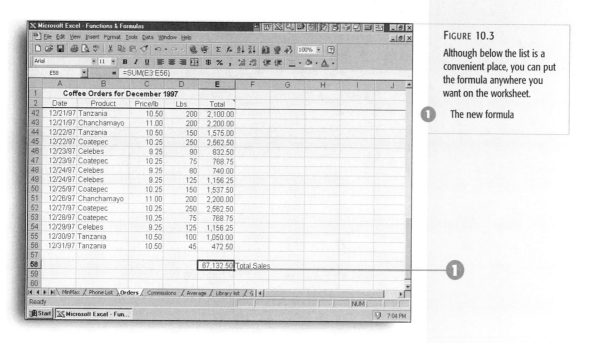

> **Use mock data**
>
> When you first write a formula, you want to test it to be sure that it's calculating properly (that is, you want to be sure you entered all the arguments correctly and the results are accurate). To test your formulas, enter *mock data* (phony numbers) in the worksheet. Use mock data that's simple: short text that's quick to type and round numbers so that you can do the math in your head and know quickly whether the results are accurate.

FIGURE 10.3

Although below the list is a convenient place, you can put the formula anywhere you want on the worksheet.

1 The new formula

Write a SUM formula

1. Click the cell in which you want to place the formula.

2. Type =.

3. Type sum(.

4. On the worksheet, drag to select the cells you want to add together (in this example, the range E3:E56).

5. Type).

6. Press Enter.

The formula is complete. If you spelled the function name, SUM, correctly, Excel converted it to upper case letters.

When you drag cells to insert them in a formula, Excel uses relative references by default; so if you copy this formula to another cell, the results change because the relative references adjust themselves. If, however, you drag the cell to *move* it elsewhere on the worksheet, Excel retains the original references and the results remain accurate. If this gets confusing and you want to be sure the references remain the same, you can change the references to absolute types.

Change the reference type

To quickly change the cell reference type, click the reference, press F4 until the type cycles to the type you want, and then press Enter.

SEE ALSO

> *To learn more about cell references, see page 139.*

> *To learn how to use the AutoSum button to quickly sum ranges, see page 138.*

MIN

The MIN function returns the minimum, or lowest, value in a range of numbers. Of course, if your range is a single column of numbers, you can also find the smallest value by sorting or filtering the list. If your range is a large table of numbers, like the one in Figure 10.4, the MIN function comes in handy.

Write your own formula with the MIN function

1. Click the cell in which you want to place the formula.

2. Type =.

3. Type min(.

4. On the worksheet, drag to select the cells you want to search for a minimum value (in this example, the range B3:M11, all the numbers in the table).

5. Type) .

6. Press Enter.

The minimum value in the table is 1006, and it would have taken a bit more time to find it yourself.

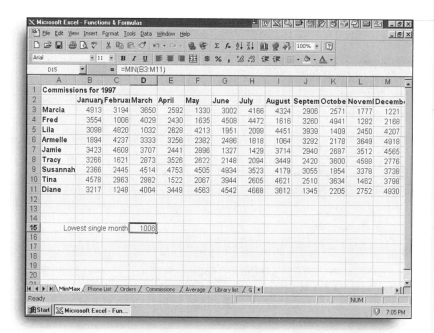

FIGURE 10.4

The MIN function finds the minimum value in the selected table of data. It's a real time-saver if the table is large.

Because the minimum value is the result of a formula, it continues to find the minimum value automatically, even if you change the numbers in the table.

SEE ALSO

➤ *To learn more about saving workbooks as templates, see page 50.*

MAX

The MAX function is the opposite of the MIN function and works exactly the same way. It finds the largest value in a selected range of cells. To write your own formula with the MAX function, you can follow the preceding procedure for the MIN function.

Save time with a template

If your business requires monthly worksheets like the one in Figure 10.4, you could save yourself time by creating a template and including the MIN formula in it. When you open a copy of the template, the formula is already in place, and as you enter numbers, the formula finds the minimum value automatically.

Write a formula with the MAX function using the Paste Function dialog box

1. Click the cell in which you want to enter the formula.

2. Click the Paste Function button f_x .

   The Paste Function dialog box appears (shown in Figure 10.5).

FIGURE 10.5

The Paste Function dialog box helps you select and write a formula using any of Excel's myriad functions.

1. Function categories

2. Description of selected function

3. Functions

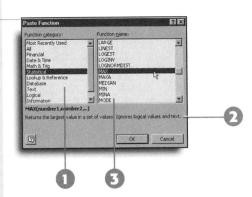

Make the MAX and MIN functions more useful

When you use the MAX or MIN function to determine the highest or lowest value in a large table, you still have to search to find that value among all those numbers. You can make it jump out visually by combining the MAX or MIN function with Conditional Number Formatting, which formats the number in the table with any formatting you choose.

3. To narrow your range of choices, click a function category in the **Function category** list. (If you know the name of the function you want but don't know in which category to find it, click **All**.)

4. Scroll through the list of functions on the right side of the dialog box and double-click the function you want (in this example, I've looked up the **MAX** function in the **Statistical** category).

5. The Formula Palette appears for the function you double-clicked (in this case, the MAX function, as shown in Figure 10.6).

6. Highlight or delete any value in the **Number1** argument and enter the entire table range by dragging to select the cells. In this example, the table range is A2:M11 (but I previously named this range Commissions, so when I select the range, Excel inserts the range name, shown in Figure 10.7).

FIGURE 10.6

The Formula Palette for the selected function explains each of the arguments.

1 Explanation of selected argument

FIGURE 10.7

Using a range name such as Commissions, instead of cell references, makes the formula more understandable.

7. Click **OK**.

The formula is complete, and the maximum value in the range, 4941, is displayed (see Figure 10.8).

SEE ALSO

➤ *To learn more about conditional number formatting, see page 231.*

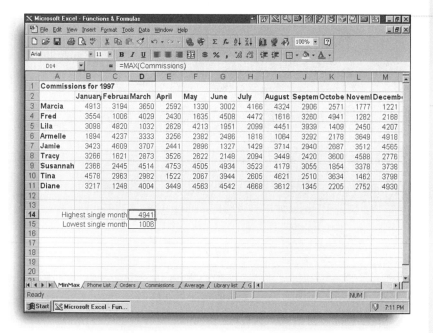

FIGURE 10.8

Whether you use the Paste Function dialog box or write the formula yourself, the result is the same.

AVERAGE

The AVERAGE function is another common and easy-to-use function. It's as simple to write as the SUM, MIN, and MAX functions, so I demonstrate it without using any dialog boxes.

The important thing to know about the AVERAGE function is that it gives a more correct result than you get by adding cells and dividing by the number of cells. When I first began using Excel, I didn't know about functions. I calculated averages by adding the cells together and then dividing by the number of cells. Occasionally, however, I got very wrong answers because if a cell didn't have a value in it, my method averaged that cell as a zero! The AVERAGE function, however, adds the cells in the selected range and then divides the sum by the number of values; so any blank cells are left out of the calculation (the comparison is shown in Figure 10.9).

FIGURE 10.9

Adding and dividing doesn't always give the correct average, but the AVERAGE function does. (I created cell comments that show the formulas for each cell.)

 Ed Hill skipped this test

 His resulting add-and-divide average is wrong

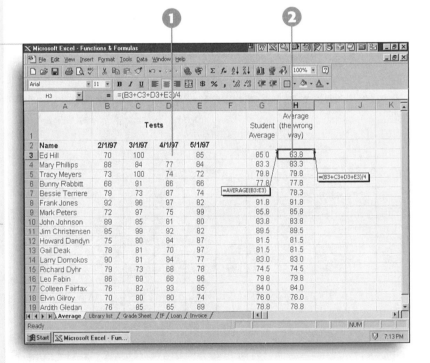

Write a formula using the AVERAGE function

1. Click the cell in which you want to place the formula.

2. Type =AVERAGE(.

3. In the worksheet, drag the range of cells you want to average (or type the range name or label).

4. Type a closing parenthesis,).

5. Press Enter.

SUMIF

In the table in Figure 10.10, I want to know how much of the product named Celebes was sold in December.

To find the answer, I use a SUMIF function, which sums values if they correspond to my criteria. (In this case, I write a formula that sums values in the Total column if they correspond to the value Celebes in the Product column.) A SUMIF formula can be written one of two ways. The Conditional Sum Wizard, an add-in, can be used, which, in my opinion, wastes a whole lot of time if you want to sum by a single criteria and only serves to make the function more mysterious. The other way is to use the Formula Palette, which is simpler and faster for single-criteria sums. I show you both ways, and you can decide for yourself which is easier.

Use the Paste Function dialog box to write a SUMIF formula

1. Click the cell in which you want to place the formula.

2. Click the Paste Function button f_x .

3. In the **All** or **Math & Trig** category, double-click **SUMIF**. The Formula Palette for SUMIF appears (see Figure 10.11).

4. In the **Range** box, enter the range of cells that contains the criteria (in this example, the Product column, because it contains the Celebes criteria).

You can drag the cells in column B (B3:B56), or you can enter the entire column (B:B) as I've done.

Why bother with the Conditional Sum Wizard?

If you want to use more than one criteria in your conditional sum formula (for example, how much Celebes and Tanzania were sold in December), using the wizard is easier.

FIGURE 10.10

For these December sales figures, I want to know the total revenues just for orders of Celebes coffee.

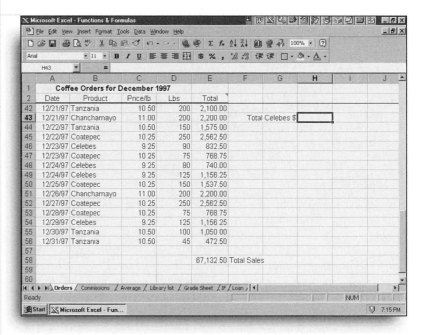

FIGURE 10.11

The Formula Palette makes the SUMIF function reasonably easy to write.

1 Range containing criteria (Product column)

2 Criteria (Celebes)

3 Range containing values to sum (Total column)

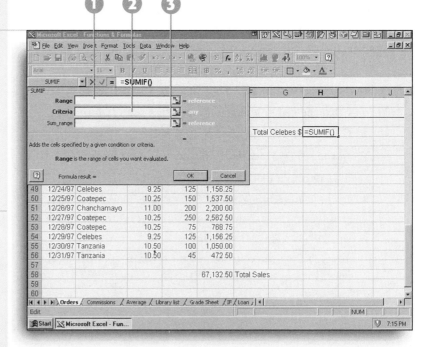

5. In the **Criteria** box, enter the criteria you want to sum values for.

- If it's a text string, as `"Celebes"` is, be sure to type quotation marks around it.

- Alternatively, you can click a cell containing the entry `Celebes`, instead of typing the text string and quotation marks.

6. In the **Sum_range** box, enter the range of values you want to sum (in this example, column E, entered as the range `E:E`)

Your SUMIF dialog box should look similar to the one in Figure 10.12.

B:B doesn't look like a cell reference

My range entry, `B:B`, designates the entire column B as the range containing my criteria. It's important that there not be any other entries on the worksheet below this table, or the formula calculates with those entries and gets messed up. Also, the range reference `B:B` is a relative reference. If I wanted an absolute reference to column B, I'd type `$B:$B`.

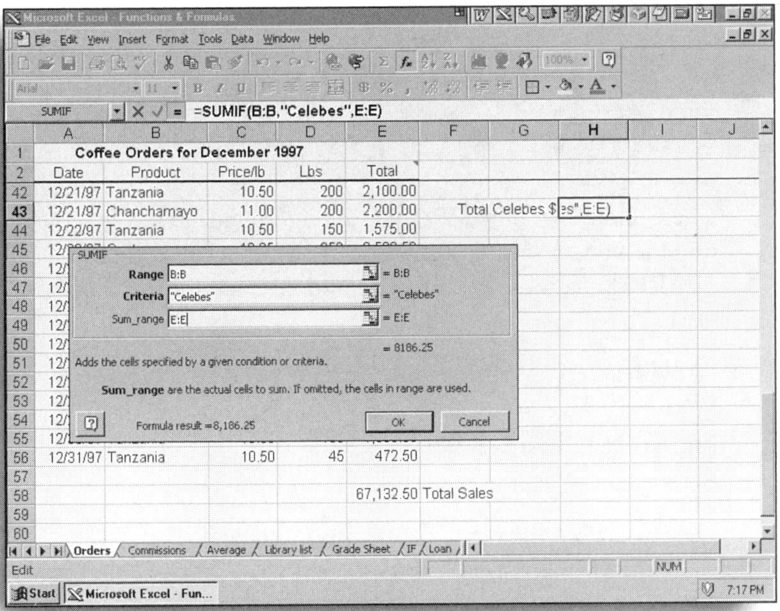

FIGURE 10.12
The SUMIF dialog box, ready to sum just `Celebes` orders.

7. Click **OK**.

The SUMIF formula is complete (shown in Figure 10.13).

FIGURE 10.13

Celebes orders totaled
$8186.25 in December. To find
the total for Tanzania, open the
cell and edit the formula:
change "Celebes" to
"Tanzania" and press
Enter.

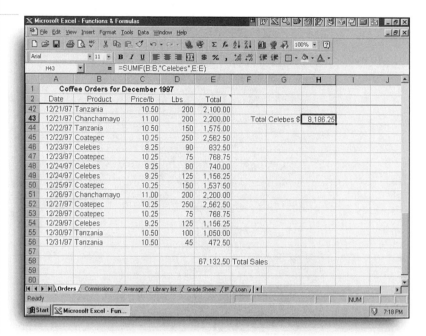

The Conditional Sum Wizard is a long, roundabout way of getting the same result for a single criteria but is better than
SUMIF if you want to write a conditional sum for multiple criteria.

SEE ALSO

➤ *To learn more about reference types, see page 141.*

Use the Conditional Sum Wizard

1. Click anywhere in the table.

2. On the **Tools** menu, point to **Wizard**, and click
   Conditional Sum.

   The Conditional Sum Wizard starts (shown in Figure
   10.14). If the selected range is wrong, change it by typing
   new references or dragging the range on the worksheet.

3. Click **Next**.

4. In step 2 of the wizard, set the column to sum (in this case,
   Total) and the criteria.

   To set the criteria for this example, select **Product**, select **=**,
   and then select **Celebes** (shown in Figure 10.15).

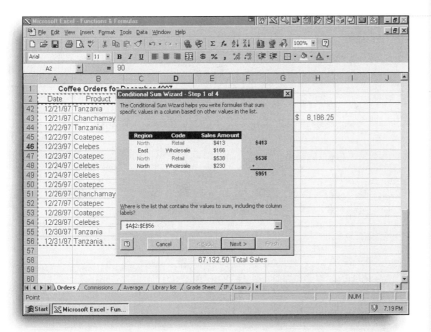

FIGURE 10.14

The Conditional Sum Wizard assumes the table you clicked is the range you want.

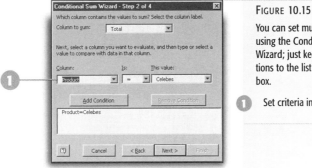

FIGURE 10.15

You can set multiple conditions using the Conditional Sum Wizard; just keep adding conditions to the list in the dialog box.

1 Set criteria in these boxes

5. Click **Add Condition** to add the conditions to a list of conditions for the sum and then click **Next**.

6. In step 3 of the wizard, you can choose to display just the sum or the sum and a label. Then click **Next**.

7. In steps 4 and 5 of the wizard, you can decide where the label and sum are to be placed on the worksheet. Click the wizard box, click a cell on the worksheet, and then click **Next**.

8. When you get to the last wizard step, click **Finish**.

The wizard result is identical to the result of the SUMIF formula (see Figure 10.16). The only real difference is that the wizard enables you to set multiple criteria for selecting cells to sum.

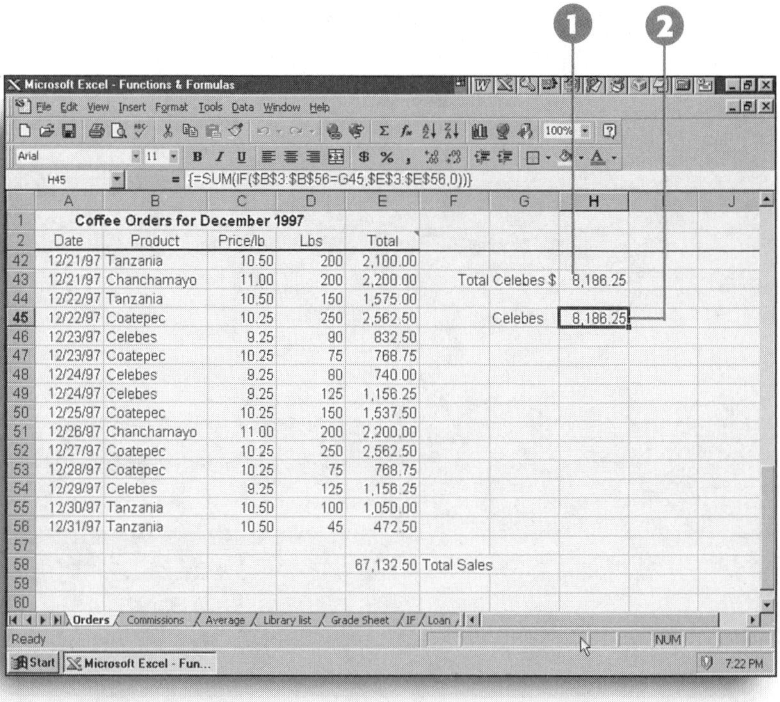

FIGURE 10.16

The SUMIF function or the Conditional Sum Wizard: different journeys, same destination.

1 SUMIF result

2 Conditional Sum Wizard result

Is there a faster way?

Another way to get a quick answer to this question is to filter the table to show only `Celebes` and then take a count of the orders by using AutoCalculate.

COUNTIF

SEE ALSO

➤ *To learn about AutoCalculate, see page 138.*

➤ *To learn about filters, see page 263.*

The COUNTIF function counts the number of values in a range that meet a specific criteria, such as "How many orders were there for Celebes coffee in December?"

The COUNTIF function works like the SUMIF function but without a wizard alternative (nor any need for one).

Use the COUNTIF function

1. Click the cell in which you want to place the result.

2. Click the Paste Function button f_x .

3. In the **All** or **Statistical** categories, double-click the **COUNTIF** function.

   The COUNTIF dialog box appears (shown in Figure 10.17).

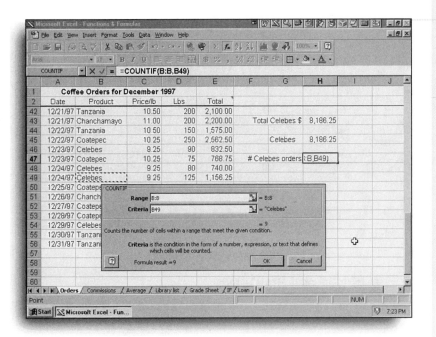

FIGURE 10.17
COUNTIF requires only a range to search and what to count in that range.

4. In the **Range** box, enter the range of cells to search (in this case, I've entered column B).

5. In the **Criteria** box, enter the criteria for counting cells (in this case, I've clicked cell **B49**, a Celebes entry, so the function counts all identical entries).

6. Click **OK**.

   The formula is complete (shown in Figure 10.18).

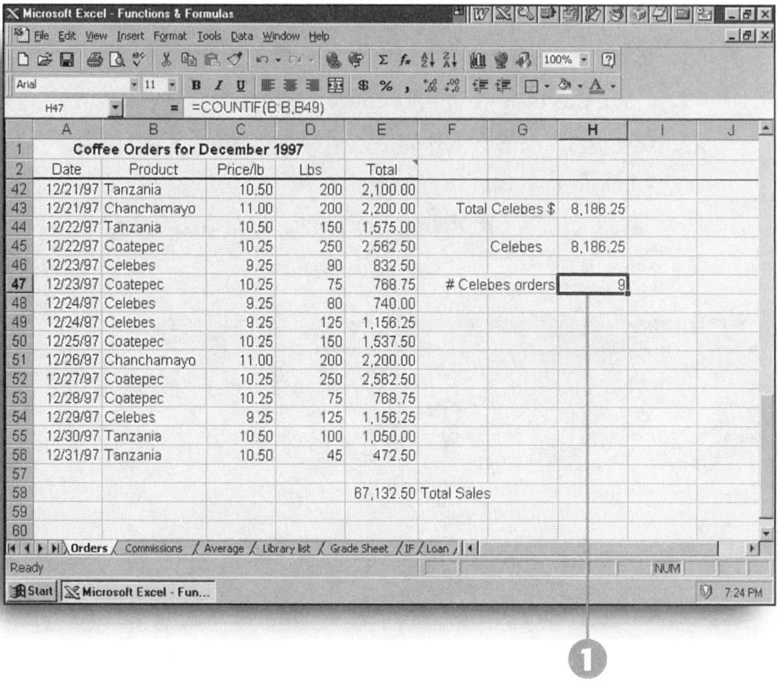

FIGURE 10.18

COUNTIF counts the number of Celebes orders in the list. I can find the average Celebes order by dividing the sum by the count.

1   Number of Celebes orders in list

SEE ALSO

➤ To learn more about AutoFilter, see page 265.

VLOOKUP and HLOOKUP

Sometimes you need to look up a value in another table. For example, in an invoice, you might want to have Excel look up the state tax rate for the shipping address, or if you're a teacher keeping grade sheets, you might want Excel to look up the letter grades corresponding to your students' test score averages.

A good function for looking up values in another table is VLOOKUP (or its transposed equivalent, HLOOKUP). These two functions are quite similar, the only difference being that one works vertically (VLOOKUP) and the other works horizontally (HLOOKUP) in the table. I demonstrate VLOOKUP, and when you understand VLOOKUP you'll be able to figure out HLOOKUP, if you ever need it.

Write a VLOOKUP formula

1. Create a lookup table that contains the values you want to look up (such as a state tax rate table or the letter grades table I use in this example).

   The table needs to be set up so that the values you are looking up (in this example, the test averages) are in the left-most column (as shown in Figure 10.19) and sorted in ascending order. The table can have several columns in it, as long as the values you look up are on the left.

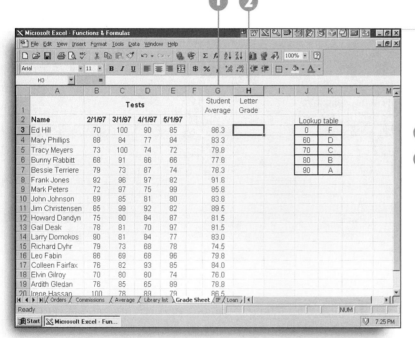

FIGURE 10.19

In my lookup table, the values I want to look up (test scores) are in the left-most column (column J), and the table is sorted in ascending order.

① What I look up

② What the formula returns

   For greater convenience, you can name the table and refer to it by name in the formula.

2. Click the cell in which you want the result to appear.

3. Click the Paste Function button ![fx].

One lookup table, a lot of lookups

A lookup table can be on the same worksheet, another worksheet, or in another workbook. For example, if you need several identical worksheets that all look up values in the same table, you can create one table on its own worksheet and use that table in the VLOOKUP formulas on all the other worksheets.

4. In the **All** or **Lookup & Reference** categories, double-click the **VLOOKUP** function.

The VLOOKUP dialog box appears (shown in Figure 10.20).

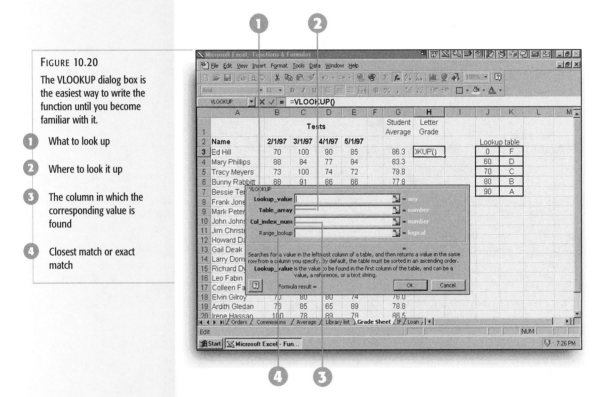

5. Click the **Lookup_value** box and click the cell that contains the value you want to look up (in this case, the test average).

6. Click the **Table_array** box and drag to select the lookup table (or enter the range name, if you named the table).

7. In the **Col_index_num** box, type the number of the lookup table column in which Excel is to find a corresponding value.

Think of the table columns as being numbered, left to right, starting with 1. In this example, the corresponding values (the letter grades) are in column 2 of the lookup table.

8. In the **Range_lookup** box, decide whether you want to find the closest match or an exact match. For the closest match, leave the box empty. For an exact match, type `false`.

In this case, each score you look up has a closest match, but probably not an exact match. So, the lookup table is sorted in ascending order, and VLOOKUP looks down the column for the closest match that's less than the test score value that it looks up.

For this example, the VLOOKUP dialog box should look like the one in Figure 10.21.

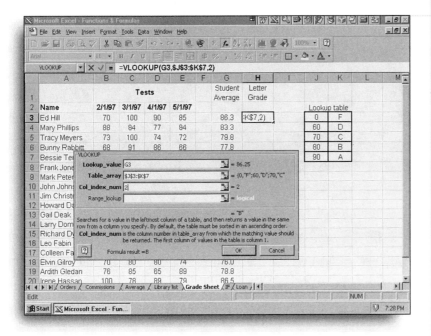

FIGURE 10.21

The VLOOKUP dialog box is ready to look up a letter grade for the test score average.

9. Click **OK**.

The VLOOKUP function looks up the score in the lookup table, finds the closest match, and returns the letter grade in the second column.

10. To copy the formula quickly down the side of the table, position the mouse pointer over the AutoFill handle and double-click.

The formula is copied down the length of the table (shown in Figure 10.22).

FIGURE 10.22

AutoFill is the fastest way to copy the formula down the length of the table. (Double-clicking the AutoFill handle works if the column is adjacent to the table, as shown here.)

1 AutoFill handle and pointer

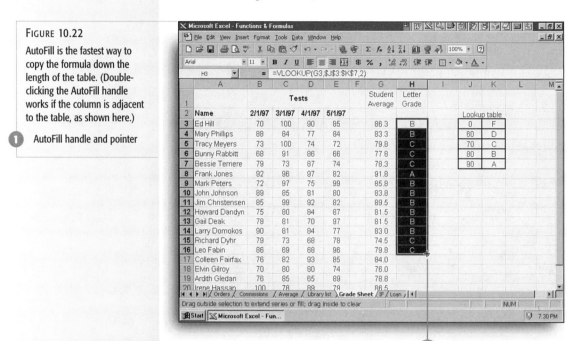

1

IF

The IF function is another way to determine a cell value based on criteria you set. The IF function works like this: IF *a statement is true*, THEN *return this first value*, OTHERWISE *return this second value*. (Figure 10.23 shows several examples of the IF function in action.)

As you can see in Figure 10.23, IF functions can be *nested* or combined within other IF functions to make them even more useful. In fact, any function can be nested in another function, up to seven levels deep, which enables you to be very creative with worksheet calculations.

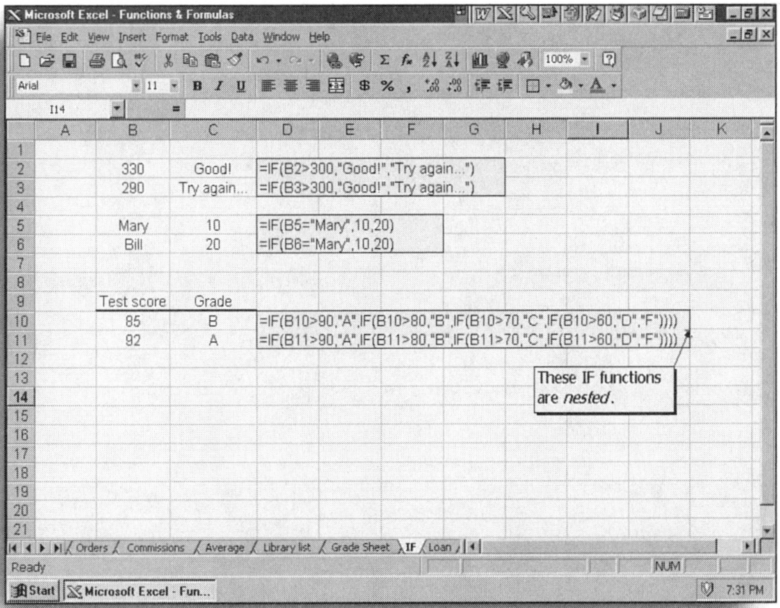

FIGURE 10.23
You can use the IF function in a lot of creative ways.

PMT

If you're shopping for a house, car, boat, or anything else that's expensive enough to require a loan, a key bit of information you want to know is what the monthly payment is. The PMT function figures it out for you quickly, if you provide the annual interest rate, number of monthly payments, and total loan amount. (Figure 10.24 shows the PMT formula—in the Formula bar—filled out with the appropriate cells in the worksheet.) If you use cell references or named cells in the formula instead of numerical values, then you can experiment with the formula results by simply changing the input values on the worksheet.

FIGURE 10.24

Use the PMT function to calculate how much of a loan you can afford.

1 Name cells with **Insert**, **Name**, **Create**

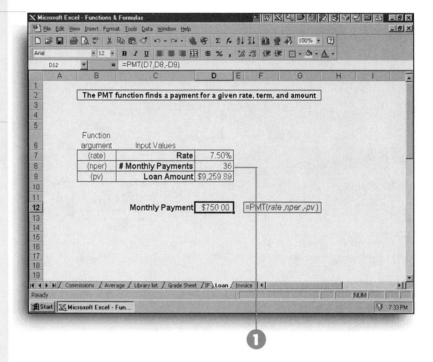

1

How can I see the serial number?

If you want to see the serial number for a date, enter the date, then format the cell as General. The serial numbers for dates begin with the number 1 on January 1, 1900; the serial number 100,000 corresponds to the date October 14, 2173 (so there won't be any Year 2000 problems in Excel 97). Time is determined by numbers on the right side of the decimal point in the serial number. For example, the decimal ".5" corresponds to 12:00:00 noon.

NOW and TODAY

The NOW function returns the current date and time. The TODAY function returns the current date. They're useful to have in the corner of a worksheet so that you can always tell how current (or old) the information in a printed page is.

NOW and TODAY have no arguments; to write them, you type =now() or =today(), and press Enter. (Be sure you include the parentheses and don't type anything in between the parentheses.) The resulting value is actually a serial number for the number of days since January 1, 1900. It's displayed as a date or time because the cell has a Date or Time format.

SEE ALSO

➤ *To learn more about formatting numbers, see page 223.*

LEFT and RIGHT

Text functions such as LEFT and RIGHT seem rather pointless unless you have a real-life use for them; then they're amazingly useful.

One of my students is a school librarian. She wants to use Excel to keep a list of the library's books, with author names, call numbers, ISBN numbers, and so forth. After typing in a long list of book titles and author names (like the list in Figure 10.25), she was going to type in the call numbers for each name. The call number, however, is composed of the first three letters of the author's last name, and she'd already done all that typing.

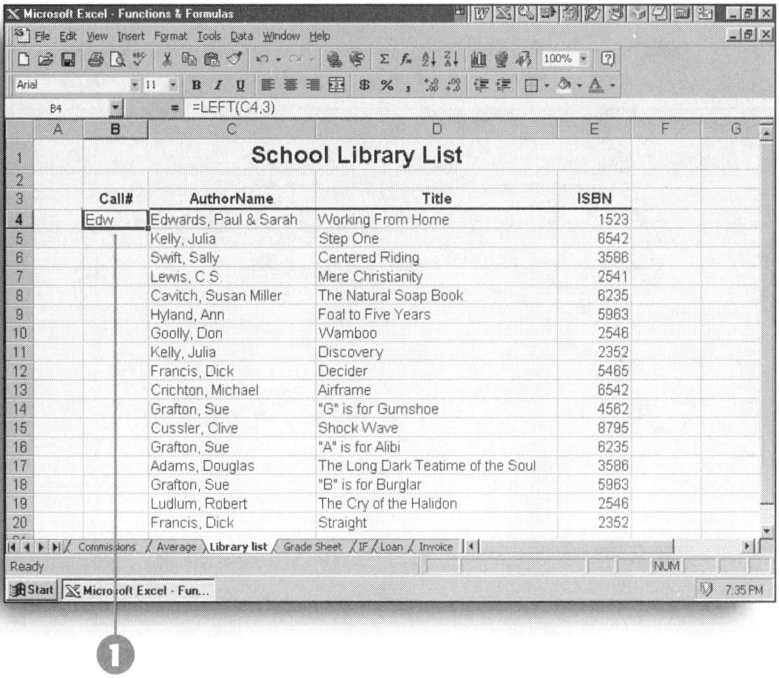

FIGURE 10.25
The LEFT function saves typing all the call signs for this long list of books.

① Call sign is first three letters of author name

At this point the LEFT function saved her a lot of redundant typing.

Write a formula using the LEFT function

1. Click the cell where you want the result of the function (in this case, the call number) to appear.

How do I know if I spelled it wrong?

Remember, typing a function name in lower-case letters is a good way to catch spelling errors. If the function name is spelled correctly, Excel converts it to upper case when you complete the formula.

2. Type =left(.

3. Click the cell containing the value from which you want to extract characters (in this case, the AuthorName cell next to the formula).

4. Type a comma (,), and then type the number of characters you want to extract (in this case, 3, for the left-most three characters).

5. Type) and press Enter.

The formula is complete, and it extracts the three left-most characters in the AuthorName cell next to it.

6. Use AutoFill to copy the formula down the length of the list.

As you can see in Figure 10.26, this saves a lot of typing.

FIGURE 10.26

After the formula is written using relative references, AutoFill copies the formula down the length of the table.

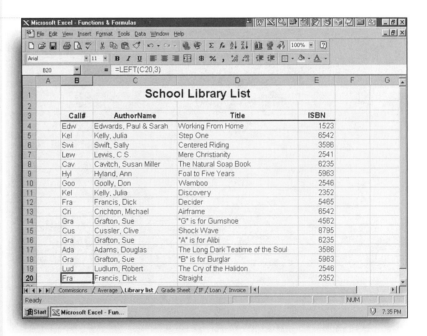

The LEFT and RIGHT functions are also useful for creating an invoice numbering system, like the one in my invoice in Figure 10.27.

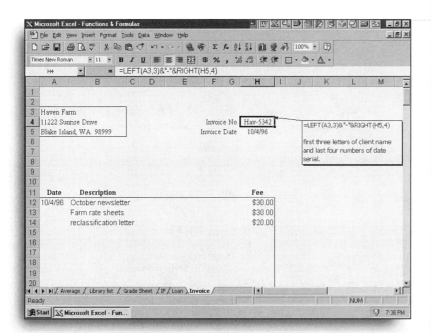

FIGURE **10.27**

The text functions work with the date serial number to help me create unique invoice numbers for good record keeping.

To create this unique-numbering system for my invoices, I combined the date serial number in the Date cell with the LEFT and RIGHT functions.

Create a unique-number invoice numbering system

1. Create a Date cell (in this case, cell H5) and a Client Name cell (in this case, cell A3).

2. Click the cell in which you want to display the formula result (in this case, the labeled Invoice No cell).

3. Enter the following formula: `=LEFT(A3,3)&"-"&RIGHT(H5,4)`

This formula extracts the left-most three characters from the Client Name cell (A3), joins or *concatenates* a dash character, and then extracts the right-most four characters from the serial number in the Date cell (H5). (In the next section you learn more about concatenation.) This makes the invoice number for each invoice unique. Because I save invoices using the invoice number as a file name, I get a clue to how ancient or recent an invoice file is when I scan a list of file names in a My Computer window.

Concatenate is a LONG name

Unlike most other functions, the CONCATENATE function name can be either spelled out ("CONCATE-NATE") or abbreviated to an amper-sand ("&"), which is much easier.

CONCATENATE (&)

The CONCATENATE function joins together the displayed values in two or more cells. It can also join a text string to the displayed value in a cell.

A situation where the CONCATENATE function comes in handy is shown in Figure 10.28. I want to join the first and last name columns into a single column of full names. I could do this slowly and inefficiently by laboriously copying and pasting every name, or I can write a single CONCATENATE formula and AutoFill copies of it down the length of the FullName column.

FIGURE 10.28

To join each pair of names into a single cell, use the CON-CATENATE function.

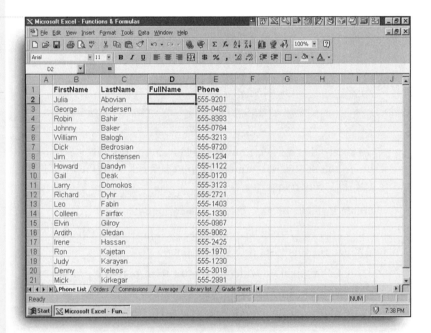

Where did these #REF! values come from?

If you later want to delete the origi-nal cells (in this case, the FirstName and LastName columns), convert the CONCATENATE formulas to val-ues first, or you get a column full of #REF! errors because the cells to which the formulas refer are gone.

Join the values of two cells in a single cell

1. Create a column where the joined value will be displayed (in this case, the FullName column).

2. Type = and click the first cell to be joined (in this case, the FirstName cell in the same row).

3. Type &.

4. Insert a space between the two names by typing " " (two quote marks with a space between them).
5. Type & again.
6. Click the second cell to be joined (in this case, the LastName cell in the same row).
7. Press Enter to complete the formula.

   The final formula is shown in Figure 10.29, in the Formula bar. The formula has been copied down the column.

SEE ALSO

➤ *To learn more about converting formula results to values, see page 188.*

A lots of uses for &

You can also join a text string like "Mr." to each cell value. To join, or concatenate, "Mr." to the LastName values in Figure 10.29, click cell F2 and enter the formula **="Mr."&" "&C2** (this formula joins Mr. and a space and the last name), and then use AutoFill to copy the formula down the list. (Of course, you'd have to edit the women's titles in this example, but it still saves time.)

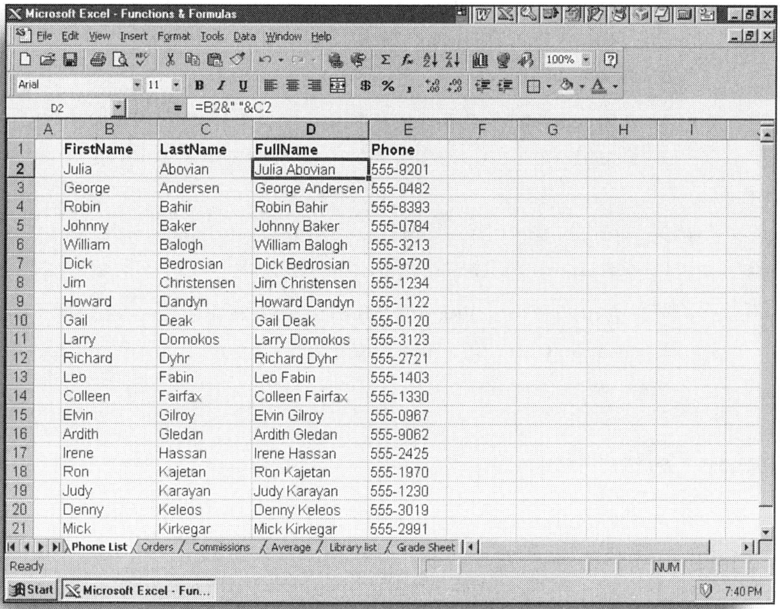

	FirstName	LastName	FullName	Phone
2	Julia	Abovian	Julia Abovian	555-9201
3	George	Andersen	George Andersen	555-0482
4	Robin	Bahir	Robin Bahir	555-8393
5	Johnny	Baker	Johnny Baker	555-0784
6	William	Balogh	William Balogh	555-3213
7	Dick	Bedrosian	Dick Bedrosian	555-9720
8	Jim	Christensen	Jim Christensen	555-1234
9	Howard	Dandyn	Howard Dandyn	555-1122
10	Gail	Deak	Gail Deak	555-0120
11	Larry	Domokos	Larry Domokos	555-3123
12	Richard	Dyhr	Richard Dyhr	555-2721
13	Leo	Fabin	Leo Fabin	555-1403
14	Colleen	Fairfax	Colleen Fairfax	555-1330
15	Elvin	Gilroy	Elvin Gilroy	555-0967
16	Ardith	Gledan	Ardith Gledan	555-9062
17	Irene	Hassan	Irene Hassan	555-2425
18	Ron	Kajetan	Ron Kajetan	555-1970
19	Judy	Karayan	Judy Karayan	555-1230
20	Denny	Keleos	Denny Keleos	555-3019
21	Mick	Kirkegar	Mick Kirkegar	555-2991

FIGURE 10.29

CONCATENATE, or &, makes it easy to join cell values.

Using Cell Names and Labels

Cell names and labels make formulas easier to read because the cells to which they refer are quickly and easily identified.

A cell *name* is an identifying name you create; it can be almost anything, as long as it's not an existing cell reference. (For example, you can name a cell "rate" or "January" or "Fred", but not "FY1998" because that's the intersection of column FY and row 1998.) Cell names use absolute cell references for identification, so using a name in a formula is just like using an absolute reference but easier to read.

The rules for cell names

- Cell names must start with a letter or an underscore (_).

- Don't use spaces; use an underscore or, better yet, use initial capitals to separate words, as in "FirstName". (Names are not case-sensitive, so you don't have to remember to type the capital letters; however, the initial capitals make the name easier to read.)

- Don't use periods (.). They're allowed but can interfere with VBA programming code, which uses periods to identify objects.

- No longer than 255 characters (but really, that's way too long to be practical, anyway.)

- No hyphens or other punctuation marks are allowed. (If Excel won't let you create the name, a punctuation mark may be the problem.)

Name Cells

You can use a few different methods for naming cells: the Name box, the Create Names dialog box, and the Define Name dialog box. Each is more convenient in particular situations. I show you how and when to use each procedure.

Use the Name Box

The Name box is the fastest way to name a cell or range if you're only creating one name or if the name is not already a label or table heading on the worksheet. For example, on my Phone List worksheet, I'm going to name the entire table "Contacts" so that I can get to it quickly from anywhere in the workbook (see Figure 10.30).

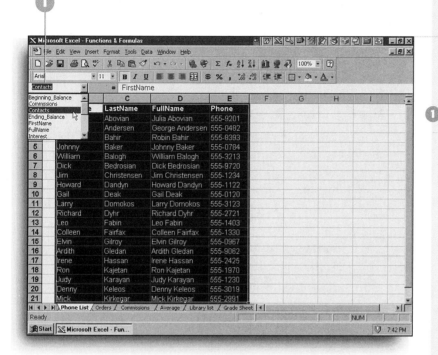

1

FIGURE 10.30

After the range is named, I can select it quickly by clicking its name on the Name box list.

1   Name box

Name cells or ranges using the Name box

1. Select the cell or range you want to name.

2. Click the Name box (shown in Figure 10.31).

FIGURE 10.31

Click the Name box once to highlight it for naming.

3. Type the name and press Enter.

When the named range is selected, the name appears in the Name box (as shown in Figure 10.32). To select the range, click the down arrow in the Name box and then click the range name.

FIGURE 10.32

When a named range or cell is selected, the name appears in the Name box.

Use the Create Names Dialog Box

The Create Names dialog box is the quickest method if the names you want to use are already in place on the worksheet as row or column labels. For example, on my Phone List worksheet, I'm going to name each column in my "Contacts" range with its column heading. The Create Names dialog box creates all four names at once.

Create names using the Create Names dialog box

1. Select the range you want to name, including the headings on the top, left, bottom, or right edges of the range (as shown in Figure 10.33).

FIGURE 10.33

To create names, select the range and include the headings or labels.

1 These headings become range names

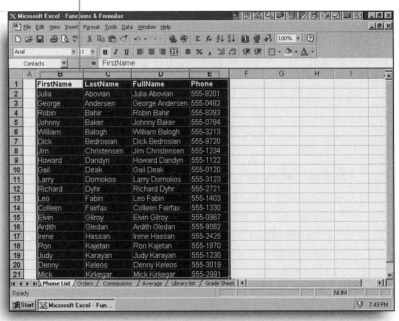

2. From the **Insert** menu, point to **Name** and then click **Create**.

3. In the Create Names dialog box, mark or clear check boxes as needed so that only the appropriate check boxes are checked. (In this example, only the **Top row** check box should be marked.)

4. Click **OK**.

The names are created, and you can select any of the ranges by clicking its name in the Name box list (as shown in Figure 10.34).

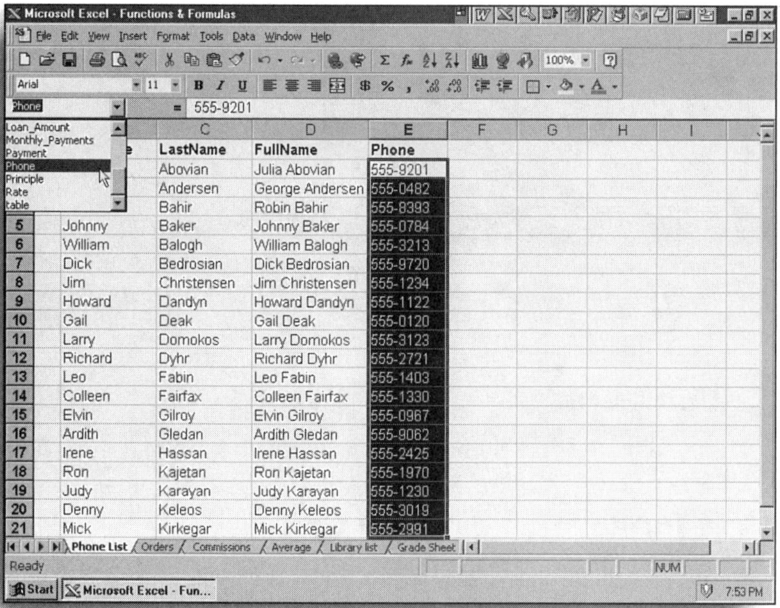

FIGURE 10.34
You can select a range name from wherever you are in the workbook.

Use the Define Name Dialog Box

The Define Name dialog box is another way to create cell and range names, although not the quickest. It is, however, the only way to name formulas or constant values. Instead of repeatedly writing, or even copying, a long and complex formula, you can write the formula one time, give it a name, and then simply write the formula name instead.

What's a constant?

A constant value is an unchanging number value, like 135 or 7.5%. Where would you use it? If the local sales tax rate is 8.17%, you can name the value TaxRate and not have to remember the exact numerical value. When the city raises the tax rate next year, you just redefine the name instead of changing it in all the cells or formulas where the number appears.

I don't see my formula and constant names

Formula names and constant value names don't appear on the Name box list, but you can type them into cells or other formulas.

Name a formula or a constant value with the Define Name dialog box

1. From the **Insert** menu, point to **Name** and then click **Define**.

   The Define Name dialog box appears.

2. In the **Names in workbook** box, type the name for your formula, range, or constant value.

3. In the **Refers to** box, type = followed by the formula or value (Figure 10.35 shows a Define Name dialog box that names a constant value).

FIGURE 10.35

You can name formulas and constant values, as well as ranges, in the Define Name dialog box.

 1 Constant value

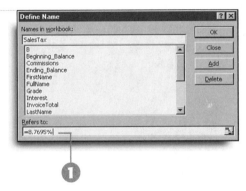

4. Click **OK**.

   (Figure 10.36 shows a named constant in use.)

Write Formulas with Named Cells

Using cell and range names in a formula is quite easy and makes the formula easier to read and understand.

Use cell and range names in a formula

It was better in the old days

Popping names into formulas used to be a lot easier; you could select names from the Name box. Microsoft, however, replaced that functionality with the altogether less useful list of functions in the Name box. Personally, I hope it returns the Name box functionality in future versions of Excel.

1. Click the cell in which you want to display the result of the formula.

2. Type your formula, beginning with an =.

3. Where you need to insert a name, type the name; or on the **Insert** menu, point to **Name**, click **Paste**, and then click the name in the list.

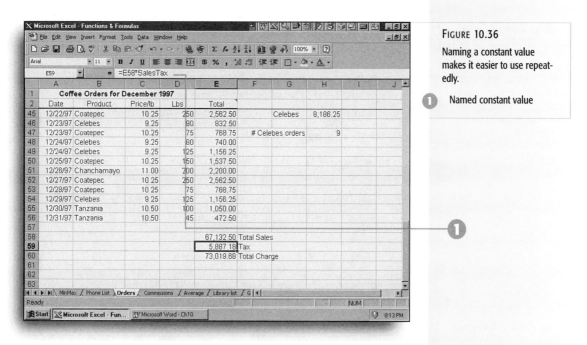

4. Complete the formula by pressing Enter. (A formula with cell names instead of references might look like the one in the Formula bar in Figure 10.37.)

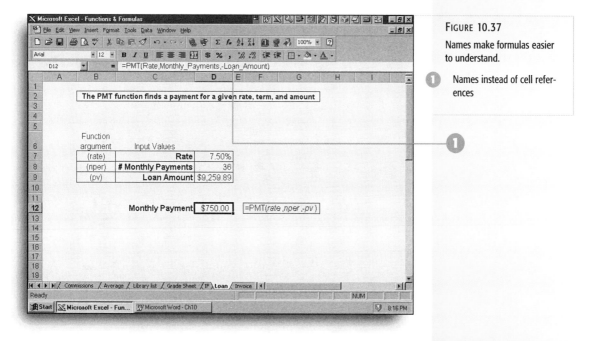

Should I use labels or names?

Labels are convenient as long as the formulas are positioned close to the table so that Excel knows to which labels the formula refers. If, however, the formula is not lined up with the columns or rows the labels identify, then the labels don't work and you need to create names instead.

Write Formulas with Labels

If your data has row and column labels, you can use them in formulas just like names but without first creating names. (In Figure 10.38, the table has column headers that I can use in formulas without first creating names with them.)

Write a formula with labels

1. Click a cell in line with the labeled columns and rows you want to use in the formula.

2. Type your formula, and type labels where the cell references are needed (as shown in Figure 10.38).

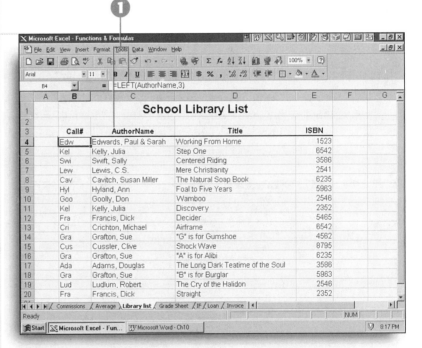

FIGURE 10.38

Labels are quick and convenient when your formulas are lined up with labeled rows and columns.

1 Column labels

Converting Formula Results to Values

If you write a formula, such as a CONCATENATE formula, then delete the referenced cells that you no longer need on the worksheet; the formulas won't work any more. You can, however, convert the formula results to values so that you can delete the unnecessary source cells without changing the results that the formulas produced.

Convert formula results to values

1. Select the formulas.

2. Click the Copy button 📋 (or use your favorite Copy method).

3. From the **E̲dit** menu, click **Paste S̲pecial**.

4. In the Paste Special dialog box (shown in Figure 10.39), click the **V̲alues** option.

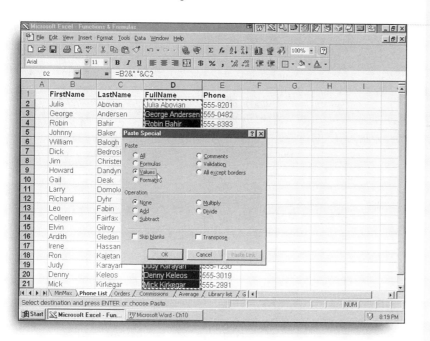

FIGURE 10.39

Use the Paste Special dialog box to convert formulas to values; then you can delete the source cells without affecting the formula results.

5. Click **OK**.

The formulas are replaced by their resulting values, and you can delete the source cells. If the moving border bothers you, you can remove it by pressing Escape.

Will I need the last name column?

In a worksheet like Figure 10.39, you might want to leave the last name column in place so that you can continue to sort the list by last name.

Locating Worksheet Errors

Errors and invalid data seem to sneak into the most scrupulously designed worksheets, but you can find and fix them with the help of a few Excel tools. If an error appears in a formula, you can use the Auditing tools to find the source of the error. (See Table 10.2 for a list of errors and what they mean.) If someone has entered invalid data in a worksheet where Data Validation is in effect, you can locate and edit the inaccuracies by using the Circle Invalid Data button on the Auditing toolbar.

TABLE 10.2 **Error values**

This Error:	Means This:	To Fix It, Do This:
#####	The column isn't wide enough to display the value.	Widen the column.
#VALUE!	Wrong type of argument or operand (for example, calculating a cell with the value #N/A).	Check operands and arguments; make sure references are valid.
#DIV/0!	Formula is attempting to divide by zero.	Change the value or cell reference so that the formula doesn't divide by zero.
#NAME?	Formula is referencing an invalid or non-existent name.	Make sure the name still exists or correct the misspelling.
#N/A	Most commonly means no value is available or inappropriate arguments were used.	In a lookup formula, be sure the lookup table is sorted correctly.
#REF!	Excel can't locate the referenced cells (for example, referenced cells were deleted).	Click Undo immediately to restore references and then change formula references or convert formulas to values.
#NUM!	Incorrect use of a number (such as SQRT(-1)), or formula result is a number too large or too small to be displayed.	Make sure that the arguments are correct, and that the result is between $-1*10^{307}$ and $1*10^{307}$.

This Error:	Means This:	To Fix It, Do This:
#NULL!	Reference to intersection of two areas that do not intersect.	Check for typing and reference errors.
Circular	A formula refers to itself, either directly or indirectly.	Click **OK** and then look at the status bar to see which cell contains the circular reference.

Locate Errors in Formulas

To locate the source of an error in a formula, begin by checking the formula itself for typing and spelling mistakes.

Find the source of an error

1. Right-click a toolbar and click <u>C</u>ustomize to display the Auditing toolbar. In the Customize dialog box, on the **Toolbars** tab, mark the **Auditing** check box and click **Close**.

2. Click the cell containing the error.

3. On the Auditing toolbar, click the Trace Errors button ◇. Tracing arrows appear and guide you visually to possible sources of error. Blue trace lines show referenced cells, and red trace lines lead to the cell that caused the error value.

Find Invalid Data in a Worksheet

If you've set up data validation in such a way that invalid data can be entered by ignoring the validation messages or if you apply data validation rules to an existing table of data, you can locate cells containing data that doesn't meet the validation rules.

Look for invalid data

1. Make sure data validation has been set up for the cells you want to check. If not, go ahead and set up validation rules.

2. Right-click a toolbar and click <u>C</u>ustomize to display the Auditing toolbar. In the Customize dialog box, on the **Toolbars** tab, mark the **Auditing** check box and then click **Close**.

3. Select the range you want to check for invalid data.

4. On the Auditing toolbar, click the Circle Invalid Data button ⊞.

All cells containing data that doesn't meet validation rules are circled in red (shown in Figure 10.40).

To remove the circles, click the Clear Validation Circles button ⊞.

SEE ALSO

➤ *To learn more about validating data during entry, see page 103.*

FIGURE 10.40

Red invalid data circles point out cells that don't meet validation rules.

① Invalid data circles

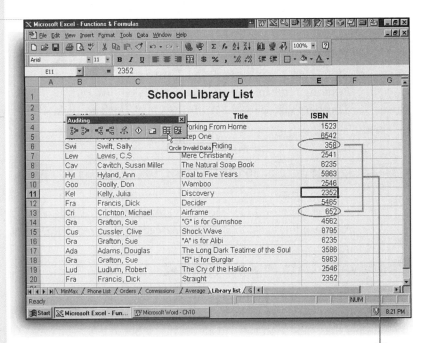

Formatting Cells

Using the Formatting toolbar

Making entries bold or italic, changing font size

Controlling how entries are displayed in a cell

Transposing table orientation

Merging multiple cells into one cell

Applying cell borders

Changing colors

Copying formatting to other cells

Formatting tables with built-in formats

Adding graphics to a worksheet

Save at each step

If you make many formatting changes at once, it might be difficult to reverse all those changes if you don't like the result. Instead, save the workbook at each stage where you like the look. If the next set of changes makes things worse instead of better, close the workbook without saving and reopen the saved version. You're back to the previous set of changes!

The Formatting Toolbar

Formatting dresses up a worksheet and makes it look nice; but more than that, formatting can make data more meaningful by visually segregating data into groups and highlighting summary information.

The Formatting toolbar, shown in Figure 11.1, holds buttons for the most commonly used formatting. It's usually displayed at the top of your Excel window, but if not, you can display it.

Display the Formatting toolbar

1. Right-click any toolbar or menu bar.

2. On the shortcut menu, click **Formatting**.

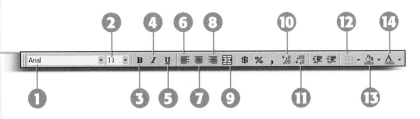

FIGURE 11.1

The default Formatting toolbar.

1. Font
2. Font size
3. Bold
4. Italic
5. Underline
6. Align left
7. Center
8. Align right
9. Merge and Center
10. Increase Decimal
11. Decrease Decimal
12. Borders
13. Fill Color
14. Font Color

If your Formatting toolbar is missing any of the buttons shown in Figure 11.1, someone might have accidentally (or purposely) removed them.

Restore the Formatting toolbar to its default configuration

1. Right-click any toolbar.

2. On the shortcut menu, click **Customize**.

3. On the **Toolbars** tab, click the **Formatting** toolbar name; then click the **Reset** button.

When asked if you're sure you want reset, click OK.

4. Click **Close**.

SEE ALSO

➤ *To learn more about customizing toolbars, see the section "Creating Personal Toolbars," page 482.*

Formatting the Font

Formatting the font means changing the look of the characters in a cell. You can change the format of all the characters in a cell, or you can select individual characters within a cell and format them differently. (For example, you can use subscript formatting to write a chemical name, superscript formatting to write an exponent, or make the first letter of a name bold and red.) Table 11.1 shows some of the ways you can format the characters in an entry.

TABLE 11.1   Font formatting possibilities

Format	Notes
Font	Typeface. Any font installed on your computer, including symbol fonts, is available in a worksheet.
Size	Size of characters, measured in points (72 points per inch).
Font Style	Bold, italic, or bold and italic together.
Underlines	Several underline styles are available in the Format Cells dialog box, on the **Font** tab. Accounting underlines leave space between the characters and the underline (which makes characters more legible because their descending tails aren't hidden by the underline).
Effects	Effects include superscript (10^3), subscript (H_2O), and ~~strikethrough~~; available in the Format Cells dialog box.
Align Left	Pushes the entry against the left side of the cell.
Center	Centers the entry in the cell.
Align Right	Pushes the entry against the right side of the cell.
Merge and Center	Merges selected adjacent cells into a single cell, and centers the entry across the merged cells.
Increase Decimal	Adds one decimal place to displayed value.
Decrease Decimal	Reduces the number of displayed decimal places by one (and rounds displayed value).
Borders	Lots of border options are available on the Borders toolbar, and there are more in the Format Cells dialog box.
Fill Color	Cell shading (background color in cell). Patterns are available in the Format Cells dialog box.
Font Color	Character color.

Apply formatting with toolbar buttons

1. Select the cell(s) or character(s) where you want to apply the formatting.
2. Click the toolbar button(s) for the formats you want.

Apply formatting with the Format Cells dialog box

1. Select the cell(s) or character(s) where you want to apply the formatting.
2. Right-click the selection; then click **Format Cells**.
3. Click tabs and select the desired formatting; when you're finished, click **OK**.

These are the basic procedures. Figure 11.2 shows a worksheet with lots of data but desperately in need of a makeover, so I'll go through individual formatting procedures in more detail (with pictures!).

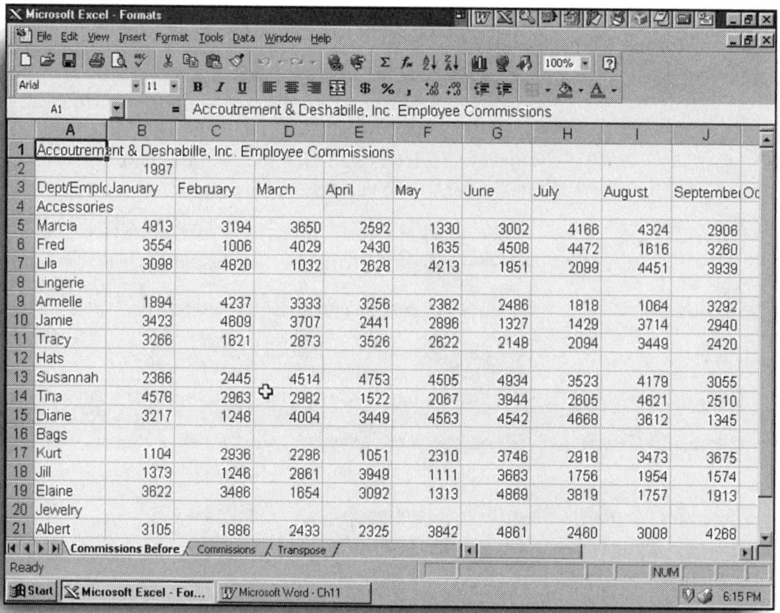

	A	B	C	D	E	F	G	H	I	J
1	Accoutrement & Deshabille, Inc. Employee Commissions									
2		1997								
3	Dept/Emplc	January	February	March	April	May	June	July	August	Septembe Oc
4	Accessories									
5	Marcia	4913	3194	3650	2592	1330	3002	4166	4324	2906
6	Fred	3554	1006	4029	2430	1635	4508	4472	1616	3260
7	Lila	3098	4820	1032	2628	4213	1951	2099	4451	3839
8	Lingerie									
9	Armelle	1894	4237	3333	3256	2382	2486	1818	1064	3292
10	Jamie	3423	4609	3707	2441	2896	1327	1429	3714	2940
11	Tracy	3266	1621	2873	3526	2622	2148	2094	3449	2420
12	Hats									
13	Susannah	2366	2445	4514	4753	4505	4934	3523	4179	3055
14	Tina	4578	2963	2982	1522	2067	3944	2605	4621	2510
15	Diane	3217	1248	4004	3449	4563	4542	4668	3612	1345
16	Bags									
17	Kurt	1104	2936	2296	1051	2310	3746	2918	3473	3675
18	Jill	1373	1246	2861	3949	1111	3683	1756	1954	1574
19	Elaine	3622	3486	1654	3092	1313	4869	3819	1757	1913
20	Jewelry									
21	Albert	3105	1886	2433	2325	3842	4861	2460	3008	4268

FIGURE 11.2
Good data, but a thoroughly dull presentation.

I'll start by making the worksheet and column headings bold.

Make the text boldface

1. Select the cells with the worksheet titles and month names (in this case, A1:M3).

2. On the Formatting toolbar, click Bold. **B**

All the month names are formatted bold, as shown in Figure 11.3.

Select a block of data fast

To select to the end of a block of data, click the first cell (B3); then hold down the Shift key and double-click the right border of the selected cell.

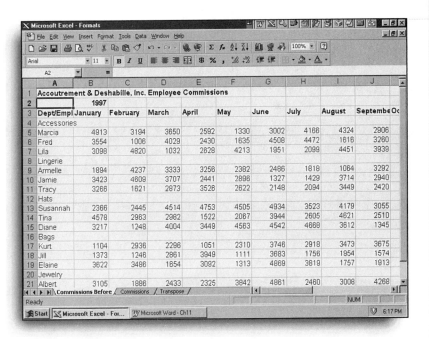

FIGURE 11.3

This is a bold beginning to a better presentation. (I couldn't resist the pun!)

I want to make the worksheet title, "Accoutrement & Deshabille, Inc. Employee Commissions," italic.

Italicize text

1. Select the cells you want to format (in this case, A1).

2. On the Formatting toolbar, click Italic. *I*

I also want to make the worksheet title much larger.

Just format the cells that need it

You can select and format the entire row, all the way across the worksheet, but it wastes system resources to apply formatting to cells you aren't going to use.

Increase or decrease font size

1. Select the cells you want to format (in this case, A1).

2. On the Formatting toolbar, click the down arrow on the Font Size box; then click **18**.

   Figure 11.4 shows the Commissions worksheet with a large, italic title.

FIGURE 11.4

Larger font and italics make the worksheet title stand out.

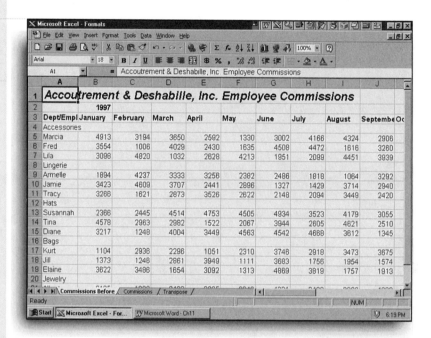

Making the Cell Fit the Text (and Vice Versa)

When you start a new worksheet, you probably won't devote much time initially to thinking about how the data will look; after all, the point of a worksheet is usually formulas and calculations, not presentation. A default worksheet has millions of cells for data entry—all the same size. As you type entries, Excel pops them into these cells and displays only what will fit. Although the worksheet will work just fine that way, it isn't very helpful for you as you try to read the cell entries, or for anyone else who tries to read the reports you print from this default setup.

When your data is entered and ready to use—or anywhere along the way—you can use Excel's many formatting features to help make the worksheet and its contents fit together.

Aligning Entries

When you enter data, Excel automatically aligns text on the left side of the cell and numbers on the right, but you can easily change alignment to make your data easier to read. I want to center the month names in my column headings.

Change cell alignment

1. Select the cells you want to align (in this case, B3:M3).

2. On the Formatting toolbar, click an alignment button (in this case, the Center button).

Figure 11.5 shows the results of centering the month names.

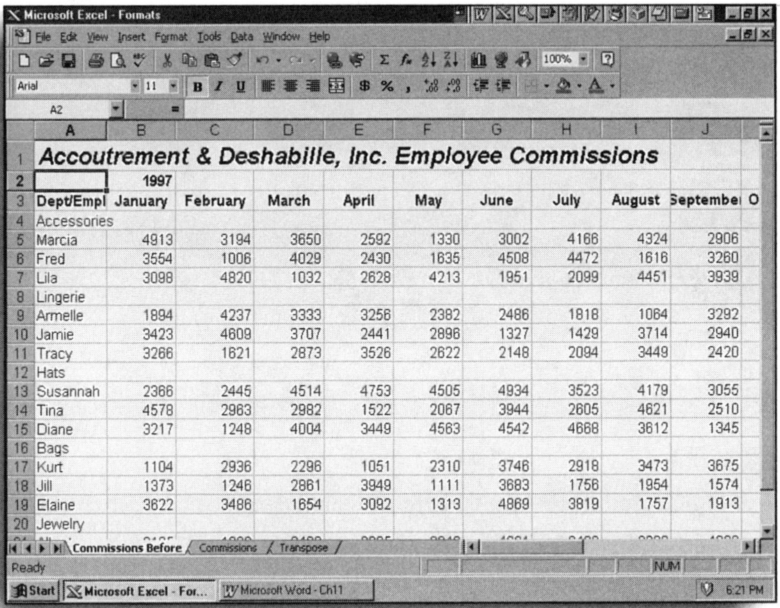

FIGURE 11.5

Month names are centered; they're also *truncated* (cut off at the right to fit in the cell), but I'll fix that later by rotating the entries and changing the column widths.

In column A, I have department names and employee names in the same column; to differentiate them, I'll leave the department names aligned on the left but indent the employee names by four characters.

Indent entries

1. Select the cells you want to indent (in this case, all the employee name cells in column A).

2. On the **Format** menu, click **Cells**.

3. On the **Alignment** tab, set a number in the **Indent** box, as shown in Figure 11.6; then click **OK**. (The Indent number is a number of character widths.)

Formatting nonadjacent cells

To select nonadjacent cells for formatting, select the first cell or range; then hold down Ctrl and select the remaining cells or ranges.

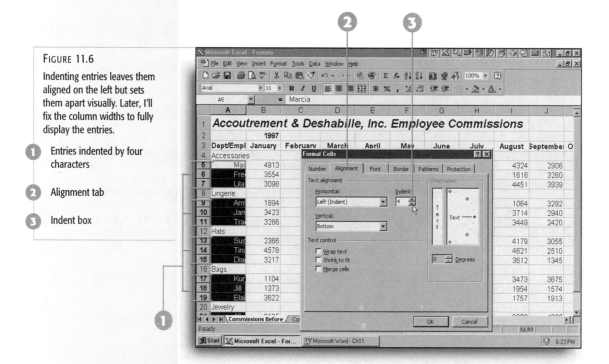

FIGURE 11.6

Indenting entries leaves them aligned on the left but sets them apart visually. Later, I'll fix the column widths to fully display the entries.

1 Entries indented by four characters

2 Alignment tab

3 Indent box

The columns are too wide to fit conveniently on my screen or on a printed page, but only because the month names are so wide. I can make the columns narrower without abbreviating the month names by rotating the month name entries.

Rotate cell entries

1. Select the cells you want to rotate (in this case, B3:M3).

2. On the **Format** menu, click **Cells**.

3. On the **Alignment** tab, under **Orientation**, click in the
half-circle to set a rotation angle, as shown in Figure 11.7;
then click **OK**.

The cell entries are rotated.

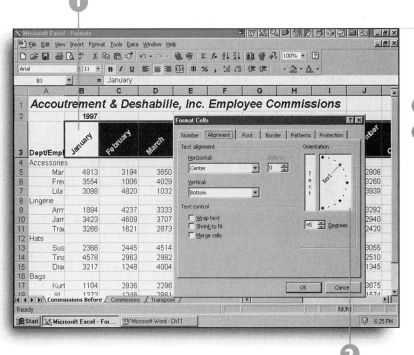

FIGURE 11.7

Row height automatically
increases to accommodate the
angle you set.

1   Rotated entries

2   Click an angle

Changing Column Width and Row Height

Most worksheets must have columns resized, and often row
heights need adjusting, too. There are several ways you can
resize rows and columns:

- Drag the borders of row and column selectors
- Set a precise width or height in a dialog box
- "Best-fit" a row or column to accommodate the tallest or
  widest entry

You can also hide rows and columns. This is useful, for example, if you have a lookup table on a worksheet, and you want worksheet formulas to reference the lookup table but don't want the table to be in view. It's also useful when you want to print a worksheet but don't want some of the rows or columns in a table printed.

Resize a column visually

1. Position the mouse pointer over the right border of the column selector for the column you want to resize.

2. When the mouse pointer becomes a two-headed arrow (as shown in Figure 11.8), drag the border to resize the column.

Resize several columns at once

To make several columns (adjacent or nonadjacent) the same width, select all the columns; then drag the border of one of the column selectors. They'll all become precisely the same width.

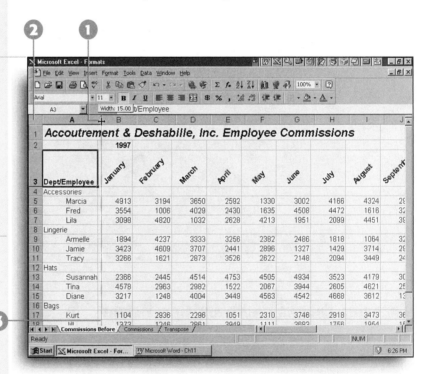

FIGURE 11.8

Resize columns and rows the same way: Drag header borders.

1 Two-headed arrow mouse pointer

2 Click here to select the entire worksheet

3 Dragging to resize

Change *all* the columns or *all* the rows

To change the column width or row height for the entire worksheet, click the gray rectangle at the upper-left corner of the worksheet, where the row selectors and column selectors intersect (this selects the entire worksheet); then change row height and/or column width by any method.

To resize rows, follow the same procedure, but drag the bottom border of the row selector for the row you want to resize.

Best-Fitting

Sometimes when you drag a column to resize it, it looks great—until you scroll down the worksheet and find a longer entry that's still truncated. You can save yourself the aggravation of guessing the appropriate width by "best-fitting" the column width (this works with row heights, too).

Best-fit a column width

1. Position the mouse pointer over the right border of the column selector for the column you want to best-fit.

2. When the mouse pointer becomes a two-headed arrow (as shown in Figure 11.8), double-click the border to best-fit the column.

   In Figure 11.9 I've best-fitted all the month columns.

Best-fit several columns at once

To make several columns (adjacent or nonadjacent) all best-fit their entries, select all the columns; then double-click the border of one of the column selectors. They'll all best-fit their own entries.

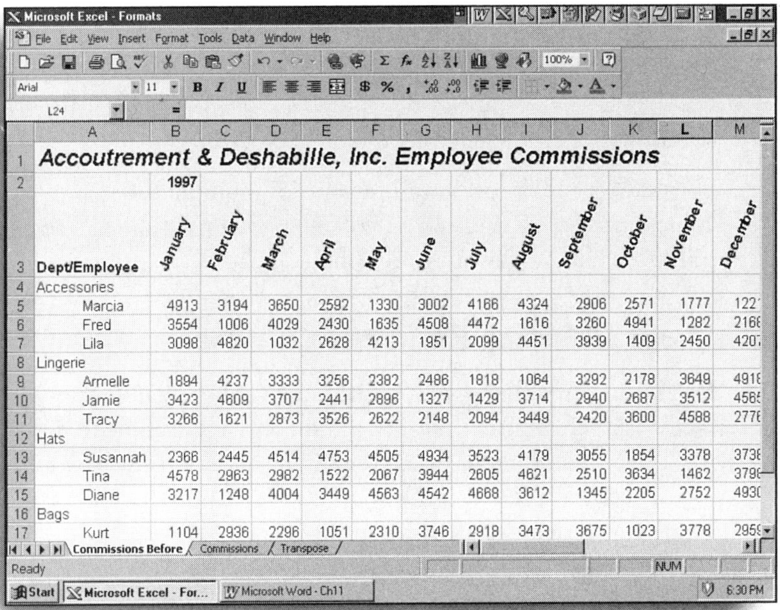

FIGURE 11.9
The month columns were best-fitted; but the Dept/Employee column was dragged to fit, because a best-fit would have widened the column to fit the worksheet title.

Remember, the worksheet title only *looks* like it's typed in cells A1 through L1. The entire title—all 52 characters—is actually entered in cell A1, and I certainly wouldn't want column A to be best-fit to 52 characters wide.

To best-fit rows, follow the same procedure, but double-click the bottom border of the row selector for the row you want to resize. Best-fitting row heights becomes most useful when you've applied or removed wrap-text formatting somewhere in a row.

SEE ALSO

➤ *To learn more about fitting entries into cells by "wrapping" the text, see the section "Wrapping Text to Multiple Lines in a Cell," page 208.*

Matching Precise Width or Height

If you want to match the measurements of rows and columns that are far apart in a worksheet or in different worksheets, you can set precise measurements for the columns/rows you want to match, and they'll match exactly.

To set a precise column width or row height, follow this procedure:

Set precise width or height

1. Right-click a column or row selector.

2. Click **Column Width** or **Row Height** (whichever is applicable).

3. Enter a new measurement; then click **OK**.

To set the same precise measurement for multiple rows or columns, select all the rows or columns; then right-click in the selection, enter a new measurement, and click **OK**.

Hiding and Unhiding Rows and Columns

It's not uncommon to have formula "machinery," like lookup tables and referenced values, that you don't want visible in the worksheet. You can hide these important but messy cells by hiding the columns and/or rows; the worksheet still functions properly, but you don't see what's going on behind the scenes.

Hide rows or columns

1. Right-click the selector for the column or row you want to hide.

To hide several columns or rows, select all the columns or rows; then right-click in the selection.

2. Click **Hide**.

The selected columns or rows are hidden. You can tell columns (or rows) are hidden because there's a gap in the selector letters (or numbers), as shown in Figure 11.10.

Someone always wants to know

The column width number is the number of characters in the default worksheet font that will fit in the cell (for example, a column width of 8.43 means that 8.43 characters, in the worksheet's default font, can be displayed in the cell); row height is measured in "points," which is a standard typeface unit of measure. (There are 72 points per inch.)

How can you find hidden columns/rows?

When columns or rows are deleted, there's no gap in the letters or numbers; the gap is how you can locate hidden columns and rows.

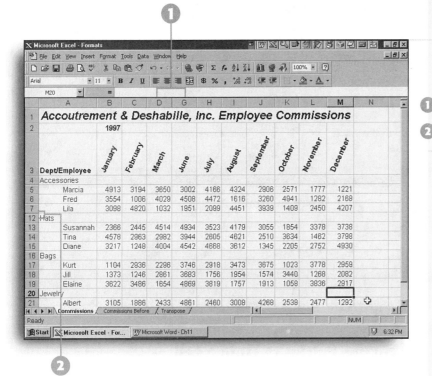

FIGURE 11.10

Columns E and F and rows 8 through 11 are hidden.

1. Letter gap

2. Number gap

Unhide hidden rows or columns

1. Select the rows or columns on *both* sides of the gap, as shown in Figure 11.11.

2. Right-click the selection.

3. Click **Unhide**.

   The hidden rows or columns are unhidden.

If you can't find the elusive hidden rows or columns, select the entire worksheet (click the gray rectangle in the upper-left corner of the worksheet, where the row and column selectors intersect); then right-click in the selected worksheet, and click **Unhide**. All hidden rows and columns in the worksheet are unhidden.

FIGURE 11.11

Select the rows and columns around the hidden rows or columns; then unhide them.

① Click here to select the entire worksheet

② Gap

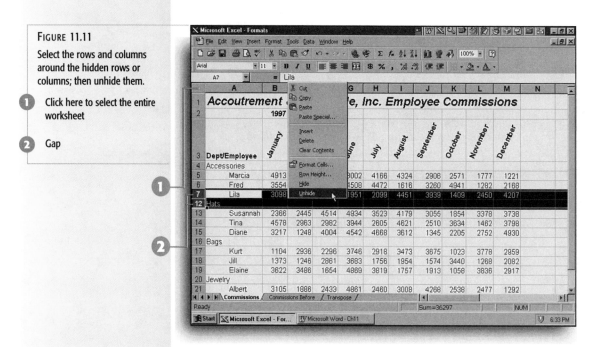

Shrinking Entries to Fit in a Cell

If you have a cell entry that doesn't quite fit and you don't want to widen the column for it, you can shrink the entry so it fits within the column width and stays neatly fitted, even if you resize the column.

Shrink an entry to fit the column width

1. Select the cell(s) where you want to shrink entries.
2. On the **Format** menu, click **Cells**.
3. On the **Alignment** tab, click the **Shrink to fit** check box.
4. Click **OK**.

Wrapping Text to Multiple Lines in a Cell

Another way to fit long entries into a narrow column width is to wrap them onto multiple lines. Wrapping text makes the row taller but keeps the characters large and the column narrow (it's practical only when the entry is two or more words).

Wrap an entry to multiple lines

1. Select the cell(s) where you want to wrap entries.

2. On the **Format** menu, click **Cells**.

3. On the **Alignment** tab, click the **Wrap text** check box.

4. Click **OK**.

You might need to resize the row and column after you apply Wrap Text formatting. To do so, drag the column to the width you want; then best-fit the row to fit the entry.

SEE ALSO

➤ *To learn about resizing rows and columns, see the section "Changing Column Width and Row Height," page 203.*

Transposing a Range from Vertical to Horizontal (or Vice Versa)

Sometimes I start a table like the one in Figure 11.12 and realize after it's gotten fairly large that it would be more practical if the orientation of the table was flipped, or *transposed*.

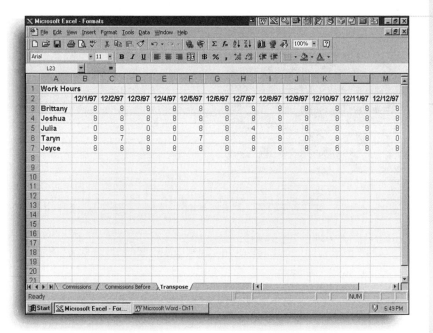

Don't like where Excel places the breaks?

To break a long entry where you want, rather than where the column width breaks it, click between the characters where you want the entry to break; then press Alt+Enter.

FIGURE 11.12

This table would be more practical if the dates ran down column A and the names were across the top.

Transpose a table or list

1. Select the entire table or list.

2. Right-click the selection.

3. Click **Copy**.

4. Right-click the cell where you want to paste the upper-left corner of the transposed table. (In Figure 11.17, I'll paste the transposed table to cell A9.)

5. On the shortcut menu, click **Paste Special**.

6. In the Paste Special dialog box, click the **Transpose** check box; then click **OK**.

The result will be similar to Figure 11.13.

Why won't this work?

You can't paste the transposed table over the copied table (Excel won't let you); you must paste it outside the area of the copied table.

FIGURE 11.13

A transposed copy of the table is pasted, and I can delete the original.

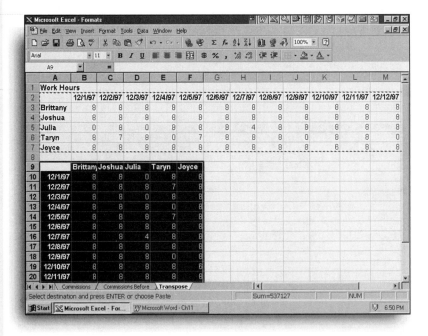

Next I'll select and delete rows 2 through 8, and the worksheet is ready to use again.

Merging Several Cells into a Single Cell (and Unmerging)

On a worksheet like the one in Figure 11.14, the worksheet title would look better if it were centered in a single cell over the length of the table.

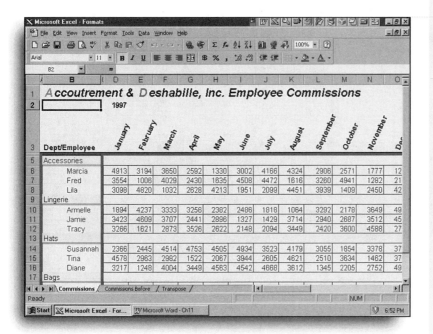

FIGURE 11.14

The title should be centered neatly over the table.

Merge several cells into a single cell and center the entry in the big, new cell

1. Select all the adjacent cells you want to merge. (In this example, I merged and centered cells B1 through O1 and then repeated the procedure to merge and center cells B2 through O2.)

2. On the Formatting toolbar, click Merge And Center.

   The cells are merged into a single cell, as shown in Figure 11.15.

FIGURE 11.15

The title looks more professional, centered in one wide cell.

1 The title is merged, centered, and text-wrapped

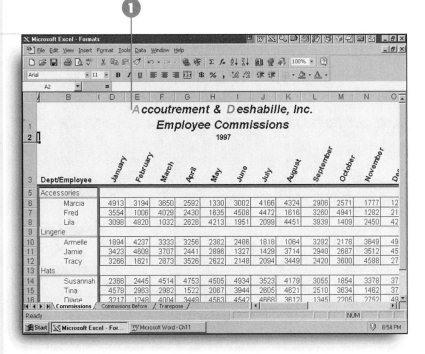

Merged cells can cause problems if you need to resize any of the columns below the merged cell.

Unmerge a merged cell

1. Right-click the merged cell.

2. Click **Format Cells**.

3. On the **Alignment** tab, clear the **Merge cells** check box; then click **OK**.

After you resize your columns, you can remerge the cells.

Formatting Borders

Borders are important, not only for dressing up a worksheet, but for segregating information so it's quickly understood. Also, if you're printing a worksheet, you need to supply your own borders because Excel doesn't print worksheet gridlines by default.

To apply cell borders quickly, use the Borders palette.

Apply borders with the Borders palette

1. On the Formatting toolbar, click the down arrow on the Borders button.

2. Drag the palette of Borders buttons away from the toolbar to "float" on the worksheet. (Drag it by its thin title bar, as shown in Figure 11.16.)

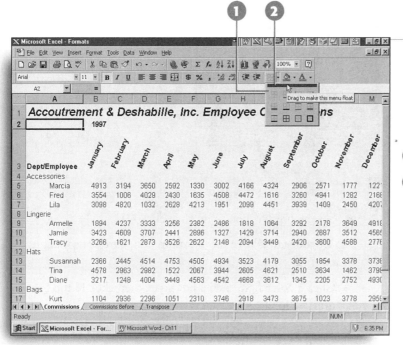

FIGURE 11.16

Floating palette toolbars are convenient ways to apply bor-ders and colors. For this illus-tration I've turned worksheet gridlines off (**Tools | Options | View**).

1. No Border button

2. Drag by title bar

3. Select the cells you want to apply a border to; then click the border you want. Repeat until all your cells have borders.

You can apply lots of borders; if it gets messy, select all the cells, click the **No Border** button, and start over.

To apply a wider variety of cell borders and change border col-ors, use the **Border** tab in the Format Cells dialog box.

Apply borders with the Format Cells dialog box

1. Select the cells where you want to apply the border.

2. On the **Format** menu, click **Cells**.

3. In the Format Cells dialog box, shown in Figure 11.17, click the **Border** tab.

FIGURE 11.17

The **Border** tab has more border options, including border colors, but you can only apply the borders to one selection of cells at a time.

1 Click to apply or remove borders

2 Line style

3 Border preview

4 Color

5 Diagonal lines

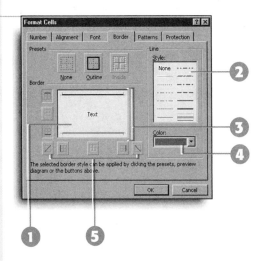

4. Set the borders you want; then click **OK**.

The **Border** tab takes a bit of exploration; here are some tips for using it:

- Click a color first, then a line style; then click in the border preview to place the line you've chosen.

- You can make each border line a different color and style to add flair to your worksheet.

- The diagonal lines serve to "X" out cells visually but don't affect the cell entries. (You might find this handy for something like marking off completed tasks in a list.)

Formatting Colors

There are two sources of color in cells: the characters (*font color*) and the background (*fill color*). The only difference between using the floating palettes and the Format Cells dialog box to set colors is that background patterns are found in the Format Cells dialog box; but the floating palettes are quicker to use because they remain ready on the worksheet.

Set the text color (font color)

1. On the Formatting toolbar, click the down arrow on the Font Color button.

2. Drag the Font Color palette away from the toolbar to float on the worksheet (as shown in Figure 11.18).

Lots of formatting buttons

There are floating palettes and buttons for almost everything in the Format Cells dialog box, but there isn't room for all of them on the Formatting toolbar, so only the most commonly used buttons are built in. You can, however, add any buttons you want by customizing your toolbars (see Chapter 26 to learn how).

FIGURE 11.18
Floating palettes make worksheet artistry easy.

3. Select the cells or individual characters you want to color.

4. Click the color you want in the floating palette.

5. When you're finished, click the floating palette's Close button to close it.

Set the cell color (fill color)

1. On the Formatting toolbar, click the down arrow on the Fill Color button.

2. Drag the Fill Color palette away from the toolbar to float on the worksheet (as shown in Figure 11.19).

3. Select the cells you want to color.

4. Click the color you want in the floating palette.

5. When you're finished, click the floating palette's Close button to close it.

Here's a trick professionals use to make worksheets look special (you'll find a bit of this in Excel's Spreadsheet Solutions Templates): Use narrow rows and columns of color around a table to create custom borders, the way I've done in Figure 11.20.

FIGURE 11.19

You can use cell colors in very creative ways to make your worksheet look great.

1 Fill Color

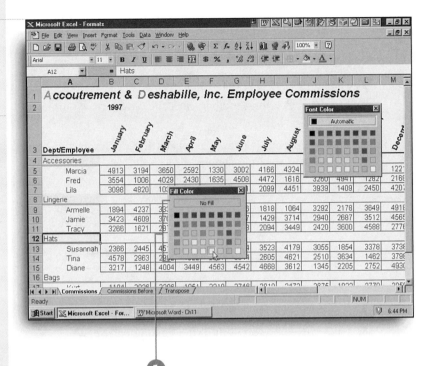

FIGURE 11.20

Create custom borders around a table by resizing and coloring cells.

1 This is made up of cells, not a cell border

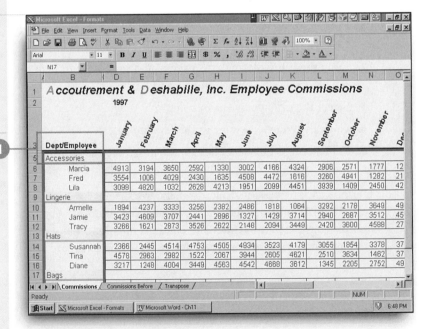

To create these custom borders, insert and resize rows and/or columns; then select and color the cells that form a border around the table.

Copying Formatting with Format Painter

When you've formatted a cell or group of cells with several formats (for example, you might have applied a cell color, font color, font size, alignment, and number format), it's daunting to think you have to repeat all that work to format other cells similarly. Well, you don't! You can copy the whole set of formats by painting them to other cells with the Format Painter.

You can copy the formatting from a single cell or a group of cells to a similar group of cells.

In Figure 11.21, I want to make the table easy to read across by coloring the rows.

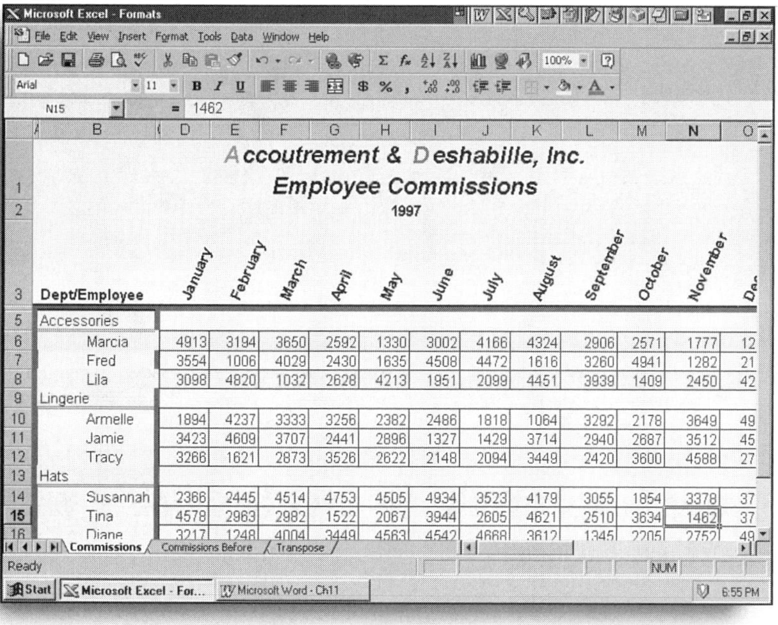

FIGURE 11.21
Select all the cells that have formatting you want to copy.

After I've colored one set of rows, I can paint the row formatting to the rest of the table.

Use the Format Painter to copy formatting

1. Select the cell(s) that contain the formatting you want to copy.

   In this case, I've selected all the cells in rows 5 through 8, so I can copy the pattern of the colors.

2. On the Standard toolbar, click Format Painter 🖌.

3. Drag the Format Painter mouse pointer over all the cells to which you want to paint the format.

   Painting the row formatting to the rest of the table results in the table shown in Figure 11.22.

Paint a format repeatedly

You can make the Format Painter "hot" by double-clicking it; it will continue to paint the same formatting until you click the Format Painter button again.

FIGURE 11.22

Coloring rows makes a wide table easier to read across (like old-fashioned computer paper).

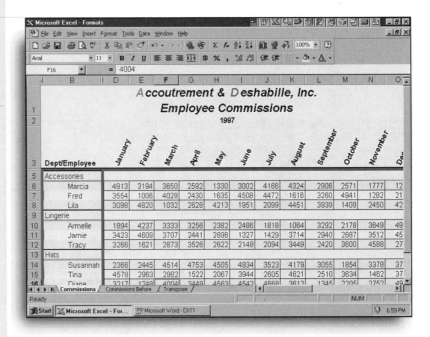

Using AutoFormat to Create a Table with Built-In Formats

If you need to format a table in a hurry, you can apply a built-in AutoFormat to the entire table much more quickly than you can apply all the individual formatting elements.

AutoFormat a table

1. Click in the table.

2. On the **Fo**rmat menu, click **A**uto**Format**.

The AutoFormat dialog box is displayed, as shown in Figure 11.23.

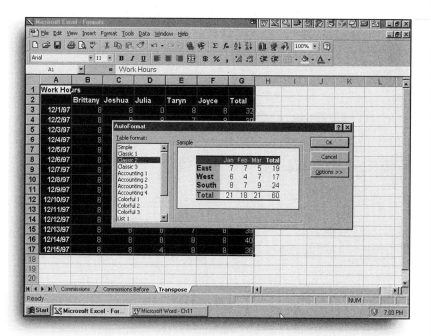

FIGURE 11.23

Choose a built-in table format in the AutoFormat dialog box.

3. Click different table formats in the list until you see one you like in the sample window.

4. Click **OK**.

The table format is applied to the entire contiguous table, as in Figure 11.24.

FIGURE 11.24

A table created using
AutoFormat.

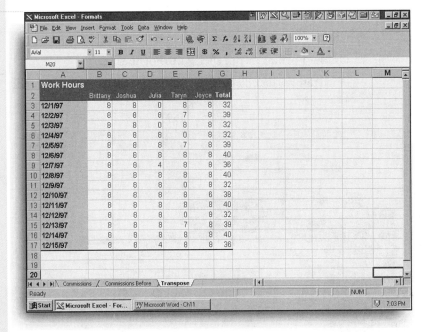

Adding a Graphic Image to a Worksheet

A logo or graphic image can really jazz up a worksheet.

Paste a graphic image into a worksheet

1. Make room in the worksheet for the image.

    Either insert several rows, or insert a single row and resize it tall enough to make room on the worksheet for the image.

2. Click in the cell where you want to paste the upper-left corner of the picture (and you can always move it later if you need to).

3. On the **Insert** menu, point to **Picture**; then click **From File**.

4. In the Insert Picture dialog box, navigate to the folder where your graphic image is saved, and double-click the image file.

    The image is pasted into your worksheet, like the one in Figure 11.25.

Add a logo to a template

Placing a logo in a workbook template can tie together a company's image, because the logo will automatically be in place in every new workbook.

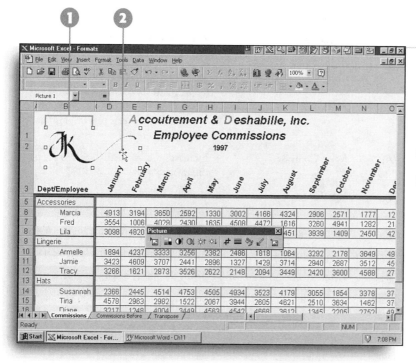

You can

- Move the graphic to reposition it
- Drag the handles around its edges to resize it
- Press Ctrl or Shift while dragging a handle to resize it without stretching it out of shape
- Use the buttons in the Picture toolbar that is displayed, or close the toolbar by clicking its Close button. (Table 11.2 shows what the buttons do.)

TABLE 11.2   Picture toolbar buttons

Icon	Button Name	Button Function
	Insert Picture From File	Opens the Insert Picture dialog box so you can insert another picture.

continues…

TABLE 11.2   Continued

Icon	Button Name	Button Function
	Image Control	Select from Automatic (displays the image's original colors), Gray Scale (converts to shades of gray), Black and White (converts to black and white), or Watermark (converts to a bright, low-contrast watermark).
	More Contrast	Increases the intensity of the colors in the image.
	Less Contrast	Reduces the intensity of the colors in the image.
	More Brightness	Adds white to lighten the image colors.
	Less Brightness	Adds black to darken the image colors.
	Crop	Trims the image when you drag a handle.
	Line Style	Sets the style of line used in an image border.
	Format Picture	Opens the Format Picture dialog box.
	Set Transparent Color	Makes a color transparent (click the button; then click the color that you want to change in the image).
	Reset Picture	Undoes the image manipulation.

Formatting Numbers

The numbers don't add up!

If the calculation on the worksheet appears to be incorrect, it's because the *actual* cell values are calculated, not the rounded-off, *displayed* values. You might want to add a label telling others who see the table that numbers might appear inaccurate because they've been rounded.

Applying Number Formats to Cells

What you see in a cell is not necessarily the value entered in the cell (or the value calculated by Excel). The actual value of an entry in a selected cell is shown in the Formula bar, but what you see in the cell is the *displayed value*, the format of which you can control with number formatting.

Some of the many ways you can change a displayed value with formatting are shown in Figure 12.1. All the numbers in column B were entered as 12345, with a variety of formats applied.

FIGURE 12.1

All these cells contain the actual value 12345, but clever formatting changes the meaning entirely.

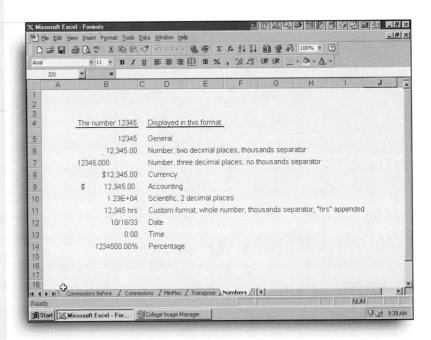

The number displayed in a cell is seldom the actual calculating value, especially if the value is the result of a formula. You can display a number in many ways by changing its format, as shown in Table 12.1.

TABLE 12.1   **Number formatting possibilities**

This Number	In This Format	Looks Like This
1.2345	Number, zero decimal places	1
	Number, two decimal places	1.23

This Number	In This Format	Looks Like This
	Currency	$1.23
	Fraction, up to one digit	1 1/4
	Fraction, up to two digits	1 19/81
12345	Number, two decimals, thousands separator	12,345.00
	Currency	$12,345.00
	Scientific, one decimal place (E indicates that 04 is an exponent)	1.2E+04
	Special, Social Security number	000-01-2345
.0012345	General	0.0012345
	Number, three decimal places	.001
	Percentage, two decimal places	.12%
	Fraction, up to three digits	1/810

Format a number value to display the way you want it

1. Select the cell or range you want to format.

2. On the **Format** menu, click **Cells**.

The Format Cells dialog box is displayed, as shown in Figure 12.2.

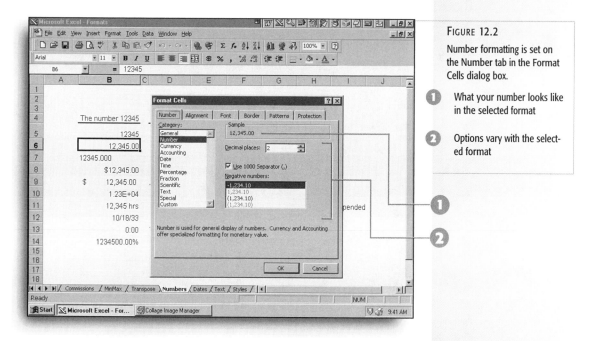

FIGURE 12.2

Number formatting is set on the Number tab in the Format Cells dialog box.

1 What your number looks like in the selected format

2 Options vary with the selected format

Can I use yen or pounds?

If you select the **Currency** category, you can choose a different currency symbol from the **Symbol** drop-down list that is displayed in the dialog box.

Some formatting tips

You can also paint number formatting to other cells by using the Format Painter toolbar button; apply number formatting to nonadjacent cells and ranges by using the Ctrl key to select them; and make a number format part of a custom style.

3. On the **Number** tab, select a format category.

Each category has specific options that customize the format further.

4. Select and set the options available for the format category.

The Sample area shows what your number looks like with the formatting options applied.

5. When the sample looks the way you want it, click **OK**.

The format is applied to all selected cells.

SEE ALSO

➤ *To learn more about using the Format Painter, see the section "Copying Formatting with Format Painter" in Chapter 11, page 217.*

➤ *To learn more about selecting nonadjacent cells, see the section "Selecting Cells in a Worksheet," page 71.*

➤ *To learn more about formatting with styles, see page 237.*

Formatting Dates and Times

Dates and times are recognized by Excel, and as such are formatted, sorted, and calculated as dates and times rather than as plain old number values. Excel can calculate dates in formulas because, although you see a date or time displayed, Excel's actual value is a serial number that corresponds to the specific date and time of day.

Some of the many Date and Time formatting options are shown in Table 12.2.

Hey! Where's my number?

Occasionally you might enter a number, such as **12345**, and be surprised to have it transformed into a date! This happens because Excel recognized the number as a date serial number, and the cell was already formatted with Date/Time formatting. To change the display to a number, change the formatting of the cell to Number or General.

TABLE 12.2   Date and Time formatting possibilities

This Date or Time	In This Format	Looks Like This
1/7/56	Date, 4-Mar	7-Jan
	Date, March 4, 1997	January 7, 1956
	3/4/97 1:30 PM	1/7/56 12:00 AM
12345	Date, March 4, 1997	October 18, 1933
	Time, 1:30 PM	12:00 AM
.75	Time, 13:30	18:00
	Time, 13:30:55	18:00:00
	Time, 1:30 PM	6:00 PM

Change the format of a date or time

1. Select the cell or range of dates (or times) you want to format.

2. On the **Format** menu, click **Cells**.

The Format Cells dialog box is displayed, as shown in Figure 12.3.

Get all the dates at once

If you want all the date or time cells in the worksheet to have the same format, hold down the Ctrl key and then click or drag across each cell or range of cells. When you apply the date format, all the selected cells will be formatted simultaneously.

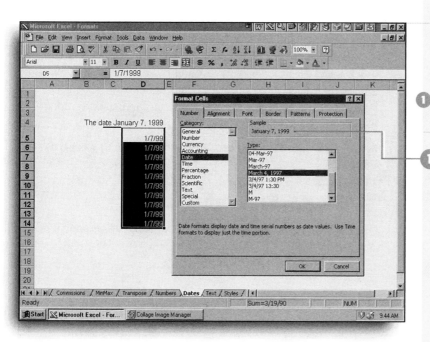

FIGURE 12.3

Date and Time formatting are set on the **Number** tab in the Format Cells dialog box.

1 What the date looks like in the selected format

3. On the **Number** tab, select the **Date** or **Time** category.

4. Select a format from the **Type** list.

The Sample area shows what your date or time looks like with the selected Type applied.

5. When the sample looks the way you want it, click **OK**.

The format is applied to all selected cells.

Formatting Text Entries

Text entries (like labels, part numbers, and zip codes) might be composed of number characters but are different from number values in that they must

- Retain any leading zeroes
- Not be included in calculations

If an entry has any character other than numbers in it (for example, the Social Security number 555-55-5555, which has hyphens in it), Excel sees the entry as text and the format is not a problem; format becomes a problem when the entry is supposed to be text but contains no letters or punctuation marks to indicate to Excel that it's text.

A quick trick for text

You can enter a number as text without changing the formatting by typing an apostrophe (') first; the apostrophe will be hidden in the cell display, but Excel will treat the entry as text.

Format cells as text, so that numbers you enter will be treated as text characters

1. Select the cells that should be text.
2. On the **Format** menu, click **Cells**.
3. On the **Number** tab, click the Text category (as shown in Figure 12.4).
4. Click **OK**.

FIGURE 12.4

Text-formatted entries are left-aligned and not calculated.

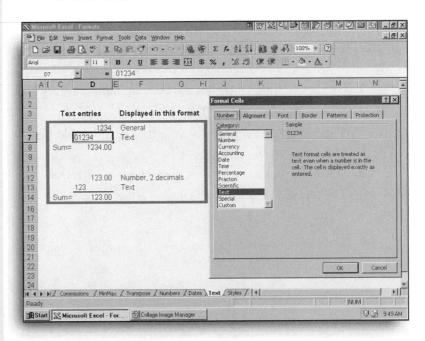

Occasionally you might want to enter calculable numbers but show text characters in the cell. This is a different problem.

One of my students wanted to create a timesheet and wanted to show the time entries with the suffix hrs, as in 8 hrs. But if you enter 8 hrs in a cell, Excel treats the entry as text; and if you concatenate the letters to the number, as in =H13&" hrs", Excel again treats the entry as text. If, however, you make the text characters part of the format rather than part of the entered value, Excel treats the entry as a number while you view it in the worksheet as text.

Include text in a number format by creating a custom number format

1. Select the cell(s) you want to custom format.

2. On the **Format** menu, click **Cells**.

3. On the **Number** tab, click the Custom category.

4. In the **Type** box, type the format code #,##0 "hrs" (as shown in Figure 12.5).

5. Click **OK**.

I want my numbers centered

When you apply number or text formatting, a default alignment is part of the format; but you can change the alignment in selected cells by clicking one of the alignment buttons on the Formatting toolbar.

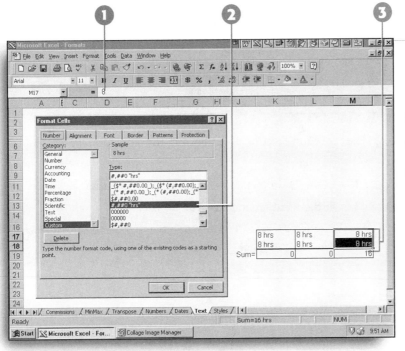

FIGURE 12.5

A custom format is the only way to display text characters in a calculable number value.

1 Cell value

2 Format code

3 Formatted display

Table 12.3 shows more useful custom format codes.

TABLE 12.3   Custom format codes

This Code	Gives This Result	Example (Value 01234.333)
#,###0	Rounds to a whole number; comma separates thousands; no leading zeroes	1,234
# ?/?	Displays decimal portion as a fraction	1234 1/3
0.00	Rounds to two decimal places; no thousands separator	1234.33
00000	Displays all digits, including leading zeroes to five places (like zip codes)	01234
000-00-0000	Placeholders for all nine digits in a Social Security number; inserts hyphens after you press Enter	
000-0000	Placeholders for all seven digits in a phone number; inserts hyphen automatically after you press Enter	
(000) 000-0000	Placeholders for area code and telephone number; inserts parentheses and hyphen after you press Enter	

For more information about custom format codes, look it up in Excel's help files:

1. On the **Help** menu, click **Contents and Index**.
2. On the **Find** tab, type Custom Number.
3. Look for the title "Custom number, date, and time format codes" in the **Click a topic, then click Display** box.
4. Double-click the topic.

SEE ALSO

➤ *To learn more about concatenating cell values, see the section "Concatenate (&)," page 180.*

➤ *To learn more about locating Excel's help files, see the section "Using the Contents and Index," page 21.*

Some special format codes are ready-made

If you want to use custom format codes for zip codes, phone numbers, and Social Security numbers (like those in Table 12.3), you can create them yourself or find them built in under the Special category.

Creating Conditional Number Formats

If you have a sea of data and want specific values to visibly leap forward from the surrounding numbers, you can create a *conditional number format*, a display format that depends on the value in the formatted cell.

For example, in Figure 12.6 there are lots of numbers, and there are formulas (MIN and MAX) that look up the minimum and maximum values in that morass of numbers. But knowing what the minimum and maximum values are doesn't make it any easier to find when and by whom they were earned.

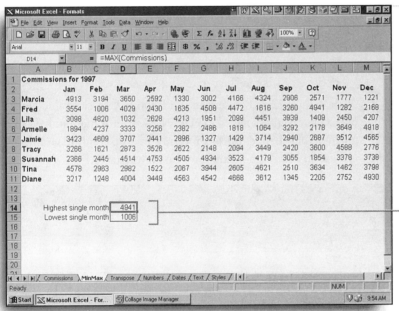

FIGURE 12.6

I'm in a hurry; who earned the minimum and maximum commissions this year?

1 MIN and MAX formulas

To make the minimum and maximum values easy to locate visually, I can apply color, bold formatting, and borders to the minimum and maximum values in the worksheet.

Apply conditional formatting

1. Select the range where you want to apply the conditional formats (in this case, cells B3:M11).

2. On the **Format** menu, click **Conditional Formatting**.

The Conditional Formatting dialog box is displayed, as shown in Figure 12.7.

FIGURE 12.7

Use the Conditional Formatting dialog box to create cell formatting that responds to cell values.

① Start here

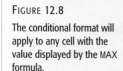

3. Select options from the boxes, starting with the **Condition 1** box on the left.

The options you choose in each box determine which options display in the remaining boxes.

In Figure 12.8, I've set the condition as "the cell value equal to the result displayed in cell D14." Even if the numbers in the table change, the MAX formula and the conditional format will still find the maximum value in the table.

FIGURE 12.8

The conditional format will apply to any cell with the value displayed by the MAX formula.

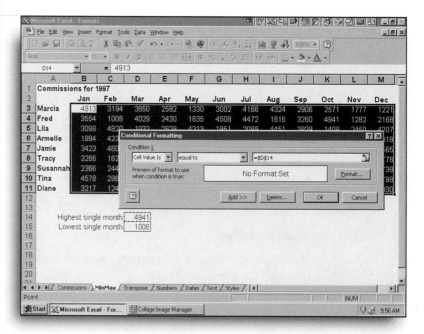

4. Click the **Format** button.

A Format Cells dialog box is displayed.

5. Set **Font**, **Border**, and **Patterns** formats; then click **OK**.

6. If you want to add more conditions, click the **Add** button to add another conditional format. (In this case, I'm going to format the minimum value in the table, also.)

7. When you finish creating conditional formats, click **OK**.

Figure 12.9 shows the results of my two conditional formats: The minimum and maximum values are easy to see among all the numbers.

SEE ALSO

➤ *To learn more about the* MIN *and* MAX *functions, see the sections* "MIN" *and* "MAX," *pages 158 and 159.*

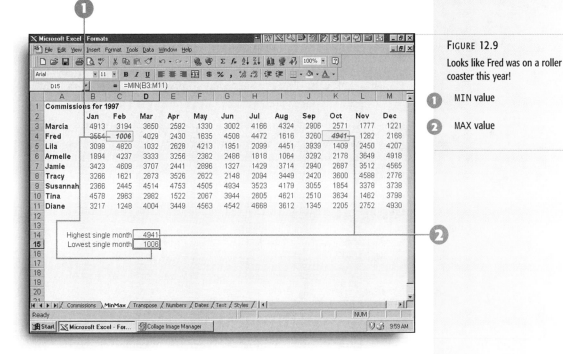

FIGURE 12.9

Looks like Fred was on a roller coaster this year!

1 MIN value

2 MAX value

Converting Actual Values to Displayed Values

If the results of your calculations end up with 11 or 12 decimal places and you want to reduce the values to whole numbers, you can permanently change the actual full-precision values to the formatted values you've displayed. For example, if you displayed 1.2345 as 1, converting to displayed value changes the actual cell value to 1, and you lose the .2345 part of the value.

You cannot, however, change just a few cells; all constant values in the workbook are changed to their displayed values and will lose accuracy in future calculations.

Convert actual values to displayed values

1. Format all values to the precision you want (for example, "Number, no decimals").

2. On the **Tools** menu, click **Options**.

3. On the **Calculation** tab, click the **Precision as displayed** check box.

4. Click **OK**. The message that you're about to lose data accuracy is your last chance to back out of the operation.

   All constant values in the workbook are permanently changed to the values that are displayed, and the change cannot be undone.

Hiding Zeroes

A worksheet full of zeroes is messy, and important values can be overlooked. Hiding unnecessary zeroes makes nonzero values more noticeable, and makes the worksheet look more professional.

There are three ways to hide zeroes:

- Hide all zeroes on the worksheet by opening the **Tools** menu, clicking **Options**, and clearing the **Zero values** check box on the **View** tab.

- To hide zeroes that are the result of a formula, nest the formula into an `IF` function, as follows: `=IF(`*`formula`*`=0,"",`*`formula`*`)` which says "If the result of the formula is zero, then display nothing, otherwise display the result of the formula."

- Create a custom number format to hide all zero values in the cells where you apply it: `#,##0;(#,##0);` (be sure you type both semicolons).

Formatting with Styles for Less Effort

Applying a Built-in Style

If you've used styles in other programs (like Microsoft Word), you already know how useful and time saving they are, and you'll be pleased to know that styles work the same way in Excel. If styles are new for you, I'll show you how easy it is to make formatting easy and fast by using styles.

A *style* is a complete package of formats that you can apply all at once. For example, a style might include red, bold Times New Roman font, size 12, centered alignment, a heavy green cell border, pale yellow cell shading, and Currency number format (that would be an eye-opener!). You can create a custom style by including any cell and number formats you want, then give the style a name, and apply the style to cells anywhere in the worksheet or workbook. You save time because all the formats included in the style are applied at once.

You save time again if you need to change a format included in the style, because you need to change only the style definition; every cell where the style is applied will automatically change to display the new style formats. For example, if you've applied a custom style to subtotal cells throughout eight worksheets in a workbook and you decide to change the font color to blue, all you need to do is change the font color in the style definition. Every subtotal cell in which you applied the style will change to blue font.

Excel comes with four built-in styles: Comma, Currency, Normal, and Percent. Normal is the default style that's applied to all cells until you apply a different style.

Currency, Percent, and Comma styles are built-in number formats, with buttons on the Formatting toolbar for easy access. If you apply one of these styles, only the number formatting is applied (no other cell formats are affected).

Apply a built-in style

1. Select the cell(s) where you want to apply the style.

2. On the Formatting toolbar, click the button for the built-in style you want to apply.

   The three number styles are demonstrated in Figure 13.1.

Where can I use styles?

All styles are available throughout the workbook where they've been created or copied.

Reformat all cells at once

You can change the formats in every cell of a workbook by changing the definition of Normal style. For example, change Normal style to include pale blue cell shading, and every worksheet in the workbook will become entirely pale blue.

Money can be deceiving

Although the button is named Currency Style, the number format it applies is actually Accounting (which lines up decimal points and dollar signs in a column), not Currency.

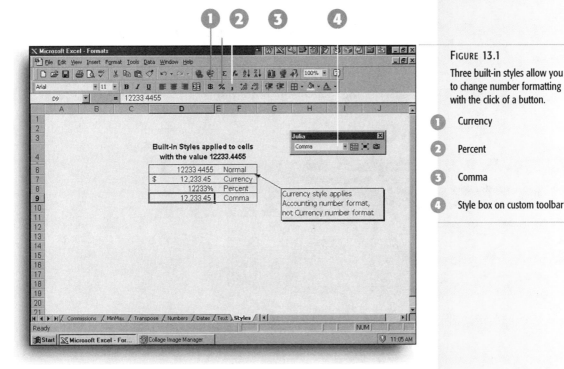

FIGURE 13.1

Three built-in styles allow you to change number formatting with the click of a button.

1 Currency

2 Percent

3 Comma

4 Style box on custom toolbar

Styles are easier if you customize a toolbar to display the Style box, shown in Figure 13.1. The Style box is in the toolbar **Customize** dialog box, on the **Commands** tab, in the Format category.

SEE ALSO

➤ To learn more about adding a new button to a toolbar, see the section "Creating Personal Toolbars" in Chapter 26, "Customizing Your Excel Screen," page 482.

Changing a Style Definition

Applying a built-in style is quick and easy, but it might not be exactly what you want. For example, you might want the built-in Comma style to apply a red font as well as a comma number format, or you might want to make a workbook-wide change to the Normal style. You can change a style definition, including built-in styles, and all cells in the workbook where the changed style is applied will automatically change to reflect the new style definition.

Change a style definition

1. Select a cell where the style is applied (in Figure 13.2, I'm going to change the Normal style).

2. On the **Format** menu, click **Style**.

   The Style dialog box is displayed, as shown in Figure 13.2.

FIGURE 13.2

One way to change style definitions is in the Style dialog box.

1   Formats included in style

   If a format check box is cleared, the style has no effect on that characteristic of cell formatting.

3. Click the **Modify** button.

   The Format Cells dialog box is displayed, as shown in Figure 13.3.

FIGURE 13.3

If you use the Style dialog box
to change a style definition,
you set and change the style's
formats in the Format Cells
dialog box.

4. In the Format Cells dialog box, set and change the formats you want the style to apply.

5. Click **OK** to close the Format Cells dialog box.

6. Click **OK** to close the Style dialog box.

   Every cell where the style was applied is changed to reflect the new style formats, as shown in Figure 13.4 (where I changed the Normal style).

Styles can be overridden

If you change a specific format, such as cell color, in a cell where a style is applied, the formatting you apply overrides the format in the style definition for that cell. (It doesn't change the style definition, it just adds another format characteristic on top of the style.)

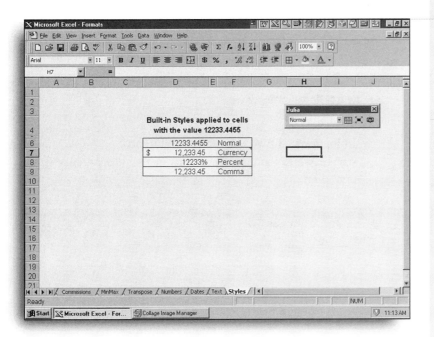

FIGURE 13.4

By changing the Normal style in this workbook, I made all the cells in the entire workbook display the new formatting.

If you use the built-in Currency, Percent, or Comma style button to apply any of those number formats to cells and then try to change workbook-wide formatting by changing the Normal style, you'll get a surprise: Cells in which Currency, Percent, or Comma style is applied don't change, because changes to Normal style don't affect them. For this reason I find it more efficient to apply Currency, Percent, or Comma formats by changing number formatting rather than using the toolbar buttons to apply styles.

If you apply a specific number format often and like the efficiency of applying it by clicking a button, you can create a quick macro and a custom toolbar button that are just as quick to use as the built-in style button.

SEE ALSO

➤ *To learn how to create macros and attach them to custom toolbar buttons, see page 489.*

Creating a Custom Style by Example

Create a new style the detailed way

If you want, you can use this same procedure to create a new style the detailed and time-consuming way: On the **Format** menu, click **Style**; in the Style dialog box, type a new **Style name** and then click **Modify**; set all the formatting in the Format Cells dialog box, and click **OK** twice to close the dialog boxes.

Creating and changing styles in the Style dialog box is sometimes the long way to go about it. It's usually faster to create and change custom styles *by example*, which means you apply all the formats you want to a single cell and then give that set of formats a custom style name.

Create a style by example

1. Format a cell.

In Figure 13.5, I've formatted a cell to be blue, bold, Arial size 14, white font, and underlined with a black double underline.

FIGURE 13.5

To create a style by example, first set up all the formatting in a cell.

① Formatted cell

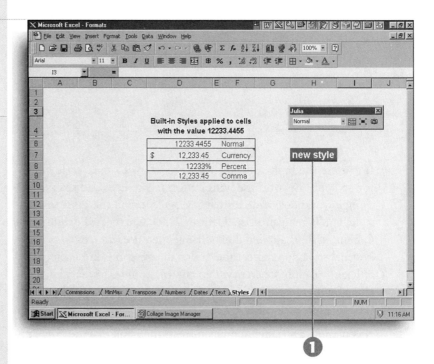

2. Select the formatted cell.

3. On the **Format** menu, click **Style**.

4. In the Style dialog box, type a name for your new style in the **Style name** box (as shown in Figure 13.6).

The toolbar Style box is faster

If you have the Style box displayed on a toolbar, click in the box and type a name for the custom style; then press Enter.

FIGURE 13.6

Type a name for your custom style, and it's ready to use.

5. Click **OK**.

The Style is ready to apply to other cells in the workbook.

In Figure 13.7, I've applied my new custom style by selecting a range and then clicking the custom style name on the drop-down list in the Style box on my custom toolbar.

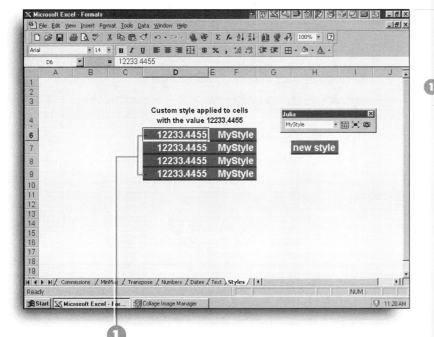

FIGURE 13.7

Custom styles can change lots of formatting characteristics quickly.

① Custom style applied

Copying Styles from Other Workbooks

Copying styles from other workbooks is especially helpful if you have several custom styles already set up in one workbook (or maybe a colleague sent you a workbook with great formatting, and you want to duplicate the formatting without having to re-create it from scratch).

You can copy a single style from one workbook to another or merge several styles at one time from one workbook to another.

Copy a style from one workbook to a second workbook

1. Open both workbooks.

2. Copy a cell that has the style applied.

3. Paste the cell into the second workbook.

   The copied-and-pasted cell carries its style with it into the second workbook, and the style name is added to the list of styles available there.

After you've pasted the cell with the custom style, you can delete the cell (or open the **Edit** menu, point to **Clear**, and click **All** to remove its contents and formatting); the custom style remains in the workbook even after you delete the cell that carried it in.

SEE ALSO

➤ *To learn about copying and pasting cells, see the section "Moving and Copying Cells to a Different Worksheet" in Chapter 8, page 126.*

Merge, or copy, several styles from one workbook to a second workbook

1. Open both workbooks.

2. In the second workbook (the workbook you want to copy styles *into*), open the **Format** menu; then click **Style**.

3. In the Style dialog box, click the **Merge** button.

4. In the Merge Styles dialog box, click the name of the workbook that contains the styles; then click **OK**.

   If there are styles in both workbooks with the same name but different formats, you'll see a message asking if you want to merge those styles.

If you click **Yes**, the styles you're merging will override the existing styles of the same name, and you can't Undo the style merger (so be careful—if you're not sure, click **No**).

The styles are merged, or copied, into the second workbook.

Deleting a Style

If you have a long list of styles in a workbook, it takes a long time to scan that list to find the style you want to apply; styles you no longer need can be deleted. Another good reason to delete a style is that it's a quick way to clean up a workbook and start over. When you delete a style, all cells with that style applied are returned to Normal style.

Delete a style

1. Under the **Format** menu, click **Style**.
2. In the **Style name** box, select the style you want to delete.
3. Click **Delete**.

    The style is deleted from the workbook, and all cells with that style applied are returned to Normal style.

Return to normalcy

If you accidentally override Normal style with an altered Normal style during a merge, here's a quick way to get your default Normal style back: Open a new workbook (it will have only the default Normal and built-in styles); then merge styles from the new, unsaved workbook into the workbook where you accidentally overrode the Normal style.

IV

Sorting, Filtering, and Summarizing Data

Sorting Lists

Sorting a List by a Single Column

After you've entered or imported a sea of data into a worksheet, you need to organize it to render it useful or meaningful. Your first line of defense against a jumble of meaningless data is to sort it. Some data-organizing procedures, such as subtotaling (covered in Chapter 16, "Summarizing Details with Consolidation or Subtotals"), require that you sort the data first.

When you sort a list, you arrange a specific column, or *field*, in the list in an ascending or descending order. The field you sort on is also known as a *sort key*. All the attached data is sorted, along with the specific column, so that if you sort a contacts list in the Last Name column, the First Name, Phone, and Address columns are sorted along with the last names, and the data remains intact.

Any data in cells adjacent to the list is sorted with the records in the list; data in cells separated from the list by a blank row or column is not included in the sort. This means that you can have two lists on a worksheet and sort them independently of one another, as long as they are separated by a blank row or column.

Sort a list quickly by a single key

1. Click in the table column (the field) you want to sort by. In Figure 14.1, I'm going to sort the list by Last Name.

   Don't select more than one cell; just click in the table column.

2. On the Standard toolbar, click a sort button:

   - To sort in ascending order (1–10 or A–Z), click Sort Ascending. ⬛
   - To sort in descending order (10–1 or Z–A), click Sort Descending. ⬛

   The list or table is sorted, as shown in Figure 14.2.

Sorting out the terminology

In general, the terms *list* and *table* mean the same thing: a rectangular block of data that pertains to a single subject (for example, contact information), in which each column, or *field*, contains the same kind of data (for example, last name or phone number).

What if I just want to sort the one column?

To sort a single column in a table without sorting the attached data along with the column, select all the cells in the table column before sorting; only that column is sorted, and the other columns are unchanged.

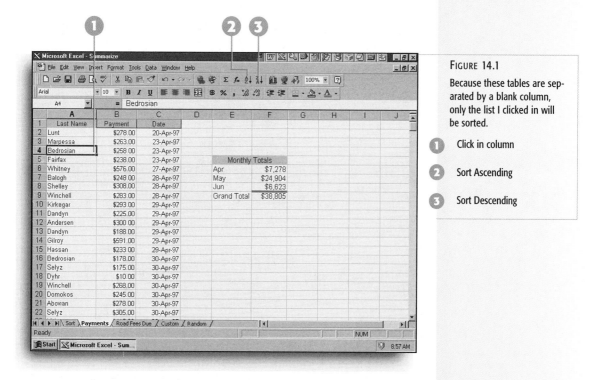

FIGURE 14.1

Because these tables are separated by a blank column, only the list I clicked in will be sorted.

1 Click in column

2 Sort Ascending

3 Sort Descending

FIGURE 14.2

The whole list is sorted, along with the column I clicked in (Last Name).

Sorting a List by Two or Three Columns

In Figure 14.3, I've got a table of nationwide sales results for baseball caps. I want to compare the sales for each color—red and black—and see if different target audiences have different cap color preferences.

FIGURE 14.3

This data needs to be sorted by Store Type, by Store Name within Store Type, and then by Cap Color within Store Name.

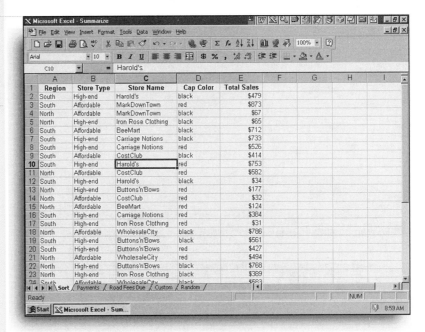

The data was entered in random order, and now I need to sort it to make sense of it. I'll sort it by Store Type (High-end or Affordable), then by the actual Store Name, and then by Cap Color.

Sort a list by two or three keys

1. Click any cell in the table.

2. On the **Data** menu, click **Sort**.

    The Sort dialog box is displayed, as shown in Figure 14.4.

3. In the **Sort by** box, click the down arrow; then click the top-level sort key (in this case, the Store Type field).

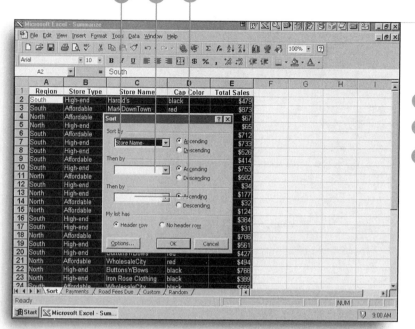

FIGURE 14.4

You can sort a table by three keys at a time in the Sort dialog box.

❶ First key

❷ Second key

❸ Third key

4. Click an option button for the sort order you want (in this case, **A**scending).

5. In the first **Then by** box, choose the second-level sort key (in this case, Store Name) and a sort order.

6. In the second **Then by** box, choose the third-level sort key (in this case, Cap Color) and a sort order.

The completed dialog box for this example is shown in Figure 14.5.

7. Click **OK**.

The table is sorted by the keys you set in the Sort dialog box; in this example, my sorted table is shown in Figure 14.6.

FIGURE 14.5

The Sort dialog box is ready to sort the table by three keys.

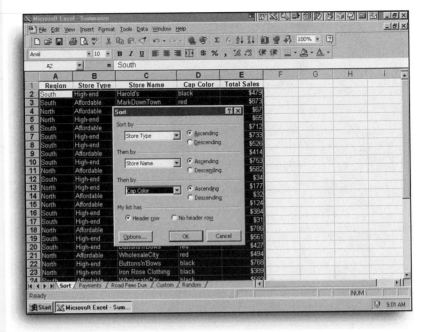

FIGURE 14.6

This table is sorted by Store Type, then by Store Name, and then by Cap Color.

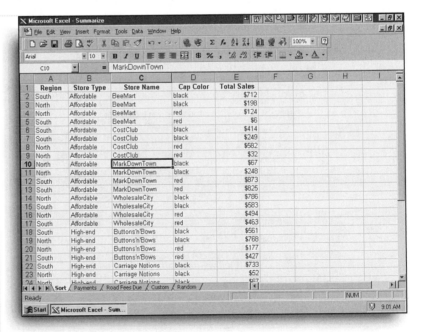

Sorting a List by More Than Three Columns

The Sort dialog box lets you sort by up to three keys; if you need to sort by four or more, there's a trick you need to know: *sort by the major, overall biggest key last*. Perform the sort on the smaller, more detailed keys first, with the Sort dialog box; then perform a second sort with the Sort dialog box, but *only* on the major sort key or keys (usually the left-most fields in the table).

For example, in the table in Figure 14.6, I want to sort sales by Region, as well as by Store Type, Store Name, and Cap Color.

Because I've already performed the sort in Figure 14.6 by the three *minor*, or more detailed, keys, I'm set up to sort on the major key: Region.

Sort a list with four keys

1. Be sure a single cell in the table is selected.
2. On the **Data** menu, click **Sort**.
3. In the **Sort by** box, select the major sort key (in this case, **Region**), and click a sort order option.
4. In the remaining **Then by** boxes, select **(none)**.

   The dialog box in Figure 14.7 is set up to perform the fourth-key sort.
5. Click **OK**.

   The fourth key becomes the top-level sort key in the table, as shown in Figure 14.8.

Sorting According to a Custom List

You can sort any key in ascending or descending order, but suppose you want to sort by a special order that's neither ascending nor descending? For example, you might want to sort a list of names of children from oldest to youngest.

FIGURE 14.7

The second sort overlays a new sort order on top of the already sorted table.

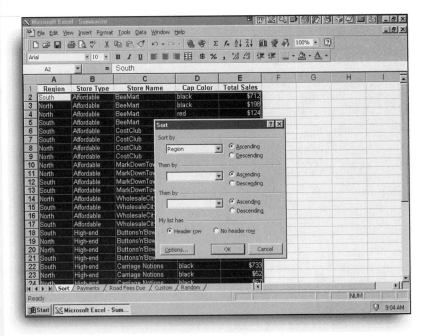

FIGURE 14.8

This table is sorted by four keys: Region, then Store Type, Store Name, and Cap Color.

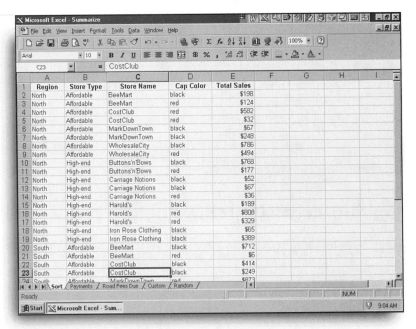

Sort options let you sort according to an order in a custom list, which includes days, months, and any custom lists you've created and saved.

SEE ALSO

➤ *To learn how to create a custom list, see page 97.*

Sort a list according to a custom sort order

1. Make sure you've created and saved a custom list. (To see the custom lists, open the **Tools** menu and click **Options**; then click the **Custom Lists** tab.)

2. Click in the custom list column in your table, also called the custom list *key*.

3. On the **Data** menu, click **Sort**.

4. In the Sort dialog box, shown in Figure 14.9, click **Options**.

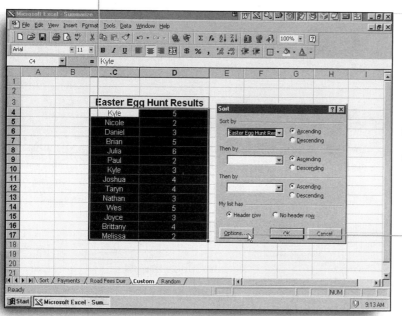

FIGURE 14.9

I previously created and saved this list of names as a custom list; it retains its original sort order, whether I enter it with AutoFill or sort it with special sorting options.

1 Custom list column

2 Options button

5. In the Sort Options dialog box, shown in Figure 14.10, click the down arrow in the **First key sort order** drop-down list box; then click the custom list you want to use as a sort order.

FIGURE 14.10

Choose a custom sort order in the Sort Options dialog box by selecting from previously saved custom lists.

① Custom list key

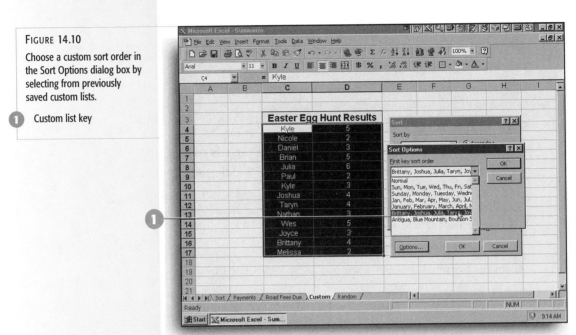

6. Click **OK**; then click **OK** again to close the Sort dialog box.

The list is sorted according to the custom sort order.

Sorting a List Randomly

Some situations call for a random assortment of items in a list, sometimes even repeated random sorting of the same list. For example, one of my students is a high school teacher, and he likes to thwart potential exam cheaters by creating several versions of the same exam. Each exam has the same long list of true/false questions but in a different order. An easy way to create several random-order versions of the exam is to combine the RAND function, which returns random numbers, and repeated sorting.

Sort a list in random order

1. Create the table or list. (For my student's example, I've created a list of exam questions in a worksheet.)

2. Add to the table a column for random numbers, like the one shown in Figure 14.11.

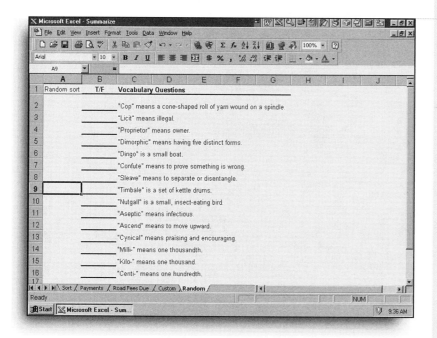

FIGURE 14.11

This table will be sorted at random every time the worksheet recalculates (which is more often than you'd think).

3. Select the entire random-number column, and type this formula:

```
=rand()
```

4. Press Ctrl+Enter to enter the formula in all the selected cells.

A formula that generates random numbers to 15-digit precision is entered in the new column.

5. Click in the random number column; then click the Sort Ascending button on the Standard toolbar.

Every time you click the Sort Ascending button, the RAND() function recalculates and the list is re-sorted, as shown in Figure 14.12.

Generating random whole numbers

To generate random numbers that are integers greater than 100, try this formula:
```
=int(rand()*100).
```

FIGURE 14.12

Random sorting is a good way to create non-identical lists that contain the same information.

1 Random numbers for sort

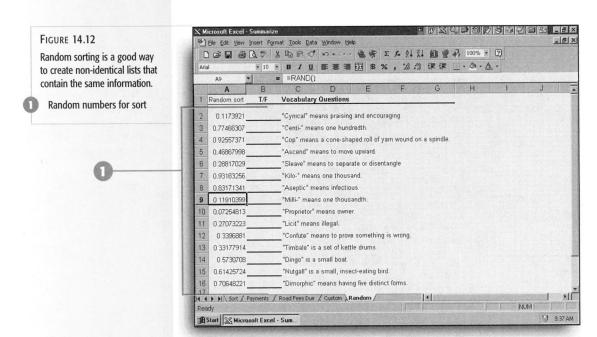

Here are some ways to "freeze" and save randomly sorted lists to create several versions:

- Copy the list without the random-number column and paste it in another worksheet

- Copy the list without the random-number column and paste it in a Word document

- Freeze the randomly sorted list by deleting the random-number formulas

SEE ALSO

➤ *To learn more about copying data to another worksheet, see page 126.*

➤ *To learn more about copying data to a Word document, see page 459.*

Undoing a Sort and Returning the List to Its Former Arrangement

You might need to sort a list for temporary information but not want to keep that sort order. There are a couple of ways to return a sorted list to its original sort arrangement:

- To undo a sort and return the list to its former arrangement, click the Undo button 🔄 on the Standard toolbar.

- To be able to return to a pre-sort arrangement after performing lots of data manipulation in a table, first insert a column of numbers, sorted in ascending order, somewhere in the table (insert a column and use AutoFill to enter the numbers). Then ignore the new column while you work with the table. When you need to return the initial sort order to the table, sort the number column you inserted.

Filtering Lists

Filtering Records

If you have a large table of data and you want to focus on particular *records*, or rows, within the table, you can *filter* the table to show only those records and hide all others. You can also use filters to *extract*, or pull out, specific records and paste them onto another worksheet (or into another file, like a Word document).

New terms

Field is the common term for a column of data in a table, and *record* is the common term for a row of data in a table. You see these terms a lot, both in this book and in Excel's help files.

The easiest, fastest way to filter a list is by using *AutoFilter*. You can filter a list by looking for a specific entry in a single *field* (for example, a specific city in a City field) or by looking for multiple criteria (such as expense amounts greater than $100 in a specific expense category).

Filter a List on a Single Criteria

I'm the treasurer for a local nonprofit organization, and the table in Figure 15.1 is similar to a table I use to keep track of who has paid their fees. It's a fairly long list, and I want to see at a glance who still owes a balance. I use AutoFilter to hide everyone who's paid up and show only those who owe fees, by filtering the nonblank cells in the Balance field.

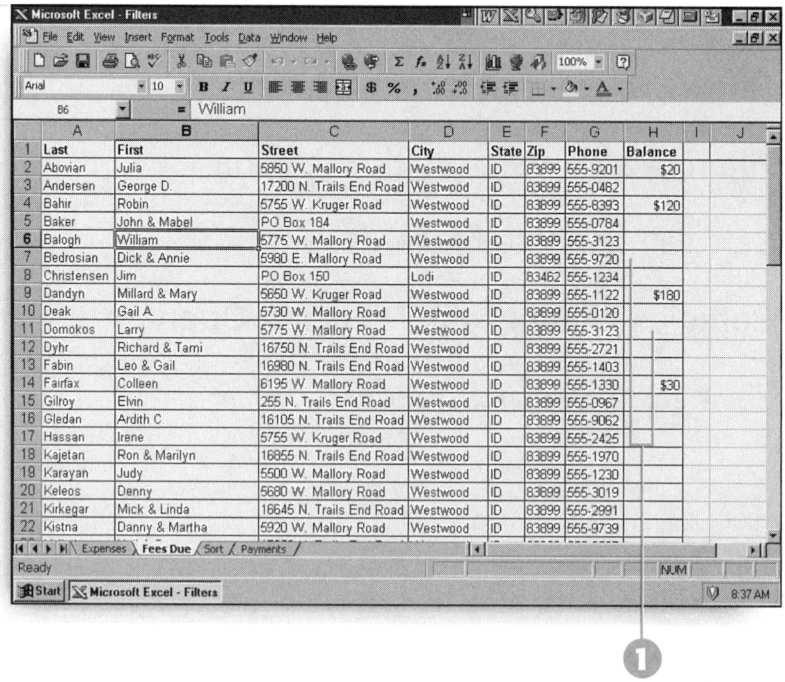

	Last	First	Street	City	State	Zip	Phone	Balance
2	Abovian	Julia	5850 W. Mallory Road	Westwood	ID	83899	555-9201	$20
3	Andersen	George D.	17200 N. Trails End Road	Westwood	ID	83899	555-0482	
4	Bahir	Robin	5755 W. Kruger Road	Westwood	ID	83899	555-8393	$120
5	Baker	John & Mabel	PO Box 184	Westwood	ID	83899	555-0784	
6	Balogh	William	5775 W. Mallory Road	Westwood	ID	83899	555-3123	
7	Bedrosian	Dick & Annie	5980 E. Mallory Road	Westwood	ID	83899	555-9720	
8	Christensen	Jim	PO Box 150	Lodi	ID	83462	555-1234	
9	Dandyn	Millard & Mary	5650 W. Kruger Road	Westwood	ID	83899	555-1122	$180
10	Deak	Gail A.	5730 W. Mallory Road	Westwood	ID	83899	555-0120	
11	Domokos	Larry	5775 W. Mallory Road	Westwood	ID	83899	555-3123	
12	Dyhr	Richard & Tami	16750 N. Trails End Road	Westwood	ID	83899	555-2721	
13	Fabin	Leo & Gail	16980 N. Trails End Road	Westwood	ID	83899	555-1403	
14	Fairfax	Colleen	6195 W. Mallory Road	Westwood	ID	83899	555-1330	$30
15	Gilroy	Elvin	255 N. Trails End Road	Westwood	ID	83899	555-0967	
16	Gledan	Ardith C.	16105 N. Trails End Road	Westwood	ID	83899	555-9062	
17	Hassan	Irene	5755 W. Kruger Road	Westwood	ID	83899	555-2425	
18	Kajetan	Ron & Marilyn	16855 N. Trails End Road	Westwood	ID	83899	555-1970	
19	Karayan	Judy	5500 W. Mallory Road	Westwood	ID	83899	555-1230	
20	Keleos	Denny	5680 W. Mallory Road	Westwood	ID	83899	555-3019	
21	Kirkegar	Mick & Linda	16645 N. Trails End Road	Westwood	ID	83899	555-2991	
22	Kistna	Danny & Martha	5920 W. Mallory Road	Westwood	ID	83899	555-9739	

FIGURE 15.1

By hiding the records with blank cells in the Balance column, I can see a list of people who still owe money.

1. Filter non-blanks

Filter a table with AutoFilter

1. Click any cell in the table.

2. On the **Data** menu, point to **Filter** and then click
   AutoFilter.

   Small gray filter arrows appear at the top of every column in
   the table (shown in Figure 15.2).

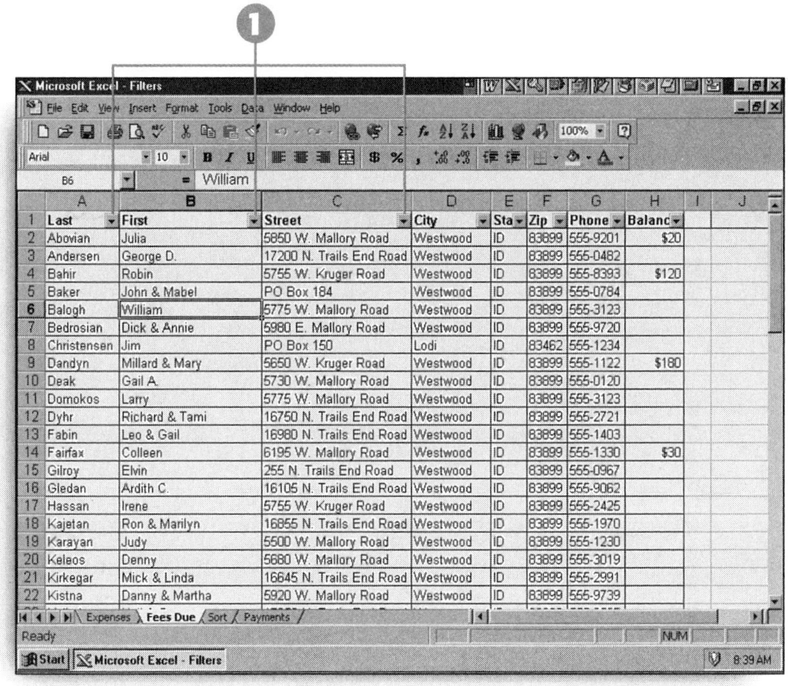

FIGURE 15.2

AutoFilter operates by means
of small gray filter arrows at
the top of each column.

❶ Filter arrows

3. Click a filter arrow in the field in which you want to set filter criteria (in this example, the Balance field, as shown in
   Figure 15.3).

4. Click the criteria on which you want to filter (in this example, I'm filtering on non-blanks).

   Records with the criteria you choose are displayed, and all
   others are hidden (shown in Figure 15.4). The filter arrow
   in the active-filter field is blue, which helps you remember
   where you set criteria.

FIGURE 15.3

The filter arrow drops a list of criteria found in that field.

1 Filter criteria

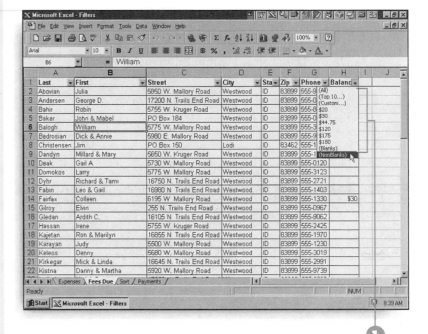

FIGURE 15.4

Filtering the table shows me at a glance who still owes what.

1 Active filter (blue arrow)

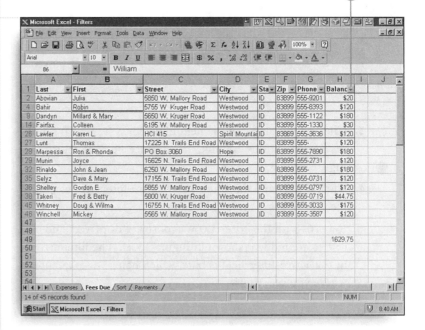

5. To keep AutoFilter on but remove the filter criteria, click the filter arrow and then click **(All)**.

To remove the filter and display all records, open the **Data** menu, point to **Filter**, and then click **AutoFilter** to turn off AutoFilter.

Filter a List on Multiple Criteria

Sometimes you need a more complex filter criteria, as I want in the expenses list in Figure 15.5.

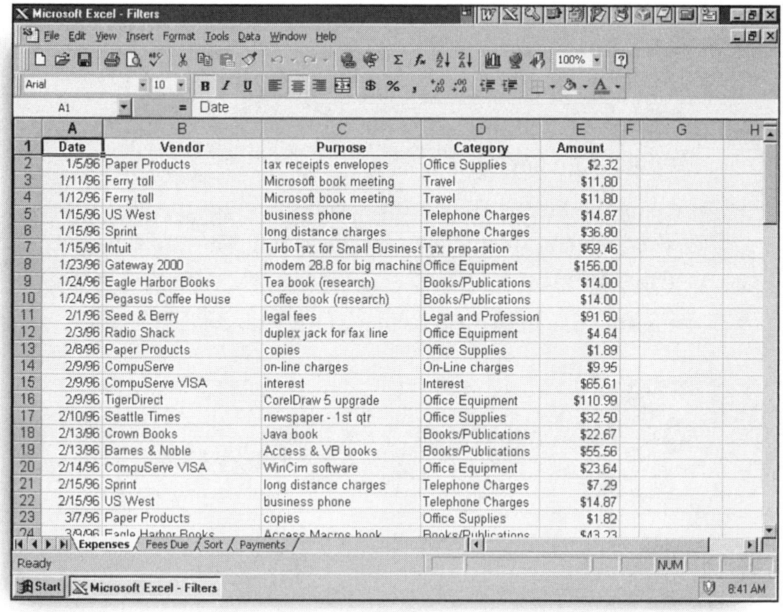

FIGURE 15.5
Filtering helps me understand better where I spent my year's expenses.

The following are several ways to narrow a filter and make it even more specific (all are covered in the following sections):

- You can filter on two different fields. (For example, I want to see the expenses for Office Supplies, specifically for the Paper Products vendor.)

- You can filter on two criteria in the same field. (For example, I want to see what I spent at Crown Books or at Barnes & Noble, both in the Vendor field.)

- You can filter on a criteria range. (For example, I want to see a filtered list of all my expenses in January.)

- You can filter on the highest or lowest numbers in a number field. (For example, I want to see the five highest expense amounts for the year.)

Filtering on Two Different Fields

I want to see the expenses for Office Supplies, specifically for the Paper Products vendor.

Filter on two different fields

1. Click the table. On the **Data** menu, point to **Filter** and then click **AutoFilter**.

2. Click the filter arrow in the first field (in this case, Category), and then click the criteria you want (in this case, Office Supplies).

3. Click the filter arrow in the second field (in this case, Vendor), and then click the criteria you want (in this case, Paper Products).

   Figure 15.6 shows the results of my two-field filter.

FIGURE 15.6

To filter on two fields, select a filter criteria in each field.

① These two fields are filtered

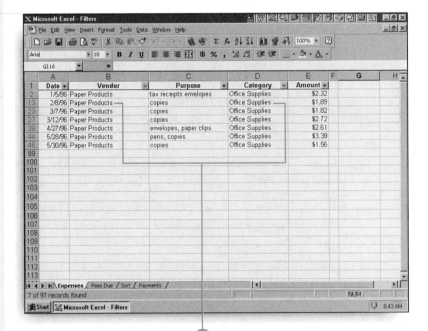

①

Filtering on Two Criteria in the Same Field

I want to see what I spent at Crown Books and Barnes & Noble, both in the Vendor field. This filter requires that I set up an OR criteria in the Vendor field to show every record where the vendor is either Crown Books OR Barnes & Noble.

Filter on two criteria in the same field

1. Click the table. On the **Data** menu, point to **Filter** and then click **AutoFilter**.

   If AutoFilter is already turned on, be sure all other AutoFilter criteria are removed (all AutoFilter arrows should be black).

2. Click the filter arrow in the Vendor field and then click **(Custom...)**.

   The Custom AutoFilter dialog box appears (shown in Figure 15.7).

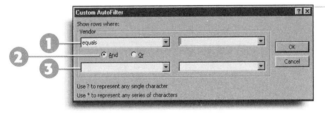

3. In the upper-left box, select a comparison operator from the list (in this example, **equals**).

4. In the upper-right box, select a value from the field (in this example, **Crown Books**).

5. Click the **Or** option button.

6. In the lower boxes, select a comparison operator and field value (in this example, **equals** and **Barnes & Noble**).

   The Custom AutoFilter dialog box in Figure 15.8 is set up to run this filter.

7. Click **OK**.

   The results of my filter are shown in Figure 15.9.

FIGURE 15.7

Set up complex filter criteria in the Custom AutoFilter dialog box by selecting items from the drop-down lists.

1. First criteria

2. And/Or

3. Second criteria

An OR criteria or an AND criteria?

An OR criteria displays records that meet either of the criteria; it reads "show me any entries that are X OR Y." An AND criteria displays records that meet both the criteria; it reads "show me each entry that's both X AND Y." If you create an AND filter and get no records displayed, you probably want an OR filter instead.

FIGURE 15.8

This OR filter displays records for both bookstores.

1 **OR** option

FIGURE 15.9

The results of my OR filter: all vendors that are Crown Books OR Barnes & Noble.

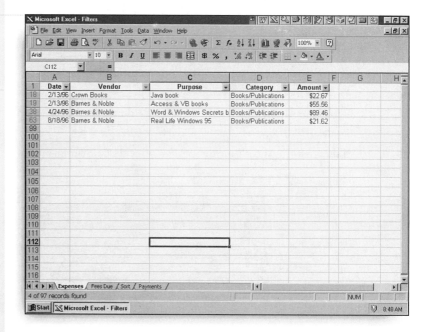

Filtering on a Criteria Range

I want to see a filtered list of all my expenses in January. This is an example of an AND filter: show all records where the Date value is greater than or equal to 1/1/96 AND less than or equal to 1/31/96.

Filter on a criteria range

1. Click the table. On the **Data** menu, point to **Filter** and then click **AutoFilter**.

   If AutoFilter is already turned on, be sure all other AutoFilter criteria are removed.

2. Click the filter arrow in the Date field and then click (**Custom...**).

The Custom AutoFilter dialog box appears.

3. In the upper-left box, select a comparison operator from the list (in this example, **is greater than or equal to**).

4. In the upper-right box, type the beginning date (in this example, **1/1/96**).

5. Be sure the **And** option button is selected.

6. In the lower boxes, select a comparison operator and field value (in this example, **is less than or equal to** and **1/31/96**).

Figure 15.10 shows the Custom AutoFilter dialog box set up to run this filter.

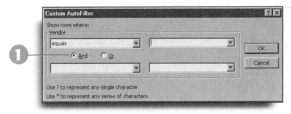

FIGURE 15.10

This complex criteria displays records with values between two dates: greater than one date AND less than another.

1 **And** option

7. Click **OK**.

The results of my AND filter are shown in Figure 15.11.

SEE ALSO

➤ *To learn more about formatting dates and times, see page 226.*

Filtering on the Highest or Lowest Numbers in a Number Field

I want to see the five highest expense amounts for the year.

Filter on the highest or lowest numbers in a number field

1. Click the table. On the **Data** menu, point to **Filter** and then click **AutoFilter**.

If AutoFilter is already turned on, be sure all other AutoFilter criteria are removed.

Excel sees your dates as serial numbers

If you open the Custom AutoFilter dialog box again, you see that Excel has converted the typed dates into date serial numbers.

FIGURE 15.11

Blue row numbers indicate
that the table is filtered and
many rows are hidden.

FIGURE 15.11

Blue row numbers indicate
that the table is filtered and
many rows are hidden.

1 Blue row numbers

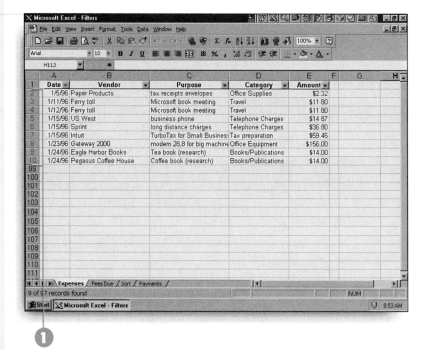

2. Click the filter arrow in a number field (in this case, the
Amount field) and then click **(Top 10...)**.

The Top 10 AutoFilter dialog box appears (shown in Figure
15.12).

FIGURE 15.12

I've set up the Top 10
AutoFilter dialog box to show
the 5 highest amounts in my
expenses table.

3. In the left-most box, select Top or Bottom (for this example,
I select **Top**).

4. In the center box, type or scroll to the number of records
you want to display (in this case, **5**).

5. In the right-most box, select Items or Percent. I select
Items; Percent shows me amounts that fall within the top
five percent of the list, but I'm not interested in percentages.

6. Click **OK**.

The results are shown in Figure 15.13.

Calculating Filtered Records

Viewing a filtered list is a good beginning, but calculations give you more information about the table. For example, I'd like to know what my average telephone charge from Sprint was. I can get that by using the SUBTOTAL function with my filtered list.

If I use the SUM or AVERAGE functions, the entire table is calculated rather than the records I display with a filter. If, however, I use the SUBTOTAL function, the formula calculates the filtered, displayed records only, rather than the entire table.

The SUBTOTAL function can calculate several different functions, depending on the arguments you enter. The function, *SUBTOTAL(function_num,Ref1)*, requires a number in the *function_num* argument that determines what specific calculation it performs. Table 15.1 shows the possible SUBTOTAL *function_num* arguments and their corresponding calculations.

Fast, temporary calculations

To get a quick, impermanent calculation of filtered records, use AutoCalculate. Filter the list, select the cells you want to sum (or average or whatever), and look at the AutoCalculate box on the status bar. AutoCalculate only calculates visible (non-hidden) cells.

AutoSUBTOTAL?

If you use the AutoSum button to create a SUM formula when the table is filtered, a SUBTO-TAL formula is created instead of a SUM formula, but the new SUBTOTAL function calculates a sum. If you want the SUBTOTAL function to calculate an average instead of a sum, you need to change the calculation argument in the SUBTOTAL function.

TABLE 15.1   **SUBTOTAL arguments and calculations**

This Argument	Performs This Calculation
1	AVERAGE
2	COUNT
3	COUNTA
4	MAX
5	MIN
6	PRODUCT
7	STDEV
8	STDEVP
9	SUM
10	VAR
11	VARP

For this example, I'm going to set up a SUBTOTAL formula that averages the filtered values in the Amount field of my expenses list.

Calculate a filtered list with the SUBTOTAL function

1. Click a cell below the list in which you want to display the result of the formula.
2. On the toolbar, click the Paste Function button f_x.
3. In the **All** or **Math & Trig** category, double-click **SUBTO-TAL**.

   The SUBTOTAL dialog box appears (shown in Figure 15.14).
4. In the **Function_num** box, type 1.

   1 is the argument that tells SUBTOTAL to calculate an average. For a different calculation, look up the argument in Table 15.1.
5. In the **Ref1** box, enter the range to calculate (in this case, the range E2:E98, in the Amount column).
6. Click **OK**.

It matters where you put the formula

If you click a cell next to the list, the cell is probably hidden when you filter the list; a cell below the list is still visible during a filter.

It could be easier

The only difficult part of the SUBTO-TAL function is figuring out what calculation argument to use. Maybe in the next version of Excel, Microsoft will make the arguments available in the dialog box, instead of making us plow through the layers of help files to find them. In the meantime, refer to Table 15.1 to find the argument you need quickly.

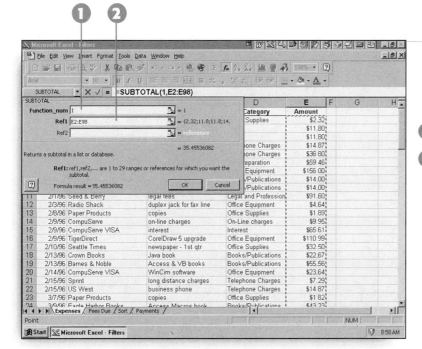

The SUBTOTAL formula calculates an average for the Amount cells that are displayed. Figure 15.15 shows the SUBTOTAL formula and the list filtered for Sprint charges.

SEE ALSO
➤ *To learn more about writing formulas, see page 143.*
➤ *To learn more about using functions, see page 154.*

The Query Wizard: A Better Filter

If you've used Microsoft Access, you probably already know what queries are. If you don't know Access however, I tell you what queries are and how and why you'd want to use them.

A query is like a *better* filter. When you use a filter you can select specific records, but you get every field in the record. When you use a query, you can select specific records and specific fields within those records (for example, in Figure 15.15, a query would enable me to extract just the Date and Amount fields for the Sprint charges).

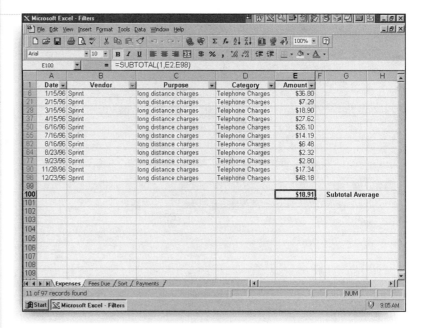

The Query Wizard in Excel helps you to pinpoint exactly the data you want to extract, and you can use the wizard to extract data from Excel lists, Access database tables and queries, and other database program files. The procedures for querying Excel, Access, and other database files are all very similar; after you know how to query an Excel list, you're able to query other database files just as easily.

Before you can use the Query Wizard, you must install the wizard and the drivers it needs on your computer. If you open the **Data** menu, point to **Get External Data**, click **Create New Query**, and a message tells you that Microsoft Query is not installed, you need to install Microsoft Query.

Installing Microsoft Query

1. Close all programs that are running on your computer.

2. Put your Office 97 CD-ROM in your computer's CD drive. (If the CD drive window opens, you can close it by clicking its Close button.)

3. Click Start, point to **Settings**, and then click **Control Panel**.

4. Double-click the Add/Remove Programs icon.

5. Click Office 97 (or Excel 97, if you installed it separately) and then click **Add/<u>R</u>emove**.

If you get a message asking you to insert your CD-ROM, click **OK** because you already did it in step 2.

6. In the next dialog box, click **<u>A</u>dd/Remove** again.

7. In the Maintenance dialog box, in the **<u>O</u>ptions** list, click **Data Access** and then click the **Chan<u>g</u>e Option** button.

8. Click the **Microsoft Query** check box to mark it.

9. Click the **Database Drivers** check box to mark it and then click the **Chan<u>g</u>e Option** button.

10. Click check boxes for the drivers that correspond to the file types you want to query.

11. Click **OK** to save the changed options. Keep clicking **OK** to close dialog boxes until you get back to the Maintenance window.

12. Click **<u>C</u>ontinue** (when asked if you're sure, click **<u>Y</u>es**).

13. When asked about removing shared Windows components, click **Remove None**.

14. Click **OK** to acknowledge that the Setup procedure is complete.

15. Click **Cancel** to close the Add/Remove Programs/Properties dialog box.

Use the Query Wizard to Extract Data

One good reason to learn how to use the Query Wizard with Excel files is that you can extract data from closed workbooks, including workbooks that a colleague may have saved as Read-only to prevent inadvertent changes. In this example, I pull data out of my expenses list in a closed workbook named Filters.

Before you run a query on an Excel table, name the range of data you're querying so that the Wizard finds the data more easily. I named my expenses list Expenses before I began this procedure, and then saved and closed the workbook.

The first time you run any query, it's a two-part process: first you define a data source (tell Query Wizard where to look for data), and then you run the Query Wizard and indicate exactly what data to extract from the data source. After you've defined a data source, the Query Wizard remembers it and you don't need to redefine it.

SEE ALSO

➤ *To learn more about naming cells and ranges, see page 181.*

Defining a Data Source

The procedure for defining a data source is very similar, whether the data source is an Excel workbook, an Access database, or another type of database file.

Create a new query

1. Open the workbook in which you want to place the queried data.

2. On the **Data** menu, point to **Get External Data**, and then click **Create New Query**.

   Microsoft Query starts, and the Choose Data Source dialog box appears (shown in Figure 15.16).

FIGURE 15.16

First, you need to define the data source you want to query.

① Previously defined data source

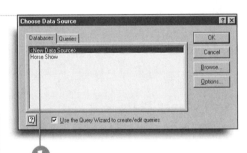

3. On the **Databases** tab, double-click **<New Data Source>**.

   The Create New Data Source dialog box appears (shown in Figure 15.17).

4. In box 1, type a name for your data source (in this example, I name the data source Expenses).

Deleting a data source name

To delete a data source name from the list, use My Computer window to navigate to your Data Sources folder and delete the name. The data source name has the extension .dsn. (In my computer, the path is C:\Program Files\Common Files\ODBC\Data Sources.) You can also click **Start**, point to **Find**, click **Files or Folders**, and search for the data source name or files with the extension .dsn.

FIGURE 15.17

I've given the new data source a name and selected the proper driver for the Query Wizard to use.

5. In box 2, click the down arrow and choose **Microsoft Excel Driver**.

6. Click the **Connect** button.

The ODBC Microsoft Excel Setup dialog box appears (shown in Figure 15.18), where you can select the workbook source from which you want to extract data.

What does ODBC stand for?

ODBC means Open Database Connectivity; it's one of those computer jargon acronyms that you don't need to think about unless you want to impress members of your local hackers' club.

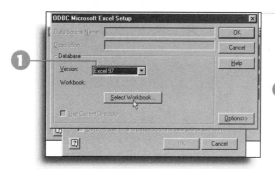

FIGURE 15.18

Make sure to indicate for the Query Wizard what version the Excel source is.

1 Excel version number

7. Make sure the Excel version is correct for the workbook you are querying, and then click **Select Workbook**.

The Select Workbook dialog box appears (shown in Figure 15.19).

8. In the Select Workbook dialog box, navigate to your workbook data source, and double-click the workbook name that contains your source data.

The workbook name and path appear in the ODBC Microsoft Excel Setup dialog box (shown in Figure 15.20.)

FIGURE 15.19

Select the workbook that contains your source data.

FIGURE 15.20

Make sure the workbook path and name are correct.

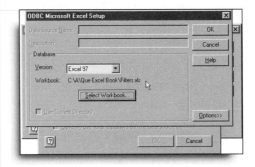

9. Click **OK**.

10. In the Create New Data Source dialog box, click **OK**.

Your new data source (in this case, Expenses) appears in the Choose Data Source dialog box (shown in Figure 15.21). You can click **OK** to close the dialog box and come back to it later, or continue with the Query Wizard in the next section.

FIGURE 15.21

The Choose Data Source dialog box keeps a list of all data sources you define, so you can use them repeatedly.

Running the Query Wizard

After you define a data source, it appears in the Choose Data Source dialog box whenever you start the Query Wizard.

Run the Query Wizard

1. Double-click your named data source (in this case, Expenses).

If the Choose Data Source dialog box isn't already open, you need to open it. On the **D**ata menu, point to **Get External Data**, and then click **Create** **New** **Query.**

Shown in the list (see Figure 15.22) are any named ranges in the data source workbook. Click the small plus (+) symbol to display the column names in the named range.

2. Double-click the column names you want to include (in this example, I include Category and Amount) and then click **Next.**

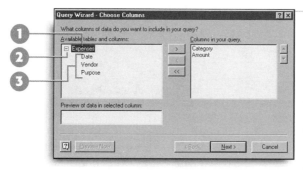

FIGURE 15.22

All named ranges in the data source are listed. Choose the fields from which you want to extract data.

① Named range

② Click to show/hide column names

③ Column names in named range

The second wizard step appears (shown in Figure 15.23).

3. In the second wizard step, you set up the filter that determines which records are extracted from the data source table. (In this case, I set the filter criteria "Category equals Office Equipment **Or** Category equals Office Supplies") and click **Next.**

4. In the third wizard step (shown in Figure 15.24), you can select a sort key (I select **Category** for a sort key, and **Ascending** for a sort order) and click **Next.**

5. If you want to use this particular query again, click the **S**ave **Query** button and follow the steps for saving and reusing a query in the next section. If you don't want to save and reuse this query, continue with step 6.

FIGURE 15.23

Set the filter criteria for the records you want to extract.

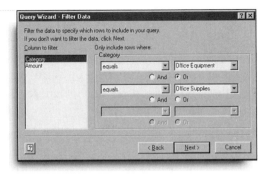

FIGURE 15.24

Selecting a sort order for the queried data saves you the time of sorting it after it's in the worksheet. You can sort on up to three keys.

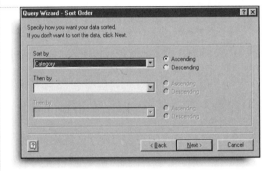

6. In the Query Wizard - Finish dialog box, click the **Return data to Microsoft Excel** option and then click **Finish**.

7. In the Returning External Data to Microsoft Excel dialog box (shown in Figure 15.25), click the **Existing worksheet** option button, click a cell on the worksheet in which you want to paste the upper-left corner of the extracted data, and click **OK**.

Query revs its engines for a few seconds and the extracted data appears in your worksheet (as shown in Figure 15.26).

Update the query with fresh data

To refresh a query with changed source data, you don't have to run the query again. Instead, click the Refresh All button on the External Data toolbar.

When queried data is pasted into a worksheet, the External Data toolbar appears, to make some tasks quicker. Table 15.2 tells about the buttons in the External Data toolbar.

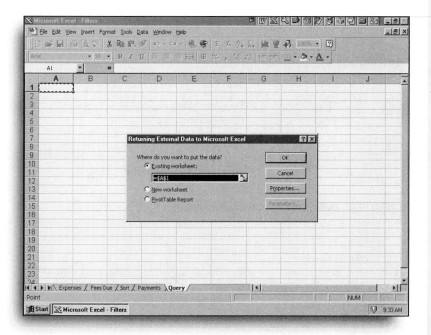

FIGURE 15.25

Indicate in the Query Wizard where you want the extracted data pasted.

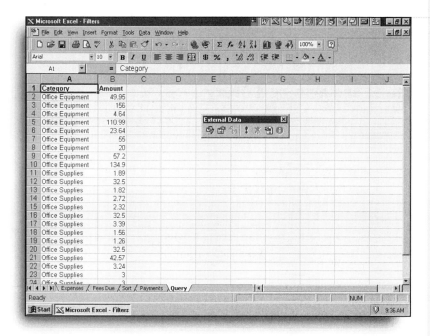

FIGURE 15.26

Raw data is extracted from the source. The cells still need to be formatted.

TABLE 15.2   Buttons in the External Data toolbar

Icon	Button Name	Function
	Edit Query	Modify an existing query: set different fields, filter criteria, sort order.
	Data Range Properties	Set advanced option on the data range or record set returned by a query.
	Query Parameters	Set parameters that ask for criteria when you run the query. Parameter queries enable you to extract different data every time you run the query.
	Refresh Data	Updates data in a PivotTable. Use this button to refresh queried data if you've returned extracted data to a PivotTable rather than to a worksheet range.
	Refresh All	Updates all queried data. Use this button to refresh queried data whether you've returned it to a worksheet range or a PivotTable.
	Refresh Status	Displays a dialog box that shows the status of a refresh procedure and how long it's taking.
	Cancel Refresh	Stops the refresh procedure if refresh is going to take a very long time and you don't want to wait for it.

Saving and Reusing a Query

If you want to run the same query repeatedly (for example, to extract the same data from an updated report every week), you can save yourself time and effort by saving and reusing the query. You need to save the query before you return the data to Excel (while the Query Wizard - Finish dialog box is open).

Save a query

1. In the Query Wizard - Finish dialog box (shown in Figure 15.27), click the **Save Query** button.

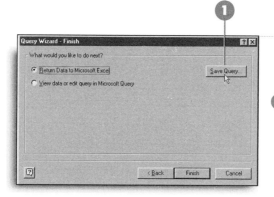

FIGURE 15.27

Saving a query you use again saves you a lot of time.

❶ Save query

2. Navigate to the folder in which you want to save the query definition.

3. Give the query a memorable name and click **Save**.

4. Click **Finish** in the Query Wizard and continue with your query operation.

Your saved query appears in the Choose Data Source dialog box on the **Queries** tab.

Reuse a saved query

1. Click a blank cell in the worksheet.

2. On the **Data** menu, point to **Get External Data**, and then click **Run Database Query**.

3. In the Run Query dialog box, navigate to the folder in which you saved the query definition.

4. Double-click the saved query name (the extension of a query is .dqy).

5. In the Returning External Data to Microsoft Excel dialog box, indicate to the Query Wizard where to put the queried data and then click **OK**.

The query runs, and current data is extracted from the data source.

Does saving a query fill up my hard drive?

When you save a query, you don't save a ton of data; you save only the query definition, a SQL statement that contains instructions for which data to extract when the query runs.

Summarizing Details with Consolidation or Subtotals

Understanding Consolidations and Subtotals

If you have a long list of data (like the expenses list in Figure 16.1), summarizing the data with subtotals makes it more meaningful. Three ways to summarize all the subcategories in a table at once are consolidation, subtotaling, and PivotTables.

Consolidation was Excel's early method of summarizing details with subtotals, and because Microsoft never throws away a functional feature, it's still available. Consolidation is quick and easy, but inflexible: The result is a list of subtotals with no underlying detail data available (like the finished consolidation shown in Figure 16.4). Occasionally, however, that's exactly what you need, and it does enable you to consolidate the details of up to 255 source ranges.

Subtotaling goes one step beyond consolidation. It creates subtotals for each subcategory in the table, but retains the detail items in the table and enables you to show or hide whichever subcategory details you want.

PivotTables are much more complex (and flexible and useful) than consolidation and subtotaling, so they're covered separately, in Chapter 17, "Summarizing Details with a PivotTable."

Make sure redundant entries are identical

The list has no misspelled Vendor or Category entries because I used AutoComplete and Pick From List to make those entries. Accuracy like this is important when you want to filter, sort, consolidate, or subtotal a table. (See Chapter 6, "Entering Data," to learn about AutoComplete and Pick From List.)

Consolidating a Table

The expenses list in Figure 16.1 is a long list of detailed expenses with repeated Vendor and Category entries.

I want to consolidate the details into a list of Vendor and Amount subtotals, with no detail data included.

Consolidate a list

1. Select a *destination area*, where the consolidated list will be pasted. (For this example, I paste the consolidated list next to my detailed list, with a blank column separating the two.)

   A destination area can be on the same worksheet or in a different worksheet or workbook.

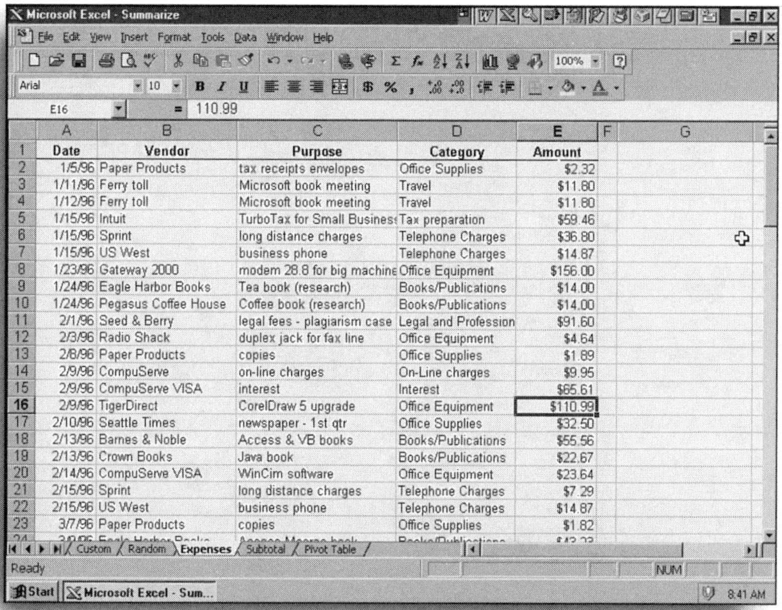

	A	B	C	D	E
1	Date	Vendor	Purpose	Category	Amount
2	1/5/96	Paper Products	tax receipts envelopes	Office Supplies	$2.32
3	1/11/96	Ferry toll	Microsoft book meeting	Travel	$11.80
4	1/12/96	Ferry toll	Microsoft book meeting	Travel	$11.80
5	1/15/96	Intuit	TurboTax for Small Busines	Tax preparation	$59.46
6	1/15/96	Sprint	long distance charges	Telephone Charges	$36.80
7	1/15/96	US West	business phone	Telephone Charges	$14.87
8	1/23/96	Gateway 2000	modem 28.8 for big machine	Office Equipment	$156.00
9	1/24/96	Eagle Harbor Books	Tea book (research)	Books/Publications	$14.00
10	1/24/96	Pegasus Coffee House	Coffee book (research)	Books/Publications	$14.00
11	2/1/96	Seed & Berry	legal fees - plagiarism case	Legal and Profession	$91.60
12	2/3/96	Radio Shack	duplex jack for fax line	Office Equipment	$4.64
13	2/8/96	Paper Products	copies	Office Supplies	$1.89
14	2/9/96	CompuServe	on-line charges	On-Line charges	$9.95
15	2/9/96	CompuServe VISA	interest	Interest	$65.61
16	2/9/96	TigerDirect	CorelDraw 5 upgrade	Office Equipment	$110.99
17	2/10/96	Seattle Times	newspaper - 1st qtr	Office Supplies	$32.50
18	2/13/96	Barnes & Noble	Access & VB books	Books/Publications	$55.56
19	2/13/96	Crown Books	Java book	Books/Publications	$22.67
20	2/14/96	CompuServe VISA	WinCim software	Office Equipment	$23.64
21	2/15/96	Sprint	long distance charges	Telephone Charges	$7.29
22	2/15/96	US West	business phone	Telephone Charges	$14.87
23	3/7/96	Paper Products	copies	Office Supplies	$1.82

FIGURE 16.1

A detailed expenses list doesn't tell you much until it's summarized.

2. At the top of the destination area, enter (or better yet, copy) the headings of the label and number columns that will be used in the consolidation. For this example, I've copied the headings from the Vendor and Amount columns, shown in Figure 16.2.
3. Select the destination area column labels, as shown in Figure 16.2.
4. On the **Data** menu, click **Consolidate**.

   The Consolidate dialog box appears, as shown in Figure 16.3.
5. Select a function in the **Function** drop-down list box (although **Sum** is most common, you can consolidate using any of several functions).
6. Click in the **Reference** box and enter the range(s) you want to consolidate. In this case, I drag to select the expenses list, making the Vendor column the left-most column in my source range. (I don't include the Date column, because Excel is looking for subcategory labels in the left column of the source range.)

How much of the data gets consolidated?

Consolidation includes only one column of labels, but can consolidate multiple columns of numbers.

Consolidation is easier with named ranges

To make source area selection easier, name the source ranges, and type the range names into the Consolidate dialog box. See Chapter 10, "Complex Calculations," to learn how to name ranges.

FIGURE 16.2

The destination area column labels tell Excel which columns to include in the consolidation. Copying them avoids misspellings.

1 Copied column labels, selected as destination area

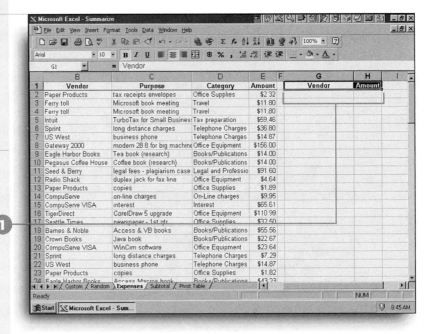

FIGURE 16.3

After the destination area is prepared, set up the Consolidate dialog box.

1 Areas in this list are consolidated

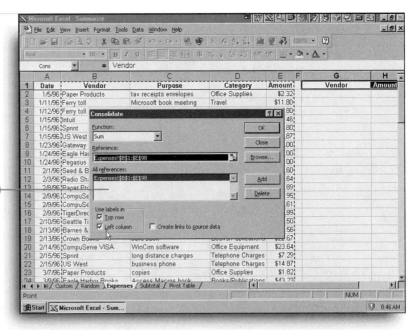

7. Click the **Add** button to add the reference to the list of source areas to consolidate.

If you are consolidating multiple ranges, add each new range to the source list by selecting it and then clicking **Add**. (See Table 16.1 for tips on selecting multiple ranges for consolidation.)

8. Click the **Top row** and **Left column** check boxes to enable Excel to look for labels in the source range(s).

9. When the Consolidate dialog box is set up, click **OK**.

The range is consolidated, as shown in Figure 16.4.

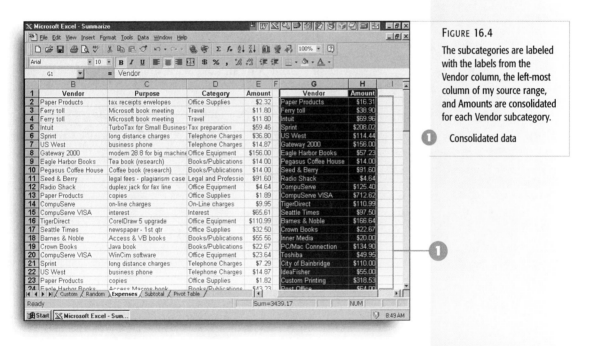

FIGURE 16.4
The subcategories are labeled with the labels from the Vendor column, the left-most column of my source range, and Amounts are consolidated for each Vendor subcategory.

❶ Consolidated data

SEE ALSO

➤ *To learn more about AutoComplete and Pick From List to ensure accurate data entry, see page 95.*

Updating a Consolidation

After you set up a consolidation, the settings are retained in the destination worksheet, and you can run the consolidation again to update it with changed source data.

Do I have to open the source to update?

When updating a consolidation, you do not need to open closed source workbooks.

Update a consolidation

1. Select the destination area column labels.

2. On the **Data** menu, click **Consolidate**.

3. Click **OK**.

The same consolidation is run again and the subtotals are updated.

Selecting Consolidation Source Areas

Consolidation has great flexibility when it comes to choosing the data you want to consolidate. *Source areas*, the details you want to consolidate, can be on any worksheet, in any open or closed workbook, and on multiple worksheets (called a *3-D source area*). The easiest way to select a source area is to drag the range in an open worksheet; but you can use closed sources, too, if you enter the workbook and worksheet names.

Table 16.1 lists more ways to enter source ranges for consolidation in the Consolidate dialog box.

TABLE 16.1   **Consolidation source area possibilities**

To Add This Range	Do This
To consolidate a range from another workbook	Click the **Browse** button, navigate to the workbook you want, and double-click the workbook name. The path to the workbook is entered, and you need to type a range name or a worksheet name and range reference. The worksheet name is separated from the range name with an exclamation mark, like this: *worksheet!range*.
To enter a range name from the active workbook	Type the range name.
To enter multiple ranges from different worksheets	Enter the first range and click **Add**. Then click a different worksheet, enter the range there, and click **Add**. Continue until all source ranges are listed in the **All references** box.

Subtotaling a Table

Subtotaling a table provides different results than a consolidation:

- A subtotaled worksheet retains detail data.
- Subtotals and outlining are added to the table so that you can show or hide the details with a click of a button.
- Subtotaling includes several levels of label columns as well as number columns.
- Data must be sorted before you subtotal it.

I'm subtotaling my expenses list and creating subtotals by both Category and Vendor within Category. I start by arranging my columns and sorting them so that the subtotal outline is well organized, and then I apply the subtotaling.

Apply automatic subtotaling

1. Arrange your table so that the columns are logically organized, and sort the columns in the order that you want to apply subtotals.

   In Figure 16.5, I've rearranged the columns and sorted them by Category and then by Vendor.

Hide columns you don't need

To remove the Date and Purpose columns from view without removing them from the table, you can hide them. Select the columns, right-click the selection, and click **Hide**.

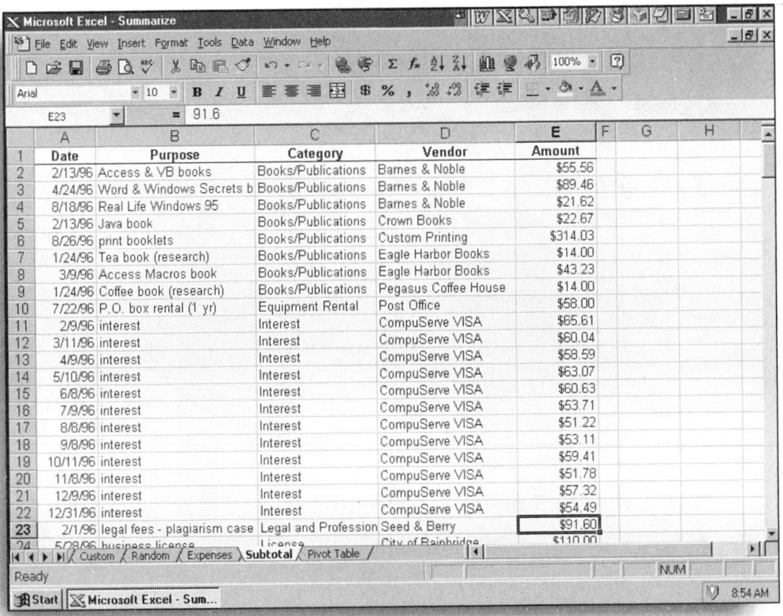

	A	B	C	D	E
1	Date	Purpose	Category	Vendor	Amount
2	2/13/96	Access & VB books	Books/Publications	Barnes & Noble	$55.56
3	4/24/96	Word & Windows Secrets b	Books/Publications	Barnes & Noble	$89.46
4	8/18/96	Real Life Windows 95	Books/Publications	Barnes & Noble	$21.62
5	2/13/96	Java book	Books/Publications	Crown Books	$22.67
6	8/26/96	print booklets	Books/Publications	Custom Printing	$314.03
7	1/24/96	Tea book (research)	Books/Publications	Eagle Harbor Books	$14.00
8	3/9/96	Access Macros book	Books/Publications	Eagle Harbor Books	$43.23
9	1/24/96	Coffee book (research)	Books/Publications	Pegasus Coffee House	$14.00
10	7/22/96	P.O. box rental (1 yr)	Equipment Rental	Post Office	$58.00
11	2/9/96	interest	Interest	CompuServe VISA	$65.61
12	3/11/96	interest	Interest	CompuServe VISA	$60.04
13	4/9/96	interest	Interest	CompuServe VISA	$58.59
14	5/10/96	interest	Interest	CompuServe VISA	$63.07
15	6/8/96	interest	Interest	CompuServe VISA	$60.63
16	7/9/96	interest	Interest	CompuServe VISA	$53.71
17	8/8/96	interest	Interest	CompuServe VISA	$51.22
18	9/8/96	interest	Interest	CompuServe VISA	$53.11
19	10/11/96	interest	Interest	CompuServe VISA	$59.41
20	11/8/96	interest	Interest	CompuServe VISA	$51.78
21	12/9/96	interest	Interest	CompuServe VISA	$57.32
22	12/31/96	interest	Interest	CompuServe VISA	$54.49
23	2/1/96	legal fees - plagiarism case	Legal and Profession	Seed & Berry	$91.60
24	5/28/96	business license	License	City of Bainbridge	$110.00

FIGURE 16.5
This table has been arranged and sorted to prepare it for subtotaling.

2. Click a cell in the table.

3. On the **Data** menu, click **Subtotals**.

   The Subtotal dialog box appears, as shown in Figure 16.6.

4. In the **At each change in** box, select the first category to which you want to add subtotals (the higher-level category—in this case, the Category field).

5. In the **Use function** box, select a function. (**Sum** is most common, but several functions are available.)

6. In the **Add subtotal to** list box, mark the check boxes for number fields you want subtotaled. Clear the check boxes for any fields you don't want calculated.

   Only fields that contain numerical values should be included, because only numerical values can be calculated.

   Use the scroll bar on the right side of the **Add subtotal to** list box to scroll through all the field check boxes.

FIGURE 16.6

The Subtotal dialog box is set up to apply the first of my two levels of subtotals.

7. Click **OK**.

   The first level of subtotals is applied to your table, as shown in Figure 16.7. If any of your subtotal labels are truncated, you can widen the column to display their full text.

   If you want to apply only a single level of subtotals, stop here; you're finished.

   For this example, I want to apply a second level of subtotals to the Vendor field.

8. On the **Data** menu, click **Subtotals**.

9. Select the second-level subtotal field (in this case, Vendor).

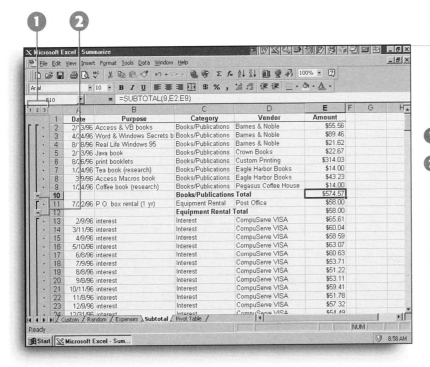

FIGURE 16.7

The Category field is subtotaled, and the worksheet is outlined so that you can show or hide details.

1 Outline levels

2 Hide buttons

10. Clear the **Replace current subtotals** check box (because I want to add a second level of subtotals, not replace the existing subtotals).

The Subtotal dialog box shown in Figure 16.8 is ready to apply the second level of subtotals.

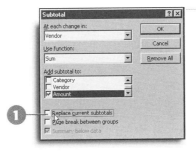

FIGURE 16.8

This Subtotal dialog box is ready to add a second level of subtotals. To replace the existing subtotals instead of adding more, mark the **Replace current subtotals** check box.

1 Clear to add more subtotals

11. Click **OK**.

The additional subtotals and outline level are added to the table, as shown in Figure 16.9.

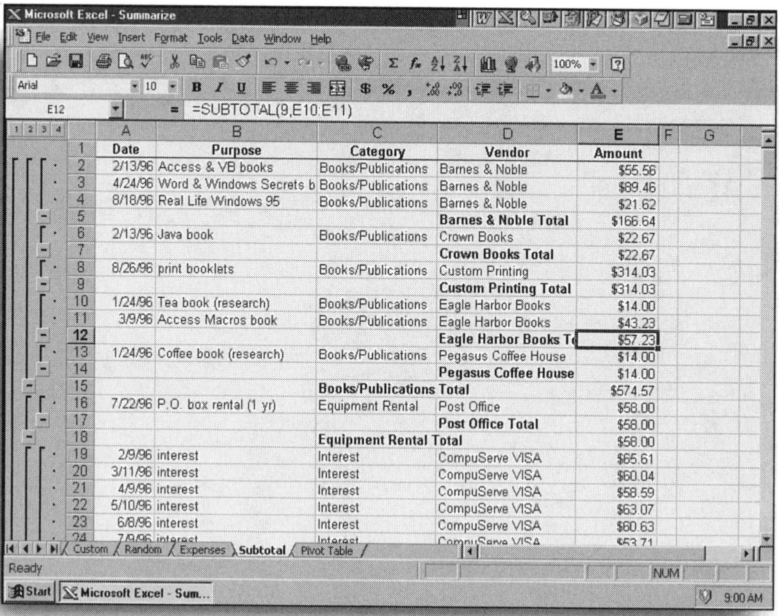

FIGURE 16.9

Now I have subtotals for each Category, and within each Category there are subtotals for each Vendor.

SEE ALSO

➤ *To learn more about sorting a list, see page 249.*

Hide Subtotal Levels

Now you learn the flexibility of subtotaling: You can hide and show the details. To hide an entire level of detail, click a Level button (shown in Figure 16.10). To hide a section of details, click a Hide button (with the minus symbol) next to the subtotal row for which you want to hide details.

In Figure 16.10, I've shown all the details by clicking Level 4 and then hidden the details for Eagle Harbor Books by clicking the Hide button next to row 12, the row with the Eagle Harbor Books subtotal.

Show Subtotal Levels

A subtotaled table is a most convenient presentation when all the details are hidden, and you can show the specific details in which you're interested.

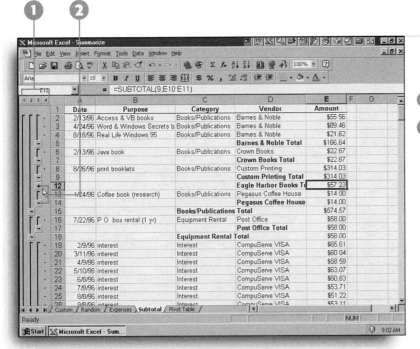

FIGURE 16.10
To show all the details, click
the Level 4 button.

1 Level buttons

2 Hide buttons

To show details in a hidden level, click the Show button (the
button with the plus symbol) next to the subtotal row for which
you want to show details—all the next-level details for that section are displayed on the worksheet. To show details for an
entire level, click a level button—all the detail items for the level
you clicked are displayed on the worksheet.

In Figure 16.11, I hid all details by clicking Level 2, so all the
Level 2 subtotals are displayed. Then I displayed subtotals with-
in the Office Supplies Total by clicking the Show button next to
row 79, which displayed the Level 3 subtotals for the Office
Supplies category. Next, I displayed the Level 4 details for the
Paper Products Total by clicking the Show button next to row 71.

If you find that more details are shown than you want, first collapse the outline sections backward by clicking Level 4, Level 3,
and then Level 2. Next, show the Level 2 subtotals you want (in
this example, Office Supplies), and then show the Level 3 details
you want (in this example, Paper Products).

FIGURE 16.11

To hide all but the Grand Total, click the Level 1 button.

1 Show buttons

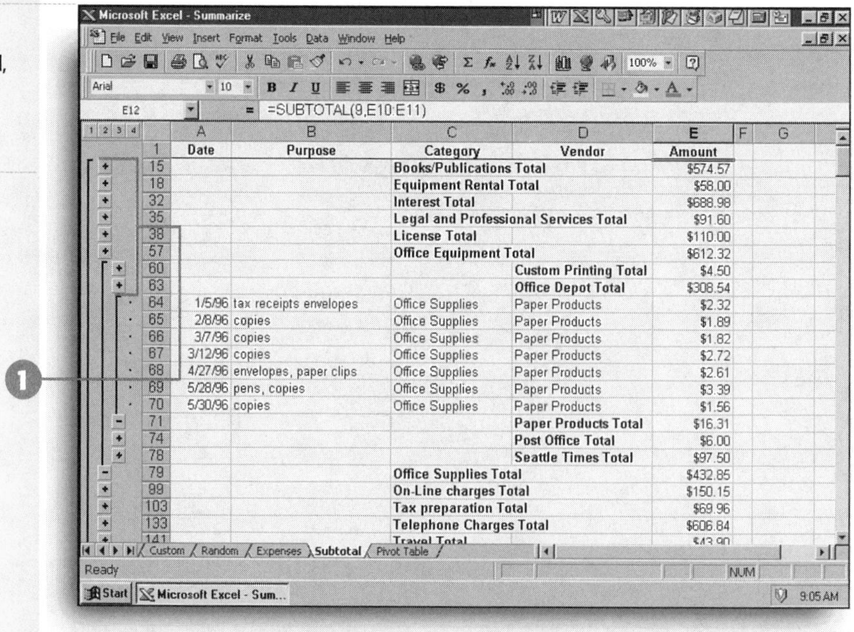

Remove Subtotaling

Return a table to details without subtotals

1. Click a cell in the table.

2. On the **Data** menu, click **Subtotals**.

3. Click **Remove All**.

Outlining a Table Manually

To add the capability of showing and hiding rows in a table without adding subtotals to the table, you can outline the table manually. An outlined table has Show buttons and Hide buttons, just like a subtotaled table, but you determine which items are hidden or shown as groups.

You might want to use manual outlining if

- You've already added subtotals to a table by writing your own formulas, rather than using the Subtotals command.

- You want to group data into categories so that you can show and hide category details, without adding subtotals to the categories.

- You want to outline only part of a table without outlining the entire table.

Outline a table manually

1. Select adjacent rows that you want to combine into a single show-or-hide group, as shown in Figure 16.12.

If you have totals in your table, don't include them in the group or they'll be hidden when you hide the group.

2. On the **Data** menu, point to **Group and Outline**, and click **Group**.

Outlining is applied to the selected group of rows, and a Hide button appears at the left side of the group (just like in a Subtotaled table), as shown in Figure 16.13. To hide the group, click the Hide button. To show the group, click the Show button.

> **You can outline columns, too**
>
> You can apply outlining to columns, also, and then show or hide groups of columns. To outline columns, follow the same procedures as for outlining rows, but select groups of adjacent columns instead of groups of rows.

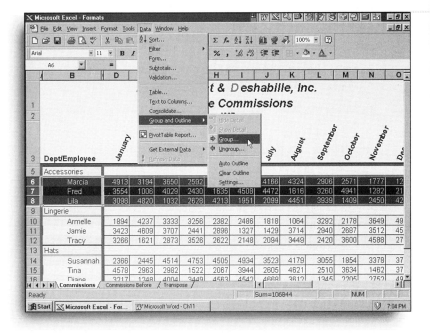

FIGURE 16.12
Select individual groups of detail rows or columns, and group them for hiding.

FIGURE 16.13

Outlining allows a reader to hide or show specific details in the table, and it makes a very large table easier to study.

1 Click to show details

2 Click to hide details

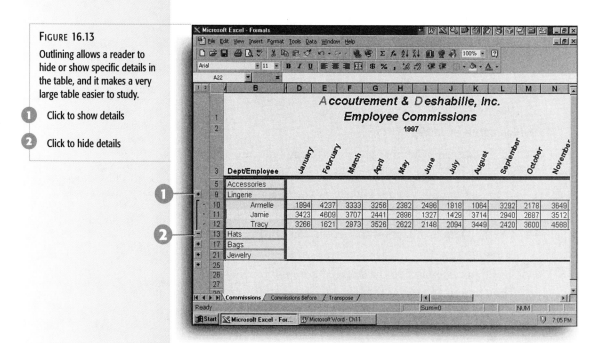

3. Repeat steps 1 and 2 for each set of adjacent rows you want to combine into a single show-or-hide group.

Remove manual outlining

1. Show the detail rows for the groups in which you want to remove outlining.

2. Select the rows that you want to remove from the outline.

You can remove a few rows from a larger outline group by selecting just those rows. You cannot, however, select nonadjacent rows; you can only remove outlining from one set of adjacent rows at a time.

3. On the **Data** menu, point to **Group and Outline** and click **Ungroup**.

Outlining is removed from the rows you selected.

To remove all outline groups in the table, click in the table, then open the **Data** menu, point to **Group and Outline**, and click **Clear Outline**.

Summarizing Details with a PivotTable

Working with PivotTables and understanding the terminology

Creating a PivotTable with the PivotTable Wizard

Using the PivotTable toolbar

Changing the arrangement of a PivotTable

Changing calculations in a PivotTable

Displaying the underlying details and formatting PivotTables

Use PivotTables for charts

PivotTables are a great data source for charts because when the PivotTable is changed, the chart changes automatically to display whatever is in the PivotTable.

Working with PivotTables

PivotTables are a very interactive and flexible presentation of data. You can change which data is presented and how it's laid out and summarized, even in the middle of an electronic presentation to a room full of people.

When you use a PivotTable to summarize data, you can

- Summarize data from several sources: Excel lists, external databases, multiple worksheets, or other PivotTables
- Pivot the table to change its orientation
- Group items in a field (for example, group dates into months or quarters)
- Change the calculation function for a field
- Show the details underlying a single summarized item
- Format the PivotTable for a professional and reader-friendly presentation

PivotTable Terms

PivotTables use some terms that you can look up here if you get lost later in the chapter. Figure 17.1 and Table 17.1 show and define important PivotTable terms.

FIGURE 17.1
Terms associated with PivotTables.

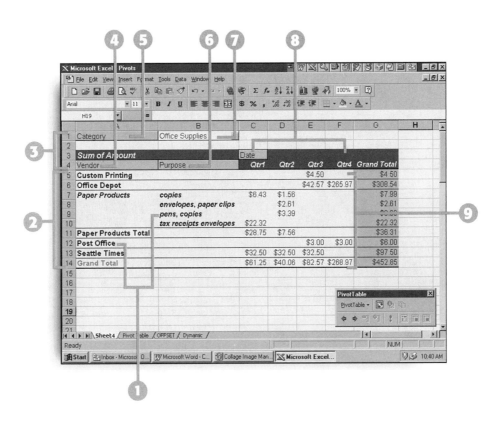

①	Item	⑥	Inner field
②	Row field	⑦	Page field item
③	Field labels	⑧	Column fields
④	Outer field	⑨	Data area
⑤	Page field		

TABLE 17.1   PivotTable terms

Term	Definition
Page field	A field that displays one item at a time. (In Figure 17.1, Category is a Page field.)
Page field item	The item displayed by the Page field. (In Figure 17.1, Office Supplies is the Page field item that's displayed.)
Row field	A field with data displayed in rows. (In Figure 17.1, Vendor and Purpose are Row fields.)
Column field	A field with data displayed in columns. (In Figure 17.1, Date is the only Column field.)
Item	A specific row or column heading. (In Figure 17.1, Custom Printing and Qtr2 are both items.)
Data area	The part of the PivotTable where data and calculations are displayed.
Field label	A label that identifies a row or column field—also called *Field heading* and *Field button*.
Outer field	When more than one field is displayed in the Row or Column area, the outermost field is the Outer field. Each Outer field encompasses one or more Inner field items.
Inner field	When more than one field is displayed in the Row or Column area, the innermost field is the Inner field. Each Inner field item is grouped within an Outer field item.
Refresh data	Updates the PivotTable with changed source data.

Creating a PivotTable

PivotTables are a bit more complex to create than subtotals or consolidations, but the PivotTable Wizard guides you through the process of creation. The wizard also guides you through editing a PivotTable if you need to change the data source (for example, if new records or fields are added to a source worksheet table). Editing a table to change the source range(s) is not the same as updating a PivotTable with current data; that's a procedure called *refreshing*, and it doesn't require the assistance of the wizard.

Using the PivotTable Wizard

You can only create a PivotTable by using the PivotTable Wizard.

If you have more than one PivotTable in a workbook, and all are based on the same source data, it's much more efficient to create the first PivotTable from the source data and create the rest of the PivotTables from the first PivotTable. This saves system resources, but more importantly it saves you time. When you refresh data in any one of the related PivotTables, all the related PivotTables are refreshed at the same time. The alternative, creating each PivotTable directly from the source data, requires that you refresh each PivotTable separately.

To create a PivotTable from another PivotTable, you click the **Another PivotTable** option in Step 1 of the PivotTable Wizard.

Create a PivotTable from a worksheet table

1. Click the worksheet source table from which you want to create a PivotTable.

   If you want to use an external data source (not a worksheet table), or create a PivotTable from another PivotTable, click anywhere in any worksheet.

2. On the **Data** menu, click **PivotTable Report**.

   The PivotTable Wizard starts (shown in Figure 17.2).

3. In Step 1 of the wizard, click an option for the type of source data (in this case, a **Microsoft Excel list or database**).

4. Click **Next**.

   The Step 2 dialog box appears, and the worksheet table you clicked is defined as the source range. (The worksheet range is outlined with a moving border, as shown in Figure 17.3.)

5. If the range is correct, click **Next**.

   If you want to use a named range instead of a range reference, type the name in the **Range** box and click **Next**.

   The wizard Step 3 appears (shown in Figure 17.4).

FIGURE 17.2

In the PivotTable Wizard Step 1, click the type of source data you're using.

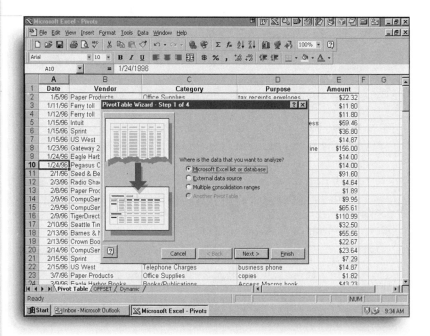

FIGURE 17.3

The range in the Range box is outlined with a moving border on the worksheet.

❶ Moving border

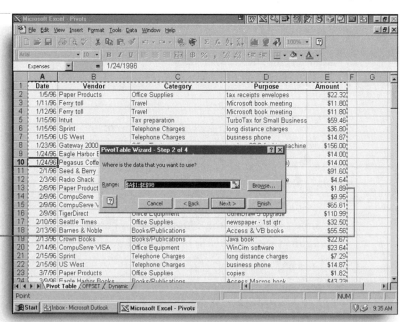

6. Drag the Field labels onto the PivotTable area diagram to lay out the structure of the PivotTable.

In this example, I'm creating a PivotTable that shows expenses by Category and Date and summarizes the Amount values with the SUM function. In Figure 17.4, Category is being dropped in the Column area, so each Category will appear in a column. Date was dropped in the Row area, so each date will have its own row. Finally, the Amount field was dropped in the Data area, to be calculated with the SUM function.

What if I want an average instead of a sum?

To change the summary function at this step, double-click the Field label in the **DATA** area (in this case, the **Sum of Amount** label). In the PivotTable Field dialog box that appears, click a different function, click **OK**, and continue building the PivotTable with the wizard.

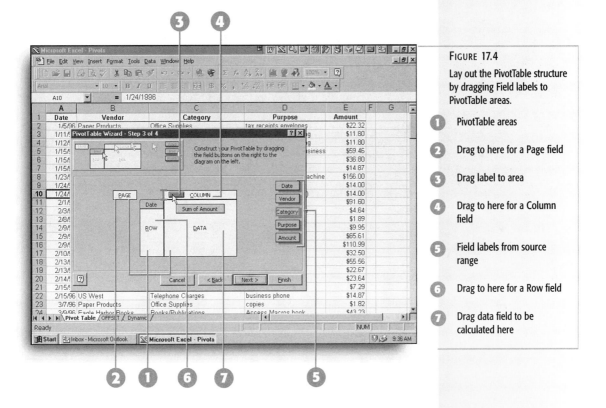

FIGURE 17.4

Lay out the PivotTable structure by dragging Field labels to PivotTable areas.

① PivotTable areas

② Drag to here for a Page field

③ Drag label to area

④ Drag to here for a Column field

⑤ Field labels from source range

⑥ Drag to here for a Row field

⑦ Drag data field to be calculated here

7. Click **Next**.

The wizard Step 4 appears (shown in Figure 17.5).

FIGURE 17.5
In Step 4 of the wizard, you can create a new worksheet to hold the PivotTable or place the PivotTable anywhere on an existing worksheet.

8. In Step 4 of the PivotTable Wizard, decide where you want the PivotTable placed and click **Finish**.

If you want to place the PivotTable on an existing worksheet rather than a new worksheet, click the **Existing worksheet** option. Next, on the worksheet, click the cell where you want to paste the upper-left corner of the PivotTable.

Your PivotTable is created. (The resulting PivotTable in this example is shown in Figure 17.6.)

FIGURE 17.6

This PivotTable was placed on a new worksheet.

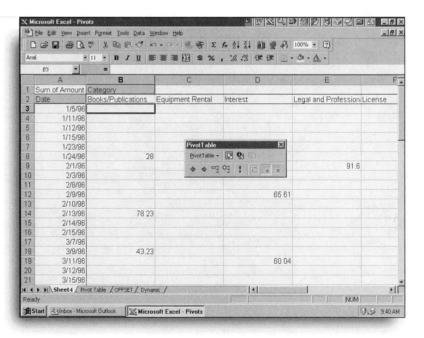

My initial PivotTable is messy and difficult to read because the data is too detailed. I make it more useful by grouping the dates into quarters and transposing the layout so that dates are across the top and categories are listed on the left.

Changing the Data Source Range

If more rows or columns of data are added to a source range, you need to change the source range for the PivotTable to include the new data. You can add the new data two ways: the straightforward way that uses the PivotTable Wizard, or the fast-and-clever way, by using a named formula to define the source range.

Changing the Source Range with the Wizard

The PivotTable Wizard is a reliable, straightforward method of updating a changed PivotTable source range.

Update a changed source range with the PivotTable Wizard

1. Click a cell in the PivotTable.

2. On the PivotTable toolbar, click the PivotTable Wizard button 🔲. (Alternatively, on the **Data** menu, click **PivotTable Report**.)

   Step 3 of the PivotTable Wizard appears, but you need to back up to Step 2 to change the source range.

3. Click the **Back** button.

4. In the wizard Step 2, drag a new source range or type new references in the **Range** box.

5. If you don't want to make any other changes using the PivotTable Wizard, click **Finish**.

   The PivotTable is updated to use the new source range.

Creating a Source Range that Changes Automatically

This method will amaze your friends and colleagues (at least, those who are not Excel experts themselves). It's a little harder to decipher at first, and if it leaves you really confused, don't bother with it. If, however, it works for you, you can create a PivotTable that updates its worksheet source ranges automatically when you refresh the PivotTable.

I closed my PivotTable toolbar

To display the PivotTable toolbar, right-click any toolbar and click **PivotTable**.

Is this only for PivotTables?

Defining a dynamic source range with the OFFSET function works well for charts and for Print Areas, too.

This method uses a named formula to define a *dynamic* worksheet source range, a range that automatically changes its defined size to include all adjacent rows and columns. The formula uses the OFFSET function, which defines a worksheet range by where it begins, how many rows it has, and how many columns it has. It uses the COUNTA function to indicate to the OFFSET function how many rows and columns to include.

A simple OFFSET formula looks like the one I've laid out in Figure 17.7.

FIGURE 17.7

A simple OFFSET formula defines this worksheet range. To select the range, open the **Edit** menu, select **Go To,** type the name of the formula in the **Reference** box, and click **OK**.

1. Anchor cell

2. Range starts this many rows away from anchor

3. Range starts this many columns away from anchor

4. Range is this many rows tall

5. Range is this many columns wide

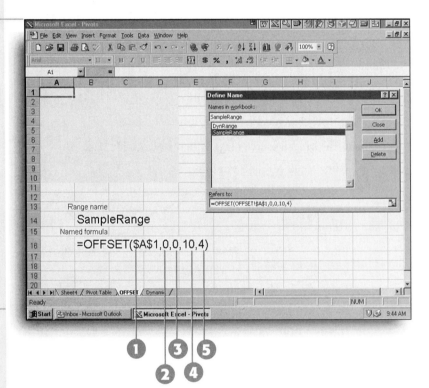

If your dynamic range has too many rows...

For a dynamic range to work correctly, make sure that you have no entries in column A or row 1 other than those in the table because the dynamic range counts all the entries in the entire column and row.

In Figure 17.7, I created a named formula, SampleRange, that defines the range I've colored in. If I filled the range with numbers, the formula =SUM(SampleRange) would sum all the numbers in the range. This named formula is a simple example of the OFFSET function. The range it defines is not *dynamic*; it's always the same size and location, just like a named range.

To make the range *dynamic*, I change the fourth and fifth arguments in the formula so that instead of the range being 10 rows tall and 4 columns wide, the range will be as many rows tall as there are entries in column A and as many columns wide as there are entries in row 1. (Figure 17.8 shows the dynamic range formula, named DynRange.)

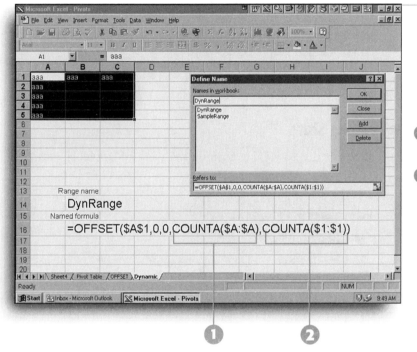

FIGURE 17.8

A dynamic range always has as many rows as there are entries in column A and as many columns as there are entries in row 1. To do this, the formula nests a couple of COUNTA functions in the OFFSET function.

1 Height argument counts entries in column A

2 Width argument counts entries in row 1

Create a dynamic range with a named formula

1. On the worksheet where you want to create the named dynamic-range formula, open the **Insert** menu, point to **Name**, and click **Define**.

2. In the Define Name dialog box (shown in Figure 17.8), type a name for your dynamic-range formula under **Names in workbook**.

3. Type the OFFSET/COUNTA formula in the **Refers to** box.

4. Click **OK**.

Easier formula construction

When I write a long, complex formula like this, I find it easier to write it in a cell without an = because I can easily see and edit the entire formula and then copy the formula and paste it into the Define Name dialog box.

Where's my named formula?

The formula name won't appear in either the Name box list or in the Go To dialog box; however, both recognize the name, so if you type it in either the Name box or the Go To dialog box, the dynamic range is selected.

5. To test your dynamic-range formula, click the **Name** box (left of the Formula bar), type the formula name, and press Enter. If the formula is written correctly, the dynamic range is selected. (Be sure there are entries in column A and row 1 for the formula to count.)

To use your dynamic range in a PivotTable, type the range name in the **R**ange box in Step 2 of the PivotTable Wizard. When you click the Refresh Data button (see the following section), a dynamic-range PivotTable is updated with both changed data and newly added rows and columns.

SEE ALSO

➤ *To learn more about naming cells and ranges, see page 182.*

Refreshing Data

Save time refreshing multiple PivotTables

If you create a PivotTable from another PivotTable, the two PivotTables are related to each other. When you refresh data in a PivotTable that's related to other PivotTables, all the related PivotTables are refreshed at the same time. (The alternative, if PivotTables are unrelated, is to refresh each PivotTable separately.)

Refresh is the PivotTable term for updating a PivotTable with current data. When you refresh data, the PivotTable Wizard goes to the PivotTable's source range and looks for changed data.

Refresh data in a PivotTable

1. Click a cell in the PivotTable.

2. Click the Refresh Data button on the PivotTable toolbar [⬍].

That's it. The PivotTable Wizard checks the source range(s) for changed data and updates your PivotTable.

The PivotTable Toolbar

Figure 17.9 shows the PivotTable toolbar, which appears whenever you display a PivotTable. Table 17.2 explains what the toolbar buttons do.

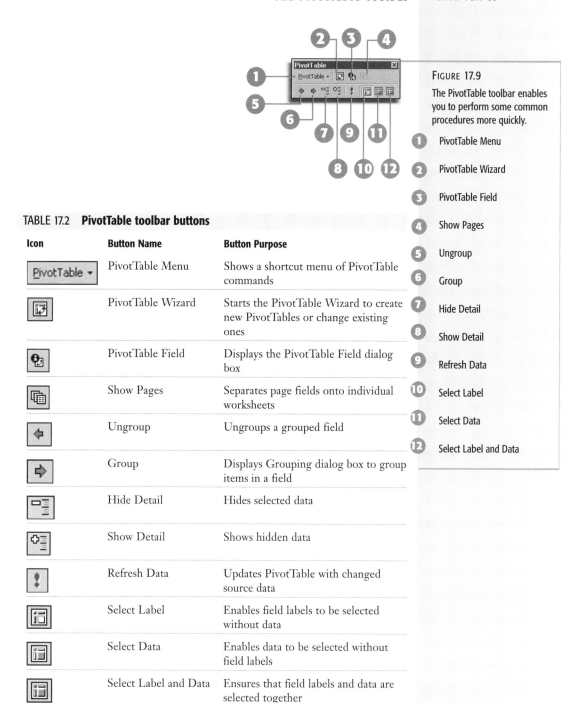

FIGURE 17.9

The PivotTable toolbar enables you to perform some common procedures more quickly.

1. PivotTable Menu
2. PivotTable Wizard
3. PivotTable Field
4. Show Pages
5. Ungroup
6. Group
7. Hide Detail
8. Show Detail
9. Refresh Data
10. Select Label
11. Select Data
12. Select Label and Data

TABLE 17.2   **PivotTable toolbar buttons**

Icon	Button Name	Button Purpose
PivotTable ▾	PivotTable Menu	Shows a shortcut menu of PivotTable commands
	PivotTable Wizard	Starts the PivotTable Wizard to create new PivotTables or change existing ones
	PivotTable Field	Displays the PivotTable Field dialog box
	Show Pages	Separates page fields onto individual worksheets
	Ungroup	Ungroups a grouped field
	Group	Displays Grouping dialog box to group items in a field
	Hide Detail	Hides selected data
	Show Detail	Shows hidden data
	Refresh Data	Updates PivotTable with changed source data
	Select Label	Enables field labels to be selected without data
	Select Data	Enables data to be selected without field labels
	Select Label and Data	Ensures that field labels and data are selected together

If you click the toolbar's Close button to close the PivotTable, you can display it again by right-clicking any toolbar and clicking **PivotTable** on the shortcut menu.

Changing PivotTable Arrangement

The PivotTable I created in Figure 17.6 is messy, hard to read, and far too detailed. The following list is some of the changes I make to it:

- Group the dates into quarters
- Pivot the table to put categories on the left (in Row fields) and dates across the top (in Column fields)
- Add the Vendor field
- Create a Page field for Category items
- Create separate pages for each Category item

Grouping Items in a Field

The dates in the PivotTable in Figure 17.6 are too detailed. I don't want to see each individual transaction, but I do want to see summaries of what expenses were in each quarter.

Group items in a field

1. Click the field that you want to group (in this example, any cell in the Date field).
2. On the PivotTable toolbar, click the Group button ⬜.

   The Grouping dialog box appears (shown in Figure 17.10).
3. Click to select the group you want and click to deselect any groups you don't want.
4. Click **OK**.

   Figure 17.11 shows the result of my grouping by quarter.

Pivoting the Table

Pivoting a PivotTable layout is similar to transposing a worksheet table, but easier and with more options. I want to pivot the PivotTable in Figure 17.11 so that Category items are listed down the side and Date fields are across the top.

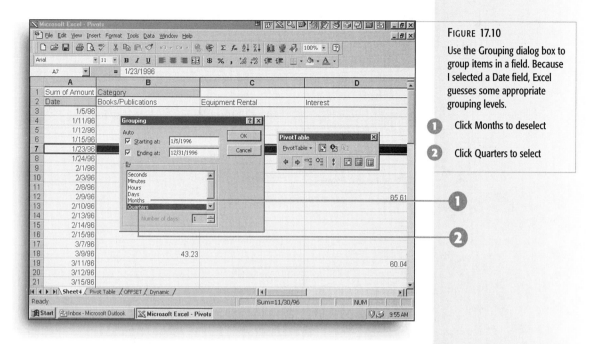

FIGURE 17.10

Use the Grouping dialog box to group items in a field. Because I selected a Date field, Excel guesses some appropriate grouping levels.

① Click Months to deselect

② Click Quarters to select

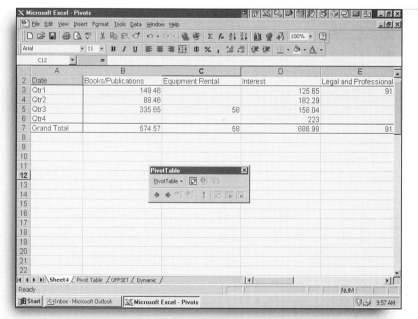

FIGURE 17.11

The PivotTable data is much more meaningful now that I've grouped it into quarterly expenses.

To pivot a PivotTable layout, you drag a Field label to a different location in the PivotTable. When you drag Field labels, the mouse pointer becomes various symbols, depending on where the dragged label is located in the PivotTable. Table 17.3 shows the different mouse pointer symbols you see when you drag Field labels around the PivotTable.

TABLE 17.3   Symbols you see when you drag field labels

Mouse Pointer Symbol	Meaning
	Dropped label becomes a Column field
	Dropped label becomes a Row field
	Dropped label becomes a Page field
	Dropped label is removed from PivotTable

Change a Row field to a Column field (in this case, move Date to the top of the PivotTable)

1. Drag the Date label to the Column field area of the PivotTable.

2. When the mouse pointer changes to a Column field symbol, drop the label.

Change a Column field to a Row field (in this case, move Category to the side of the PivotTable)

1. Drag the Category label to the Row field area of the PivotTable.

2. When the mouse pointer changes to a Row field symbol, drop the label.

I pivoted the PivotTable in Figure 17.11 and got the results shown in Figure 17.16.

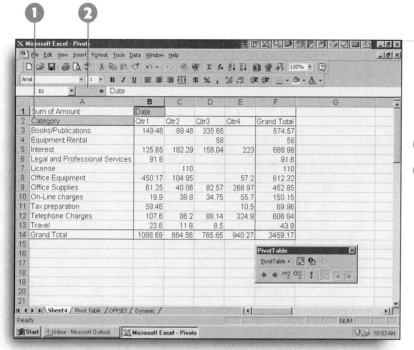

Adding Fields

I want to add the Vendor field to my PivotTable so that I can show more of the details in my expenses list.

Add a field to a PivotTable

1. Click the PivotTable.

2. On the PivotTable toolbar, click the PivotTable Wizard button 📊.

Step 3 of the PivotTable Wizard appears.

3. Drag the field you want to add to a PivotTable area.

In Figure 17.17, I dragged the Vendor field to the **ROW** area.

4. Click **Finish**.

FIGURE 17.17

Dropping the Vendor field below the Category field makes the Vendor field an inner field in the PivotTable. (You see what that means in Figure 17.18.)

① Vendor field dropped here

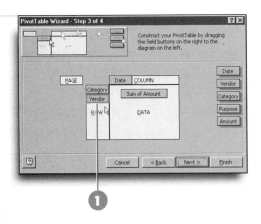

Figure 17.18 shows my PivotTable after I added the Vendor field.

FIGURE 17.18

The Vendor field I added is an inner row field that I can hide or show.

① Vendor field

	A	B	C	D	E	F	G
1	Sum of Amount		Date				
2	Category	Vendor	Qtr1	Qtr2	Qtr3	Qtr4	Grand Total
3	Books/Publications	Barnes & Noble	55.58	89.46	21.62		166.64
4		Crown Books	22.67				22.67
5		Custom Printing			314.03		314.03
6		Eagle Harbor Books	57.23				57.23
7		Pegasus Coffee House	14				14
8	Books/Publications Total		149.46	89.46	335.65		574.57
9	Equipment Rental	Post Office			58		58
10	Equipment Rental Total				58		58
11	Interest	CompuServe VISA	125.65	182.29	158.04	223	688.98
12	Interest Total		125.65	182.29	158.04	223	688.98
13	Legal and Professional Services	Seed & Berry	91.6				91.6
14	Legal and Professional Services Total		91.6				91.6
15	License	City of Bainbridge					110
16	License Total						110
17	Office Equipment	CompuServe VISA	23.64				23.64
18		Gateway 2000	156				156
19		IdeaFisher		55			55
20		Inner Media	20				20
21		PC/Mac Connection	134.9				134.9

Showing and Hiding Inner Field Details

The Vendor field I added to the Row field area in Figure 17.18
is an *inner* row field, which means the Vendor items are subordinate to the Category items. I can show or hide the Vendor field
items for each Category item. To show or hide inner field items,
double-click the outer field where you want to show or hide
inner field items. (In Figure 17.19, I hid the inner field items for
all Category items, and then I showed the inner field items for
the Books/Publications Category.)

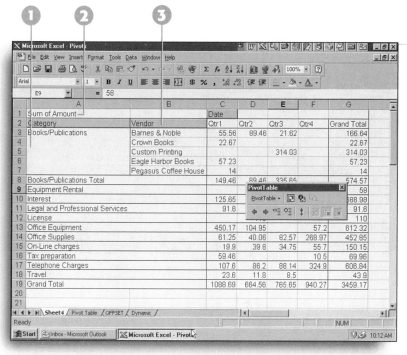

FIGURE 17.19

The Books/Publications
Vendors are shown; all other
Vendors are hidden.

① Double-click to show or hide
Vendors in this Category

② Outer field

③ Inner field

Creating Page Fields

Another way I can make this PivotTable more useful is to make
the Category field into a Page field. Then I can show only the
Vendors in a specific Category.

Create Page fields any time

To create Page fields when you
initially create the PivotTable,
drag a Field label to the **PAGE**
field area in Step 3 of the
PivotTable Wizard.

Change a Row or Column field to a Page field

1. Drag the Field label to the upper-left corner of the PivotTable.

2. When the mouse pointer changes to a Page field symbol, drop the label.

A Page field is created for the field you dragged. To show data for a specific Page field item, click the down arrow in the Page field item box, and select the item (as shown in Figure 17.20).

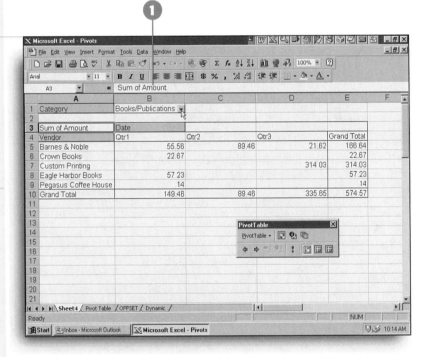

FIGURE 17.20

I made my expenses Category field into a Page field and then selected the Books/Publications Category. The data for the Vendors in my Books/Publications Category is displayed.

① Page field item box

Creating Separate Pages

I want to create separate tables for each of my expense Category items so that I can print them all at once.

Create separate Page field tables

1. Click the PivotTable.

2. On the PivotTable toolbar, click the Show Pages button. 🔲 The Show Pages dialog box appears (shown in Figure 17.21).

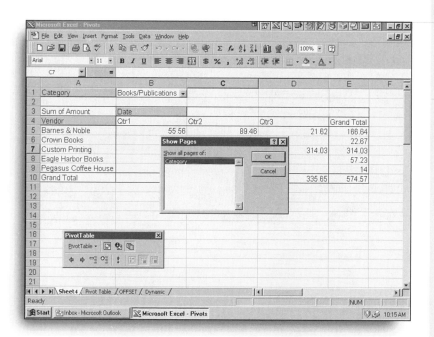

FIGURE 17.21

If I had more than one Page field, they'd all be listed in the Show Pages dialog box.

3. Double-click the field name for which you want to create pages (in this case, **Category**).

A new worksheet is created for each item in the field (as shown in Figure 17.22), and each worksheet has an identical Pivot-Table with the item's data displayed. The new worksheets are named with the names of the Page field items, so you can navigate easily.

SEE ALSO

➤ *To learn more about printing worksheets, see page 421.*

Print all the new worksheets

To print all the new worksheets with a single command, open the **File** menu, select **Print**, click the **Entire workbook** option, and click **OK**.

FIGURE 17.22

When you use Show Pages, you create a new worksheet and PivotTable for each item in the original Page field.

① Worksheets are named for their displayed Page fields

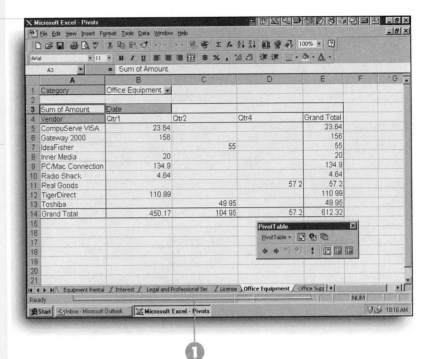

Removing Fields

I want to remove the Vendor and Date field from the PivotTable so that only the total expenses in each Category are displayed.

Remove fields from a PivotTable

1. Drag the Field label away from the PivotTable until it becomes a remove field symbol (shown in Figure 17.23).

2. Drop the Field label.

   The field is removed from the PivotTable.

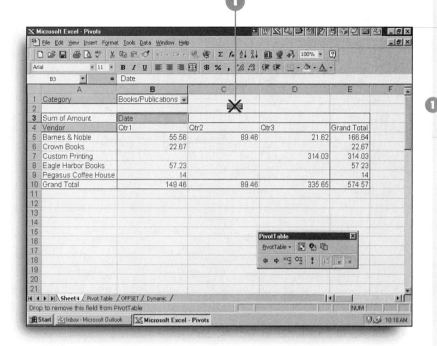

FIGURE 17.23

The big X is your clue that you lose the field from the PivotTable if you drop it.

① Remove field mouse pointer symbol

Changing PivotTable Calculation

Although SUM is the most common calculation used in data summaries, you can change the calculation in a PivotTable field to any of several functions, including AVERAGE, MIN, MAX, COUNT, and others.

Change the calculation function for a field

1. Click a field or data cell for the field in which you want to change the function.

2. On the PivotTable toolbar, click the PivotTable Field button ⊞.

   The PivotTable Field dialog box appears (shown in Figure 17.24).

FIGURE 17.24

Change a field's calculation function in the PivotTable Field dialog box.

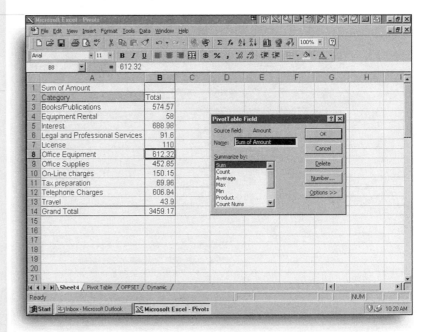

3. In the **Summarize by** list, click the function you want.

4. Click **OK**.

In Figure 17.25, I've changed the Amount calculation to AVERAGE.

Showing Underlying Details

I want to know what individual expenses make up the Books/Publications average shown in Figure 17.25.

To display the source data underlying a data cell in the PivotTable, double-click the data cell for which you want to see source data.

To show underlying data for the Books/Publications average in Figure 17.25, double-click its data cell in the Total column. This is called drilling down for the source data. A new worksheet is created (shown in Figure 17.26) with a table that shows all the source table entries that were calculated to produce the Books/Publications average.

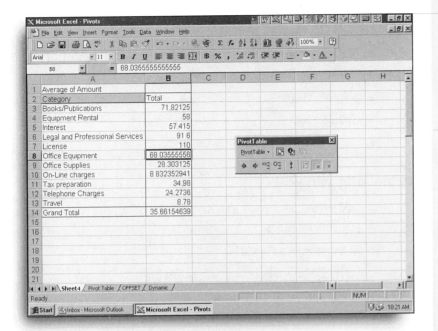

FIGURE 17.25

This PivotTable shows my average expense in each expense Category. The numbers still need to be formatted, however, to be displayed as dollar amounts.

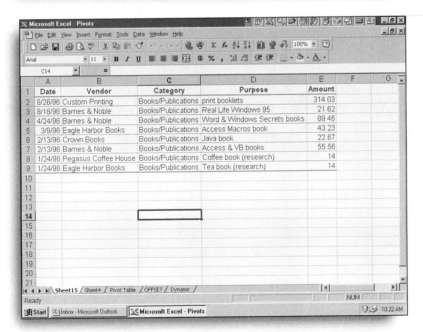

FIGURE 17.26

The new worksheet table displays source data for the PivotTable cell I drilled down.

Formatting a PivotTable

PivotTables are candidates for formatting just like other worksheet tables. You can format the following:

- Number display
- Cell and font color
- Field labels to display different text

Formatting Numbers

Wasn't formatting previously more work?

In earlier versions of Excel, Number formatting was a longer procedure, but now it's as easy as formatting worksheet tables. If you find that formatting disappears when you refresh a PivotTable, you need to activate the Preserve Formatting option: right-click the PivotTable, select **Options**, click the **Preserve formatting** check box, and then click **OK**.

The easiest way to format numbers in a PivotTable is the same way you format them in a worksheet table.

Format numbers in a PivotTable

1. Select the number cells you want to format.

2. On the **Format** menu, select **Cells**.

3. In the Format Cells dialog box, click the **Number** tab.

4. Set the Number formatting you want, and click **OK**.

   The PivotTable in Figure 17.27 looks a lot better now that it's formatted in a Currency number format.

FIGURE 17.27

The Currency format shown in the Format Cells dialog box is appropriate for my Amount field.

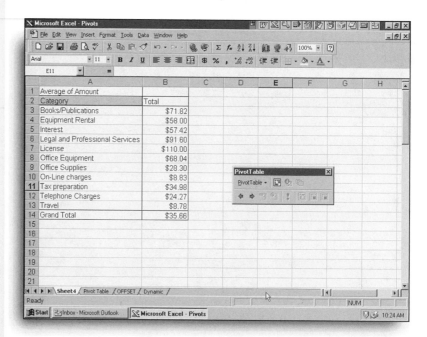

SEE ALSO

➤ *To learn more about formatting numbers, see page 223.*

Formatting Tables

You can format PivotTables using the same techniques as for worksheet tables, but AutoFormat works especially well for PivotTables.

AutoFormat a PivotTable

1. Click any cell in the PivotTable.

2. On the **Format** menu, select **AutoFormat**.

3. Click a format in the **Table format** list.

4. Click **OK**.

   The PivotTable in Figure 17.28 is formatted with the Colorful 2 format. The AutoFormat remains when you change, pivot, or refresh the PivotTable.

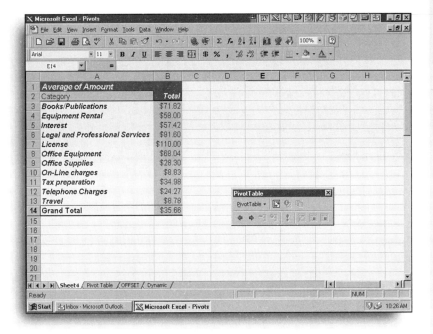

FIGURE 17.28

AutoFormat is a quick, easy way to apply a complete format to a PivotTable.

Changing Label Text

Sometimes a data source has field names that are abbreviated, obscure, or unintelligible to anyone who didn't create the table. Those field names become the Field labels in your PivotTable, but you can change the Field labels in the PivotTable to display any text you want.

Change Field label text

1. Click the Field label you want to change.

   If the label isn't selected the first time you click it, click it a second time (not a double-click).

2. Type the label text you want and press Enter.

The label text changes to your entry.

The button isn't really a button

The Field label looks like a button, but it's really just a cell.

Finding Answers and Making Decisions

Using Goal Seek to find answers to simple questions

Using Goal Seek to solve more complex problems

Using Scenario Manager to create alternative scenarios

Editing a scenario

Summarizing multiple scenarios

Goal Seeking for Answers

One of a computer's most important functions is to help us make better decisions. The capability to calculate and summarize large quantities of data is a good beginning; but there are two more areas where Excel can help you make better decisions. If you have several possible situations, or scenarios, it's wise to compare the results of different courses of action before moving ahead with one of them; Excel's Scenario Manager can help you compare different scenarios. If you're working on a problem and you know what result, or solution, you want to arrive at, Excel can help you figure out what you need to do to get there; the Goal Seeking tool will work problems "backward" to figure out what input values will give you a specific answer.

Excel was designed to perform calculations, and if you know what input values a function or formula requires, Excel gives you an answer. But what if you know what answer you want but don't know what input values will give you that specific answer?

This chapter covers how to use Goal Seek to do "backward" math: You know the answer you want, so you have Excel figure out what the input values should be to arrive at that answer.

For example, you can use the PMT function to figure out what a loan payment will be when you know the interest rate, number of payments, and loan amount; but suppose you want to know how large a loan amount you can get for a specific payment size? This question works the formula in reverse: You know what the answer should be (the payment), and you want to know how to get that answer (the loan amount).

Goal Seeking an Answer to a Simple Question

To demonstrate using Goal Seek to find a solution to the problem posed previously, I'm going to determine how big a loan I can get if I can afford a payment of $750 per month, with an interest rate of 7.5 percent and monthly payments for three years (36 payments).

Use Goal Seek to determine a loan amount

1. Enter the formula and its input values (*arguments*) in a worksheet, as shown in Figure 18.1.

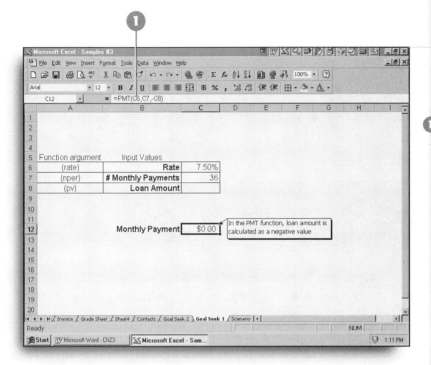

FIGURE 18.1

First, set up the equation; then, run Goal Seek to find new answers.

1 PMT formula

2. Fill in the input values that won't change (in this case, the interest rate and number of payments).

3. On the **Tools** menu, click **Goal Seek**.

The Goal Seek dialog box is displayed, as shown in Figure 18.2. The currently active cell is displayed in the **Set cell** box; if you click the cell you want in the **Set cell** box before you start Goal Seek, steps 4 and 5 will already be done.

A PMT function idiosyncrasy

In the **PMT** formula, the loan amount argument is entered as a negative number so that your payments appear as positive values. You can enter either a negative value or the minus sign in the function argument, as I've done here; or you can enter the loan amount as a positive value and your payments will show up as negative values.

FIGURE 18.2

Work a problem "backward" in the Goal Seek dialog box.

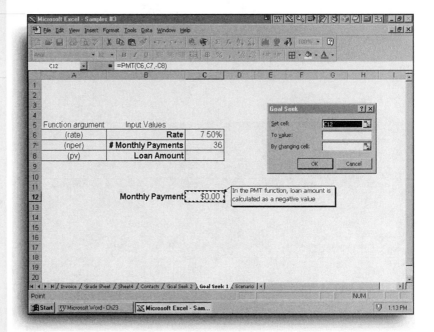

4. Be sure the value in the **Set cell** box is highlighted; if it's not, select it or delete it, because you're going to replace it in the next step.

5. On the worksheet, click the cell you want to set a value in (in this case, cell C12, the PMT formula cell, because I want to calculate a specific payment value).

6. Click in the **To value** box, and type the value you want to arrive at (in this case, the payment I can afford, $750).

7. Click in the **By changing cell** box.

8. On the worksheet, click the cell that contains the input value that you want Excel to figure out (in this case, cell C8, the loan amount cell).

   In this example, the worksheet and Goal Seek dialog box resemble Figure 18.3.

9. Click **OK**.

   Excel finds an answer and changes the data on the worksheet, as shown in Figure 18.4.

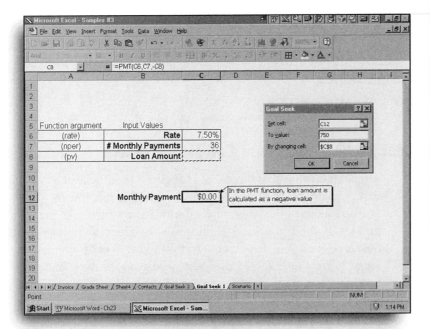

FIGURE 18.3

This Goal Seek dialog box is ready to calculate the loan that a specific payment will cover.

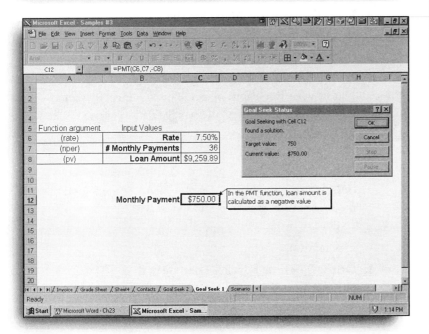

FIGURE 18.4

Goal Seek found the solution—a loan amount of $9,259.89, as shown in cell C8.

To keep the new worksheet data, click **OK**; to return the worksheet to its previous values (if you want to run Goal Seek again with different numbers), click **Cancel**.

SEE ALSO

➤ *To learn more about writing formulas, see page 143.*

➤ *To learn more about using functions, see page 154.*

Goal Seeking in a More Complex Problem

Although Goal Seek is limited to changing one variable at a time, you can use it to find answers to problems that involve many more cells. In this example, I'm working a right-triangle problem; I know how long the long side (side b) is, and I know how long I want the hypotenuse (side c) to be. What I want to know is, How long should the short side (side a) of the triangle be to give me the hypotenuse I need? Refer to the illustration in Figure 18.5 for a visual approach to the problem.

Use Goal Seek to solve a complex problem

1. Enter the input values and formula in your worksheet.

The cells in the Length Squared column are named Asq (for A squared), Bsq, and Csq. The cells in the length column are named a_, b_, and c_.

I know what the length of side b is, so I enter that length; then I enter formulas in all the cells that calculate (as shown in Figure 18.5).

Formulas are entered in Asq and Bsq to calculate the squares (a_*a_ and b_*b_); the right-triangle formula is entered in cell Csq; and the formula for the length of the hypotenuse, the square root of Csq, is entered in cell c_.

2. Click cell c_ (the cell with the formula for the length of the hypotenuse).

3. On the **Tools** menu, click **Goal Seek**.

The Goal Seek dialog box is displayed, with the selected cell in the **Set cell** box.

The right triangle equation

The mathematical formula for a right triangle, which this problem is based on, is

$$a^2+b^2=c^2$$

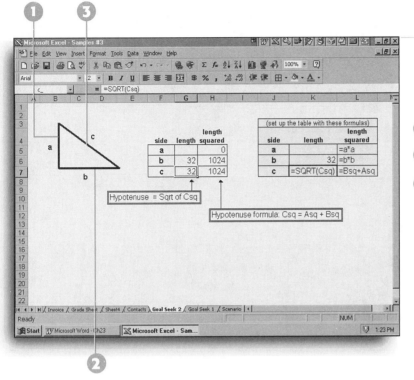

FIGURE 18.5

I want to know what value I need for side a to get a value of 35 for the hypotenuse, side c.

1 Short side

2 Long side

3 Hypotenuse

4. In the **To value** box, type 35 (the length I want for the hypotenuse).

5. Click in the **By changing cell** box; then click cell a (the side I want to know the length of).

The dialog box should look similar to the one shown in Figure 18.6.

6. Click **OK**.

If you watch closely, you'll see the numbers on your worksheet change rapidly as Excel tries different values and recalculates the formulas with each try. Your results should be similar to Figure 18.7.

7. To keep the new values, click **OK**.

If you don't have this decimal display

I formatted these cells to display numbers with no decimal places. (See Chapter 12, "Formatting Numbers," to learn how.)

FIGURE 18.6

One click and I'll have my answer.

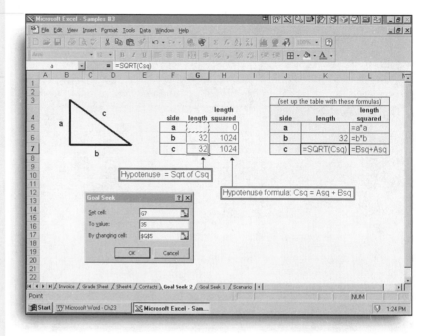

FIGURE 18.7

Goal Seek found the short-side length that gives me the hypotenuse length I want.

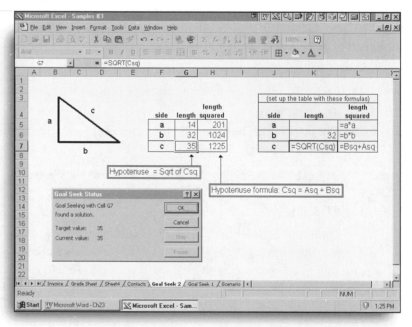

SEE ALSO

➤ *To learn more about naming cells, see page 182.*

➤ *To learn more about formatting cells, see page 195.*

Creating and Comparing Scenarios

Scenarios are alternative solutions to a business question; by comparing different scenarios, you can make well-informed decisions.

Scenario Manager is a tool for comparing alternative solutions to a question. You can set up a worksheet with formulas and values and then change and save different sets of values so that you can compare them at your leisure. As a simple example, you can set up alternative loan scenarios, edit them if you need to, and then summarize them for easier comparison.

Create alternative scenarios

1. Lay out your worksheet with formulas and input values, as shown in Figure 18.8.

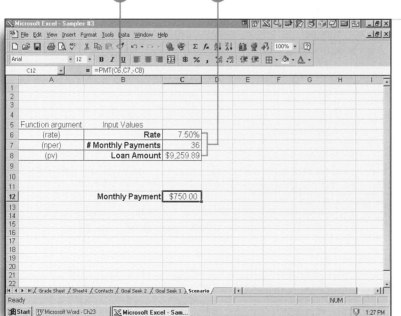

What's the easiest way to name these cells?

To name the cells used in these scenarios, I used the Create Names dialog box. Select the cells and their labels; then open the **Insert** menu, point to **Name**, and then click **Create**.

FIGURE 18.8

Start by setting up a worksheet with the first of the scenarios to be compared.

❶ PMT formula

❷ Input values for formula

2. On the **Tools** menu, click **Scenarios**.

The Scenario Manager dialog box is displayed, as shown in Figure 18.9.

FIGURE 18.9

Use Scenario Manager to save, edit, and summarize scenarios.

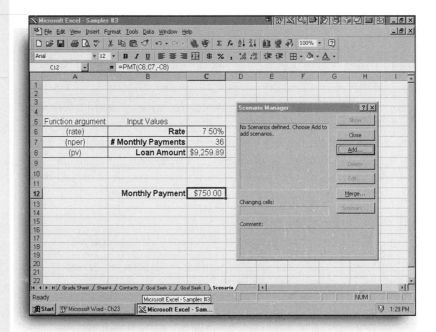

3. Click **Add**.

The Add Scenario dialog box is displayed (shown in Figure 18.10).

4. In the **Scenario name** text box, type a name to identify the first scenario.

5. Click in the **Changing cells** box; then on the worksheet, click the cells where you want to change values to create different scenarios.

In this example, I clicked cells C6 and C7, the Rate and # Monthly Payments values. Your dialog box should look similar to Figure 18.11.

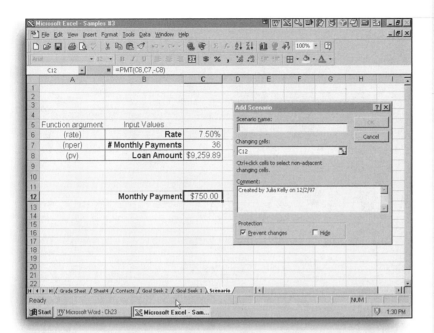

FIGURE 18.10

To add a scenario, name it and identify the cells that change in the different scenarios.

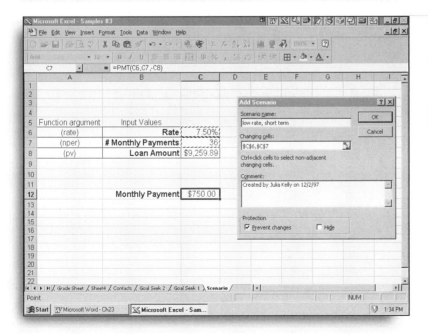

FIGURE 18.11

In this example, I'm going to create scenarios with interest rates and numbers of payments.

Use cell names for easy reading

To have the cell names display in your scenarios instead of references, name the changing cells first.

FIGURE 18.12

To save the first scenario, leave the values that are displayed; then click **Add**.

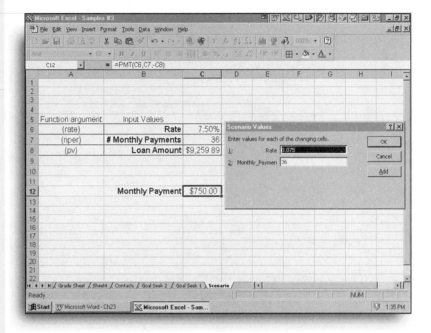

6. Click **OK**.

The Scenario Values dialog box is displayed, as shown in Figure 18.12.

To save your initial set of values, leave the values that are displayed.

7. Click **Add** to add a second scenario.

8. In the Add Scenario dialog box, type a name for the next scenario; then click **OK**.

9. In the Scenario Values dialog box, type new scenario values that you want to compare to other scenarios; then click **Add**.

Repeat steps 8 and 9 to add more scenarios. When you've added all the scenarios you want, finish step 9 by clicking **OK** instead of **Add**.

All your named scenarios are displayed in a list in the Scenario Manager dialog box, as shown in Figure 18.13.

To show values for a specific scenario in the worksheet, click the scenario name; then click **Show**.

To close the Scenario Manager, click **Close**.

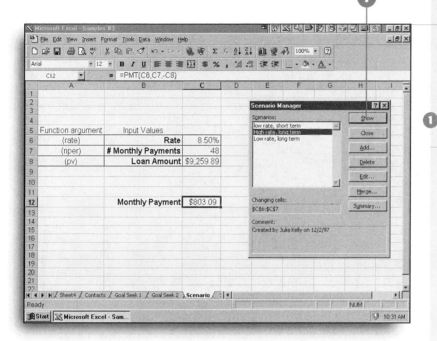

FIGURE 18.13

Click the scenario name you want to see; then click **Show** to see the scenario on the worksheet.

❶   Show selected scenario on worksheet

To change values in a specific scenario (or a misspelled scenario name), you can edit that scenario.

Edit a scenario

1. On the **Tools** menu, click **Scenarios**. In the Scenario Manager dialog box, click the name of the scenario you want to edit.

2. Click **Edit**.

3. In the Edit Scenario dialog box, change the scenario name and/or select new changing cells.

4. Click **OK**.

5. In the Scenario Values dialog box, set the values you want to use in the changing cells.

6. Click **OK**; then click **Close** to close the Scenario Manager.

You can summarize the results of all scenarios in one place, which allows you to compare them more easily.

To delete a scenario

To delete a scenario, select the scenario name in the Scenario Manager dialog box and click **Delete**.

Summarize multiple scenarios

1. On the **Tools** menu, click **Scenarios**. In the Scenario Manager dialog box, click **Summary**.

The Scenario Summary dialog box is displayed, as shown in Figure 18.14.

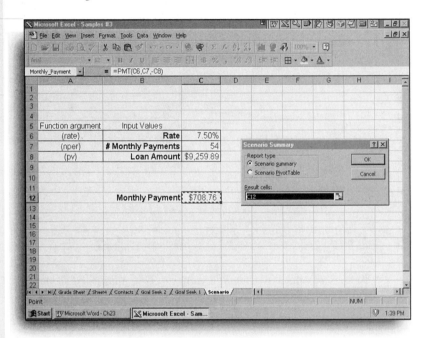

2. Be sure the **Result cells** box shows the cell that contains your formula.

3. Click **OK**.

A new worksheet is added to your workbook (shown in Figure 18.15), and a table is created that shows the values and results for all your scenarios.

The summary table is outlined so you can show and hide details:

- To hide details in a section, click the small minus (–) button in the left or top margin.

- To show details in a section, click the small plus (+) button in the left or top margin.

Did you use named cells?

If you used named cells in your scenarios, the Summary makes much more sense.

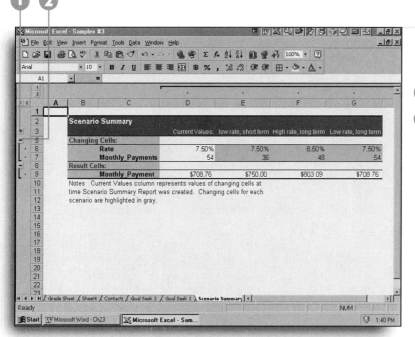

FIGURE 18.15
A summary makes scenarios much more useful.

❶ Click to expand section

❷ Click to collapse section

SEE ALSO

➤ *To learn more about worksheet outlines, see page 287.*

Charts

Creating a Chart

Creating a Chart with the Chart Wizard

A lot of folks are visually oriented and grasp data and comparisons much more easily when it's presented graphically rather than as a bunch of numbers.

Excel's Chart Wizard guides you through the process of creating charts; and if you change your mind about the chart after you finish it, you can change and reformat any part of it.

Creating a chart in Excel is a quick procedure: You select the data you want to chart and then let the Chart Wizard help you build the chart. You have a multitude of choices available in the Chart Wizard, but any choice you make is easy to change after the chart is finished.

Chart your data

1. Select the data you want to include in your chart.

Do the following when selecting data to chart:

- Drag to select a rectangular range of data, including any row and column labels that you want to appear in the chart.

- Press the Ctrl key to select nonadjacent rows or columns.

- Don't include grand totals in your data selection; they make the chart hard to read.

2. On the Standard toolbar, click **Chart Wizard**. 📊

The Chart Wizard starts (shown in Figure 19.1).

3. Click **Next**.

Step 2 of the Chart Wizard appears (shown in Figure 19.2).

4. Click the data orientation you want—**Rows** or **Columns**—and click **Next**.

Step 3 of the Chart Wizard appears (shown in Figure 19.3).

Is a chart the same thing as a graph?

Yes, it's the same thing. The term *graph* is commonly used for graphically displayed data, but in Excel you only see the term *chart*.

Too many steps in the wizard?

Want to create a chart really fast? Select your data, click the Chart Wizard button on the toolbar, and click **Finish** in Step 1 of the Chart Wizard.

What are Custom chart types?

Excel's Custom chart types consist mostly of interesting formatting (except for user-defined, where you save your own custom chart formats). Play with the custom formats, and see whether they display your data in a way that makes sense.

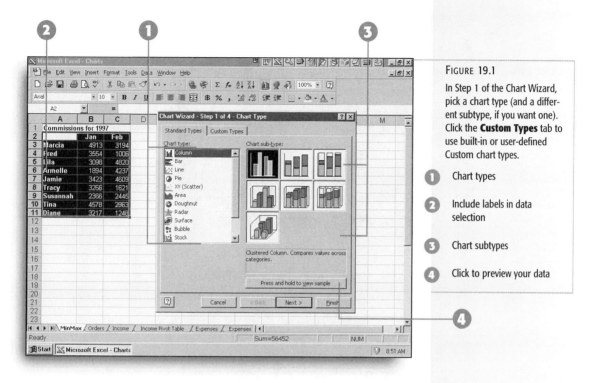

FIGURE 19.1

In Step 1 of the Chart Wizard, pick a chart type (and a different subtype, if you want one). Click the **Custom Types** tab to use built-in or user-defined Custom chart types.

1 Chart types

2 Include labels in data selection

3 Chart subtypes

4 Click to preview your data

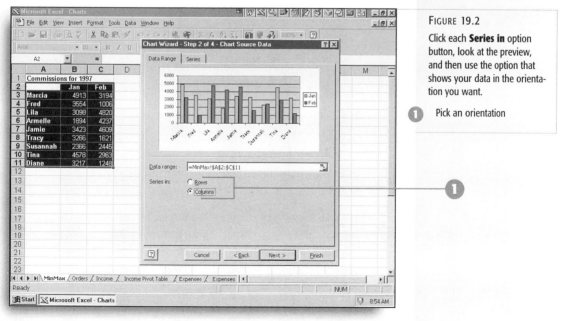

FIGURE 19.2

Click each **Series in** option button, look at the preview, and then use the option that shows your data in the orientation you want.

1 Pick an orientation

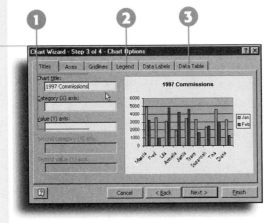

FIGURE 19.3

A lot of chart options are available in Step 3 of the Chart Wizard. Whatever you don't set here, you can easily change after the chart is finished.

① Type titles

② Remove or reposition legend on this tab

③ Show an attached data table on this tab

5. Set the chart options you want (such as chart titles, gridlines, and a legend) and click **Next**.

Step 4 of the Chart Wizard appears (shown in Figure 19.4).

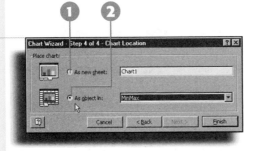

FIGURE 19.4

A chart sheet is a separate sheet in the workbook, like a worksheet but containing only a full-size chart.

① Create chart sheet

② Create chart object on worksheet

6. Click an option to create the chart as an object in the worksheet (as shown in Figure 19.5) or on a separate chart sheet, and click **Finish**.

If you change the data in the worksheet, the chart updates automatically to reflect the changed data.

That's all there is to creating a chart. The real fun and magic happen when you format the chart, which is covered in Chapter 20, "Formatting a Chart." Some of the formatting changes I would make in the chart in Figure 19.5 are: change the number format on the Y-axis to Currency, change the X-axis to show every category label, make the chart object larger, and change the colors in the chart.

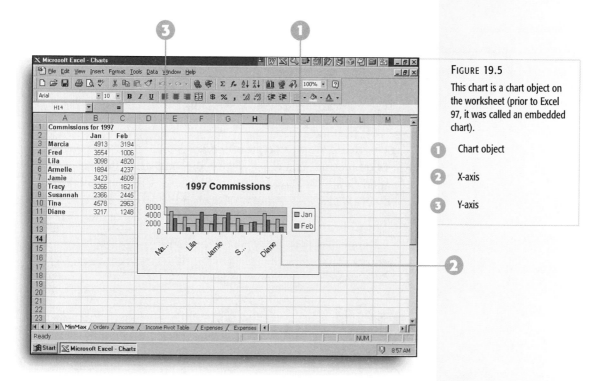

FIGURE 19.5

This chart is a chart object on the worksheet (prior to Excel 97, it was called an embedded chart).

❶ Chart object

❷ X-axis

❸ Y-axis

SEE ALSO

➤ *To learn more about formatting charts, see page 365.*

Types of Charts

When you create a chart, the first step is to choose a chart type. Many different types of charts are available, and some may seem very unusual because you're not accustomed to seeing them or interpreting the data they present. The key ideas to keep in mind when you choose a chart type are as follows:

- What kind of data are you charting? Are you showing discrete comparisons between categories of data? Changes over time? Percentages of a whole? Correlations between two numeric values? Three sets of values, which are most easily displayed in a three-dimensional format?

Using different series markers in one chart

To change the chart type of a single series (as I did in the Cylinder-Cone-Pyramid chart in Figure 19.6), right-click the series, click **Chart Type**, click the type you want for the series, and click **OK**.

- What kinds of charts is your audience accustomed to seeing and interpreting? If you choose a chart type your audience isn't familiar with, they're less likely to understand the data you're presenting.

The following figures show and explain different kinds of charts you can create in Excel.

The charts shown in Figure 19.6 are familiar to most audiences. The Line and Area charts display the same data. They are a good choice for showing changes in values over time because their lines suggest continuity between the data points.

The Column, Bar, and Cylinder-Cone-Pyramid charts all display the same data and are all good for comparing discrete categories of data at a specific point in time (such as total sales in each department for the month of January).

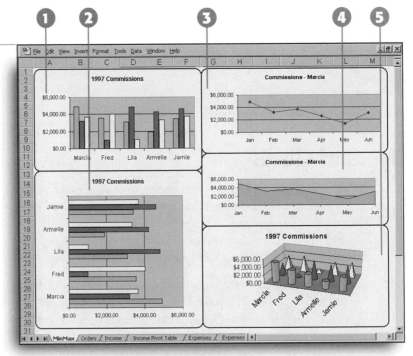

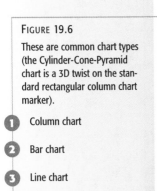

FIGURE 19.6

These are common chart types (the Cylinder-Cone-Pyramid chart is a 3D twist on the standard rectangular column chart marker).

1. Column chart

2. Bar chart

3. Line chart

4. Area chart

5. Cylinder-Cone-Pyramid series

When you want to show how data breaks down into percentages of a total amount (for example, how your expense budget was spent), the chart types shown in Figure 19.7 work best. The Pie chart is very effective, but can only display a single series of data. The Doughnut chart is less familiar to most audiences. It does the same job as the Pie chart, but for two or three series. If you want to compare percentages of a whole for more than two or three series, your best bet is the 100% Stacked Column chart. In any of these charts, however, your chart has more impact if you limit each series to a half-dozen data points.

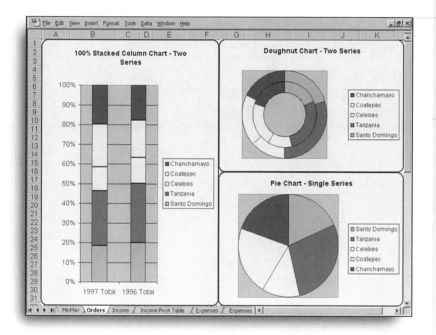

For keeping track of investment performance, Excel has several versions of the Stock chart that you see in financial reports. (Two of them are shown in Figure 19.8.) The important thing to remember about creating a Stock chart is that the data source you want to chart must be laid out in the same order as the name of the chart. For example, the data for the Volume-Open-High-Low-Close chart is organized in the source table in this order: Date, Volume, Open, High, Low, Close.

FIGURE 19.8

Stock charts are ideal for tracking the performance of stocks and futures prices.

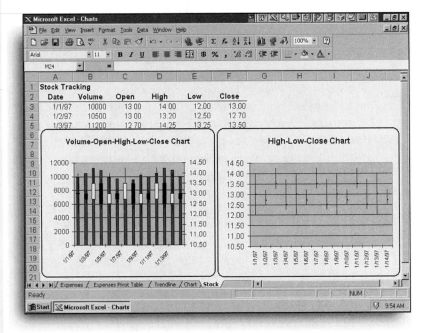

Which chart element is which?

If you hold your mouse pointer over any chart element, a ChartTip appears with the name of the element and other information, depending on what's selected in the chart.

The charts shown in Figure 19.9 have fairly specific applications and are all best used when your audience is familiar with the chart type. For example, Radar charts are not seen much in North America, and those audiences are usually baffled by the presentation.

XY (scatter) charts are common in scientific applications where two values are correlated, such as comparing the height and weight of individuals in a test population. Bubble and surface charts both give three-dimensional representations of three sets of data: The Surface chart shows an X-axis, a Y-axis, and a Z-axis and can give an audience a feel for the data after they become familiar with the Surface chart type. In the Bubble chart, the size of each bubble point represents the Z-axis value for the point.

SEE ALSO

➤ *To learn more about formatting chart lines, colors, and fonts, see page 366.*

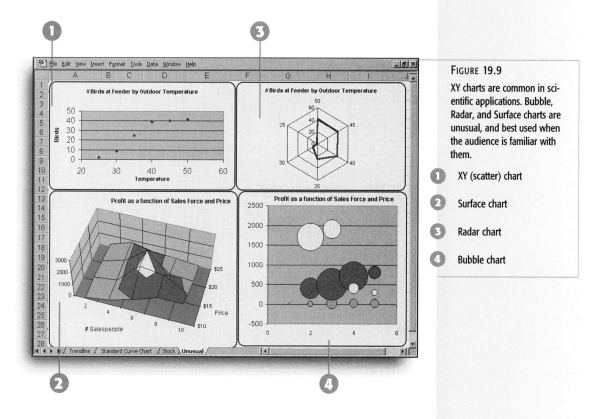

FIGURE **19.9**

XY charts are common in scientific applications. Bubble, Radar, and Surface charts are unusual, and best used when the audience is familiar with them.

1 XY (scatter) chart

2 Surface chart

3 Radar chart

4 Bubble chart

The Chart Toolbar

The Chart toolbar appears automatically whenever a chart object is active (that is, when you click a chart object), *unless* you close the toolbar to get it out of your way. After you've closed the Chart toolbar, you need to open it again to return its automatic behavior. (The Chart toolbar is shown in Figure 19.10, and Table 19.1 explains each button on the toolbar.)

My Chart toolbar isn't automatic

To open the Chart toolbar and return it to automatic behavior, click a chart object (to activate it), right-click any toolbar, and click **Chart**. Now the Chart toolbar appears when you click a chart object and disappears when you click the worksheet.

FIGURE 19.10

The buttons on the Chart tool-bar help you make some com-mon changes to your chart quickly.

1 Chart Type

2 Chart Objects

3 Format

4 Legend

5 Data Table

6 By Row

7 By Column

8 Angle Text Downward

9 Angle Text Upward

TABLE 19.1 **Buttons on the Chart toolbar**

Icon	Name	Purpose
Chart Area	Chart Objects	A list of all chart elements. To select a specific element, drop the list and click the element name.
	Format Selected Object	Opens a Formatting dialog box for the selected chart element.
	Chart Type	Opens a palette of chart types. To float the palette, drag its title bar away from the toolbar.
	Legend	Click to remove or replace the chart legend. When you remove the legend, the plot area resizes to fill the chart.
	Data Table	Click to add or remove a data table at the bottom of the chart.
	By Row	Changes orientation to put rows along the X-axis.
	By Column	Changes orientation to put columns along the X-axis.

Icon	Name	Purpose
✂	Angle Text Downward	Angles labels along selected axis to read from the upper left to the lower right.
✂	Angle Text Upward	Angles labels along selected axis to read from the lower left to the upper right.

Changing the Chart Type

After you've created a chart, you may decide that a different chart type would display your data better.

Change the chart type

1. Click the chart to select it.

2. On the <u>**Chart**</u> menu, click **Chart <u>Type</u>**.

The Chart Type dialog box appears. (It's identical to the Step 1 dialog box shown in Figure 19.1.)

3. Select a chart type (and a different subtype, if you want one).

4. Click **OK**.

The chart type changes.

Changing Chart Data

Charts update automatically when the values in source ranges change, but if you add or insert rows and columns of data in a source range, charts don't automatically include the new rows and columns.

You have two easy ways to change the source range, depending on what kind of change you want to make:

- To add more rows or columns to the existing source range, drag the data border.

- To switch to a different source range, use the Chart Wizard.

Both techniques are shown in the following sections.

Change chart type quickly

For a quick but limited selection of chart types, click the down arrow on the Chart Type button on the Chart toolbar and then click a chart type button. To switch between chart types rapidly, you can drag the Chart Type palette away from the toolbar and use it as a floating palette.

How can I change just one series?

To change the chart type of a single series (for example, to create a line series in a Column chart), click a marker in the series that you want to change and select a chart type for the series.

Adding More Data to a Source Range

In Figure 19.11, I've got a chart for three months of data. I added another month of data to the source range and need to add the new data to the chart.

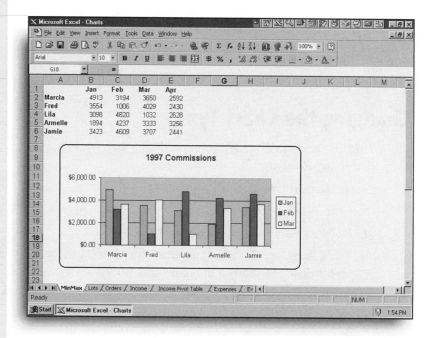

SEE ALSO:

➤ *To learn about using the OFFSET and COUNTA functions, see page 310.*

Add more data to an existing source range

1. Click near the chart perimeter to select the Chart Area.

   When the Chart Area is selected, the Name box reads Chart Area and handles appear around the chart border.

   When you select the Chart Area, colored borders appear around the source data range (shown in Figure 19.12).

2. Drag the Fill handles on the colored source range borders to increase or decrease the source data range.

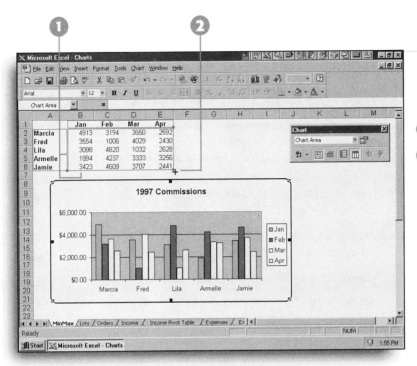

FIGURE 19.12

The source data in the chart is surrounded by colored borders.

① Source data range borders

② Drag Fill handle

Changing the Data Source Range

If you've created a great chart and want to switch the data it displays to a different source range, either on the same worksheet or on another worksheet, using the Chart Wizard is the easiest way.

Change the data source range

1. Click the chart to select it.

2. Click the Chart Wizard button on the Standard toolbar. 📊 Step 1 of the Chart Wizard appears.

3. Click the **Next** button.

4. In Step 2 of the Chart Wizard, delete the reference in the **Data range** box, and enter a new source range by dragging to select the worksheet range you want.

   If you've named the worksheet range you want, type the range name in the **Data range** box.

5. Click <u>**Finish**</u>.

The chart's data source is changed.

Changing Chart Orientation

You can select the orientation you want in Step 2 of the Chart Wizard. You can put row labels along the horizontal axis or use column labels on the horizontal axis. When you create a chart, it's a good idea to take advantage of the opportunity to preview what each orientation looks like before you move on to the next step in the Chart Wizard.

After you finish the chart, however, you may change your mind about the orientation you chose. Fortunately it's easy to change.

Change the orientation of an existing chart

1. Click the chart to select it and to display the Chart toolbar.

2. On the Chart toolbar, click the By Row or By Column button.

- Click the By Row button to put row labels along the chart's X-axis.

- Click the By Column button to put column labels along the chart's X-axis.

The chart orientation is switched.

Moving and Resizing a Chart

A newly created chart object is unlikely to be the right size or in the right position, but moving and resizing a chart are simple.

Move a chart

1. Click the chart near its perimeter so that the Chart Area is selected.

You can tell the Chart Area is selected because the name Chart Area appears in the worksheet Name box and in the Chart Objects box. Handles appear around the chart border (as shown in Figure 19.13).

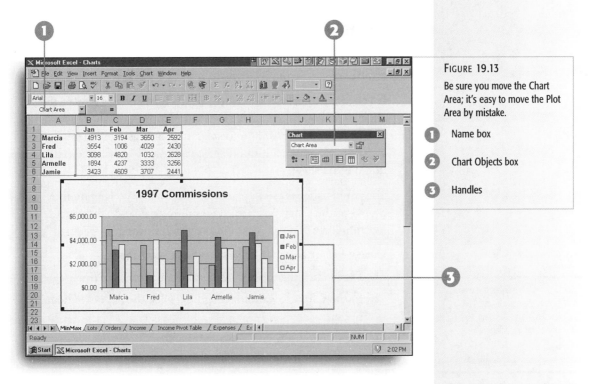

FIGURE 19.13

Be sure you move the Chart Area; it's easy to move the Plot Area by mistake.

1 Name box

2 Chart Objects box

3 Handles

2. Drag the Chart Area to move the chart.

You can grip the chart anywhere inside the Chart Area. If you accidentally drag the Plot Area or another element by mistake, click the Undo button on the toolbar and start again.

Resize a chart

1. Click the chart near its perimeter so that the Chart Area is selected.

2. Drag a chart handle (refer to Figure 19.13) to resize the chart.

- Hold down the Shift key while you drag a corner handle to resize the chart proportionally. (The chart retains its original height-to-width ratio.)

- Hold down the Ctrl key while you drag any handle to resize a chart symmetrically (both sides or top and bottom, move in or out the same distance).

- Hold down the Alt key while you drag any handle to align the border with the worksheet gridlines.

Use gridlines for perfect alignment

To align the chart with worksheet gridlines, press the Alt key while you drag the chart. Release the Alt key *after* you release the mouse button to drop the chart.

Changing the Chart Location

You can easily move a chart from a worksheet to its own sheet in a workbook, or from its own sheet onto a worksheet.

If you want to print a worksheet with a chart object next to the chart data, you need to have the chart on the worksheet as a chart object. If you want to display the chart as a full-size sheet so that you can see a lot of details, it's easier to make the chart into a chart sheet.

You can decide where to place the chart when you create it in Step 4 of the Chart Wizard. If you need to change the chart location after you've created it, use the following procedures.

Print chart and worksheet separately

If you want to print either the worksheet or the chart separately, you don't need to move the chart, just set printing options differently.

Sheet names do double duty

Because the sheet name is the default page header when you print a chart or worksheet, you can save yourself time by naming the chart sheet with a good printed-page title.

Change a chart object on a worksheet to a chart sheet

1. Right-click the chart object and then click **Location**.

2. In the Chart Location dialog box, click the **As new <u>s</u>heet** option.

3. Type an appropriate name for the chart sheet (something more meaningful than Chart1).

4. Click **OK**.

   The chart becomes a separate chart sheet in the workbook (shown in Figure 19.14).

Change a chart sheet to a chart object on a worksheet

1. Right-click the Chart Area or Plot Area and click **Location**.

2. In the Chart Location dialog box, click the **As <u>o</u>bject in** option.

3. In the **As <u>o</u>bject in** drop-down list box, select the worksheet in which you want to place the chart object (as shown in Figure 19.15).

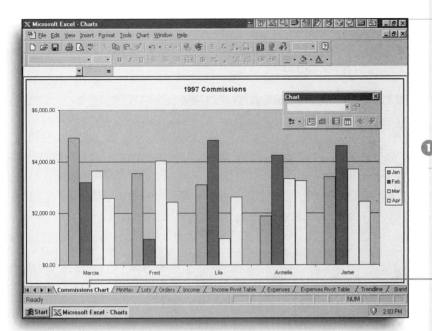

FIGURE 19.14

This chart was stretched to fill the window by opening **View** and selecting **Sized with Window**. To return it to its original dimensions, I'd open **View** and select **Sized with Window** again.

1 Renamed sheet tab

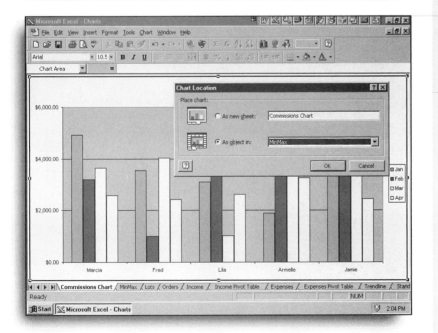

FIGURE 19.15

Pick a worksheet in the active workbook in which you want to place the chart object.

4. Click **OK**.

The chart becomes an object on the worksheet (shown in Figure 19.16).

FIGURE 19.16

After you place the chart object in the worksheet, you can move and resize it.

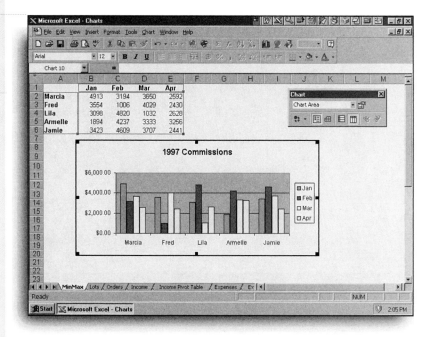

SEE ALSO

➤ *To learn more about printing worksheets and charts, see pages 412 and 416.*

Formatting a Chart

Formatting Chart Colors, Lines, and Fonts

Like worksheets, charts can present data in a utilitarian manner, or you can format them to make them look professional or graphically striking or silly, depending on your audience.

When you first create a chart, you get Excel's default colors, fonts, and so on, and your chart looks like every other chart ever created in Excel 97. But after you've created a chart, your options for changing the look of the chart are countless.

And after you've spent a lot of time formatting a chart, you can save and reuse the entire formatting package for a chart as a custom chart format.

To keep your audience's attention during a presentation, make your charts visually attractive with color, line, and font formatting (as shown in Figure 20.1). To make a presentation involving several charts coherent and professional, give all the charts a uniform look by using the same formatting for all of them.

To format any element's color, line weight, font, or other characteristics, you select the element and then open the Format dialog box for that element. Sometimes selecting an element is a little difficult because the element is small or overlapped by another element; but there are a few different ways you can use to select the chart element you want to format.

Quick change artist

For quick color changes, select the element; then use the **Fill Color** or **Font Color** button on the Formatting toolbar. The selection is limited compared with what the dialog box offers, but it's much faster.

Change the formatting of chart colors, lines, or fonts

1. Do one of the following to select a chart element for formatting:

   - Click the element
   - On the Chart toolbar, in the **Chart Objects** box, click the down arrow; then click the name on the list
   - Click any element; then press the right or left arrow key to cycle through all elements in the chart

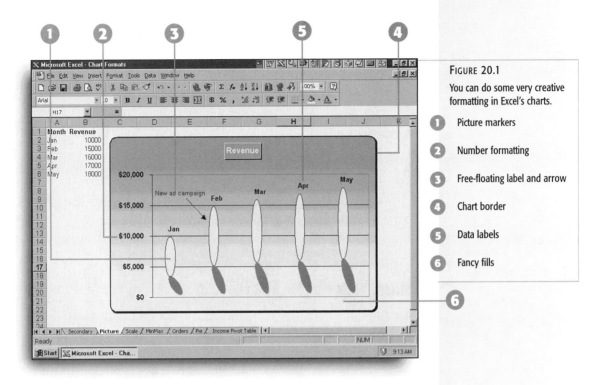

FIGURE 20.1

You can do some very creative formatting in Excel's charts.

1 Picture markers

2 Number formatting

3 Free-floating label and arrow

4 Chart border

5 Data labels

6 Fancy fills

2. Do one of the following to open the Format dialog box for the selected element:

- Double-click the selected element
- On the Chart toolbar, click the **Format** button (the button name is **Format** *element*, depending on which element is selected) 📇
- Right-click the selected element; then click the **Format** command (the command name is **Format** *element*, depending on which element is selected)

3. In the Format dialog box, select the formatting options you want.

4. Click **OK**.

Deleting a Chart Element

You can delete any element from a chart: individual series, elements you've added (such as a trendline), legend, data table, axes, gridlines; anything in the chart can be deleted in the interest of showing only what you want to show and nothing else.

Delete a chart element

1. Select the element.

2. Press **Delete**.

    If you change your mind about a deleted element, click the **Undo** button (on the Standard toolbar) to replace the element.

Changing Axis Scale

Changing the scale of a chart axis can persuade an audience to accept your point of view. For example: Suppose OkeyDokey forest has a chemical factory built along one side of it, and there's an argument about whether the factory is making life difficult for the trees in the forest. You've counted the number of trees per acre in four quadrants of the forest, and the counts are all between 100 and 200.

If you want to persuade an audience that there's no important difference between quadrants, you can show the data on a scale that runs from 0 to 200 (as shown in Figure 20.2); to persuade the audience there's a big problem in Quad2 (next to the chemical factory), show the data on a narrow scale that runs from just below the minimum data point to just above the maximum data point (as shown in Figure 20.3). The data is valid, and it's perfectly fair to present the data either way; but you can control your audience's perception of the data by changing the scale you use to present it.

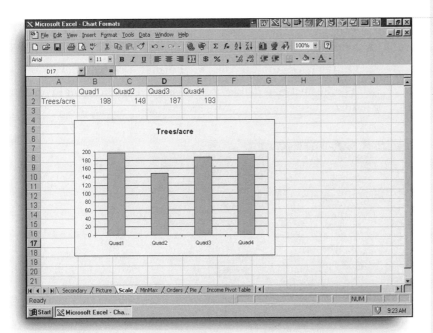

FIGURE 20.2
To persuade an audience that
there's little difference in the
data, use a large axis scale.

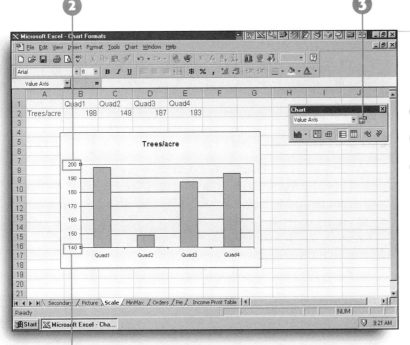

FIGURE 20.3
Use a narrow axis scale to
show clear differences
between data point values.

① Minimum

② Maximum

③ Format Axis

Change the axis scale in a chart

1. Select the axis.

2. On the Chart toolbar, click the **Format Axis** button.

The Format Axis dialog box is displayed, as shown in Figure 20.4.

FIGURE 20.4

I've set the axis scale to run from 140 to 200.

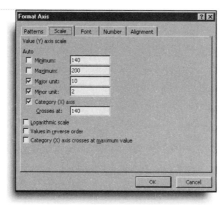

3. On the **Scale** tab, type the maximum number for your custom scale in the **Maximum** box.

4. Type the minimum number you want in the **Minimum** box.

5. Click **OK**.

The scale on the selected axis is changed.

Reordering the Series

When you create a chart, your data series are plotted in the order that Excel finds them in the chart's source range, but you are not limited to that series order. You might want to rearrange the series order in the chart, especially if you've created a 3-D chart, in which a tall series in front can hide shorter markers behind it (like the chart in Figure 20.5).

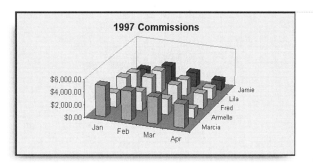

FIGURE 20.5

In this 3-D column chart, the series in front hides the series behind it.

Reorder the series in a chart

1. Double-click any series in the chart.

   The Format Data Series dialog box is displayed, as shown in Figure 20.6.

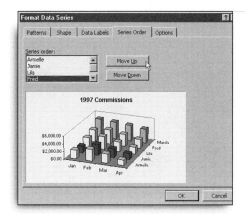

FIGURE 20.6

On the **Series Order** tab, you can rearrange the series in any order you want.

2. Click the **Series Order** tab.

3. Rearrange the series order: click a series name and then click the **Move Up** and **Move Down** buttons to reposition it.

4. When you're finished, click **OK**.

   The resulting series order, shown in Figure 20.7, is more readable.

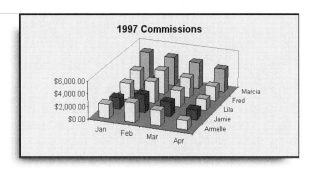

Resizing and Exploding a Pie Chart

Pie charts are great for showing how much of the total "pie" belongs to each data point; if you make the pie larger and *explode* it by separating the slices (or pulling out a single slice), you can call attention to individual items in your data.

I'll demonstrate resizing and exploding a Pie chart using the chart shown in Figure 20.8.

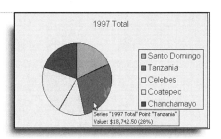

Making the Pie Bigger

I want to make the pie bigger; to do this, I'll make the legend smaller to make more room in the chart and then drag the plot area to make it larger.

Make the legend smaller

1. Click the legend border to select it.

2. On the **Formatting** toolbar, select a smaller font size in the **Font Size** box.

   The entire legend is resized to accommodate the changed font size.

Make the plot area larger

1. Select the plot area.

   If it's difficult to locate the plot area with the mouse pointer, click the arrow on the **Chart Objects** box (on the Chart toolbar); then click **Plot Area** on the list.

2. Make the plot area larger by dragging a corner; move the resized plot area by dragging inside a corner (as shown in Figure 20.9).

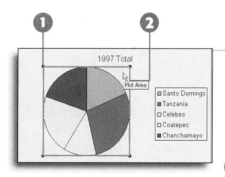

FIGURE 20.9

By changing the font size in the legend, I made the legend smaller; then I made the plot area larger by dragging a corner handle and then repositioning the enlarged pie.

1 Drag handle to resize

2 Drag inner corner to move

Exploding the Pie

To call attention to a specific data point in a Pie chart, you can drag that slice out of the pie; you can also *explode* the entire pie by dragging all slices away from the center of the pie.

Drag a single slice out of the pie

1. Click anywhere inside the pie.

   The series (the whole set of slices) is selected.

2. Click the slice you want to drag out.

   The single slice is selected, as shown in Figure 20.10.

3. Drag the slice away from the center of the pie.

   Figure 20.11 shows the results of dragging a single slice out.

To rejoin the slice to the pie, select the single slice and drag it back to the center of the pie.

Can I have two slices?

You can drag two or more slices out of the pie; just drag each slice away individually.

FIGURE 20.10

Click a slice twice (not a double-click) to select it.

1 Drag away from the center

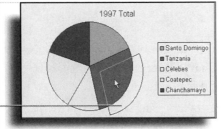

FIGURE 20.11

The Tanzania slice draws attention because it's separated from the pie.

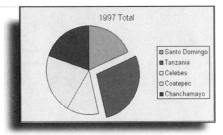

Explode the entire pie

1. Click the pie to select the entire series (all the slices).

2. Drag any of the slices away from the center of the pie.

All the slices separate from the pie, as shown in Figure 20.12.

FIGURE 20.12

Explode the whole pie by dragging a slice in the selected series, rather than a single selected slice.

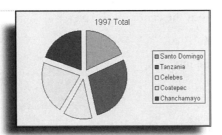

To rejoin the slices, select the series and drag a slice back to the center of the pie.

Changing 3-D Perspective

A 3-D chart can be a very effective way to get your point across, but sometimes it's difficult to see all the markers in a 3-D chart because they hide behind one another.

To bring hidden markers into view, you can rotate a 3-D chart on all three axes; you can rotate it quickly by dragging a corner of the plot area or more carefully by opening a dialog box that gives you more precise control of the rotation.

A 3-D chart has a few elements that 2-D charts don't have: *walls* and a *floor*. Think of the chart as a box of markers with two of the sides cut away; the walls are the remaining sides of the box, and the floor is under the markers. If you click the walls or the floor, that element will display handles on each corner, and you can rotate, or spin, the chart in any direction by dragging a handle.

Changing Perspective by Dragging

Change the perspective of a 3-D chart by dragging

1. Select the chart walls or floor.

The element you select (walls or floor) will display a handle at each corner.

2. Drag a corner handle to rotate the chart, as shown in Figure 20.13.

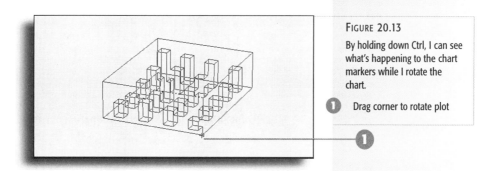

FIGURE 20.13

By holding down Ctrl, I can see what's happening to the chart markers while I rotate the chart.

1 Drag corner to rotate plot

Here are a couple of hints for more precise dragging:

- Drag a front floor corner for greater precision and control
- Hold down **Ctrl** while you drag to display a wire frame of the chart markers

Changing Perspective Using a Dialog Box

Changing perspective by dragging a chart corner takes some practice (your chart can easily end up upside down and inside out), so here's a rotation technique that gives you more precise control over your chart's perspective.

Change perspective using a dialog box

1. Right-click anywhere in the chart or plot area.
2. Click **3-D View**.

   The 3-D View dialog box is displayed, as shown in Figure 20.14.

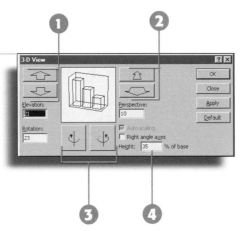

FIGURE 20.14

Use the 3-D View dialog box for more precise control of 3-D perspective.

1 Rotate up or down

2 Increase or decrease depth

3 Spin left or right

4 Change height-to-width ratio

3. Rotate the chart around any of three axes (elevation, rotation, or perspective) by clicking the buttons.
4. When you're finished, click **OK**.

If your chart seems too small, you can often make it larger by changing the height-to-width ratio in the 3-D View dialog box: changing the **Height** setting to 50 percent of base makes the chart wider and larger.

Adding a Trendline

Trendlines are of real value and are commonly used in the scientific arena. To create a trendline, Excel uses specific equations that calculate the data points in a chart and then draws the trendline that the equation calculates. Excel also calculates how well the points in the chart correlate to the trendline. (The *R-squared value* is the measure of how well the points and trendline correlate.)

The best chart type for a trendline is an XY (scatter) chart, because the data normally charted in a scatter chart—two sets of numeric values—is of the sort that a trendline was designed to analyze; also, any other lines or solid markers tend to obscure the trendline. A trendline is a visual representation of a *regression analysis* of the data points; a regression analysis is a mathematical measurement of how closely data points fit a perfect line or curve.

Here's an example of a linear trendline in action. At a biotech company I once worked for, I performed chemical analyses of water samples, testing for trace amounts of a biochemical called endotoxin. Endotoxin reacts with a test chemical that turns it yellow; the concentration of endotoxin in a sample is determined by how long it takes the sample to turn yellow. The faster it turns yellow, the higher the concentration of endotoxin. (Endotoxin is measured in EU/ml, which means endotoxin units per milliliter.)

To make this work, a standard curve (a trendline) is produced by using endotoxin samples of known concentration; then the water samples are tested and the results compared with the standard curve (the trendline) to determine endotoxin concentration in the water samples.

In the following example, known concentrations and dilutions of endotoxin were tested, and the results are shown in Figure 20.15.

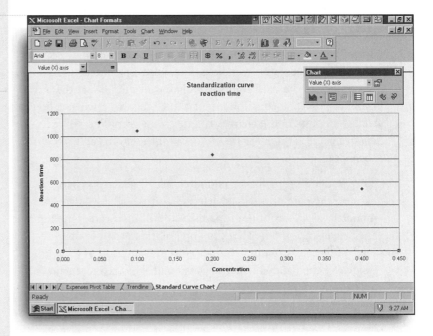

FIGURE 20.15

This XY scatter chart plots concentration against reaction time.

What are the trendline equations?

To see the equation for each trendline: In the Add Trendline dialog box, on the **Type** tab, click the **Help** button in the upper-right corner; then click a trendline type. A ScreenTip is displayed with the equation.

What's an R-squared value?

The R-squared value tells me whether the trendline is a valid measuring stick for endotoxin concentration: An R-squared value of 1.0000 (or –1.0000) is perfect correlation; to be valid, the trendline R-squared value must be at least 0.98. In Figure 20.17, the R-squared value of 0.9949 tells me the trendline is valid for measuring endotoxin concentration.

Add a trendline to a chart

1. Select the chart.

2. On the **Chart** menu, click **Add Trendline**.

The Add Trendline dialog box is displayed, as shown in Figure 20.16.

3. On the **Type** tab, click the type of trendline you want to apply to your data.

For more information on the mathematics of various trendline types, use Help to look up *trendline equations* (on the **Help** menu, click **Contents and Index**; then click the **Find** tab).

4. On the **Options** tab, click the **Display equation on chart** and **Display R-squared value on chart** check boxes (if you want to include the supporting mathematical results).

5. Click **OK**.

The linear trendline for my chart is shown in Figure 20.17.

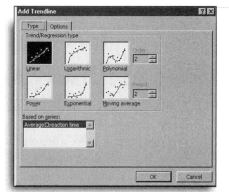

FIGURE 20.16

The type of trendline you choose depends on the data you've charted.

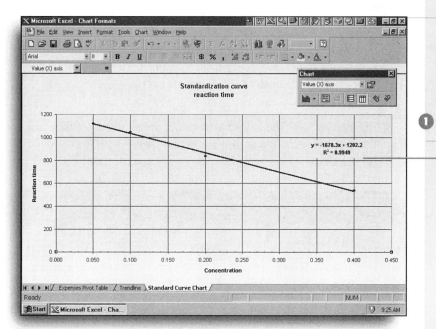

FIGURE 20.17

To use this trendline, I draw a line from the Y-axis value (reaction time) to the trendline and then down to the X-axis to find the concentration.

1 Supporting math results

I used a linear trendline (which is appropriate for this data), and the trendline equation and resulting R-squared value are shown on the chart.

To use this trendline to determine the concentration of endotoxin in water samples, I mix the samples with the test chemical and then use the machine to time the color reaction. Next I plot the reaction time against the trendline on the chart, and I find the corresponding endotoxin concentration. For example, in

Figure 20.17, a reaction time of 800 seconds is equivalent to a concentration of approximately 0.24 EU/ml.

Adding a Secondary Axis

A secondary axis is ideal for comparing data that's related but is on two different scales. For example, suppose you are in charge of a department store sales staff, and your burning questions are: How are total sales related to the number of salespeople on the staff? Does adding salespeople result in more total sales revenue? At what point does a larger sales staff result in marginally larger sales revenues?

You might find an answer by charting total revenue versus number of salespeople for several months. But if total revenue is in excess of $10,000 and salespeople number between 10 and 20, how can you put both sets of numbers on the same chart? By using a secondary axis.

In Figure 20.18, the Sales Force values are so much smaller than the Revenue values that they're "off the scale" and don't show up on the chart. This is my clue that I need a secondary axis.

FIGURE 20.18

With a single axis, the Sales Force series is completely hidden because the numbers are too small to show on the same scale as the Revenue series.

1 The Sales Force data is hidden

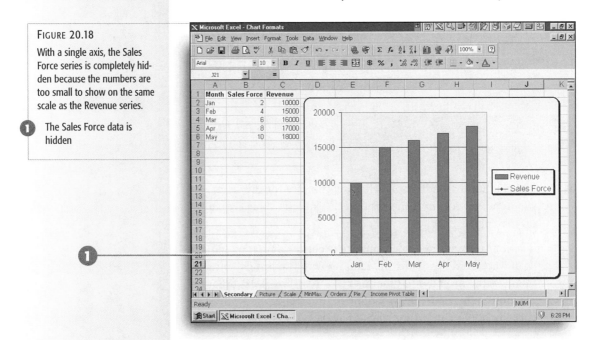

Add a secondary axis to a chart

1. Select the chart.

2. On the Chart toolbar, in the **Chart Objects** box, select the hidden series.

3. On the Chart toolbar, click the **Format Data** Series button.

4. In the Format Data Series dialog box (shown in Figure 20.19), on the **Axis** tab, click the **Secondary axis** option.

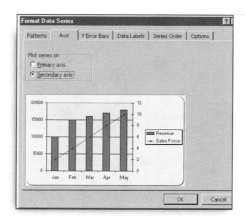

FIGURE 20.19
FIGURE 20.19

When you click the **Secondary axis** option, it is displayed in preview in the dialog box.

5. Click **OK**.

The selected series is plotted on a secondary axis, as shown in Figure 20.20.

Adding Data Labels

Data labels add value to a chart by positioning data labels or values right next to their markers in the chart, as shown in Figure 20.21. The labels show text or values from the source range, so if you change text or values in the source range, the data labels on the chart are automatically updated. Data labels can be moved, formatted, and deleted as a group or individually.

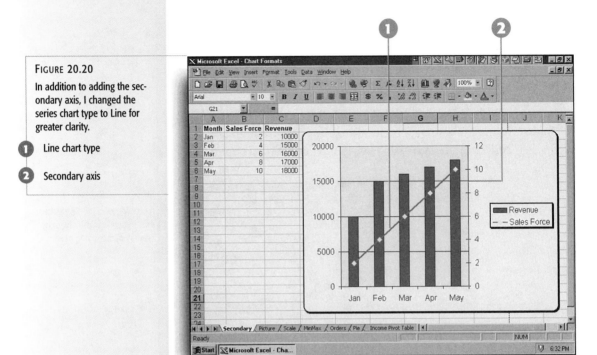

FIGURE 20.20

In addition to adding the secondary axis, I changed the series chart type to Line for greater clarity.

❶ Line chart type

❷ Secondary axis

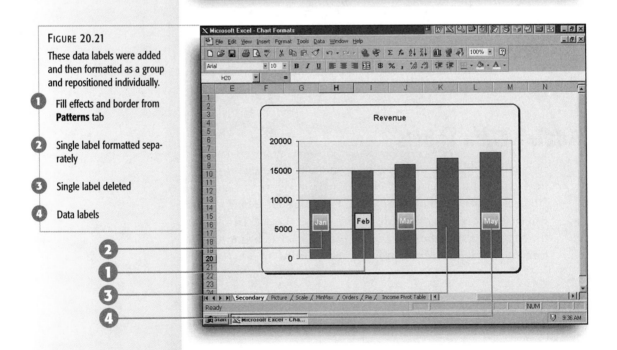

FIGURE 20.21

These data labels were added and then formatted as a group and repositioned individually.

❶ Fill effects and border from **Patterns** tab

❷ Single label formatted separately

❸ Single label deleted

❹ Data labels

SEE ALSO

➤ *For more information on drawing objects, see "Basic Drawing," page 520.*

Add data labels to a chart

1. Select the series you want to add data labels to.

2. On the Chart toolbar, click the **Format Data Series** button.

   The Format Data Series dialog box is displayed, as shown in Figure 20.22.

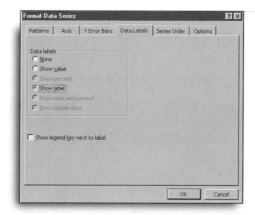

> **FIGURE 20.22**
>
> The types of data labels available depend on the type of chart you're adding them to.

3. On the **Data Labels** tab, click an option for the type of data label you want.

   For this example, I selected **Show label**, so that my category labels would display with the chart markers.

4. Click **OK**.

Format data labels

1. Click one of the labels.

   The set of labels for the series is selected.

2. Use the buttons on the Formatting toolbar to make quick changes to color, font, and font size.

3. Double-click one of the labels to open the Format Data Labels dialog box, where you can make a wider variety of formatting changes. (Be sure to double-click the data label, not the data point.)

Add your own labels

To add a free-floating label anywhere on the chart: Select the chart area; then type your label text (your text is displayed in the Formula bar); and then press Enter. The label will display somewhere on the chart; you can format it and move it wherever you want. (To call attention to a specific item, use the Drawing toolbar to draw an arrow from the label to the item.)

Remove those data labels

To remove data labels, select the set of labels; then press **Delete**. To remove a single data label, select the single label by clicking it twice (not a double-click); then press **Delete**.

Format one unique label

To select a single label, click the label twice (not a double-click). Only the selected label is formatted.

Add a data table

To add (or remove) a data table at the bottom of a chart, click the **Data Table** button on the Chart toolbar. A data table is a picture of the chart's source data, attached to the bottom of the chart; you can use it to show all source values without showing the worksheet.

4. Click **OK** to close the Format Data Labels dialog box when you're finished.

Creating Picture Markers

Picture markers can wake up a drowsy audience by adding a touch of whimsy to a chart. You can use any picture you want as data markers: clip art, objects you've created in Windows Paint, or even a company logo graphic (see Figure 20.23).

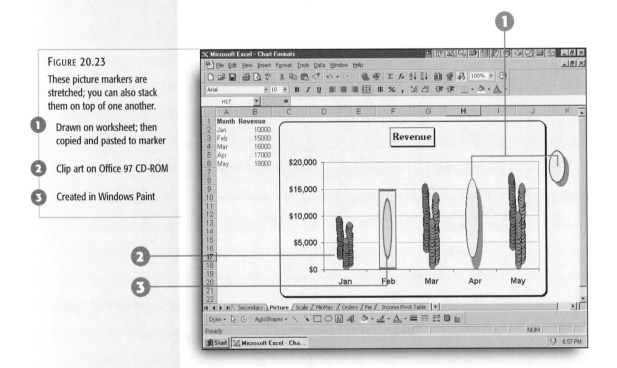

FIGURE 20.23

These picture markers are stretched; you can also stack them on top of one another.

1. Drawn on worksheet; then copied and pasted to marker

2. Clip art on Office 97 CD-ROM

3. Created in Windows Paint

Create one unique marker

To create a picture marker for a single data marker, click the marker twice to select it (not a double-click); then double-click the single marker and use the **Patterns** tab in the Format Data Point dialog box to create the new marker.

Create picture markers

1. Double-click the data series.

   The Format Data Series dialog box is displayed, as shown in Figure 20.24.

2. On the **Patterns** tab, click the **Fill Effects** button.

   The Fill Effects dialog box is displayed, as shown in Figure 20.25.

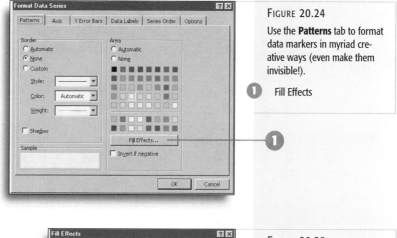

FIGURE 20.24

Use the **Patterns** tab to format data markers in myriad creative ways (even make them invisible!).

1 Fill Effects

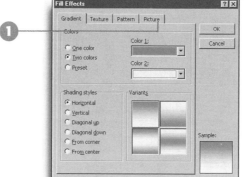

FIGURE 20.25

Spend some time playing with the colors on the **Gradient** tab; you might like them better than a picture marker.

1 **Picture** tab

3. In the Fill Effects dialog box, click the **Picture** tab.

4. On the **Picture** tab, shown in Figure 20.26, click the **Select Picture** button.

The Select Picture dialog box is displayed, as shown in Figure 20.27.

5. Navigate to a folder that contains the picture you want to use.

Click the **Preview** button to look at the pictures before you choose one.

Draw your own markers

Here's a quick way to create a simple picture marker: Use the Drawing toolbar to draw an object on the worksheet. Select and copy the object; then select a data series (or single marker) and paste the object to replace the marker(s).

FIGURE 20.26

There's nothing to see here until you select a picture.

1 Select Picture

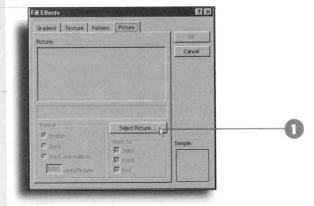

FIGURE 20.27

Clip art names are not always helpful; previewing them saves a lot of guessing.

1 Preview

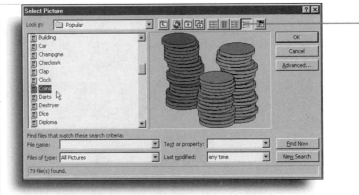

6. Double-click the name of the picture you want.

The picture is displayed on the **Picture** tab in the Fill Effects dialog box (shown in Figure 20.28).

FIGURE 20.28

Stretch is usually the most interesting option, unless you want to retain the original picture proportions.

7. Decide whether you want to stretch, stack, or stack and scale the picture marker in the chart:

- **Stretch** fills the picture marker to its value by stretching a single picture out of proportion.

- **St<u>a</u>ck** fills the picture marker to its value by stacking several pictures on top of one another; the picture retains its original size and proportions and might be cut off at the value level.

- **Stac<u>k</u> and scale to** also stacks pictures on top of one another, retaining their original proportions, but it resizes the picture smaller so that each picture equals a specific number of data units in the chart (which you specify in the **<u>U</u>nits/Picture** box).

8. Click **OK** to close the Fill Effects dialog box.

9. Click **OK** to close the Format Data Series dialog box.

Your data markers are replaced by picture markers.

SEE ALSO

➤ *For more information on drawing objects, see "Basic Drawing," page 520.*

Beware Stack and scale

A smaller number of units per picture means more pictures per marker, which uses more computer memory and takes the chart longer to redraw.

Saving and Reusing Your Custom Chart Format

When you've put a lot of time into formatting all the elements of a chart (or if someone sends you a workbook containing a beautifully formatted chart that you want to use), you can save all that formatting work as a custom chart format. Then you can apply all that painstaking formatting to new charts with just a couple of clicks.

To demonstrate, I'm going to save and then apply the formatting shown in Figure 20.29.

FIGURE 20.29

I spent a lot of time on this format. (I wish you could see it in color!)

1 Markers drawn on work-sheet and then pasted to series

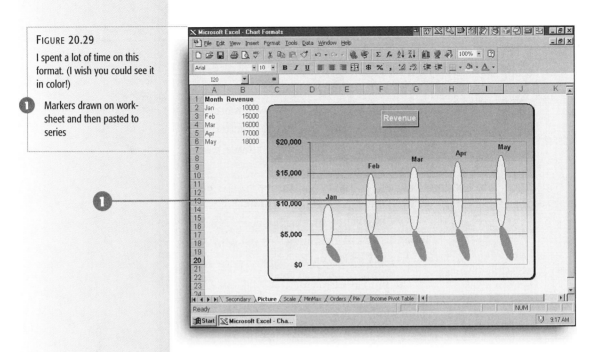

Save chart formatting as a custom chart format

1. Right-click the formatted chart.

2. Click **Chart Type**.

In the Chart Type dialog box, click the **Custom Types** tab (shown in Figure 20.30).

FIGURE 20.30

The **Custom Types** tab looks like this after you click the **User-defined** option.

1 Add new custom format

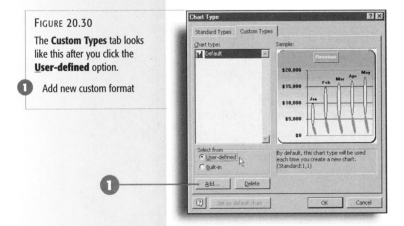

3. Click the **Add** button.

4. In the Add Custom Chart Type dialog box that is displayed, type a name and memorable description for your custom format; then click **OK**.

The name is added to the **Chart Type** list, and when the name is selected, your description and a preview of the format are displayed in the dialog box.

5. Click **OK** to close the Chart Type dialog box and save the custom format.

Apply a custom chart format

1. Select your data and click the **Chart Wizard** button on the Standard toolbar to begin creating the chart.

2. In Step 1 of the Chart Wizard, click the **Custom Types** tab.

3. In the **Custom Types** tab, click the **User-defined** option.

4. In the **Chart Type** list, click the name of your custom format.

5. Continue creating the chart using the Chart Wizard.

If you've already created a chart, you can switch the chart type to your custom format. Right-click the chart area; then click **Chart Type**. On the **Custom Types** tab, click **User-defined**; then double-click the name of your custom format.

Putting Data on a Map

Are there more maps?

Microsoft Map is a separate program included with Excel that generates predrawn maps on which
you can display your data. A limited
number of maps come with Excel;
you can buy more maps from the
company that originally created the
map program, MapInfo Corporation.
To find them, click a map, and on
the **Help** menu, click **How to Get
More Data**.

Where is Microsoft Map?

To use Microsoft Map, you must
install it from your Office 97 or
Excel 97 CD-ROM. You'll find it in
the Excel category.

Introducing Microsoft Map

If you have data that's geographically oriented, such as sales by
state, you might want to display the data on a geographical map
instead of on a chart.

In this chapter I'll show you how to get started using maps to
display your data and how to create a map with no data (called a
pin map) to which you can add your own labels and information.

The Microsoft Map program has its own toolbar, with buttons
that you don't see elsewhere in Excel. This toolbar is displayed
only when a map is active. Table 21.1 explains what each button
does.

TABLE 21.1 **Map toolbar buttons**

Icon	Name	Purpose
	Select Objects	Allows mouse pointer to select objects for moving, sizing, and deleting
	Grabber	Allows mouse pointer to drag image around within map object
	Center Map	Turns mouse pointer into an "X-marks-the-spot" symbol, for designating a new map center (click it where you want to create a map center point)
	Map Labels	Turns mouse pointer into a labeler, to add labels to clicked map elements
	Add Text	Creates free-floating labels
	Custom Pin Map	Turns mouse pointer into a pushpin, to add pushpins to a pin map
	Display Entire	Zooms out so entire original map is displayed
	Redraw Map	Redraws flat map proportions after you move the image with the Grabber

Icon	Name	Purpose
	Map Refresh	Updates map with changed worksheet data (becomes available if worksheet data changes)
	Show/Hide Microsoft Map Control	Turns Microsoft Map Control dialog box on and off
	Zoom Percentage of Map	Changes (zooms) map magnification
	What's This? Help	Turns mouse pointer into a What's This? pointer, for quick identification of map elements and toolbar buttons

Creating a Geographical Data Map

If you want to show your data on a map, the data layout is important: The first column must contain geographical entries, such as cities, states, or countries. An appropriate data layout is shown in Figure 21.1. (Excel recognizes standard two-letter state abbreviations as well as full state names.)

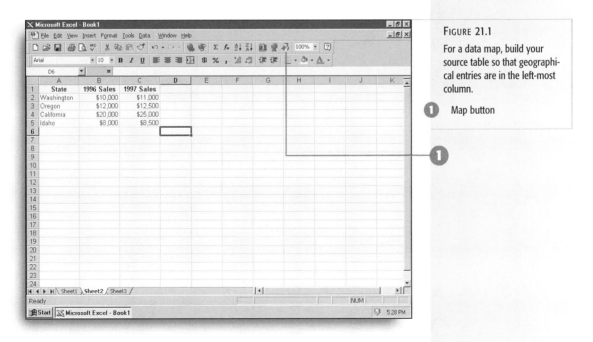

FIGURE 21.1

For a data map, build your source table so that geographical entries are in the left-most column.

❶ Map button

1. On the worksheet, select the data you want to map. (If you want the legend to include category names, include the column and row labels in your selection.)

2. On the Standard toolbar, click the **Map** button. 🌐

Your mouse pointer becomes a crosshair, as shown in Figure 21.2.

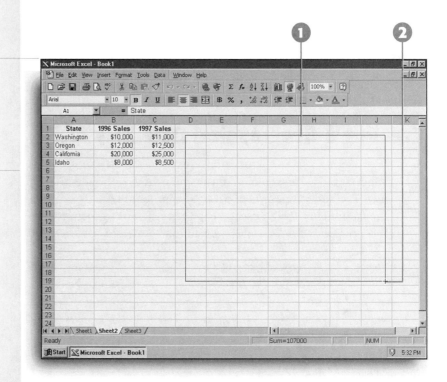

3. Drag the crosshair diagonally across the worksheet to draw a rectangle.

The rectangle will be your data map; don't worry about the dimensions, because you can change size and shape later.

If Microsoft Map can guess which map you want from your data, that map is displayed. If not, you'll see one of two dialog boxes after you draw the map rectangle (both are shown in Figure 21.3).

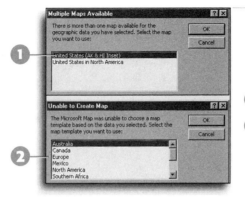

FIGURE 21.3

Which dialog box you see at this point depends on what Microsoft Map can guess from your data.

1 Maybe one of these?

2 Not a clue

4. Whichever dialog box you see, double-click the map you want.

The map is displayed, along with the Microsoft Map Control dialog box and the Map toolbar, as shown in Figure 21.4. Initially, only the data from the first category (in this case, 1996 Sales) is displayed. You add the remaining data and choose the format you want by using the Microsoft Map Control dialog box.

To resize or reshape the map, click the map to select it; then drag the handles on the map border.

To return to the worksheet, click a cell. The map becomes a worksheet object, and the Map toolbar is replaced by worksheet toolbars. To activate the map again, double-click the map object.

SEE ALSO

➤ *To learn more about adding and formatting data series in a map, see the section "Using the Map Control," page 400.*

Adding Features to Your Map

You can add geographical features—such as cities, highways, and airports—to your map and then label the specific features you want to call attention to.

Add geographical features to your map

1. Right-click the map; then click **Features**.

FIGURE 21.4

Your map is created; use the Map Control to determine which data is shown on your map and how it's displayed.

1 Map toolbar

2 Map Control

3 Handles

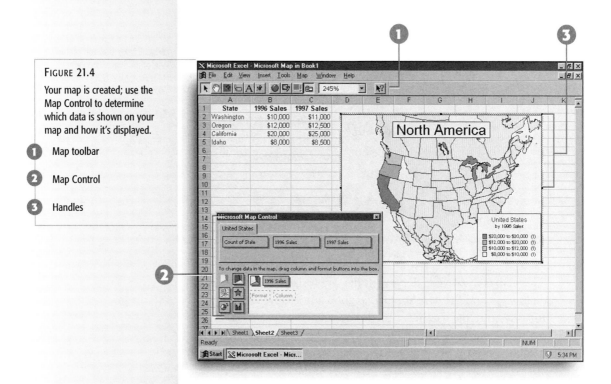

2. In the Map Features dialog box (shown in Figure 21.5), click check boxes for the features you want displayed on the map.

There are lots of different features available for each map; to add more features (such as Airports or Postal Codes) to the list in the Map Features dialog box, click the **Add** button, select a feature from the list, and click **OK**.

3. Click **OK**.

FIGURE 21.5

Several features are already attached to each map; you can choose to make them visible.

1 Add more features to list

2 Remove features from list

3 Click to pick your own symbol

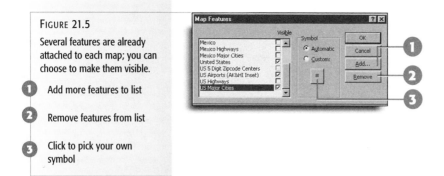

Airports and major cities are shown on the map in Figure
21.6. I added Airports to the list in the Map Features dialog
box, so that I could show airports on the map.

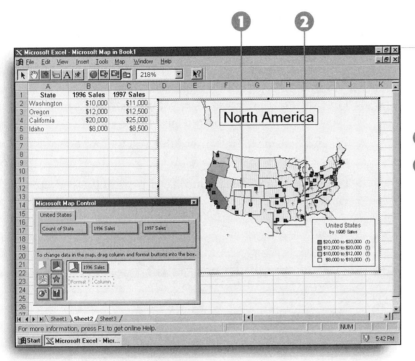

FIGURE 21.6

You can show airports, cities,
and highways and then label
just those you want to point
out.

❶ Major cities

❷ Airports

Labeling Map Items

When you show map features, lots of them are displayed. You'll
want to label only those specific features on your map that you
want to point out to your audience.

Label map items

1. On the **Tools** menu, click **Labeler**.

   The Map Labels dialog box is displayed, as shown in Figure
   21.7.

2. In the Map Labels dialog box, click the down arrow in the
   Map feature to label box, and click the feature category
   you want to create labels for (in Figure 21.8, I'm going to
   label a few airports).

FIGURE 21.7

Label just a few features to make your map more readable.

1 Select feature to label

3. Click **OK**.

The mouse pointer becomes a crosshair again.

4. Hold the mouse crosshair over features on your map; feature names are displayed in ScreenTips.

5. When a ScreenTip is displayed that you want to use as a label, click it.

Figure 21.8 shows labels for some airports in the Western United States.

FIGURE 21.8

Lots of airports are shown, but only a few are labeled. I repositioned and zoomed this map image to focus on my four states (see the following section to learn how).

1 Select Objects

2 Grabber

3 Center Map

4 Zoom Percentage of Map

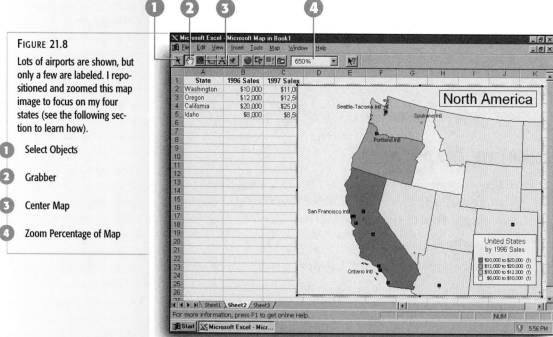

6. On the toolbar, click **Select Objects** to turn off the labeler.

   After you create labels, you can reposition them on the map by dragging their borders.

Repositioning and Enlarging a Map

You can resize and reposition a map object on your worksheet the same way you resize and reposition any graphical object; but with a map object, you can also do two more things:

- Reposition the map image within the object frame, to help your audience focus on a specific portion of the map

- Zoom into a specific portion of a large map, again to help your audience focus on a specific portion of the map

Move a map around within its object frame

1. On the Map toolbar, click the **Grabber** button.

2. Click the map image, and drag it to a new position within its frame.

3. To recenter the map image in its frame, on the toolbar, click **Center Map**; then click the map-spot that you want to put in the center of the map frame.

Zoom, or enlarge, the map

1. On the Map toolbar, click the down arrow on the **Zoom Percentage** of Map button. 100% ▾

2. Click a higher zoom percentage to zoom in on the map.

   If the default percentages aren't quite right, you can type your own zoom percentage in the **Zoom Percentage of Map** button; then press Enter.

3. On the Map toolbar, click the **Grabber** button; then drag the zoomed image around in its frame to position it precisely.

Using the Map Control

Your data can be shown on the map in several ways, including

- Regions colored by value
- Regions colored by category
- Small Column charts overlaid on regions
- Small Pie charts overlaid on regions
- Colored dots or symbols

To change the way data is displayed in your map, use the Microsoft Map Control dialog box, shown in Figure 21.9.

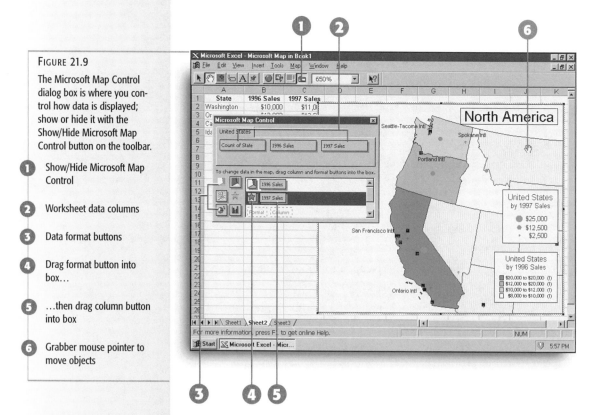

FIGURE 21.9

The Microsoft Map Control dialog box is where you control how data is displayed; show or hide it with the Show/Hide Microsoft Map Control button on the toolbar.

1 Show/Hide Microsoft Map Control

2 Worksheet data columns

3 Data format buttons

4 Drag format button into box...

5 ...then drag column button into box

6 Grabber mouse pointer to move objects

Table 21.2 identifies the buttons in the Map Control.

TABLE 21.2 **Map Control buttons**

Icon	Name	Purpose
	Value shading	Shows each value level in a different color (can display only a single category of data values, as shown in Figure 21.10)
	Category shading	Shows each category in a different color, instead of each value level
	Dot density	Shows values as lots of small dots; more dots (higher density) represents higher values
	Graduated symbol	Shows values as symbols of different sizes; larger symbols represent higher values (as shown in Figure 21.10)
	Pie chart	Shows multiple categories of data as small pie charts overlaid on each region
	Column chart	Shows multiple categories of data as small column charts overlaid on each region

Control your data display with the Map Control

1. On the toolbar, click the **Show/Hide Microsoft Map Control** button.

If the Microsoft Map Control dialog box is already displayed, clicking the button will hide it; to do this procedure, make sure the Microsoft Map Control is displayed.

The Microsoft Map Control dialog box is displayed.

2. Drag a data format button from the lower left portion of the dialog box into the big white box in the Map Control.

In this example, I dragged the **Symbol** format button into the box.

3. Drag a data column button into the big white box in the Map Control.

In this example, I dragged the 1997 Sales data button into the box.

The format button lines up with the data button; that column of data is displayed on your map in the format you paired with it (as shown in Figure 21.10).

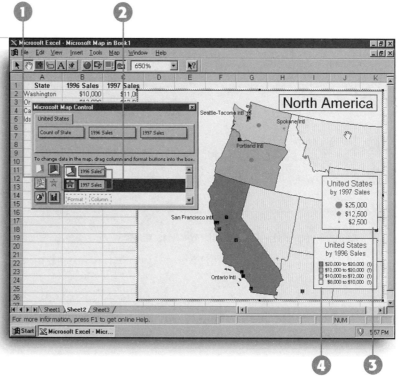

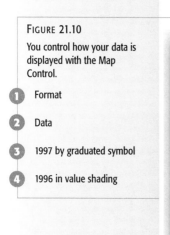

To remove data, or redo the data display, drag the format and data buttons away from the big white box in the Map Control (a wastebasket symbol indicates removal).

Creating Custom Pin Maps

A *pin map* is a map with pushpin markers in it; you can use push-pin markers in maps with data, but they are also a great way to customize a map with no data. You can use a pin map to show information such as where events are held or where you traveled on your vacation. In this example, I'll show you how to create a no-data map and then add your own push-pins and labels.

Create a pin map

1. On the Standard toolbar, click the **Map** button (don't select any data).
2. Drag the crosshair to draw a rectangle for your map object.
3. In the Unable To Create Map dialog box, double-click a map.

    Your map object is created on the worksheet.
4. On the Map toolbar, click the **Custom Pin Map** button. 🖫
5. In the Custom Pin Map dialog box (shown in Figure 21.11), type a name for the pin map (something like Summer Events or European Travels).

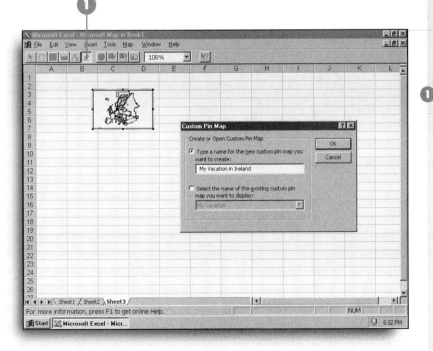

FIGURE 21.11

Name your pin map before you place and label the pins.

1 Custom Pin Map

6. Click **OK**.

Your mouse pointer becomes a pushpin symbol.

7. Click the map to place each pushpin you want.

8. When you finish placing pins on the map, click the **Select Objects** button on the Map toolbar.

9. To label your pushpins, create free-floating labels on the map with the **Add Text** button on the Map toolbar. $\boxed{\text{A}}$

To create free-floating labels, click the **Add Text** button; then click in the map where you want your label. Type the label and click **OK**.

Figure 21.12 shows a pin map with free-floating labels and an active pushpin mouse. Any label on the map can be moved around after you click the **Select Objects** button.

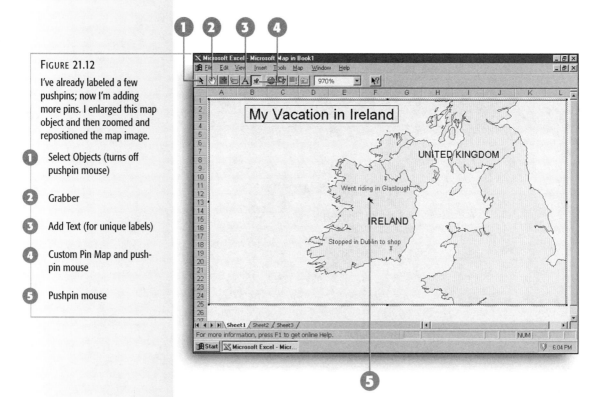

FIGURE 21.12

I've already labeled a few pushpins; now I'm adding more pins. I enlarged this map object and then zoomed and repositioned the map image.

1 Select Objects (turns off pushpin mouse)

2 Grabber

3 Add Text (for unique labels)

4 Custom Pin Map and push-pin mouse

5 Pushpin mouse

To either change the symbol of a pushpin or make it larger, double-click the pushpin you want to change. In the Symbol dialog box that is displayed, you can click a different symbol. To change the size of the pushpin, click the **Font** button, and in the Font dialog box, make your changes; click **OK** twice to close both dialog boxes.

Deciding What to Print

Previewing your worksheet before you print

Printing a quick copy of an entire worksheet

Printing a portion of a worksheet

Printing a chart, with or without its worksheet data

Printing an entire workbook

Previewing Printed Pages

While Bill Gates envisions a utopian "paperless office," you and I know that it's a long, long way off. We still need to print information: to mail out, to pass around at company meetings, to give to the CEO who's still a bit computer-phobic, and to file as a backup to fragile electronic information storage.

You can print a worksheet with one click of a toolbar button; but you might not get the easy-to-read printed pages you want. You can save yourself time and paper if you develop the habit of *always* looking at your pages in Print Preview before you print.

Preview the worksheet before you print

1. Display the worksheet on your screen, as shown in Figure 22.1.

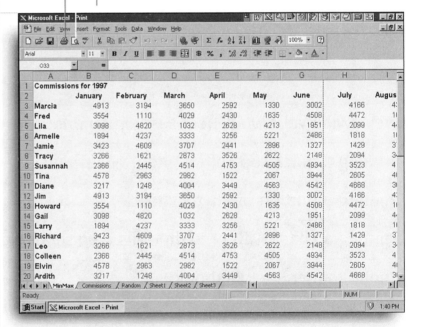

FIGURE 22.1

I'll preview this worksheet before I print it.

1 Print

2 Print Preview

2. On the Standard toolbar, click the Print Preview button. 🔍
Your worksheet is displayed as printed pages, as shown in
Figure 22.2.

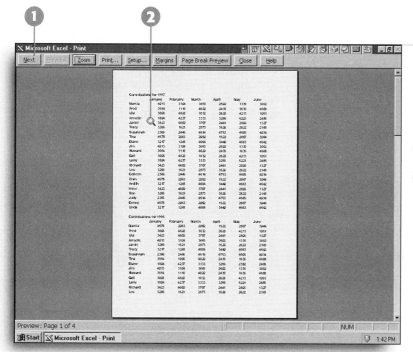

FIGURE 22.2

My worksheet in Print Preview;
to zoom in on part of the page,
click there with the zoom
pointer; click again to see the
whole page.

❶ Button bar

❷ Zoom pointer

There are nine buttons on the Print Preview button bar; Table
22.1 tells you what they do.

TABLE 22.1 **Print Preview button bar**

This Button	Does This
Next	Shows the next page
Previous	Shows the previous page
Zoom	Zooms in and out on the printed page, the same as the Zoom pointer; you can zoom with greater accuracy by clicking on the page instead of the button
Print	Opens the Print dialog box

continues…

TABLE 22.1	**Continued**
This Button	**Does This**
<u>S</u>etup	Opens the Page Setup dialog box
<u>M</u>argins	Shows and hides page margins; you can change margins by dragging them with the mouse
Page Break Pre<u>v</u>iew	Switches to Page Break Preview, where you can see the page breaks and page order for the whole worksheet; to return to Print Preview from Page Break Preview, click the Print Preview button on the Standard toolbar; to return to the worksheet from Page Break Preview, open the <u>V</u>iew menu and click <u>N</u>ormal
<u>C</u>lose	Returns to the worksheet
<u>H</u>elp	Opens a Print Preview help file

SEE ALSO

➤ *To learn more about working in Page Break Preview, see page 424.*

Printing a Quick Copy of a Worksheet

You can print a single copy of everything on a worksheet very quickly.

Use the Print button to quickly print a worksheet

  1. Display the worksheet on your screen.

  2. On the Standard toolbar, click the Print button 🖨.

   A copy of the entire worksheet is printed, using the default print settings.

Printing Part of a Worksheet

Hiding columns or rows before you print

To print nonadjacent columns or rows in a table, rather than the entire table, hide the columns or rows you don't want to print (select the rows or columns; then right-click the selection and click **Hide**).

You won't always want to print your entire worksheet. You can set a specific range as a *Print Area*, which will always be printed without the rest of the worksheet. You can also select a specific range of cells for a single printing (the selection overrides a Print Area for the specific printing).

Setting a Print Area

If you print the same worksheet table every week, you can set a Print Area that allows you to print the table quickly without selecting it first.

Set a Print Area in the worksheet

1. Select the range of cells you want to include in your Print Area, as I've done in Figure 22.3.

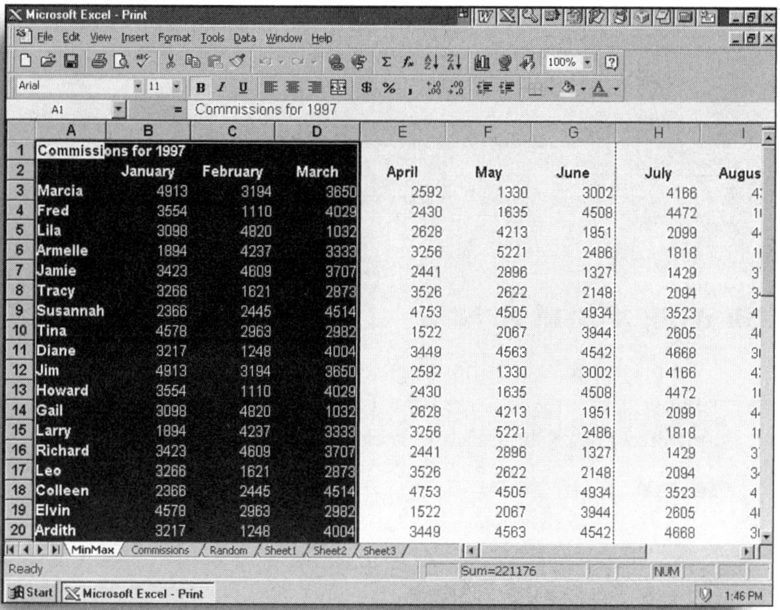

More about the Print Area

The Print Area is really a range named "Print_Area" (you can see it in the Define Name dialog box). To create a self-adjusting, dynamic Print Area, define the name Print_Area with the **OFFSET / COUNTA** formula discussed in Chapter 17, "Summarizing Details with a Pivot-Table," in the section titled "Creating a Source Range that Changes Dynamically."

FIGURE 22.3

You can set any range in a worksheet as a Print Area; the remainder of the worksheet isn't printed.

2. On the **File** menu, point to **Print Area**; then click **Set Print Area**.

The Print Area is set, and a dashed line is displayed around it in the worksheet. You can check it by clicking the Print Preview button; only the Print Area is displayed, as shown in Figure 22.4.

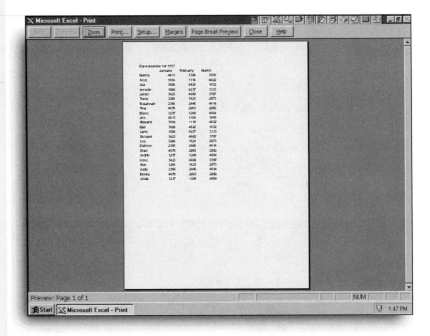

FIGURE 22.4

Only the Print Area is displayed in the preview.

Changing the Print Area

You don't need to remove a Print Area to set a new one; just set the new Print Area, and it will replace the previous Print Area.

Removing a Print Area

When a Print Area is no longer useful, you can remove it. To remove a Print Area, open the **File** menu, point to **Print Area**, and then click **Clear Print Area**.

SEE ALSO

➤ *To learn more about formatting printed pages, see page 421.*

Print several ranges with one click

To set several different, nonadjacent print areas on the same worksheet, select one range; then press Ctrl while you select the remaining ranges. On the **File** menu, point to **Print Area**; then click **Set Print Area**. Each Print Area is printed on a separate page, and you can print them all with a single Print command. To print them all on the same page, hide the rows and columns between the nonadjacent ranges, and then set a single print area that encompasses all of them.

Printing a Selected Range

To print a worksheet range "on the fly" or "just one time, right now," you can print a worksheet selection without setting a Print Area.

Print a selected range

1. Select the range you want to print.

2. On the **File** menu, click **Print**.

The Print dialog box is displayed, as shown in Figure 22.5.

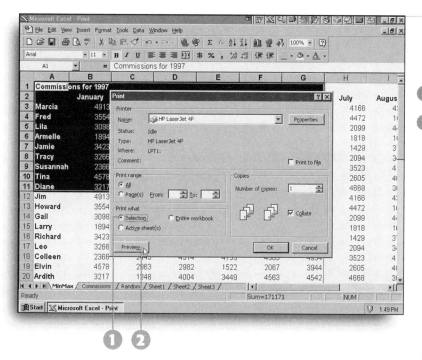

FIGURE 22.5

The Print dialog box is where you change default print settings.

① Selection

② Preview

3. Under **Print what**, click **Selection**.

If you want to check your selection in Print Preview, click the **Preview** button before you click OK; from the Print Preview window you can click the **Print** button (on the button bar) to print, or the **Close** button to return to the worksheet and make further changes before printing.

4. Click **OK**.

Your selected range is printed.

Printing Specific Pages

Sometimes I catch an error after I've printed a worksheet that's several pages long. I have to change and reprint the page(s) with the corrections, but it's a waste of time and paper to reprint the entire worksheet.

Print specific pages from a worksheet

1. Display the worksheet in Print Preview (or look at your printed copy), and determine which page(s) you want to print.

2. On the **File** menu, click **Print**.

   The Print dialog box is displayed, as shown in Figure 22.6.

FIGURE 22.6

To print just page 2, set **From:** and **To:** to 2. To print pages 3 through 5, set **From:** to 3, and **To:** to 5.

1   Print these pages

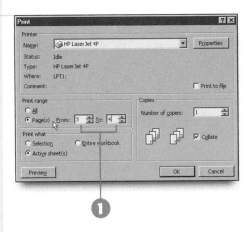

3. Under **Print range**, click the **Page(s)** option.

4. Type the beginning and ending page numbers you want to print in the **From:** and **To:** boxes.

5. Click **OK**.

The pages you specified are printed.

SEE ALSO

➤ *To learn how to fit printed data onto a specific number of pages, see page 431.*

Printing a Chart

A chart can exist as a chart object on a worksheet, or it can stand alone as a separate chart sheet. If the chart is an object on a worksheet, you have three print choices:

- Print the chart alone
- Print the worksheet alone
- Print the worksheet with the chart on it

SEE ALSO

➤ *To learn more about creating charts, see page 347.*

➤ *To learn more about formatting printed charts, see page 435.*

Printing a Chart Sheet

If a chart exists as a chart sheet, it is printed alone.

Print a chart sheet

1. Display the chart sheet.

   Check the chart page in Print Preview before you print, so you won't be surprised (beautiful color charts often require color changes to be readable when printed on a black and white printer).

2. On the Standard toolbar, click the Print button.

The chart is printed. See Chapter 23 to learn about changes you can make to a printed chart.

SEE ALSO

➤ *To learn more about formatting printed pages, see page 421.*

Printing a Chart Object

When a chart is an object on a worksheet, you can print it alongside the worksheet data, print the chart alone, or print the worksheet alone without removing the chart.

Printing the Chart Alone

You can print a chart object without its underlying worksheet by selecting the chart before you print.

Print a chart object without the worksheet data

1. Click in the chart. It doesn't matter which chart element is selected, so you can click anywhere in the chart.

   It's a good idea to check Print Preview at this point, in case you need to make color changes for printing.

2. On the Standard toolbar, click the Print button.

The chart is printed as a full page, just as if it were a chart sheet.

Printing the Worksheet Alone

If you want to print the underlying worksheet without any charts, you need to make a minor change to the chart's properties to prevent it from printing.

Print the worksheet without the chart object

1. Right-click the chart area.

2. Click **Format Chart Area**.

The Format Chart Area dialog box is displayed, as shown in Figure 22.7.

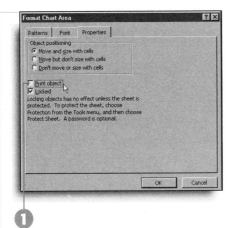

3. Click the **Properties** tab; then click the **Print object** check box to clear it.

4. Click **OK**.

If you check your worksheet in Print Preview at this point, the chart won't display.

To set the chart to print with the worksheet again, repeat the procedure to mark the **Print object** check box in step 3.

Printing the Worksheet with the Chart

Unless you make changes to the chart object's Print properties (as in the procedure described previously), the chart object will be printed with the worksheet when you print the worksheet.

If you set a Print Area and the chart object is positioned outside the Print Area, the chart won't be printed unless you include it in the Print Area.

Printing an Entire Workbook

If you have several worksheets in a workbook and need to print all of them, you can save yourself time by printing the entire workbook instead of printing each worksheet separately.

Print an entire workbook

1. On the **File** menu, click **Print**.

2. Under **Print what**, click the **Entire workbook** option.

   If you want to preview the pages that will be printed, click the **Preview** button. All the pages in the workbook will be displayed in Print Preview; to page through them one by one, click the **Next** button on the Print Preview button bar.

3. Click **OK**.

Print more efficiently

To print a workbook efficiently, set up the Print Area and page orientation on each worksheet so that extraneous pages aren't printed.

Formatting the Printed Page

Changing page breaks, orientation, and paging order

Changing alignment and margins of the data on the page

Fitting data to a specific number of pages

Changing how data is labeled on each page

Creating page headers and footers

Printing worksheet gridlines (or not)

Changing worksheet colors

Printing charts

Changing Page Breaks

Excel automatically sets page breaks at the page margins, but the automatic page breaks often break information at inappropriate places in a table. You can change page breaks so that large tables are broken into pieces where you choose. There are two ways to set your own page breaks: the old way, in the worksheet; and the new Excel 97 way, in Page Break Preview.

Changing Page Breaks in the Worksheet

Set page breaks

1. Display the worksheet in Print Preview (as shown in Figure 23.1), and determine where you need to reset page breaks.

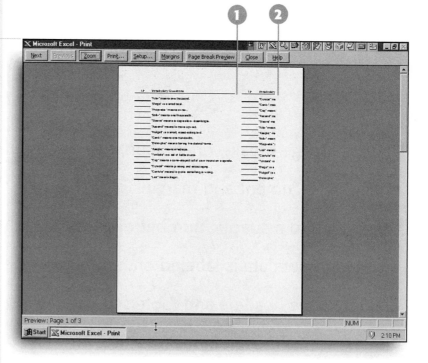

FIGURE 23.1

These page breaks are inappropriate for this table.

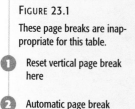

1 Reset vertical page break here

2 Automatic page break

2. Click **Close** to close Print Preview and switch to Normal view.

After you've opened a worksheet in Print Preview, the worksheet shows dashed lines where Excel has set automatic page breaks.

3. To set a new vertical page break, select the column on the right side of the new page break (as shown in Figure 23.2).

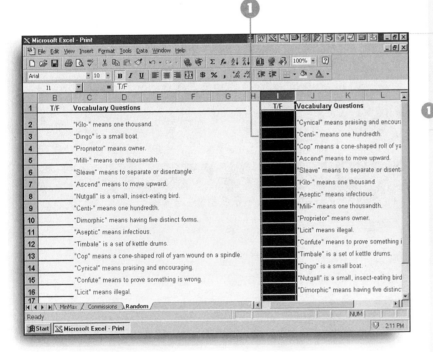

FIGURE 23.2

The new page break is created on the left side of the selected column.

1   Manual page break

4. On the **Insert** menu, click **Page Break**.

A manual page break is created; it's a dashed line with longer dashes than the automatic page break.

5. To create a horizontal page break, select the row below the new page break.

6. On the **Insert** menu, click **Page Break**.

A new horizontal page break is inserted.

Remove a page break

To remove a manual page break, click a cell below or on the right of the break line; then open the **Insert** menu and click **Remove Page Break**.

Using Page Break Preview

Page Break Preview is a new Excel 97 feature that shows you page breaks and page ordering from an "aerial view" and allows you to reset page break lines and print areas by dragging the lines.

You can also format cells, resize rows and columns, write formulas, and do just about anything you can do in Normal view.

Switch to Page Break Preview and change page breaks

1. On the **View** menu, click **Page Break Preview**.

   If you see a message welcoming you to Page Break Preview, click **OK**.

   The worksheet from Figure 23.1 is shown in Page Break Preview in Figure 23.3.

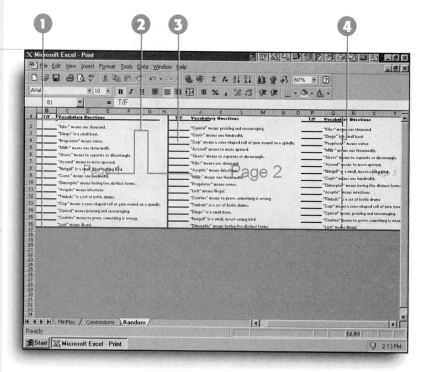

FIGURE 23.3

Page Break Preview puts page breaks, print areas, and page ordering all in one place.

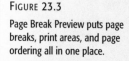

1 Print Area border

2 Page order

3 Manual page break

4 Automatic page break

2. Point to the page break you want to move.

3. When the mouse pointer becomes a two-headed arrow, drag the break line to a new position.

4. To switch back to normal worksheet view, open the **View** menu and click **Normal**.

SEE ALSO

➤ *To learn more about setting print areas, see "Setting a Print Area," page 413.*

Set or reset a Print Area quickly

To reset a Print Area in Page Break Preview, drag the Print Area border lines to new positions.

Changing the Page Layout

There are several aspects of the page layout that usually need your attention, such as the following:

- Orientation, either landscape or portrait
- Paging order, either over then down or down then over
- Centering the information on the page
- Changing page margins

All these items, and others, are set in the Page Setup dialog box.

Changing the Page Orientation

Some worksheets and charts need to be printed in a *landscape*, or wide, orientation, whereas others are better presented in a *portrait*, or tall, orientation.

Change page orientation

1. On the **File** menu, click **Page Setup**.

   The Page Setup dialog box is displayed, as shown in Figure 23.4.

2. On the **Page** tab, under **Orientation**, click the **Portrait** or **Landscape** option.

3. Click **OK** to close the dialog box, or **Print Preview** to see the result of your change.

FIGURE 23.4

Use the **Page** tab to set the orientation.

1 Page tab

2 Orientation

3 Print Preview

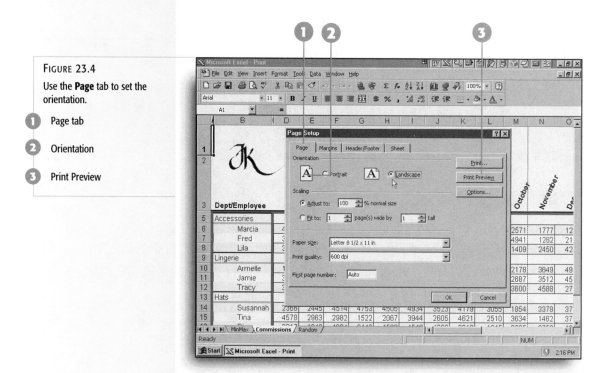

Changing the Paging Order

Paging order is the order in which the pages in the worksheet are printed; if you have a worksheet that's several pages wide and several pages long, you can choose whether to have pages numbered across the width of the worksheet (as shown in Figure 23.5) or down the length (as shown in Figure 23.6).

Change paging order

1. On the **File** menu, click **Page Setup**.

2. On the **Sheet** tab, shown in Figure 23.7, click an option under **Page order**.

3. Click **OK** to close the dialog box or **Print Preview** to see the new layout.

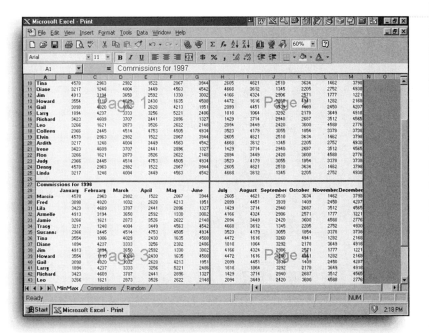

FIGURE 23.5

This page order is over then down.

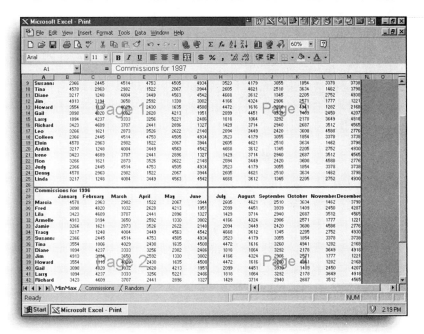

FIGURE 23.6

This page order is down then over.

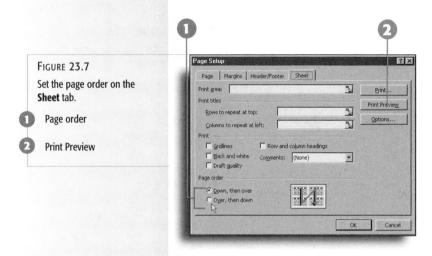

FIGURE 23.7

Set the page order on the **Sheet** tab.

① Page order

② Print Preview

Changing the Centering

By default, the data on printed pages is aligned against the top and left margins. Often your data looks better if it's centered horizontally (and sometimes vertically).

Center data on the printed page

1. On the **File** menu, click **Page Setup**.

2. On the **Margins** tab, shown in Figure 23.8, under **Center on page**, click check boxes for the centering you want.

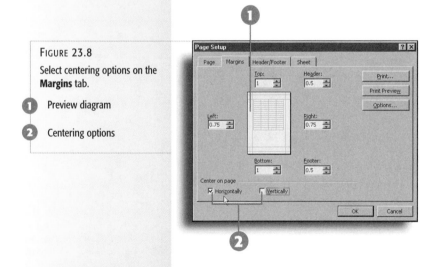

FIGURE 23.8

Select centering options on the **Margins** tab.

① Preview diagram

② Centering options

The Preview diagram shows you the results of your choices.

3. Click **OK**.

Changing Page Margins

Two common situations exist when you might want to change the margins on your printed pages: to reduce the number of pages by fitting more rows or columns on each page and to change the size of a printed chart.

You can change margins precisely and identically by setting numerical margin measurements in a dialog box; or you can change them quickly by dragging the margin lines in Print Preview.

Changing Margins Precisely by Using the Dialog Box

To set margins with precision (for example, to make each margin exactly 1.5 inches), set them in the Page Setup dialog box.

Change margins using the Page Setup dialog box

1. On the **File** menu, click **Page Setup**.

2. On the **Margins** tab, shown in Figure 23.9, type margin measurements in the **Top**, **Bottom**, **Left**, and **Right** boxes.

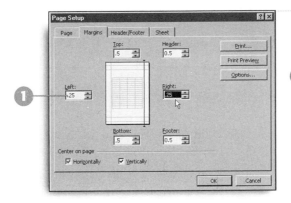

FIGURE 23.9

Set precise margins on the **Margins** tab.

① Type precise measurements

3. Click **OK** to close the dialog box or **Print Preview** to see the changed pages.

Changing Margins Quickly by Dragging Them

Often you don't need precise margin measurements but want to change margins quickly.

Change margins quickly

1. Switch to Print Preview.

2. On the Print Preview button bar, click the **Margins** button (shown in Figure 23.10) to display margin lines on the page.

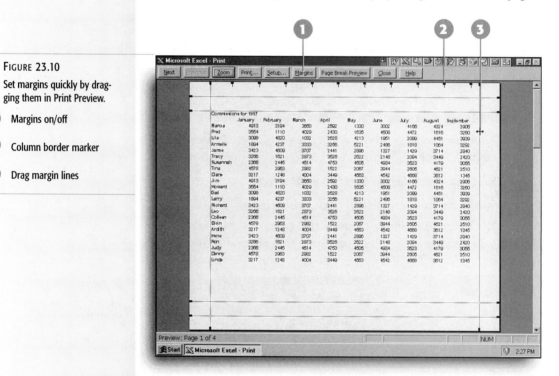

FIGURE 23.10

Set margins quickly by dragging them in Print Preview.

① Margins on/off

② Column border marker

③ Drag margin lines

3. Point to a margin line; when the mouse pointer becomes a two-headed arrow, drag the line to a new position.

4. If you notice that a column is too narrow or too wide in Print Preview, drag its column border marker to resize it.

Printing a Worksheet on a Specific Number of Pages

Suppose you have a table of data that's just a few rows too long for three pages, but you don't want to print a fourth page. You can spend time messing with the margins and page layout to make the data fit on three pages, or you can have Excel shrink the data to fit precisely on three pages.

Fit data on a specific number of pages

1. On the **File** menu, click **Page Setup**.

2. On the **Page** tab (shown in Figure 23.11), under **Scaling**, click the **Fit to** option; then type numbers in the **page(s) wide by** and **tall** boxes.

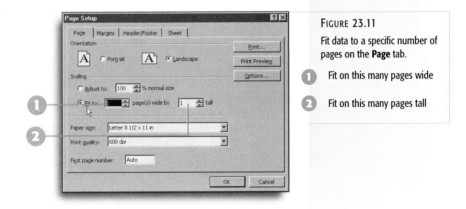

FIGURE 23.11

Fit data to a specific number of pages on the **Page** tab.

  1 Fit on this many pages wide

  2 Fit on this many pages tall

3. Click **OK** to close the dialog box or **Print Preview** to see the changed pages.

Printing Row and Column Labels on Every Page

When you're printing a table that's several pages long or wide, only the first page has both column labels and row labels; on the

remaining pages, where rows and/or columns don't have identifying labels, the data becomes rather meaningless. The solution
to this problem is to set the rows and columns that contain
labels as *print titles*, and rows and columns that are printed on
every page as labels to identify the data.

Create print titles

1. Display the worksheet in Normal view.

2. On the **File** menu, click **Page Setup**.

3. Click the **Sheet** tab (shown in Figure 23.12).

4. Under **Print titles**, click in the **Rows to repeat at top** box.

5. In the worksheet, click or drag the row selectors for the
   rows that contain column labels.

   The row references are entered in the box; these rows are
   repeated at the top of the data table in each printed page.

6. Click in the **Columns to repeat at left** box.

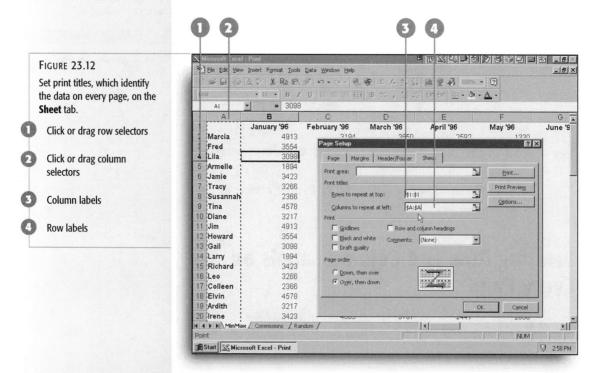

FIGURE 23.12

Set print titles, which identify
the data on every page, on the
Sheet tab.

1 Click or drag row selectors

2 Click or drag column
selectors

3 Column labels

4 Row labels

7. In the worksheet, click or drag the column selectors for the columns that contain row labels.

   The column references are entered in the box; these columns are repeated on the left side of the data table in each printed page.

8. Click **OK** to close the dialog box or **Print Previe**w to see the changed pages.

Creating a Custom Header or Footer

Headers and footers are an important part of the printed page; they can be displayed on every page and show information that's not part of the worksheet. Information that is often put in headers and footers includes a report title, page numbers, and date and time the report was printed.

Headers and footers are created the same way; the only difference is that a header displays at the top of each page, and a footer displays at the bottom of each page.

Create a header (or footer)

1. On the **File** menu, click **Page Setup**.

2. Click the **Header/Footer** tab (shown in Figure 23.13).

Save time on headers

The default header is always the worksheet name; so you can save yourself time by naming the worksheet with a suitable printed-page header. See the section titled "Naming Worksheets" in Chapter 4 to learn about naming worksheets.

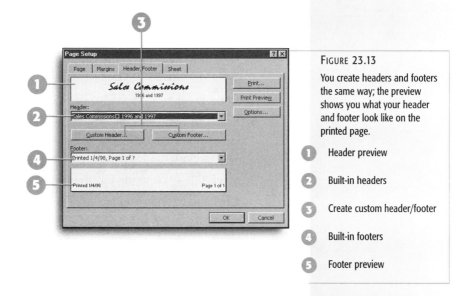

FIGURE 23.13

You create headers and footers the same way; the preview shows you what your header and footer look like on the printed page.

1 Header preview

2 Built-in headers

3 Create custom header/footer

4 Built-in footers

5 Footer preview

3. To use a built-in header or footer, click the down arrow in the **He_ader** box; then click the header/footer you want.

Your selection is displayed in the preview window.

4. To create a custom header or footer, click the **C_ustom Header** or **C_ustom Footer** button.

The Header (or Footer) dialog box is displayed, with default entries. The dialog box (shown in Figure 23.14) has three windows; entries in the left window are left-aligned in the header/footer, entries in the center window are centered in the header/footer, and entries in the right window are right-aligned in the header/footer.

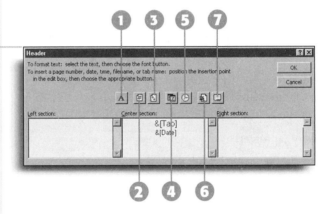

FIGURE 23.14

Custom headers and footers can be formatted and can show automatically updated information such as page numbers and dates.

1 Font

2 Page number

3 Total pages in document

4 Current date

5 Current time

6 Workbook name

7 Worksheet name

5. Click in the window for the alignment you want; then type your custom header/footer text or click buttons to enter automatically updated information.

Press Enter to start a new line in the header/footer.

6. Select text you want to format; then click the Font button (shown in Figure 23.14) and apply font formatting; click **OK** to close the Format Font dialog box.

7. Click **OK** to close the Header (or Footer) dialog box.

Check the header/footer in the preview window to be sure it's what you want.

8. Click **OK** to close the Page Setup dialog box, or click **Print Preview** to see the changed pages.

Printing Worksheet Gridlines

In previous versions of Excel, worksheet gridlines were printed by default, and you had to turn them off. Now they don't print by default, which is usually what you want. There might be times when you do want to print the gridlines, however.

Print worksheet gridlines

1. On the **File** menu, click **Page Setup**.

2. On the **Sheet** tab, click the **Gridlines** check box.

3. Click **OK** to close the Page Setup dialog box, or click **Print Preview** to see the changed pages.

Printing in Black and White

I like to use cell colors in my worksheets to highlight important cells, but I don't want the cell colors (or shades of gray) printed. Instead of removing the cell colors, printing, and replacing the cell colors, I can tell Excel to print the worksheet in black and white, which hides any cell colors.

Print in black and white

1. On the **File** menu, click **Page Setup**.

2. On the **Sheet** tab, click the **Black and white** check box.

3. Click **OK** to close the Page Setup dialog box, or click **Print Preview** to see the changed pages.

SEE ALSO

➤ *To learn more about formatting worksheet cells with colors, see the section titled "Formatting Colors," page 214.*

Formatting Printed Charts

You might want to make two changes to your charts before printing:

- Change the size and/or proportions of the printed chart
- Switch the colors of the data markers to black-and-white patterns, for clear differentiation on a black-and-white printer

Customize your page numbers (or other fields)

To create a footer that reads Page 1 of 4, type Page and then a space; then click the Page number button; then type a space, of, and a space; then click the Total Pages button. You can use this technique to customize any automatic fields in a header or footer.

SEE ALSO

➤ *To learn more about creating charts, see the section titled "Creating a Chart with the Chart Wizard," page 348.*

Resizing a Printed Chart

When you're about to print a chart without a worksheet (whether it's a chart sheet or a chart object), take a look at the chart page in Print Preview before you click the Print button. What you see might need some tweaking.

A printed chart is automatically stretched to fit within the margins of the printed page, which can stretch a tall or wide chart completely out of proportion. You can change the size and/or proportions of your printed chart in the following ways:

- Change the page margins to resize and reposition the chart on its page.
- Select from three options in the Page Setup dialog box, on the **Chart** tab. Table 23.1 explains the three options.

TABLE 23.1 **Printed chart size/scale options**

This Option	Does This
<u>U</u>se full page	Changes the size and shape of the chart to fill all the space within the margin lines
Scale to <u>fi</u>t page	Resizes the chart to fit within the margins, without altering the chart's original height/width proportions
<u>C</u>ustom	Makes the printed chart the same size and shape as the chart object on the worksheet (has little effect on a chart sheet)

Resize and reposition the chart on the page by changing the page margins

1. Display the chart in Print Preview.

2. On the button bar, click the **<u>M</u>argins** button to turn on margin lines.

3. Drag the margin lines (as shown in Figure 23.15); the chart will remain within them, in accordance with the size/scale options set in the Page Setup dialog box.

Chart options in the Page Setup dialog box

The chart options in the Page Setup dialog box only display when a chart object or chart sheet is selected before you open the **File** menu and click **Page Setup**.

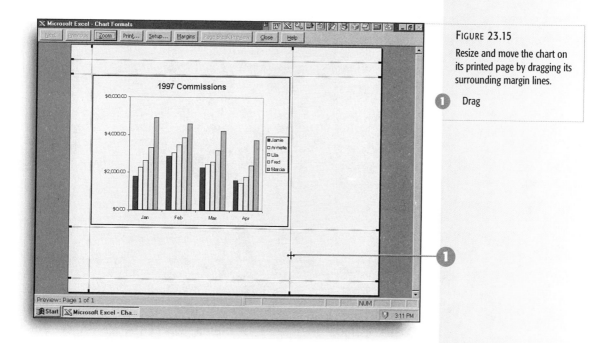

Control the size and proportions of a chart within the printed-page margins

1. On the **File** menu, click **Page Setup** (or click the **Setup** button on the Print Preview button bar).

2. On the **Chart** tab (shown in Figure 23.16), click one of the three options under **Printed chart size**.

   Table 23.1 explains what each option does.

3. Click **OK** to close the Page Setup dialog box, or click **Print Preview** to see the changed page.

FIGURE 23.16

Set printed-chart size and scale options on the **Chart** tab.

1 These options control size and proportion

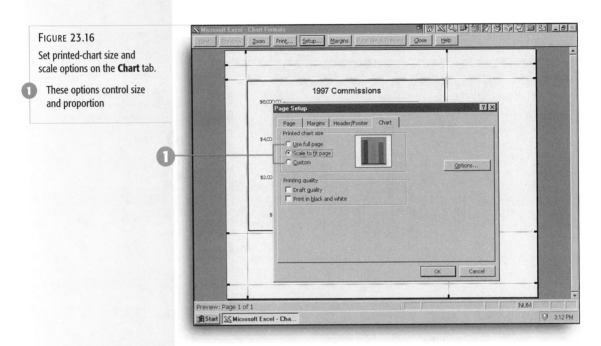

Printing Data Markers in Black and White

If you're printing on a black-and-white printer, you'll be disappointed at what happens to your beautifully colored chart; sometimes the markers are difficult to differentiate and identify because they're all in shades of gray.

To solve this problem, you can print your chart with gray-shaded background fills and borders but have Excel switch the marker colors and their corresponding legend keys to black-and-white patterns, as shown in Figure 23.17.

Print data markers in black-and-white patterns

1. On the **File** menu, click **Page Setup**.
2. On the **Sheet** tab, click the **Black and white** check box.
3. Click **OK** to close the Page Setup dialog box, or click **Print Preview** to see the changed pages.

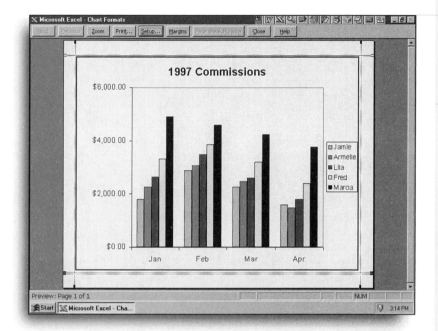

FIGURE 23.17

There's no question which marker is which in this chart, now that the data markers are in black-and-white patterns.

Sharing Data with Other Users and Other Applications

Sharing a Workbook with Other Users

Finding out who's using a shared workbook

Saving a shared workbook

Reviewing changes and resolving conflicts in a shared workbook

Tracking changes in a shared workbook

Accepting and rejecting tracked changes

Merging shared workbooks

Printing a history of changes

Unsharing a workbook

Saving a workbook as read-only

Sharing a Workbook

If you share a workbook with others on a network, two or more people can use the workbook simultaneously. This comes in handy if a team is working feverishly on a project deadline or if several people need access to a list of common data such as expenses, orders, or purchases. When a workbook is shared, no one has to wait his or her turn to open and make changes in the workbook.

If a workbook isn't shared and someone else has it open when you try to open it, you'll get a message box that allows you to choose between opening the workbook read-only (so you can read it but not make changes) or being notified by an onscreen message when the workbook is closed and available to you.

You can also work on two separate but identical copies of a shared workbook and then merge the two workbooks into one for the same results as simultaneously sharing the same workbook. This is handy if someone needs to take a copy of a workbook "on the road" and work on it away from the network and then come back to the office and combine his or her changes quickly into the original workbook.

Before you can use a workbook simultaneously with another user (or use copies of a workbook you want to merge later), you must open the workbook and set its shared setting.

Does this really work?

To test and practice sharing workbooks, you'll need to enlist the help of someone else on your network who can open a shared workbook simultaneously with you.

Share a workbook

1. On the **Tools** menu, click **Share Workbook**.

   The Share Workbook dialog box is displayed, as shown in Figure 24.1.

2. On the **Editing** tab, click the **Allow changes by more than one user at the same time** check box.

3. Click **OK**.

   A message tells you the workbook will be saved and asks if you want to continue. If your workbook is brand-new and hasn't been saved yet, you'll be asked to save it and give it a name at this point.

4. Click **OK**.

FIGURE 24.1

One quick click and the work-book is available to all.

The workbook is now shared, and the word [Shared] is displayed in the title bar as a reminder.

When you work in a shared workbook, you might find yourself unable to perform a task. To save you the frustration of wondering why it won't work, here are some things you can't do in a shared workbook:

- Delete worksheets
- Insert or delete ranges (however, you can insert or delete entire rows and columns)
- Merge multiple cells into a single cell
- Create conditional formats
- Create or change data validation settings
- Create or change charts, pictures, objects, or hyperlinks
- Draw graphical objects with the Drawing toolbar
- Create, change, or view scenarios
- Create automatic subtotals
- Group or outline data
- Create or change PivotTables
- Do anything involving macros

SEE ALSO

➤ *To learn more about saving workbooks, see the section titled "Saving a File," page 46.*

Removing a user

Any user can remove any other user from a shared workbook by selecting his or her name and clicking the **Remove user** button; this might be necessary if someone is finished using the shared workbook but left it open. For more details about removing a user, right-click the **Remove user** button; then click the **What's This?** button that is displayed.

Who's Using a Shared Workbook?

When you open a shared workbook, the word [Shared] in the title bar tells you it's available to others, but you can't tell from the title bar whether someone else is currently using the workbook (or who the current users are).

See who's currently using a shared workbook

1. On the **Tools** menu, click **Share Workbook**.

2. On the **Editing** tab, look at the **Who has this workbook open now** list (shown in Figure 24.2).

FIGURE 24.2

Three people currently have this workbook open. Names come from Excel's **Tools**, **Options** dialog box, **General** tab, in the **User name** box.

1 Disconnects selected user

3. Click **OK** or **Cancel** to close the dialog box.

Saving a Shared Workbook

If more than one user has made entries in a shared workbook, you'll see the other entries when you save the workbook. Whoever saves the workbook gets to decide which changes to keep.

Save a shared workbook

1. On the toolbar, click Save. 🖫

A message that other users have made changes might be displayed; if it is, read it and click **OK** to close it.

Changed cells have colored borders and a colored triangle in the upper-left corner; the color identifies who made the change. The colored borders and triangles will disappear after changes are accepted or rejected (which you'll learn about in the following sections).

2. Point to a changed cell.

A comment like the one in Figure 24.3 is displayed, with information about the changes.

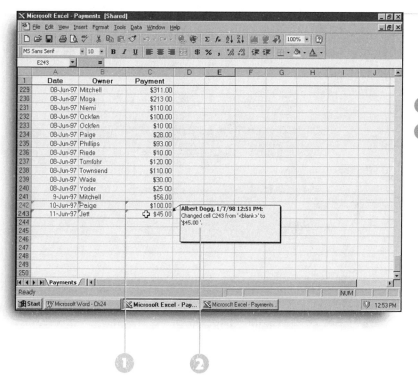

FIGURE 24.3

Every time the workbook is saved, each worksheet shows you where changes were made since you last saved.

1 Change indicator

2 Change comment

Reviewing Changes in a Shared Workbook

If two or more people have made changes to the same cell, a conflict arises when the workbook is saved: Which changes should Excel keep?

Excel keeps track of all the changes made in a shared workbook; you can review all the changes and decide individually which changes to keep, either when you save the workbook or later when you want to see what's been happening in the workbook while you were away.

Resolving Conflicts in a Shared Workbook

When you save a workbook that contains conflicting changes, you can resolve the conflicts in the Resolve Conflicts dialog box (shown in Figure 24.4) and accept or reject any changes.

FIGURE 24.4

The Resolve Conflicts dialog box is displayed only when there are two or more saved changes to a cell.

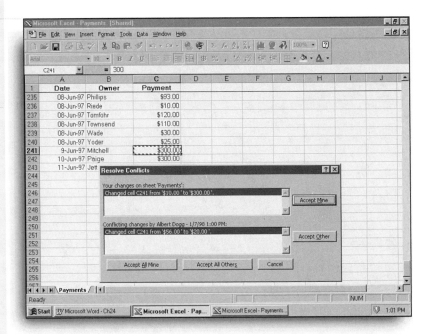

I'm not conflict oriented

To set up the shared workbook so that whoever saves the workbook gets his or her changes saved, open the **Tools** menu and click **Share Workbook**; on the **Advanced** tab of the Share Workbook dialog box, click the option for **The changes being saved win**. There won't be any conflicts to resolve.

If the Resolve Conflicts dialog box is displayed when you save the workbook

- To keep your change (displayed in the dialog box), click **Accept Mine**.

- To keep the other change displayed in the dialog box, click **Accept Other**.

- To keep only your changes throughout the worksheet, without reviewing them, click **Accept All Mine**.

- To keep all the other changes in the worksheet without reviewing them, click **Accept All Others**.

- To postpone the conflict resolution until later, click **Cancel**. (You'll see a message that the worksheet hasn't been saved; click **OK** to continue.)

The Resolve Conflicts dialog box closes itself when you finish.

Tracking Changes in a Shared Workbook

If you've just opened a shared workbook and want to see what changes have been made in your absence, you can highlight every changed cell on a worksheet and accept or reject any changes that were made.

Highlighting Changed Cells

You can see which cells have been changed by highlighting them.

Highlight changed cells

1. On the **Tools** menu, point to **Track Changes**; then click **Highlight Changes**.

   The Highlight Changes dialog box is displayed, as shown in Figure 24.5.

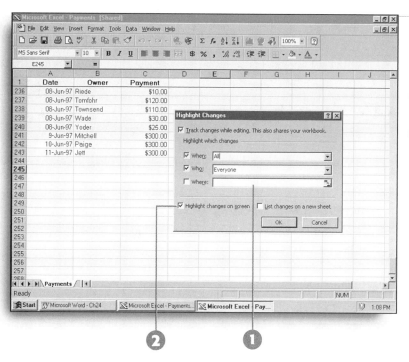

FIGURE 24.5

To save time, you can be quite specific about which changes you want to see.

1 Drag to enter a specific worksheet range

2 Show the changed cells

2. Select the changes you want to see by clicking the **When**, **Who**, and/or **Where** check boxes and selecting alternatives from the drop-down lists.

3. Click **OK**.

All the changes you elected to see are highlighted with colored borders and change indicators, like the changed cells in Figure 24.6.

FIGURE 24.6

The cell borders and change indicators are different colors depending on who made the change. (The person's Excel username is displayed in a comment when you point at a changed cell.)

1 Change indicator

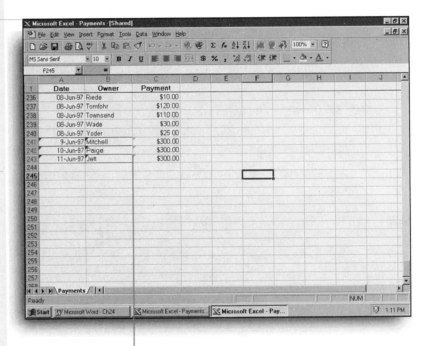

Accepting and Rejecting Tracked Changes

After you highlight changed cells, you can accept or reject the changes; you can review the changes individually, to accept some and reject others, or you can accept or reject the whole set of highlighted changes.

Accept or reject changes

1. On the **Tools** menu, point to **Track Changes**; then click **Accept or Reject Changes**.

At this point you might see a message that the workbook will be saved; click **OK** to continue. Then you might see the Resolve Conflicts dialog box; you'll have to accept or reject conflicting changes to satisfy the dialog box. (You might or might not see this message and dialog box before you see the Select Changes to Accept or Reject dialog box, depending on what has transpired among users of the shared workbook.)

The Select Changes to Accept or Reject dialog box is displayed, as shown in Figure 24.7.

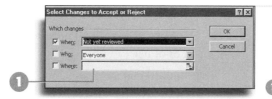

FIGURE 24.7

You can save time by narrowing the range of changes to accept or reject.

① Click here; then drag to limit worksheet range

2. In the Select Changes to Accept or Reject dialog box, click the **When**, **Who**, and/or **Where** check boxes and select alternatives from the drop-down lists to limit the changes you want to see.

3. Click **OK**.

If there are changes within the limits you set, the Accept or Reject Changes dialog box is displayed, as shown in Figure 24.8. (If there are no changes, you'll see a message to that effect; click **OK** to continue.)

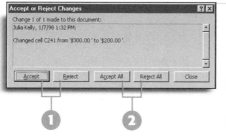

FIGURE 24.8

Sort through the changes individually or accept/reject the whole lot.

① Accept/reject the displayed change

② Accept/reject all the changes you specified

4. To accept or reject changes, either individually or en masse, click the appropriate buttons in the dialog box.

When all changes have been reviewed, the dialog box closes itself.

Merging Shared Workbooks

You can send identical copies of a workbook to others, let each make his or her own changes and additions to the workbook, and then merge all the copies back into a single workbook.

There are specific requirements that workbooks must meet so that they can be merged:

- The original workbook must be shared before you make copies of it.

- In the original workbook, you must set a number of days to track the change history (on the Share Workbook dialog box, **Advanced** tab). By default, Excel keeps a change history for 30 days.

- The workbook copies must be merged before the change history days run out. (So if you don't change any default settings, you've got a month.)

- You can only merge copies of the original workbook with each other. (Workbooks that are similar but not copies won't merge.)

- Each copy of the workbook must have a different filename.

When you've made copies of a shared workbook and made changes to one or all of the copies, you can merge them all back together into a single workbook. In the merged workbook, you can highlight, accept, and reject changes and conflicting information just as if the changes had been made to a single shared workbook.

Merge copies of a shared workbook

1. Open the copy of the shared workbook that will become the main shared workbook.

2. On the **Tools** menu, click **Merge Workbooks**.

   If the merge workbook has any unsaved changes in it, you'll see a message asking you to save the workbook. Click **OK**.

The Select Files to Merge Into Current Workbook dialog box is displayed; it looks and works like the Open and Save dialog boxes you're familiar with.

3. In the Select Files to Merge Into Current Workbook dialog box, click the name of a shared copy you want to merge.

4. Click **OK**.

5. Repeat steps 2 through 4 for each copy you want to merge into the main shared workbook.

The main shared workbook shows changes and conflicts with changed-cell colored borders and indicators.

Printing a History of Changes

By default, Excel keeps track of the changes that have been made to a shared workbook for the past 30 days. For example, if a specific cell has been changed back and forth several times, each change in the tussle is tracked. You can print a change history—a separate worksheet that lists all changes made to cells in your worksheet—as long as the workbook is shared.

Print a history of all the changes Excel has kept track of

1. On the **Tools** menu, point to **Track Changes**; then click **Highlight Changes**.

2. Clear the **When**, **Who**, and **Where** check boxes.

3. Click the **List changes on a new sheet** check box.

4. Click **OK**.

A new worksheet is created, like the one shown in Figure 24.9. The worksheet has AutoFilter buttons so that you can filter to hide changes you're not concerned with and then print the history (to show others who's been wrangling over which data).

SEE ALSO

➤ *For more information on using AutoFilter, see the section titled "Filter a List with a Single Criteria," page 263.*

Merge several copies at once

If you're merging multiple shared copies that are all in the same folder, you can select all their names in step 3 and merge them all at once.

How much history can I keep?

You can change the number of days, or not keep track of the history at all, by changing the option under **Track changes**, on the **Advanced** tab of the Share Workbook dialog box.

FIGURE 24.9

You can limit the change history with choices in the Highlight Changes dialog box and then further limit the display by filtering the changes with the AutoFilter buttons.

① AutoFilter buttons

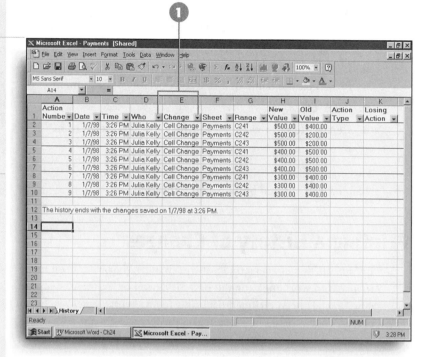

Unsharing a Workbook

The time might come when you need to be proprietary about a workbook; for example, if you want to create PivotTables or charts for a presentation. Because you can't do these things (or other important stuff) in a shared workbook, you'll need to unshare the workbook.

Unshare a workbook

1. On the **Tools** menu, click **Share Workbook**.

2. On the **Editing** tab, clear the **Allow changes by more than one user at the same time** check box; then click **OK**.

   A confirmation message is displayed.

3. If you're sure you want to unshare the workbook, click **Yes**. Otherwise, click **No**.

   The workbook is now available to only one user at a time. If you had a change history worksheet in the workbook, it's removed permanently.

Saving a Workbook as Read-Only (The Opposite of Sharing)

The opposite of sharing a workbook is to save it as read-only, so that others are reminded not to use it. (In its read-only state, others can read it but cannot save changes to it unless they save it with a different filename.)

If you have an unshared workbook open, anyone else who tries to open it can *only* open it read-only. You can make the read-only setting permanent to remind others not to change it, even when you're not using it, but if the workbook isn't in use when they open it, the read-only message is only a reminder.

Save a workbook as read-only

1. On the **File** menu, click **Save As**.

2. In the Save As dialog box, click the **Options** button.

3. In the Save Options dialog box, click the **Read-only recommended** check box; then click **OK**.

4. In the Save As dialog box, click **Save**.

    A message is displayed asking if you want to replace the existing file of the same name with the "new" file. (It's the same file, but this is how Excel makes the change.)

5. Click **Yes**.

    Other people will be able to open the file and read its contents. (They'll see a message like the one in Figure 24.10, and they should, you hope, heed your request to open the file read-only by clicking **Yes**.)

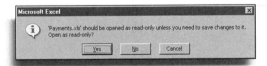

If they want to make changes, they'll have to either click **No** (and the file will open normally) or click **Yes** and then save the file with a different name.

I don't want anyone to see my workbook at all

To protect the workbook so that nobody can open it without a password, in the Save Options dialog box, type a password in the **Password to open** box. (This is a great idea for teachers who want to protect grade sheets from their bright young hacker students.) Be careful: Passwords are case-sensitive (j k is different from JK), and if you forget the password, you're out of luck.

Read-only is only a reminder

If someone clicks **No** in the **Open as read-only?** message, the workbook opens normally, and they can save changes to it. The read-only status of the file is only a reminder, not true file security.

Figure 24.10

This message is a reminder to anyone who opens the workbook.

To undo the read-only setting, repeat the steps to save a workbook as read-only, but clear the **Read-only recommended** check box in step 3.

SEE ALSO

➤ *To learn more about saving workbooks, see the section titled "Saving Files as Workbooks," page 46.*

Sharing Data Between Applications

Pasting, embedding, and linking objects

Sending data from Excel to Word

Sending data from Word to Excel

Changing the source of a link

Using Excel data in a PowerPoint slide

Sharing Data: Pasting, Embedding, and Linking Objects

The biggest advantage in having the Microsoft Office suite of programs on your computer is that they cooperate and share data with one another so well. By sharing data between programs, you can create reports that combine data from Word documents and Excel worksheets on the same page.

A table of data or chart in Excel can be copied to a Word document as simple data or a picture, as an embedded object that can be changed with Excel tools (without opening Excel), or as a linked object that's always current. Information in a Word document can be copied to an Excel worksheet by using the same procedures.

There are several different ways to share data between programs, depending on what results you need:

- Pasting copied data from one program into another
- Embedding an object of copied data and formatting from one program into another
- Linking an object of information from one program into another

This chapter uses several new terms—*object*, *embed*, and *link*—that I'll explain before I show you how to use them to share data between programs. Refer to Table 25.1 for definitions and other useful information.

TABLE 25.1 Shared data definitions

Term	Definition	Double-click Results	Editing Results
Object	A "container" of information that's inserted in another file.	Depends on whether the object is linked or embedded (see following).	
Paste	Pasted data is inserted as text; it becomes part of the file into which it's pasted.	No special results; pasted data is not connected to its source.	

Term	Definition	Double-click Results	Editing Results
Embed	An *embedded* object is connected to the program in which it was created, but not to its source file.	The source program opens, so you can change the object with its own editing and formatting tools.	Editing changes only the embedded object, not the source file. A file containing an embedded object is larger because it contains all the object's data and formatting.
Link	A *linked* object is connected directly to its source file.	The source file and program both open, so you can change the source file.	Editing changes a linked object's source file; all linked copies reflect changes. A file containing a linked object is smaller because it contains only the link.

Sending Data from Excel to Word

If you're creating a report that's primarily a Word document, but you need to include an Excel chart or table, you can paste, embed, or link the Excel data into the Word document. The figures in the following sections show you what happens when you paste, embed, and link data from Excel to Word.

Copying and Pasting Data

When you copy and paste data from Excel into Word, the data becomes a table in the Word document. (If you copy and paste a chart, the chart is pasted as an embedded object.)

Paste data from Excel into Word

1. Open both the Excel worksheet and the Word document.

2. In the worksheet, select the data you want to copy and paste.

3. Right-click the selection; then click **Copy.**

4. Switch to Word.

Isn't drag and drop faster?

If you drag cells from a worksheet and drop them in the document, you'll get an embedded object instead of a pasted table. (It's faster, if an embedded object is what you want.) Hint: to prevent window scrolling when you drag and drop, press Alt while you drag. (If you want to copy, not move, press Ctrl when you drop the cells in the Word document.)

   5. Right-click in the document where you want to insert the
       table.

   6. Click **Paste Cells**.

   The data is pasted as a table in the document, as shown in
   Figure 25.1. The worksheet cells become cells in a Word
   table and carry their formatting with them.

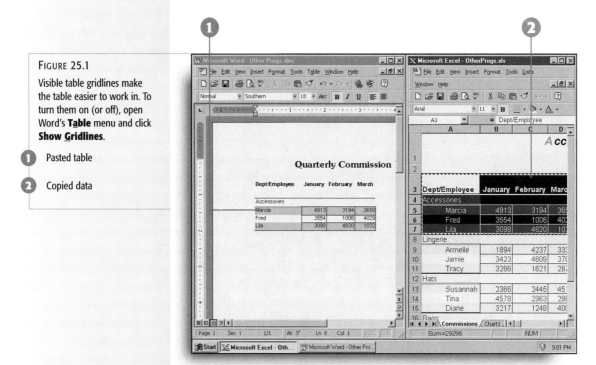

   You can work with the pasted data as you would any other Word
   table.

Embedding an Object

   An embedded object is a picture of the data (table or chart) that's
   connected to its *source* program (the program in which it was
   created). The embedded object can be changed from within
   Word, using Excel's menu and toolbars.

   In this example I'll paste an embedded worksheet table. (You can
   use the same procedure to paste an embedded chart.)

Embed Excel data in a Word document

1. Open both the Excel worksheet and the Word document.
2. In the worksheet, select the data you want to embed.
3. Right-click the selection; then click **Copy.**
4. Switch to Word.
5. Click in the document where you want to embed the object.
6. On the **Edit** menu, click **Paste Special**.
7. In the Paste Special dialog box, be sure the **Paste** option is selected, and double-click **Microsoft Excel Worksheet Object**.

   The data is pasted as an embedded object in the document, as shown in Figure 25.2. The object "floats" on top of the document and can be moved anywhere. (Word text moves around to make room for it.)

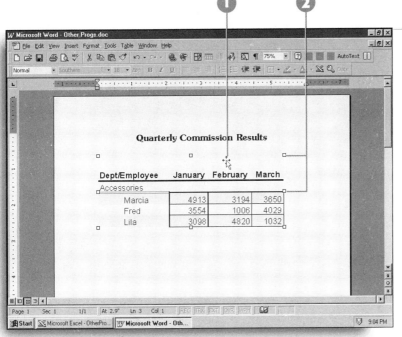

FIGURE 25.2

If you drag the object handles, the object will stretch out of proportion; to resize the object proportionally, hold down Shift or Ctrl while you drag a corner handle.

① Four-arrow "move" pointer

② Object handles

To select the object, click it; to move it, drag from anywhere within the object with the four-arrow "move" pointer; to resize the object to fit your page, drag one of the handles around the border.

Change the embedded object

1. Double-click the embedded object.

   Excel opens within Word. (The title bar still says Word, but the menu and toolbars are Excel's, as shown in Figure 25.3.)

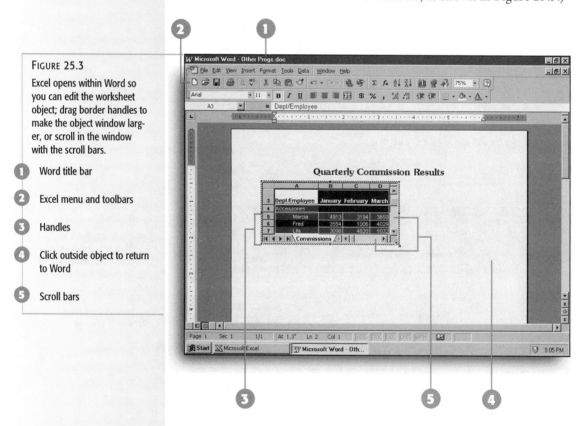

FIGURE 25.3

Excel opens within Word so you can edit the worksheet object; drag border handles to make the object window larger, or scroll in the window with the scroll bars.

1   Word title bar

2   Excel menu and toolbars

3   Handles

4   Click outside object to return to Word

5   Scroll bars

How do I delete an embedded object?

To delete an embedded object, click it; then press Delete.

2. Make changes using Excel's tools. (Because the object is embedded, changes you make don't affect the source file.)

   Be careful about dragging handles and scrolling: Whatever is displayed in the Excel window when you return to Word is what your object will display. (It could be a completely different part of the worksheet than you originally copied.)

3. To close Excel and return to Word, click in the Word document.

Linking to the Source File

Pasting a linked object is similar to pasting an embedded object, but the result is quite different. A *link* is just a short set of directions to the location of the source file (and if the source file is moved, the link might be broken). Linked data is especially useful if you need to make several copies of the same data, because if you need to make a change in the source data (such as correcting a misspelling), you only need to make the change once, in the source file; linked copies are all updated with the change automatically.

For this example, I'll paste a linked chart from Excel to Word. (You can use the same procedure to paste a linked worksheet table.)

Paste linked Excel data into a Word document

1. Open both the Excel workbook and the Word document.

2. In the workbook, right-click the chart you want to link; then click **C**opy.

3. Switch to Word.

4. Click in the document where you want to paste the linked chart.

5. On the **E**dit menu, click **Paste S**pecial.

6. In the Paste Special dialog box, be sure the **Paste l**ink option is selected, and double-click **Microsoft Excel Chart Object**.

   The chart is pasted as a linked object in the document, as shown in Figure 25.4. Like an embedded object, it can be moved anywhere in the document with the four-arrow "move" pointer.

Because the object is linked, you change it by changing the source file.

Change the linked object

1. Double-click the linked object.

   Excel opens, and the source file opens in Excel (as shown in Figure 25.5).

FIGURE 25.4

Click the object to select it and display its handles; to resize the linked chart object proportionally, hold down Shift or Ctrl while you drag a corner handle.

1 Four-arrow "move" pointer

2 Object handles

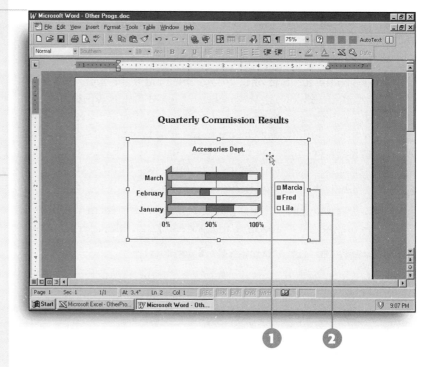

FIGURE 25.5

When you double-click a linked object, the source file opens in its original program. Changes are updated in the linked object immediately.

1 Linked object in Word

2 Source file in Excel

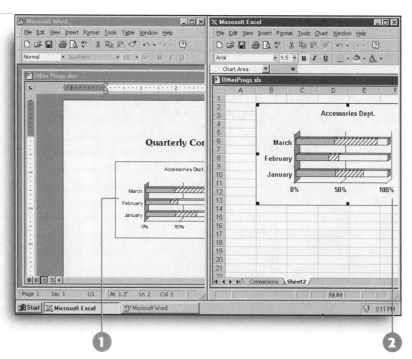

2. Make changes in the source file.

Changes in the source file are automatically reflected in the linked object.

3. To close Excel and return to Word, save the source file; then close the file and close Excel.

If you don't save the source file, the linked object won't show your changes (because it only shows what's in the source file).

When you open a document or workbook that contains linked objects, a message might ask you if you want to update the linked information; click **Yes** to update the file immediately or **No** to preserve the previous values.

Bringing Data from Word into Excel

Bringing data from Word into an Excel worksheet works exactly the same way as pasting, embedding, and linking Excel data into a Word document. The biggest difference is that if you copy Word text and paste it in a worksheet, each paragraph is pasted into a single cell; however, if you copy a Word table into Excel, each cell in the Word table is pasted into a cell in the worksheet.

In Word, select the paragraphs (or table) you want to copy; then follow the procedures described previously to paste, embed, or link them into a worksheet.

Changing a Link's Source

If a linked object's source is renamed, you'll need to update the link so your object can find its data. I'll demonstrate updating a linked Excel object from within Word (but you update a link in a workbook the same way).

Update a link

1. Open the file that contains the linked object.

2. On the **Edit** menu, click **Links**.

The Links dialog box is displayed, as shown in Figure 25.6. It lists all the links in the open workbook or document.

How do I delete a linked object?

To delete a linked object, click it; then press Delete.

To ask or not to ask

If you want Excel to prompt you before updating linked information, open the **Tools** menu and click **Options**; on the **Edit** tab, click the **Ask to update automatic links** check box. To update automatically without being asked, clear the check

Do you have a bitmap logo?

You can use these procedures to paste or embed a bitmap (`.bmp`) graphic; when you double-click an embedded graphic to edit it, Windows Paint opens (unless you have another paint program, like CorelPaint, that opens instead).

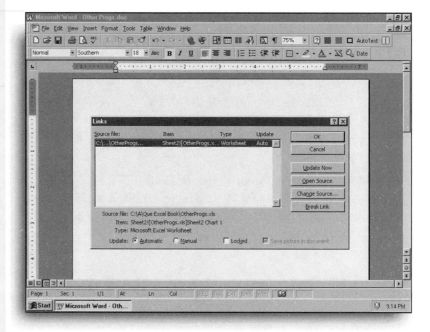

3. Select the link you want to update; then click **Change Source**.

   The Change Source dialog box is displayed, as shown in Figure 25.7.

4. In the Change Source dialog box, browse to the folder.

5. Double-click the new filename.

   The link in the Links dialog box is updated to the new filename.

6. In the Links dialog box, click **OK**.

Now your linked object can display current data again.

Pasting Excel Data to a PowerPoint Slide

Slide presentations that include Excel charts are colorful and powerful. Pasting a chart in a PowerPoint slide is usually a better idea than linking or embedding because it's more easily transportable: You don't need to have either Excel or the source workbook on your laptop computer to support the object in the slide. Also, the charting feature in PowerPoint is the same lame charting feature that's in Word and Access; it's not as powerful, flexible, or easy to use as Excel's charting feature, so if you want to show a great chart in a PowerPoint slide, you'll get better results if you create the chart in Excel and paste it into the PowerPoint slide.

FIGURE 25.7

The Change Source dialog box works just like the Save and Open dialog boxes: Browse to the folder and double-click the filename.

Paste a chart into a PowerPoint slide

1. Start PowerPoint, and open the slide you want to paste the chart into. (See a good PowerPoint book to learn about using PowerPoint.)

2. Switch to Excel.

3. Select the chart object or chart sheet you want to copy and paste.

4. On the toolbar, click the Copy button.

5. Switch to PowerPoint.

6. Click in the slide where you want to paste the chart.

7. On the **Edit** menu, click **Paste Special**.

8. In the Paste Special dialog box, be sure the **Paste** option is selected; then double-click **Microsoft Excel Chart Object**.

Your chart is pasted into the slide; you can close Excel and finish creating your PowerPoint presentation.

SEE ALSO

➤ *To learn more about creating Excel charts, see the section titled "Creating a Chart with the Chart Wizard," page 348.*

➤ *To learn more about exporting Excel data to an Access database, see the section titled "Sending Excel Data to Access," page 112.*

Customizing Your Excel Screen

Using the Full Screen and Zoom features

Moving, hiding, and showing toolbars

Changing buttons in built-in toolbars

Creating your own personal toolbar

Adding and removing commands from the menu bar

Creating a new menu

Customizing Screen Elements

The default screen display for your workbooks is functional and useful just the way it is, but on occasion certain changes come in handy (especially if your monitor is only 15 inches or less, like mine).

Some customizing changes that come in handy are

- Switching to Full Screen, to remove all extraneous clutter and see the maximum amount of worksheet possible
- Changing the magnification of your worksheet, or *zooming*, to see specific details close up and enlarged or lots of the worksheet, all reduced
- Personalizing your toolbars so that all the buttons, and only the buttons, you use are displayed
- Personalizing your menus to add and remove commands

I'll show you how to do all these things; you might find some of them quite useful.

Changing Your Screen Display

Two very useful methods of changing how much Excel "real estate" you see on your screen are Full Screen and Zooming. Both allow you to see much more of your worksheet; Full Screen does so by hiding everything except the menu bar and sheet tabs, and Zooming does so by reducing the size of the cells. Which method you choose depends on what you want to do.

If you're formatting or setting page breaks, you don't need to see cell contents, but you do need to see as much of the worksheet as possible. In this case, you'd want to zoom out and see lots of small worksheet cells.

If you're working with the contents of cells but need to see more of the worksheet to maintain your train of thought, you might want to give Full Screen a try. Also, sometimes folks accidentally switch to Full Screen and can't find their way back to Normal view, so I'll tell you how to recover from Full Screen.

Esoteric display changes

Other screen display changes aren't universally useful, but for unusual situations you'll want to know about them. On the **Tools** menu, click **Options**, and on the **View** tab you'll find several check boxes under **Window options**. Those check boxes change settings for the active worksheet.

Using the Full Screen

To get a big view of your worksheet, without extra screen elements taking up scarce screen space, you can switch to Full Screen.

To switch to Full Screen view, open the **View** menu and click **Full Screen**.

Full Screen view hides the toolbars, the title bar, status bar, and the taskbar and leaves only your sheet, the scroll bars, and the menu bar in view (as shown in Figure 26.1).

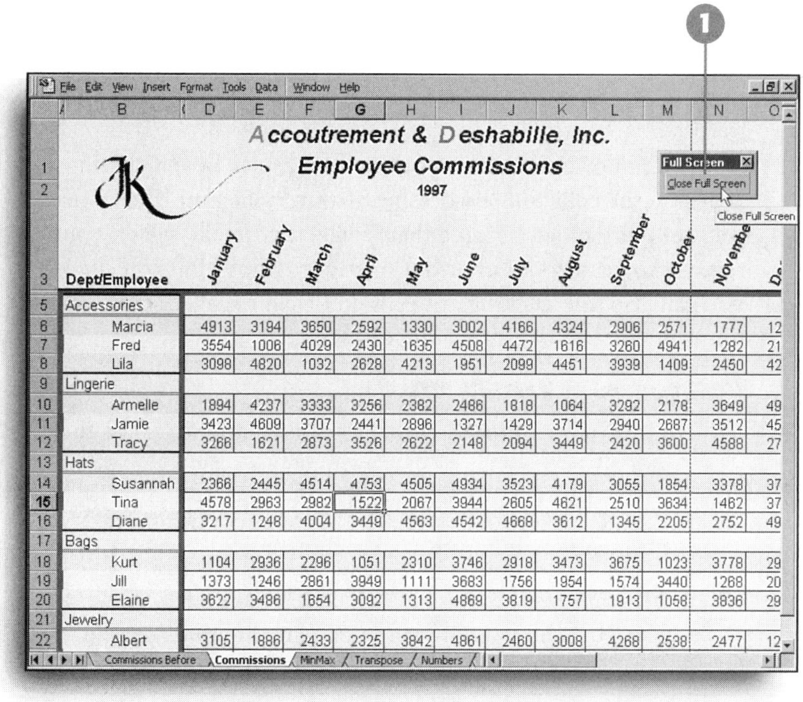

FIGURE 26.1

Full Screen view can be a bit scary at first, because all your familiar landmarks are gone.

1 Full Screen toolbar

You won't want to work in Full Screen all the time. There are two ways to return to Normal view, and you need to be aware of both of them: the toolbar button method and the menu/command method. The toolbar button method is fastest, but if you hide the toolbar (either purposely or accidentally), you'll need to use the menu/command method.

To return your screen to Normal view, do one of the following:

- Click the **Close Full Screen** button on the Full Screen toolbar.

- On the **View** menu, click **Full Screen**.

The Full Screen toolbar has only the one necessary button: **Close Full Screen**; it's an ideal toolbar candidate for adding one or two other buttons you find essential. To learn how to add other buttons to any toolbar, see the section "Personalizing Your Toolbars" later in this chapter.

SEE ALSO

➤ *To learn more about other ways to change your on-screen view, see the section titled "Using Multiple Windows," page 86.*

Zooming In and Out

It's like page break preview

Page Break Preview (see Chapter 23, "Formatting the Printed Page") is a zoomed-out view with a bit more information displayed than in Normal view.

Zooming in or out changes your screen display by magnifying or reducing the cells in the worksheet. It's very helpful when you want to format a larger area than you can normally see on your screen. You can zoom in or out to any magnification you choose; you can also select a range of cells and have Excel zoom in or out to frame just that range in your screen.

Zoom in or out by a specific percentage

1. On the Standard toolbar, click the down arrow next to the Zoom box.

   The Zoom list drops down to show built-in Zoom percentages, as shown in Figure 26.2.

2. Click a percentage.

   Figure 26.3 shows two windows zoomed to different percentages.

To return the worksheet to a standard magnification, repeat steps 1 and 2, and click the 100% zoom setting.

Sometimes a setting of 85% or 120% is preferable to any built-in settings; you can zoom the view to any percentage you want.

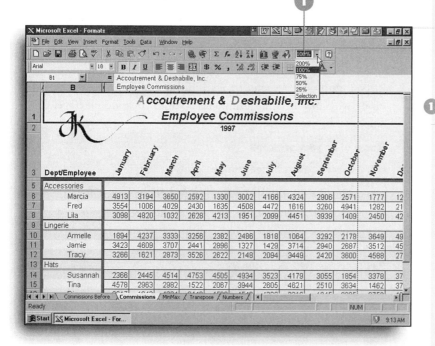

FIGURE 26.2

Pick a built-in Zoom setting from the list, or type your own setting in the box.

1 Zoom

FIGURE 26.3

The left window is zoomed to 75%; the right window is zoomed to 200%.

Zoom to a custom percentage that's not on the list

1. On the Standard toolbar, click in the Zoom box.

2. Type your own percentage.

3. Press Enter.

If you want your selected range to fill the screen, without fiddling with finding the right zoom setting, you can tell Excel to zoom to fit your selection.

Zoom to fit your selection

1. Select the worksheet range.

2. On the Zoom button list, click **Selection**.

Figure 26.4 shows a worksheet zoomed to fit a selected table.

FIGURE 26.4

To view only your selection, zoom to it.

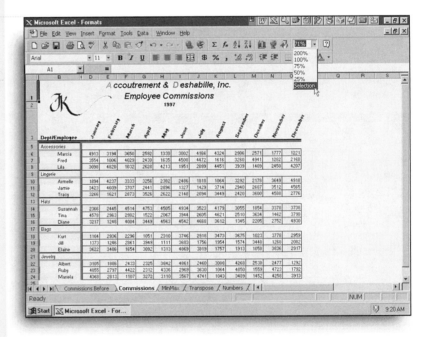

Personalizing Your Toolbars

Excel has several built-in toolbars that you can personalize by deleting seldom-used buttons and adding new buttons. The

Standard and the Formatting toolbars start with Excel by default, and you've probably already used these toolbars. Other useful toolbars are the Chart toolbar that displays when you create a chart (see Chapter 19), the PivotTable toolbar that displays when you create a PivotTable (see Chapter 17), the Drawing toolbar (see Chapter 29), and others that you can show and explore when you're curious. All of them can be personalized.

Some of the things you'll want to know how to do with toolbars are

- Moving them around your screen, including "floating" and "docking"
- Showing them and hiding them
- Changing the buttons they display
- Creating a new toolbar

Many toolbar buttons are multifunctional with the Shift key (so you can reduce the number of buttons on a toolbar and make room for other buttons). For example, you can click the Sort Ascending button to sort a list in ascending order, or you can hold down Shift while clicking the same button to sort a list in descending order. Other multifunctional buttons include Save/Open, Print/Print Preview, Align Left/Align Right, and Center/Merge and Center.

Moving Toolbars

The usual position for a toolbar is "docked," or attached to the top of your Excel window (right below the menu bar); but you can also dock toolbars against the bottom and sides of your Excel window, or "float" them in the middle of the screen, as shown in Figure 26.5.

Move a toolbar to a different location

1. Click the double vertical bar at the left end of the toolbar, or click a space between buttons.

Which buttons are multifunctional?

To figure out if a button is multifunctional, hold down the Shift key and click the button; if the button face changes, it's multifunctional. But don't release the mouse button while you're pointing at the button, or the button action will take effect; instead, slide the mouse pointer away from the toolbar before you release the mouse button.

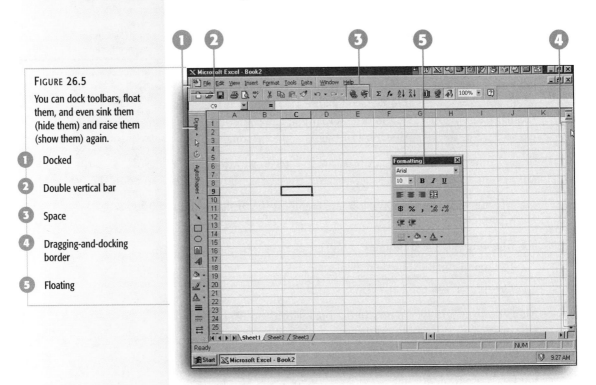

FIGURE 26.5

You can dock toolbars, float them, and even sink them (hide them) and raise them (show them) again.

❶ Docked

❷ Double vertical bar

❸ Space

❹ Dragging-and-docking border

❺ Floating

2. Drag the toolbar to a new position in the Excel window, and drop it.

- If you drop the toolbar in the middle of the Excel window, it will float there; you can reposition a floating toolbar by dragging its title bar.

- If you drag the toolbar to the bottom or side of the Excel window, it will dock against the edge of the window. (The border you drag changes to a light broken line, shown in Figure 26.5, when the toolbar is in docking position.) This takes just a little practice.

- To change the shape of a floating toolbar (like the Formatting toolbar in Figure 26.5), drag one of its borders.

The toolbars stay where you left them, even after you close and reopen Excel.

Hiding and Showing Toolbars

Hiding and showing toolbars is important when you learn to create your own personal toolbars; you'll want to hide the built-in toolbars and show your own instead.

Hide or show toolbars

1. Right-click any toolbar or the menu bar.

The toolbar shortcut menu is displayed, as shown in Figure 26.6.

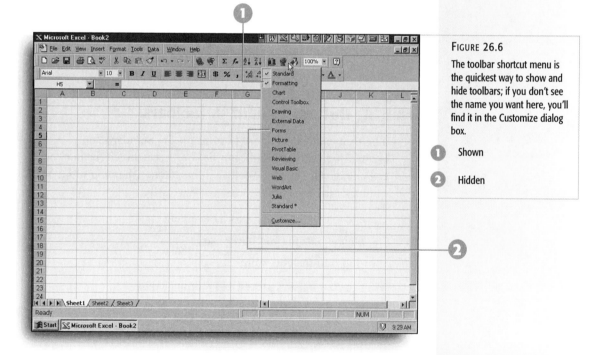

FIGURE 26.6

The toolbar shortcut menu is the quickest way to show and hide toolbars; if you don't see the name you want here, you'll find it in the Customize dialog box.

1 Shown

2 Hidden

2. Click the name of the toolbar you want to hide or show.

The commands are all toggle commands: Click to show, and click again to hide. A toolbar name with a check mark is shown; no check mark means the toolbar is hidden.

3. If you don't see the name of the toolbar you want to hide or show, click **Customize**.

The Customize dialog box is displayed, as shown in Figure 26.7.

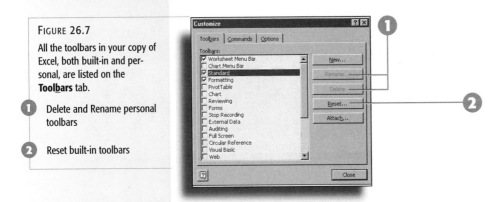

FIGURE 26.7

FIGURE 26.7

All the toolbars in your copy of Excel, both built-in and personal, are listed on the **Toolbars** tab.

1 Delete and Rename personal toolbars

2 Reset built-in toolbars

4. Click check boxes for toolbars you want to show; clear check boxes for toolbars you want to hide.

5. Click **Close** to finish.

Changing Buttons in Built-in Toolbars

The tremendous variety of buttons on the Standard and Formatting toolbars might not fit your needs precisely, but you can change any built-in toolbar to be exactly what you want. You can make these changes to any toolbar easily:

- Move buttons around for convenience
- Delete buttons you never use
- Add buttons you want

Move toolbar buttons around and rearrange them

1. Press and hold down the Alt key.

2. Drag buttons to new positions on the toolbar, as shown in Figure 26.8.

Drop a button between two other buttons to rearrange them; add a space between buttons by dragging a button just a bit to one side.

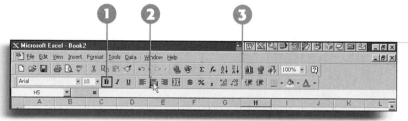

FIGURE 26.8

When you move a button, an insertion marker shows you where it will be inserted.

1 Moving this button

2 Insertion marker

3 Space

Delete buttons from a toolbar

1. Press and hold down the Alt key.

2. Drag the button away from the toolbar and drop it anywhere on the worksheet.

The button is removed from the toolbar.

If the toolbar is one of Excel's built-in toolbars and you make it unrecognizable, you can reset it to its original configuration.

Reset a built-in toolbar's original configuration

1. Right-click any toolbar; then click **Customize**.

2. On the **Toolbars** tab, click the name of the toolbar you want to reset.

3. Click the **Reset** button.

If a message asks if you're sure, click **OK**.

4. Click **Close** when you're finished.

Add buttons to a toolbar

1. Show the toolbar you want to add buttons to.

2. Right-click any toolbar; then click **Customize**.

3. On the **Commands** tab, click the category of commands where you'll most likely find the button you want.

Toolbar buttons are all quick ways to use a menu command, so the buttons are sorted into categories that correspond to Excel's menus.

4. Scroll through the **Commands** list until you find the toolbar button you want.

5. Drag the button away from the dialog box and drop it on the toolbar, as shown in Figure 26.9.

Resetting toolbars

You can reset built-in toolbars, but you cannot delete them; you can delete personal, custom toolbars, but you cannot reset them.

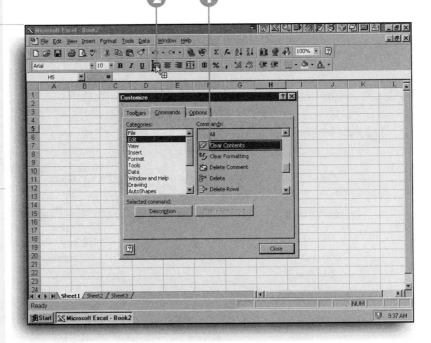

FIGURE 26.9

There are lots more buttons available to you than are on the built-in toolbars; it's worth your time to cruise through the buttons in the **Commands** tab.

1 Drag from here

2 Drop here

6. In the Customize dialog box, click **Close** when you finish.

SEE ALSO

➤ To learn how to create a button or command to run a macro, see the section titled "Attaching a Macro to a Toolbar Button or Menu Command," page 496.

Creating Personal Toolbars

Personal toolbars are about as customized as you can get in Excel; they're a great boon to efficiency and productivity because you have exactly the buttons you want at hand. And, if you share a computer with someone else, you can cause them great strife if you mess with shared built-in toolbars; instead, you can use personal toolbars, which allow you to customize your workspace without messing up your coworker's workspace.

Create a personal toolbar

1. Right-click any toolbar; then click **Customize**.

2. On the **Toolbars** tab, click **New**.

The New Toolbar dialog box is displayed, as shown in Figure 26.10.

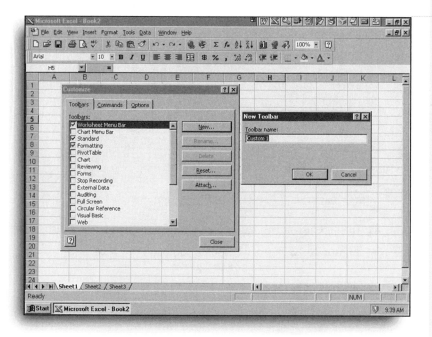

3. Type a name for your toolbar; then click **OK**.

The new, empty, very small toolbar is displayed on your worksheet (shown in Figure 26.11).

4. On the **Commands** tab, click a category of commands that lists the buttons you want.

5. Scroll through the **Commands** list until you find the toolbar button you want.

6. Drag each button away from the dialog box and drop it on your new toolbar.

7. Repeat steps 4 through 6 until you've added all the buttons you want.

FIGURE **26.11**

The new toolbar is empty and small; be careful that you don't lose sight of it behind another dialog box.

1 New toolbar

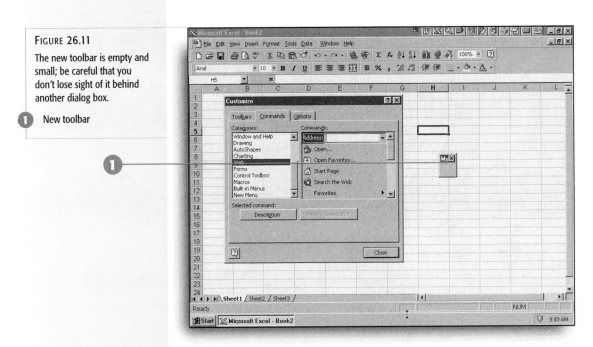

8. In the Customize dialog box, click **Close** when you finish.

Figure 26.12 shows a personal toolbar I use a lot.

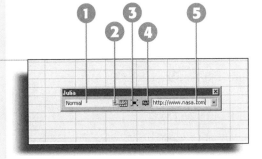

FIGURE **26.12**

My personal toolbar has very useful buttons that aren't displayed on any built-in toolbars.

1 Style

2 Unmerge Cells

3 Select Current Region

4 Camera

5 Address

Customizing Your Menu Bar

You can customize your menu bar to remove commands you never use, add commands you want, and even add commands to run macros (which you learn more about in Chapter 27).

To alter your menu bar, you can remove an entire menu by holding down the Alt key while you drag the menu name away and drop it on the worksheet.

To restore the menu bar to its original configuration, with all its original menus and commands: In the **Customize** dialog box, on the **Tool̲b̲ars** tab, click the name **Worksheet Menu Bar**; then click the **R̲eset** button.

Add a command to a menu

1. Right-click the menu bar; then click **C̲ustomize**.

2. On the **C̲ommands** tab, click the category and then locate the command you want to add to a menu.

3. Drag the command from the dialog box to the menu bar, and hold the mouse pointer over the specific menu item you want to add the command to.

    The menu drops down so you can place the command where you want it, as shown in Figure 26.13.

4. Drop the command in position on the menu.

5. When you're finished, click the **Close** button to close the Customize dialog box.

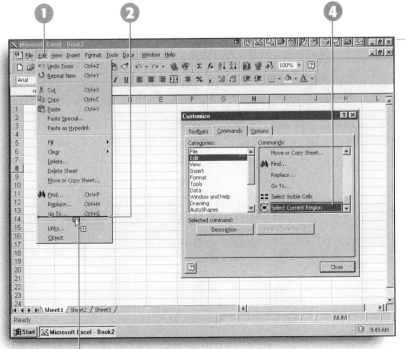

Don't mess with someone else's workspace

If you share a computer with someone else, I strongly advise you not to mess with the menus, because a coworker who doesn't know what you did to his or her menu bar can become irate when he or she can't find the command needed.

FIGURE 26.13

Hold the dragged command over the menu name until the menu drops; then move the dragged command down the menu list until the insertion bar is where you want to park the command.

1 Wait here until the menu drops

2 Insertion bar

3 Drop here

4 Dragged from here

Remove a command from a menu

1. Right-click the menu bar; then click **Customize**.

You won't actually use the Customize dialog box, but it must be displayed to render the menus customizable.

2. Click a menu to display it; then drag the command away and drop it on the worksheet.

3. When you're finished, click **Close** to close the Customize dialog box.

Create a new menu for your menu bar

1. Right-click the menu bar; then click **Customize**.

2. On the **Commands** tab, scroll to the bottom of the category list, and click **New Menu**.

3. From the **Commands** list, drag the **New Menu** command from the dialog box and drop it on the menu bar (as shown in Figure 26.14).

A new, empty menu is added to the menu bar.

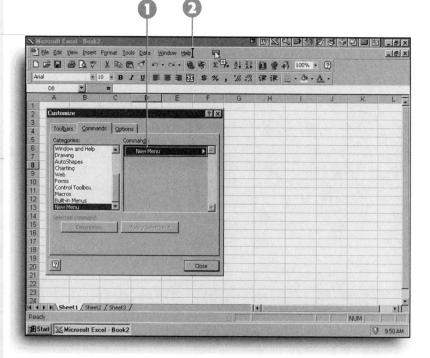

FIGURE 26.14

After you create a new menu, you get to add any commands you want.

 Drag from here

2 Drop here

4. Right-click the new menu.

A shortcut menu is displayed, as shown in Figure 26.15.

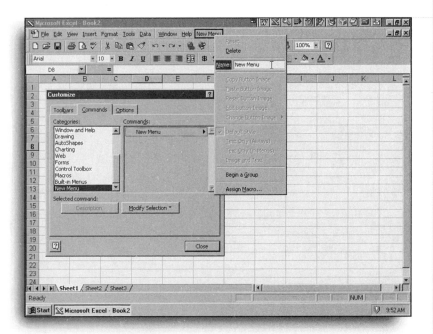

FIGURE 26.15
Create a hotkey by typing & in the name, just left of the hotkey letter.

5. In the **Name** box, delete the default name New Menu and type the menu name you want; then press Enter.

6. Use the procedure "Add a command to a menu" described previously to add commands.

Your new menu will be blank, and therefore very small, until you add commands to it; so be careful that you don't drop that first command on the menu bar by mistake.

7. When you're finished, click **Close** to close the Customize dialog box.

To remove a custom menu, press the Alt key while you drag the menu name away from the menu bar; then drop the dragged menu name anywhere on the worksheet.

Can I make a shortcut key?

You can designate a shortcut key, or *hotkey*, for a menu or command name by adding an ampersand (&) to the left of the letter. For example, to make the *u* in the menu name "Stuff" a hot key: In the **Name** box, type the name St&uff. The new menu name will be **St<u>u</u>ff**.

Automating Repetitive Work with Macros

Recording a macro

Running a macro

Editing a macro

Attaching a macro to a toolbar button or
menu command

Creating a toggle macro

Plan and test your macro

It's a good idea to rehearse your planned macro steps before you actually record the macro and then test the macro after you record it.

Introducing Macros

Some of your Excel tasks are bound to be repetitive. For example, you might import and consolidate sales information on a weekly basis and then format and subtotal the new table the same way every time. Rather than performing the same formatting and subtotaling tasks over and over again, you can create a macro that will perform the sequence of tasks for you.

A *macro* is a series of instructions, written in a programming language called Visual Basic for Applications (VBA), that Excel can follow. To create a macro, you don't need to understand the programming language; you only need to know what Excel commands you want the macro to perform for you. You record the commands by performing them (clicking and typing and so forth), and the *macro recorder* translates them into VBA, which Excel reads as if a professional programmer had written it. Recording a macro is similar to recording music on a tape recorder: You don't need to understand how the music is recorded onto the tape; you only need to know what music you want to record.

After your macro is recorded, you can run it from the Macro dialog box, or you can attach it to a menu command or toolbar button.

Recording a Macro

Before you record a macro, plan out exactly what you want the macro to do and in what order. After you start the macro recorder, every cell you click, everything you type, and every command you select is recorded in a manner similar to a tape recorder.

Name your macro to reflect the actions it performs, so that it is easy to identify later. Macro names cannot include spaces or periods, so if you include more than one word, you must separate the words with an underscore, as in My_Cool_Macro, or use initial capitals to separate the words, as in MyCoolMacro.

Record a macro

1. On the **Tools** menu, point to **Macro**; then click **Record New Macro**.

The Record Macro dialog box is displayed, as shown in Figure 27.1.

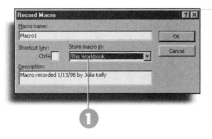

FIGURE 27.1

A macro stored in This Workbook is available only in this workbook; to make a macro always available, store it in the Personal Macro Workbook.

① Where macro is available

2. In the **Macro name** box, type an identifiable name for the macro.

No spaces or periods are allowed in the name, and it must begin with a letter.

3. In the **Shortcut key** box, type a shortcut key, or *hotkey*, that you can click to run the macro.

Be careful that you don't assign a keyboard shortcut that you use for other workbook activities, such as Ctrl+C to copy or Ctrl+V to paste.

4. In the **Store macro in** list, select a workbook to store the macro in.

A macro stored in This Workbook is available only when this particular workbook is open. To make a macro available all the time, in any workbook, click the down arrow on the **Store macro in** box and select **Personal Macro Workbook**.

5. Select the text in the **Description** box, and type your own memorable macro description.

6. Click **OK**.

The macro recorder starts recording immediately, and the Stop Recording toolbar (shown in Figure 27.2) is displayed with two buttons on it: Stop Recording and Relative

A shifty shortcut

You can include the Shift key in your keyboard shortcut, if you click in the **Shortcut key** box and press Shift+*key*. For example, if you press Shift+d, your shortcut key is Ctrl+Shift+d. (You press all three keys at the same time.)

What's the Personal Macro Workbook?

The Personal Macro Workbook is a hidden file that Microsoft Excel creates when you select the Personal Macro Workbook option; it opens automatically whenever you start Microsoft Excel, but you won't see it because it's hidden.

Reference. You can move this toolbar out of the way while you record the macro, if you need to; moving the toolbar won't be recorded.

- Click the Stop Recording button to stop the macro recorder when you finish performing the macro steps.

- Click the Relative Reference button to switch between recording relative and absolute references.

FIGURE 27.2

These are the buttons you'll need when you're in the middle of recording a macro.

1 Stop Recording

2 Relative Reference

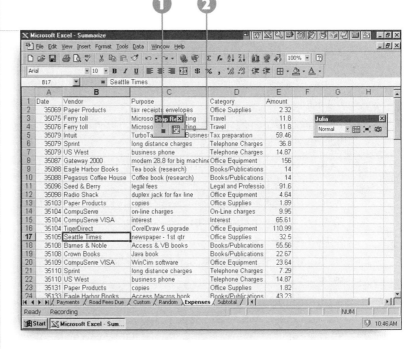

7. Perform all the steps you want the macro to perform for you when you run it.

8. When you finish, click the Stop Recording button on the Stop Recording toolbar.

The macro recorder stops recording your actions, and the Stop Recording toolbar is no longer displayed.

Running a Macro

After you've recorded a macro, it's a good idea to test it and iron out any little glitches before you store it permanently or pass it along to someone else.

When you run a macro, it carries out all the actions that you performed while you were recording.

Run a macro

1. On the **Tools** menu, point to **Macro**; then click **Macros**.

   The Macro dialog box is displayed.

2. Click the macro name; then click **Run**.

   The macro runs, and the macro actions you recorded are carried out.

If you started your recorded macro by selecting a cell and absolute references were used by the recorder, the cell you selected will be selected by the macro. But here are two other possibilities:

- If your macro begins by selecting a cell and the recorder was using relative references, the macro selects a cell relative to the cell that's already selected when you run the macro. If you have problems with your macro beginning in an unexpected cell, this could be the source of your trouble; either re-record the macro with the Relative Reference button turned off (not highlighted or depressed), or edit the macro to replace the relative reference with an absolute reference.

- If you didn't intend for the macro to begin by selecting a cell, but instead to begin carrying out procedures in whatever cell you select before running the macro, either re-record your macro and don't select a starting cell after you turn on the recorder, or edit the macro to remove the cell selection at the start of the macro.

Am I recording relative or absolute?

If the Relative Reference button is depressed or highlighted, you're recording relative references; if the button isn't depressed or highlighted, you're recording absolute references.

Editing a Macro

Just as comments in your worksheets can document how they are set up, you can add comments to your macro to document it so that later you and other users can understand what it's doing. You can also edit a macro by changing recorded actions, to correct a problem, or to refine the macro. Because macros are written in VBA, you need to understand VBA and programming to make serious changes to a recorded macro; but there are smaller changes you can make that don't require a course in programming. (For example, if you misspell a word while recording a text entry, you can edit the spelling in the module rather than re-recording the entire macro.)

Macros are stored in a Visual Basic module hidden in the workbook. To read and edit your macros, you open the module using the Visual Basic Editor. With the Visual Basic Editor, you can add comments to the macro to explain individual steps, and you can edit the steps themselves to change or correct them without recording the macro again.

Edit a macro

1. On the **Tools** menu, point to **Macro**; then click **Macros**.

   The Macro dialog box is displayed.

2. Select the macro name you want to edit; then click **Edit**.

   The Visual Basic Editor opens (shown in Figure 27.3), with the selected macro displayed in the window on the right.

In the macro, some text is displayed in green, some in blue, and some in black. Green text indicates a comment and is ignored by Microsoft Excel when the macro is run. Blue text indicates *keywords* that Microsoft Excel recognizes (in this case, Sub, With, False, End With, and True). Black text indicates macro steps. Comments are always preceded by an apostrophe, which tells Microsoft Excel that they are comments.

The macro begins with the word Sub in blue text, followed by the macro name and a pair of parentheses (in this example, FormatExpenses()). Everything else after this line is a step in the macro, until you reach the line that reads End Sub (in blue).

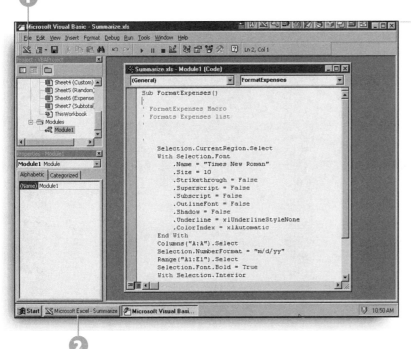

FIGURE 27.3

The Visual Basic Editor is a separate program within Excel that gives you access to your macros. You can switch between a workbook and your macro by clicking the buttons on either the taskbar or toolbar.

1 Return to Excel

2 Return to Excel

To document a macro, add comments to individual sections, either immediately above the section, on the same line as the section, or immediately following the section. It doesn't matter which you choose, as long as you are consistent.

Add a comment to a macro

1. Type an apostrophe and then the comment.

2. Click away from the comment line, or press Enter.

The comment automatically turns green after you click away from the line (as shown in Figure 27.4). The apostrophe tells Microsoft Excel that the text is a comment rather than a step. Adding comments will not affect the macro when you run it, as long as you remember to add the apostrophe at the beginning of the line. (If you forget, you'll see an error message when you try to run the macro again.)

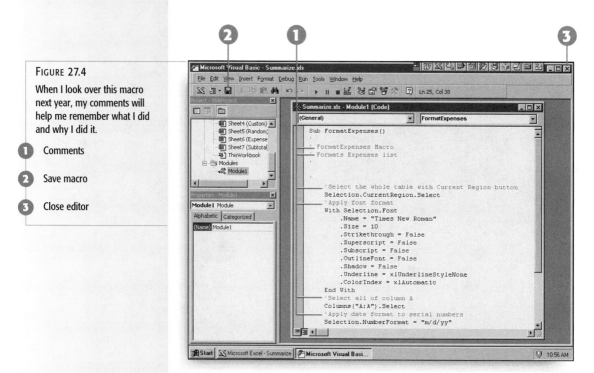

FIGURE 27.4

When I look over this macro
next year, my comments will
help me remember what I did
and why I did it.

1 Comments

2 Save macro

3 Close editor

3. When you finish editing the macro, click the Save button on
the toolbar.

4. To close the Visual Basic Editor and return to Excel, click its
Close button.

Attaching a Macro to a Toolbar Button or Menu Command

After you record a macro, you can run it more quickly by attaching it to a button or menu command.

Create a menu command or toolbar button to run the macro

1. Right-click a toolbar; then click **Customize**.

2. On the **Commands** tab, scroll down the list of categories,
and click **Macros**.

3. In the **Commands** list (shown in Figure 27.5), do one of the following:

- To create a menu command, drag **Custom Menu Item** up to the menu bar, hold it over the menu you want, and then drop it into position on the menu.

- To create a toolbar button, drag **Custom Button** onto a toolbar.

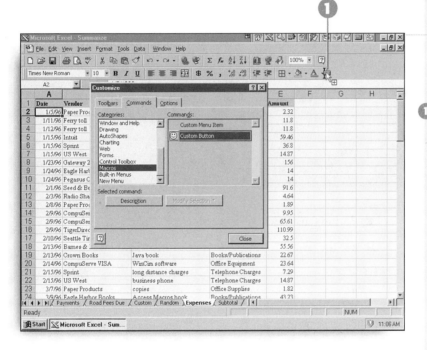

FIGURE 27.5

First, create the custom menu command or toolbar button; then assign the macro to it.

1 Drag Custom Button to toolbar

4. Right-click the new button or menu command.

5. In the shortcut menu that is displayed (shown in Figure 27.6), give the button or command a name in the **Name** box.

6. In the shortcut menu, click **Assign Macro**.

The Assign Macro dialog box is displayed.

7. Click the macro name you want to assign to the button or command; then click **OK**.

How about a command shortcut key?

To create a shortcut key for your new menu command, type an ampersand (**&**) to the left of the shortcut key letter in the command name. For example, to create the command name MyMacro, type the name M&yMacro in the **Name** box.

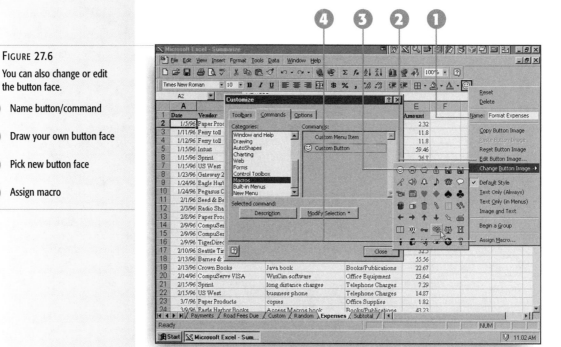

FIGURE 27.6

You can also change or edit the button face.

1. Name button/command

2. Draw your own button face

3. Pick new button face

4. Assign macro

8. In the Customize dialog box, click **Close**.

To test the macro, click the button or menu command.

SEE ALSO

> To learn more about creating custom menus and commands, see the section titled "Creating Personal Toolbars," page 482.

> To learn more about creating custom toolbar buttons, see the section titled "Customizing Your Menu Bar," page 484.

Creating a Toggle Macro

A toggle is something you click to turn on and click again to turn off (like the Bold formatting button or the AutoFilter command). There are commands you can reduce to a single click by creating a macro and then edit the macro to turn it into a toggle macro. To explain more clearly, I'll show you how to create one of my favorite toggle macros: to turn fixed-decimal entry on and off.

This macro is simple to record and then requires a minor edit in the Visual Basic Editor to make it a toggle.

Fixed-decimal entry is something I use whenever I have lots of currency figures to enter in an expenses list; it allows me to type just the dollars and cents, and it inserts the decimal point for me at the two-decimal-place position (it's a lot faster). I don't want it on when I'm not entering currency figures, however, so I want to be able to turn it on and off easily. For clarity in this demonstration (and to make your macro match the one shown in the figures), be sure the fixed-decimal setting is turned off (check box cleared) before you begin recording.

Record the initial macro

1. On the **Tools** menu, point to **Macro**; then click **Record New Macro**.

    The Record Macro dialog box is displayed.

2. In the **Macro name** box, type the name `ToggleDecimal`.

3. Leave the **Shortcut key** box empty, unless you're sure you want (and can remember) a shortcut key.

4. Store the macro in the Personal Macro Workbook.

    The Personal Macro Workbook is a hidden workbook that makes the macro available to any workbook you're working in.

5. Select the text in the **Description** box, and type `Toggles two fixed decimal places on and off`.

6. Click **OK**.

    The macro recorder starts, and the Stop Recording toolbar is displayed.

7. On the **Tools** menu, click **Options**; then click the **Edit** tab.

8. Click the **Fixed decimal** check box, and leave **Places** set at `2`.

9. Click **OK** to close the dialog box.

10. On the Stop Recording toolbar, click the Stop Recording button.

    The macro recorder stops recording your actions.

Where's this fixed-decimal feature?

To find the actual on/off check box, open the **Tools** menu, click **Options**, and then click the **Edit** tab. To turn the fixed-decimal setting on or off, click the **Fixed decimal** check box (leave **Places** set at 2). To make this macro simple, leave the **Fixed decimal** check box cleared (off) before you begin recording the macro.

More about the Personal Macro Workbook

The Personal Macro Workbook doesn't exist until you store a macro in it; Excel creates it to hold the macro, keeps it hidden (unless you unhide it), and opens it every time you start Excel—which is how your macro is made *global*, or available to every workbook you open. To keep it out of your way, keep it hidden unless you're editing a macro that's stored in it.

Next you'll edit the macro to make it a toggle, but because the macro is stored in a hidden workbook (the Personal Macro Workbook), you'll have to unhide the workbook before you can edit the macro. (A macro stored in This Workbook or New Workbook is not hidden; only the Personal Macro Workbook is hidden.)

Edit the macro to make it toggle on/off

1. On the **Window** menu, click **Unhide**.

2. In the Unhide dialog box, be sure **Personal** is selected; then click **OK**.

   The Personal Macro Workbook looks like an empty workbook; don't type anything in it. You're only going to edit the macro stored there.

3. On the **Tools** menu, point to **Macro**; then click **Macros**.

4. Select the name **ToggleDecimal**; then click **Edit**.

   The Visual Basic Editor opens, and your macro should look similar to the one in Figure 27.7. Right now the macro tells Excel to turn on the fixed-decimal setting. I'm going to change the macro action to read as follows:

   `Application.FixedDecimal = Not Application.FixedDecimal`

   This tells Excel that whatever the setting is, it should make it the opposite.

5. In the module, select the words `Application.FixedDecimal`; then press Ctrl+C to copy it.

6. Double-click the keyword `True` to select it; then click Ctrl+V to paste the copied words in its place.

7. Enter the word `Not` after the equal sign; then click away from the line. (Leave a space between the word `Not` and the pasted words.)

   Your module should look like the one in Figure 27.8. The word `Not` is changed into a blue keyword.

Mine says False, not True

If you had **Fixed Decimal** turned on before you started this macro and cleared the check box instead of marking it in the previous procedure, your macro will read `False` instead of `True` and have an extra line. To make your macro match the figures in this demonstration, be sure you start recording the macro with **Fixed Decimal** turned off.

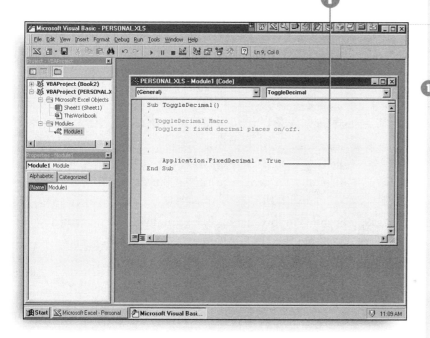

FIGURE 27.7

I'm going to edit this simple macro into a toggle macro.

1 Macro action

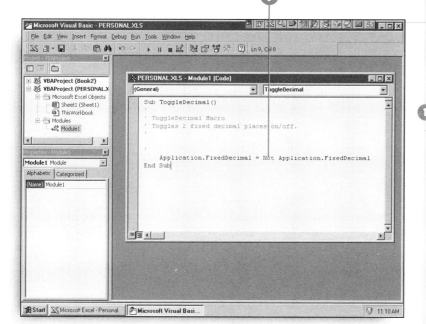

FIGURE 27.8

Now it's a toggle macro: Whatever the state of the setting is, the macro sets the opposite.

1 Keyword

8. On the **File** menu, click **Close** and return to Microsoft Excel.

The VB Editor closes, and the Personal workbook is open. (The title bar should read Microsoft Excel - Personal.) You'll hide the Personal workbook before you exit Excel, but first you'll finish working with your macro. You won't save Personal until after it's hidden and you exit Excel; when you exit Excel, you'll be asked if you want to save Personal.

9. Assign the macro to a button or menu command before you hide the Personal Macro Workbook (see the section "Attaching a Macro to a Toolbar Button or Menu Command" earlier in this chapter).

10. On the **Window** menu, click **Hide** to hide the Personal Macro Workbook. (Don't close it, just hide it.)

When you exit Excel, you'll be asked if you want to save changes to Personal.xls; at that point, you'll click **Yes**; Excel will save the hidden workbook and then exit.

Now you can give it a try.

Open a new workbook. In any cell, type 123 and press Enter. Then click your toggle button or command, type 123, and press Enter again. When the toggle is "on," your entry will read 1.23; when the toggle is "off," the entry reads 123.

When you close Excel after working in the Personal Macro Workbook, you'll be asked if you want to save your changes. Click **Yes**. (If you click **Yes To All**, you'll save changes to any and all open workbooks, which you might not want to do.)

Do macro stuff before you hide the workbook

When you hide the Personal workbook, you'll discover that you can't assign, edit, delete, or mess with its macros in any way without unhiding it; so save yourself a step by making toolbar buttons and menu commands now, before you hide it.

Hiding the Personal workbook is important

If you don't hide the Personal workbook, it will open every time you start Excel; to get it out of your way, you must remember to hide it.

Please don't forget you did this!

Please don't forget you created this macro and then call Microsoft Product Support for help, because they'll probably get mad at *me* for having taught you this. To help you remember, make the button or command name very obvious and easy to find again later.

Using Excel's Built-in Templates

Working with templates

Installing the Template Wizard add-in

Entering automated information in the template

Setting up a database for a new template

Setting up a database for an existing template

Saving copies of a template to collect summary data

Working with Templates

What's a template?

A template is like a preprinted pad of paper. You can tear off new, ready-to-use copies that only need new data entered. All the labeling, formatting, and formulas you need are already in place.

Excel comes with three built-in Spreadsheet Solutions templates, including Invoice and Expense Statement templates, that can save you considerable time by automating data collection. The Template Wizard sets up the automatic data collection for you, links each saved copy of the template to its appropriate database, and collects the summary data from every saved copy of the template. The resulting workbook database is a list of data from which you can subtotal or create PivotTables, like any other list in Excel.

You can use the built-in templates, as described in Chapter 3, "Saving Files and Using Templates," without installing the Template Wizard. The difference is that without the Template Wizard you won't be able to compile and track data from copies of the template.

Why isn't every add-in loaded?

Each loaded add-in uses more of your system resources and memory and slows down Excel just a bit. For maximum performance, you should install only the add-ins that you use. Load an add-in when you need to use it, and unload it when you don't need it.

To collect summary data from every saved copy of a Spreadsheet Solutions template, you need to have the Template Wizard add-in installed and loaded. *Installing* copies the add-in from the CD-ROM into your computer. Loading the add-in makes it available for Excel to use.

SEE ALSO

➤ *To learn more about templates, see page 50.*

Installing the Template Wizard Add-In

Are there more Spreadsheet Solutions templates?

You can download more Spreadsheet Solutions templates from Microsoft for free. Open the **Help** menu, select **Microsoft on the Web**, and click **Free Stuff** to launch your Internet browser and go directly to the electronic ware-

To find out if you've already installed the Template Wizard add-in, open the **Tools** menu, select **Add-Ins**, and look for the **Template Wizard with Data Tracking** check box in the list of add-ins (shown in Figure 28.1). If it's there, it's already installed. Click the **Template Wizard with Data Tracking** check box to load the Template Wizard (and clear the check box to unload it when you're finished using it).

If the **Template Wizard with Data Tracking** check box isn't listed with the available add-ins, you need to install it from your Office 97 (or Excel 97) CD-ROM.

FIGURE 28.1

Load add-ins when you need to use them; unload them for better system performance when you're not using them; uninstall the ones you never use to free up hard drive space.

Install the Template Wizard add-in

1. Close all open programs, and put your Office 97 (or Excel 97) CD-ROM in your computer's CD-ROM drive. If a window to your CD-ROM drive opens, close it.

2. Open **Start**, select **Settings**, and click **Control Panel**.

3. Double-click the Add/Remove Programs icon.

4. Click **Microsoft Office 97** (or **Microsoft Excel 97**, if you installed it separately) and then click the **Add/Remove** button.

   Whether your CD-ROM is in the drive or not, you're instructed to insert it. Click **OK** and continue.

5. In the Setup dialog box, click **Add/Remove**.

6. In the Maintenance dialog box, under **Options**, click **Microsoft Excel** and then click the **Change Option** button.

7. Click **Add-ins** and then click **Change Option**.

8. In the Add-ins dialog box, click the **Template Wizard with Data Tracking** check box and then click **OK**.

9. In the Microsoft Excel dialog box, click **OK**.

10. Click **Continue** (when asked if you're sure, click **Yes**).

11. If asked about removing shared Windows components, click **Remove None**.

12. Click **OK** to acknowledge that the Setup procedure is complete.

13. Click **Cancel** to close the Add/Remove Programs/Properties dialog box.

Load other templates

Before you move on to step 9, you can click **Spreadsheet Templates**, click **Change Option**, and select any of the three Spreadsheet Solutions templates that shipped with your CD-ROM.

To uninstall any add-ins, repeat these steps, but clear the check box in step 8.

SEE ALSO

➤ *For more information on personalizing Excel's Spreadsheet Solutions templates, see page 55.*

Entering Automated Information in the Template

Some of the Spreadsheet Solutions templates, like the Expense Statement template, require employee information that gets collected in the summary database along with the totals.

The macros in the Spreadsheet Solutions templates enable you to enter automatically customized information, such as names, addresses, and employee numbers. These save time and prevent errors for everyone who uses a copy of the template.

Customize a Spreadsheet Solutions template with automated information

1. Open the **File** menu and select **Open**.

2. Navigate to your Library folder (the default path is C:\ Program Files\Microsoft Office\Office\Library). The path in your computer may be different if you changed the folder during installation.

3. Double-click the workbook named **Common**.

   The Common workbook opens (shown in Figure 28.2); it's a workbook of information shared by all the Spreadsheet Solutions templates. It has sample employee data in it to guide you in filling in your own company data.

   You can also enter company data on the Product and Service Catalog worksheet.

4. In the Common workbook, delete the sample data and enter your own data.

5. Save and close the Common workbook.

I forgot how to open my Spreadsheet Solutions template

Open the **File** menu, select **New**, and double-click a template on the **General** tab, where your customized templates are stored.

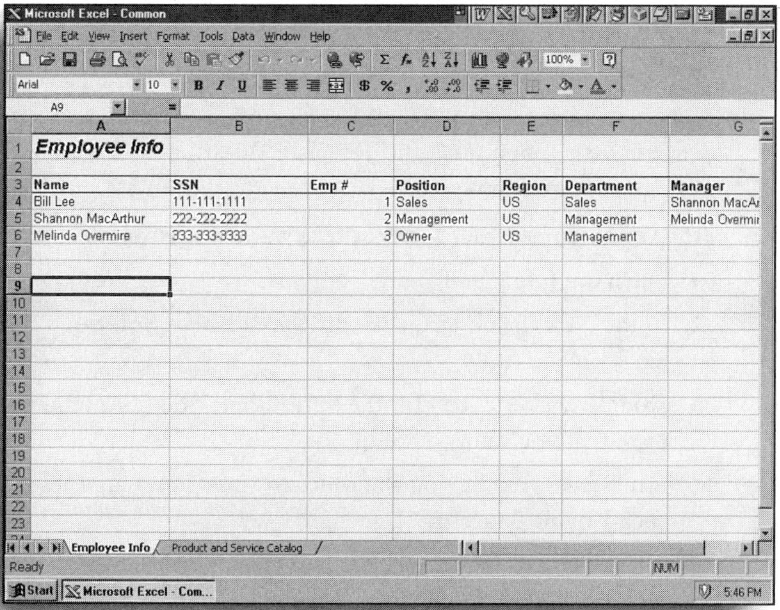

FIGURE 28.2

The Common workbook is a file in the Excel Library in which you can keep employee data that some of your Spreadsheet Solutions templates require.

Now you can open a copy of any Spreadsheet Solutions template that requires employee data, and enter employee information from a list rather than typing it. For example, if you have the Expense Statement template installed, you notice a **Select Employee** button in the Employee Information area. Click the button, select a name, click **OK**, and all the correct employee information is automatically entered.

SEE ALSO

➤ *For more information on opening copies of templates, see page 51.*

Setting Up the Collection Database

You can set up the link between a Spreadsheet Solutions template and its collection database when you first customize the template, or after you've customized and saved the template.

Templates for everyone

If you want to give others access to copies of a customized template, be sure the Templates folder where you save the customized template is a public-access folder on your network.

Setting Up a Database While You Set Up a New Template

If you are customizing a Spreadsheet Solutions template and database for the first time, the Template Wizard guides you through the entire process.

Set up a new Spreadsheet Solutions template and collection database

1. Open the **File** menu and select **New**.

2. In the New dialog box, click the **Spreadsheet Solutions** tab.

3. Double-click the icon for the Spreadsheet Solutions template that you want to set up.

   A message warning you about macro viruses may appear; click **Enable Macros**.

   A new copy of the template appears (a copy of the Invoice template is shown in Figure 28.3).

FIGURE 28.3

A new Invoice template that I want to customize.

1 Customize

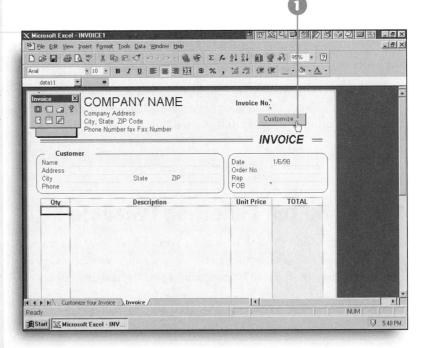

4. Click the **Customize** button.

5. Fill in all the customization information you want on the Customize Your Invoice worksheet.

SEE ALSO

➤ *For more about customizing the template, see page 45.*

6. Find the **Template Wizard Database** box in the Default Information area (shown in Figure 28.4). The path and workbook name you see there lead to the linked database for this template.

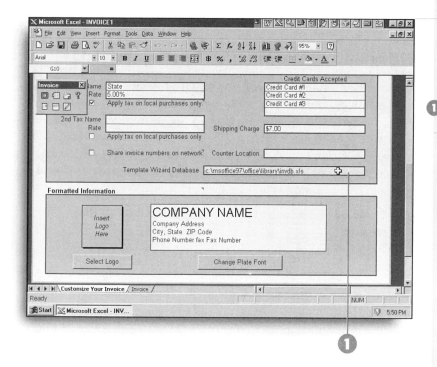

FIGURE 28.4

You want to remember where the collection database is so that you can find the collected data later.

① Database path and name

Because you're creating the template with the Template Wizard installed and loaded, its link to its database is automatically set up for you. If you want, you can change the database using the procedures in the next section, "Setting Up a Database for an Existing Template."

7. At the top of the customizing worksheet, click the **Lock/Save Sheet** button.

The **Lock/Save Sheet** button saves your changes and protects the worksheet from further inadvertent changes.

8. In the Lock/Save Sheet dialog box, click **OK**.

9. In the Save Template dialog box, give the template a name and click **Save**.

    You see a message with information about your new template. Read it and click **OK** to continue.

10. Close the template.

Now you can open copies of your template, enter data, save and close them, and the data is collected in the linked database.

Setting Up a Database for an Existing Template

In the previous procedure, you set up a new Spreadsheet Solutions template and linked it to an automatic-tracking database; however, you can also set up a Spreadsheet Solutions template without linking it to a database and later change your mind about tracking the data. This procedure begins with an existing Spreadsheet Solutions template that's not linked to a database and creates a linked database for it.

Create a linked database for an existing Spreadsheet Solutions template

1. Open the **File** menu and select **New**.

2. In the New dialog box, double-click the icon for the customized template that you want to link to a database.

    Because you're linking a template you've already created (like my Cookies Invoice, shown in Figure 28.5), you find it on the **General** tab.

    Be sure you click the **Enable Macros** button in the macro warning message that appears.

3. In the new template copy, click the **Customize** button.

    The hidden customizing worksheet appears (shown in Figure 28.6).

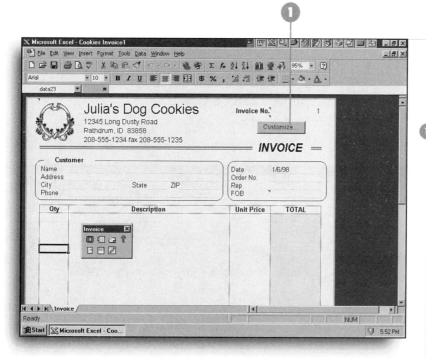

FIGURE 28.5

I set up this invoice template in
Chapter 3, without the Data
Tracking link. Now I'm going to
link it to its collection database.

1 Customize the invoice

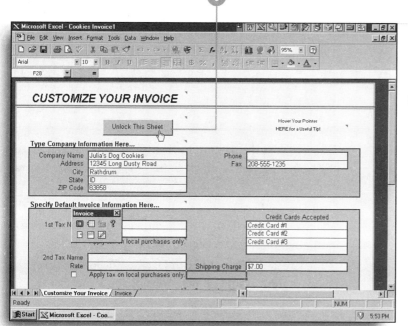

FIGURE 28.6

The hidden worksheet in the
template does the automation
work.

1 Unlock the worksheet

This worksheet is a bit confusing

To learn about any particular data cell on the customize worksheet, click the cell or point to a comment indicator. A comment or text box appears with explanatory information.

4. Click the **Unlock This Sheet** button so that you can make changes to the template and click **OK** in the warning message that appears.

5. Scroll to the Default Information area and look for the **Template Wizard Database** box shown in Figure 28.7 (each template is a little different).

FIGURE 28.7

Each template serves a different purpose and requires different automation information.

1 Capture data in a database

2 Path to database

3 Text box appears when I click the cell

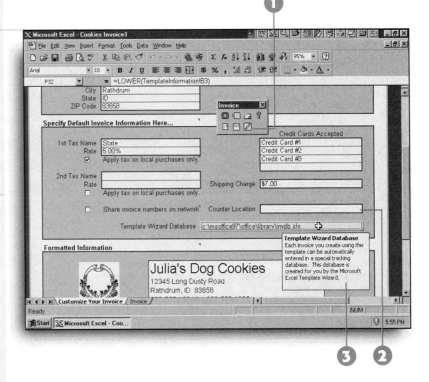

Take a look at the path in the **Template Wizard Database** box so that you know where to find the data collection database later.

6. To create a different database for the template or change the data that's collected, click the **Capture Data in a Database** button on the Invoice template toolbar.

7. In the Create and Interact with Database dialog box, click the **Create a new Template Database** option and click **OK**.

Create a new database for your template

To change the database, you must first save a workbook to be the database in the Library folder. The contents must be recognizable to the Template Wizard, so the easiest way is to create a copy of the default database (the name in the **Template Wizard Database** box) and give it a new name.

The Template Wizard starts.

8. Follow the steps in the Template Wizard to set up a new database for your template.

If anything in the Template Wizard is confusing, click the **Help** button in the wizard step. The Template Wizard help files are remarkably direct and helpful.

Saving Copies of the Template to Collect Summary Data

When a template is linked to its collection database and you open a copy of the template to create an invoice (or whatever) for a customer, saving the template-copy workbook involves an extra step. Excel asks whether you want to create a new record in the collection database.

In this procedure, you are no longer customizing a template; you've opened a copy of the template, which is a normal workbook.

Collect summary data from template copies in the collection database

1. Open and fill out the template-copy workbook and click the Save button on the Standard toolbar. 🖫

The Template File - Save to Database dialog box is displayed (shown in Figure 28.8).

2. To save the data in the database, be sure the **Create a new record** option is selected and then click **OK**.

If, instead, you want to save the workbook without saving the data to a database, click the **Continue without updating** option and click **OK**.

The Save As dialog box appears.

3. Continue saving the workbook normally. Be sure to navigate to the folder in which you save your business workbooks, and give the workbook an identifiable name.

At this point the template copy is a normal workbook, and you can save it with file properties (such as keywords) to make it easier to locate later.

4. Close the workbook.

> **Just one record is saved**
>
> By default, the collection database collects only a single line of summary data from each copy of the template. To collect more or different data from a template, click the **Capture Data in a Database** button on the Invoice template toolbar, follow the Template Wizard steps, and click the wizard's **Help** button when you need more information.

FIGURE 28.8

You can choose whether to save the data in the collection database or not.

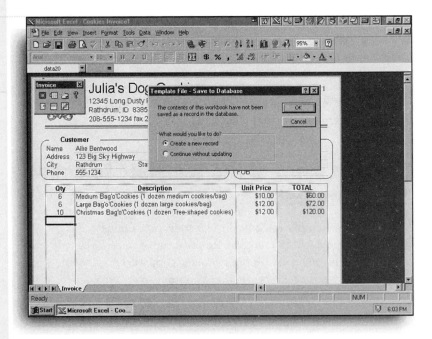

FIGURE 28.8

You can choose whether to save the data in the collection database or not.

SEE ALSO

➤ *For more information on saving workbooks as templates, see page 45.*

➤ *For more information on opening copies of templates, see page 51.*

➤ *For more information on personalizing Excel's Spreadsheet Solutions templates, see page 55.*

Using the Collection Database

After you've saved a couple of template workbooks that are linked to a collection database, you can open the database to work with the collected data.

Open a collection database

1. On the Standard toolbar, click Open.

2. In the Open dialog box, navigate to your Library folder (the default path is C:\Program Files\Microsoft Office\Office\Library; it may be different in your computer).

3. Double-click the name of the collection database linked to your template.

The name of the default database for the Spreadsheet Solutions Invoice template is INVDB. The default name for the Expense Statement's database is EXPDB. For other templates, be sure you remember what the database name is.

Your collection database opens. You can consolidate, subtotal, chart, and add PivotTables to the collected data to evaluate it.

SEE ALSO

➤ *To learn more about consolidating and subtotaling lists, see page 288.*

➤ *To learn more about charting data, see page 347.*

➤ *To learn more about creating PivotTables, see page 304.*

Can't remember the database name?

In the Open dialog box, you can right-click a likely filename and click **Quick View** to glimpse what's in the mysterious file.

Creative Excel

Drawing Objects

Draw basic shapes

Create AutoShapes

Draw text boxes

Change your graphical objects

Convert objects to 3-D

Create WordArt objects

Basic Drawing

Excel isn't about art; nevertheless, like other Office 97 programs it has extensive tools for drawing graphical objects. What's more, your graphical objects can be very functional. You can assign a macro to a drawn object and run the macro by clicking the object.

I give you a basic overview of drawing objects. If you're artistic by nature, you can further investigate and practice drawing objects after I get you started in the right direction.

To draw anything in Excel, start by displaying the Drawing toolbar: right-click any toolbar and click **Drawing**. The Drawing toolbar most likely appears docked at the bottom of your Excel screen (shown in Figure 29.1). Table 29.1 explains the buttons on the Drawing toolbar.

You can more quickly access the Drawing toolbar

You can show and hide the Drawing toolbar even more quickly by clicking the **Drawing** button on the Standard toolbar.

FIGURE 29.1

Some of the buttons on the Drawing toolbar have floating palettes that you can drag away from the toolbar.

1   Drawing button

2   Drawing toolbar

3   Floating palettes

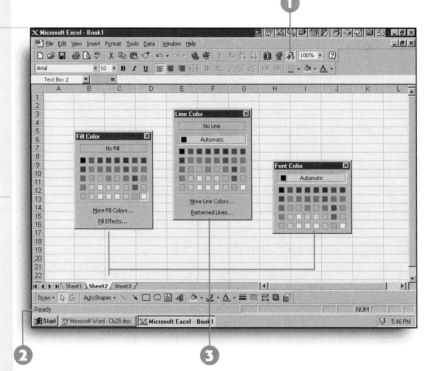

TABLE 29.1 Buttons on the Drawing toolbar

Icon	Name	Purpose
	Draw	Shows a menu with more drawing commands
	Select Objects	Enables the mouse pointer to select objects; click to deactivate it when you want to select a worksheet cell
	Free Rotate	Enables you to rotate an object with the mouse
	AutoShapes	Shows a menu of AutoShape categories
	Line	Draws a straight line
	Arrow	Draws an arrow
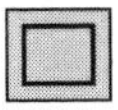	Rectangle	Draws a rectangle or square
	Oval	Draws an oval or circle
	Text Box	Draws a box that holds text
	Insert WordArt	Starts the WordArt program
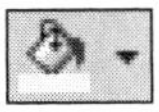	Fill Color	Shows a palette of colors to fill a selected object
	Line Color	Shows a palette of colors for selected lines, arrows, or object borders
	Font Color	Shows a palette of colors for selected text
	Line Style	Shows a palette of line weights (thickness) for selected lines, arrows, or object borders
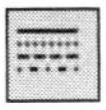	Dash Style	Shows a palette of line dash styles for selected lines, arrows, or object borders
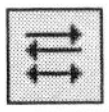	Arrow Style	Shows a palette of arrow styles for selected lines or arrows
	Shadow	Shows a palette of shadows for selected objects
	3-D	Shows a palette of 3-D styles for converting selected objects

Basic shapes include lines/arrows, rectangles, and ovals.

Draw a basic graphics object

1. Click the button for the shape you want to draw (line, arrow, rectangle, or oval).

The mouse pointer becomes a crosshair for drawing.

2. Click and drag the crosshair across the screen, diagonally to create an oval or rectangle, or in the direction you want to create a line or arrow (shown in Figure 29.2).

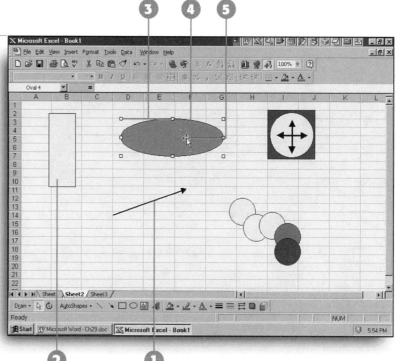

FIGURE 29.2

Drag the crosshair to draw the shape. If your object isn't quite the shape or location you want, you can move it and reshape it later.

1 Arrow

2 Rectangle

3 Handles

4 Oval

5 Four-arrow Move pointer

The following are some tips for drawing and formatting basic shapes:

- To draw a perfectly vertical or horizontal line, hold down Shift while you draw the line. (Shift forces the line into 15-degree angles.)
- To draw any object from the center out, hold down Ctrl while you draw.

I want them all to be the same

To format several objects at once, select them as a group: either press and hold down Shift while you click to select individual objects, or click the Select Objects button and then draw a rectangle around the group of objects that you want to select.

- To draw a perfect square or circle, hold down Shift while you draw a rectangle or oval.

- To convert an arrow to a line, a line to an arrow, or change the direction of an arrow, select the line or arrow object and choose a different style from the Arrow Style button.

- To change line or border weight (thickness), select the object, and then select a line weight from the Line Style button.

- To move an object, click it and drag it with the four-arrow Move pointer.

- To resize or reshape an object, click it and drag a handle.

- To align an object with worksheet gridlines, press Alt while you move the object or drag a handle. The object border snaps to the nearest gridline.

- To draw several lines, arrows, rectangles, or ovals, double-click the button for the shape you want and draw a lot of objects. Click the button to deactivate it when you're finished.

- To copy a shape, press Ctrl while you drag and drop the object.

- To assign a macro to an object, right-click the object, click **Assign Macro,** click the macro name, and then click **OK**.

SEE ALSO
➤ *For more information on creating macros to automate a worksheet, see page 489.*

Creating AutoShapes

AutoShapes are built-in complex shapes, such as banners, flow-chart symbols, and block arrows, that you can select from a menu. After you create an AutoShape, you can move, resize, reshape, and color it just like any other object.

Create an AutoShape graphic

1. On the Drawing toolbar, click the **A̲utoShapes** menu.

2. On the **A̲utoShapes** menu, point to a category and click a shape (shown in Figure 29.3).

FIGURE 29.3

Check out all the AutoShapes available on the different sub-menus.

1 AutoShapes menu

2 AutoShapes object

3. Either click the worksheet to create an instant AutoShape, or drag the crosshair across the worksheet to draw the AutoShape.

The AutoShape is created and all the moving, shaping, and formatting tips listed above apply to AutoShapes.

Many AutoShapes have an adjustment handle—a small yellow diamond that appears when the AutoShape is selected. You can drag the adjustment handle to alter a prominent feature of the shape, such as the shape or size of an arrow's point. You have to drag the handle on your specific shape to see what changes it makes.

Charts, too

Although I'm only talking about worksheets in these procedures, all these objects can also be drawn in charts.

Drawing Text Boxes

Text boxes are free-floating text labels that you can use to add information to a worksheet or chart. You can format them as colored, bordered rectangular objects and change their font. You can also leave them as transparent and place them on top of other graphics to make it look as though the graphic object contains text (shown in Figure 29.4).

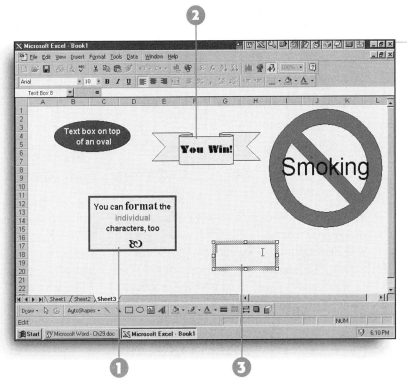

Create a text box

1. On the Drawing toolbar, click the Text Box button.

The mouse becomes a sword shape, which changes to a crosshair when you begin to draw the box.

2. In the worksheet, drag the mouse pointer diagonally to draw the text box.

When you release the mouse button, a text box is created, and an insertion point flashes in the box.

3. Type the text you want.

You can edit and format the text the same way you would text in a cell.

4. Click away from the text box to finish.

To edit text in a finished text box, click the text box. The text box is selected, and the insertion point appears in the text.

To delete a text box, click it, click its border, and then press Delete.

The sword-shaped mouse pointer

If you click the sword-shaped pointer, rather than drag across the worksheet, a small text box is created that precisely fits the text you type in it.

Converting Objects to 3-D

Most objects can be converted to a 3-D shape. If a selected object is not convertible, you know it because the shapes on the 3-D menu are grayed out.

Convert a drawn object to a 3-D shape

1. Select the object.

2. On the Drawing toolbar, click the 3-D button.

3. On the 3-D palette, click a 3-D shape.

The object is converted to 3-D.

For more interesting 3-D effects, click the **3-D Settings** button on the 3-D palette. (Table 29.2 explains what the buttons on the 3-D Settings toolbar do for you.) A few effects are shown in Figure 29.5, but the best way to learn what these settings can do for you is to create an object and test the different effects yourself.

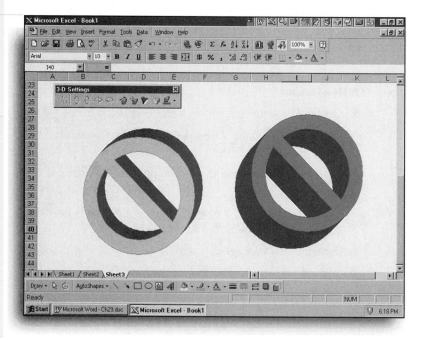

FIGURE 29.5

Be careful with three-dimensional effects; you could get hooked! These identical objects have different directions, surfaces, and 3-D colors.

TABLE 29.2   **3-D Settings toolbar**

Icon	Name	Purpose
	3-D On/Off	Toggles the 3-D effect on and off
	Tilt Down	Tilts perspective down
	Tilt Up	Tilts perspective up
	Tilt Left	Tilts perspective left
	Tilt Right	Tilts perspective right
	Depth	Enables you to choose the depth of the third dimension
	Direction	Enables you to change the three-dimensional direction
	Lighting	Enables you to change the directional source of light and shadow on the object
	Surface	Enables you to choose a material-surface effect
	3-D Color	Enables you to change the color of the third dimension

Creating WordArt Objects

WordArt in Office 97 is a more powerful, more memory-intensive version of the mini-program that creates curved and shaped pictures from your text. WordArt creates really arresting graphics, but a word of caution is in order: Don't plan on printing it unless your printer has a lot of memory. My printer is an out-of-the-box Hewlett-Packard LaserJet 4P, with the standard 2MB of memory that it came with. It's a little workhorse of a printer, but 2MB of memory isn't enough to print a page with even the smallest WordArt graphic in it.

Create a WordArt graphic

1. On the Drawing toolbar, click the Insert WordArt button.

The WordArt palette of text shapes appears (shown in Figure 29.6).

FIGURE 29.6
Start by choosing a shape.

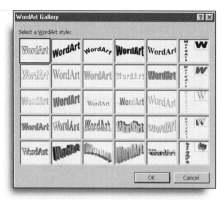

2. Double-click a shape.

The Edit WordArt Text dialog box appears (shown in Figure 29.7).

FIGURE 29.7

The best way to learn what looks good in WordArt is to test different ideas.

1   Formatting tool

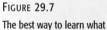

3. Type your text in the **Text** box.

4. Use the formatting tools in the Edit WordArt Text dialog box to format your text.

5. Click **OK**.

Your WordArt object is created, and the WordArt toolbar appears (shown in Figure 29.8). Table 29.3 explains what the WordArt toolbar buttons do.

FIGURE 29.8
Don't get too carried away, or your data is overshadowed by the graphics.

TABLE 29.3   **WordArt toolbar buttons**

Icon	Name	Purpose
	Insert WordArt	Adds a new WordArt object
	Edit Text	Enables you to change text in a selected WordArt object
	WordArt Gallery	Enables you to change the shape of a selected WordArt object
	Format WordArt	Opens the Formatting dialog box for a selected WordArt object
	WordArt Shape	Gives you more WordArt shapes from which to choose
	Free Rotate	Enables you to rotate the object (drag a corner dot to rotate)
	WordArt Same	Makes all letters in WordArt object the Letter Heights same height
	WordArt Vertical Text	Changes WordArt text alignment to vertical

continues…

TABLE 29.3   Continued

Icon	Name	Purpose
	WordArt Alignment	Lets you change how words are stretched and aligned
	WordArt Character Spacing	Enables you to tighten or loosen letter spacing in a WordArt object

Creative Worksheets

Kurt's invoice, an invoice that combines AutoFilter, macros, and printing in a creative business solution

A theatre seating chart, a creative Excel approach that makes business in a theatre reservations office more efficient

Creative Approaches to Worksheet Applications

This chapter is about creative ways to combine different techniques covered in this book. It's by no means exhaustive, and if you really get interested in creative worksheet techniques, there is a lot more to learn. I hope these two examples inspire you to look for ways to be creative with your own Excel work.

I show you two real-life Excel projects that I created as solutions for clients' questions. First I show you the finished project and explain how it works and then guide you through the creation of a simple example of each. The procedures for creating these projects are loose and general because I want you to inject your own creativity into the process.

Kurt's Invoice—A Creative Invoice Solution

My friend Kurt wanted to figure out how to make an invoice out of a long parts-and-prices list. His original idea was to write a VBA program; however, I'm not a programmer by nature, so I always look for an easier route. In this case, I thought AutoFilter might be the perfect answer.

To demonstrate the solution, I've created an invoice for the fictitious Stony Keep Soap and Pottery company, which sells handmade vegetable soaps and handmade pottery pieces.

How Kurt's Invoice Works

Figure 30.1 shows the finished worksheet. To create the invoice for an order, you type a quantity for each item ordered. The worksheet has formulas that automatically calculate item totals and an invoice total.

The two text boxes on the worksheet run macros. One macro filters and prints the invoice, and the other macro returns the worksheet to its original condition, ready to take another order.

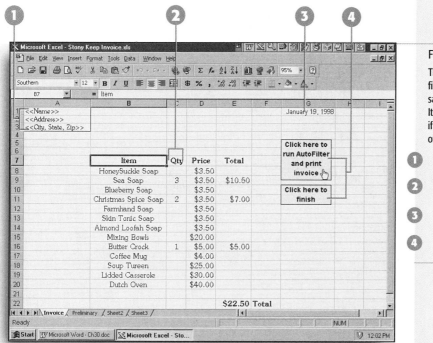

FIGURE 30.1

This invoice is designed to be filled out and printed, but not saved as individual Excel files. It could be saved as a template if you wanted to keep a copy of each separate invoice.

1 Enter customer information

2 Enter item quantities

3 Automatic current date

4 Run macros by clicking

After you type quantities for each item ordered, click the upper text box. Its assigned macro activates AutoFilter, filters the table for nonblanks in the Qty column, and then sends the page to the printer (Figure 30.2 shows a sample invoice in print preview). The macro is edited to print two copies, one for the customer and one for the business.

After the invoice is sent to the printer, click the lower text box. Its assigned macro removes the AutoFilter and deletes the data in the Qty column, so the invoice worksheet is ready for another order.

The invoice is not designed so that each individual invoice is saved electronically because for many small businesses with small hard drives that's impractical; instead, paper invoices are kept in file cabinets.

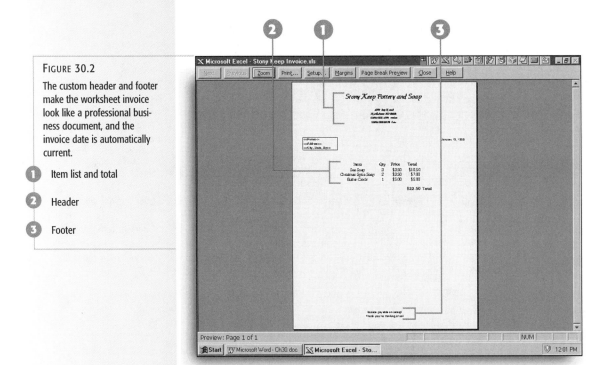

FIGURE 30.2

The custom header and footer make the worksheet invoice look like a professional business document, and the invoice date is automatically current.

① Item list and total

② Header

③ Footer

Setting Up the Invoice Worksheet

First, set up your invoice with all the product entries, formulas, and formatting that's needed to make the printed invoice look professional.

Create the invoice worksheet

1. Open a new workbook, and save it with an appropriate name.

2. Create a custom header and footer for the invoice:

   • Enter your business name, address, and phone number in the header.

   • Format the header text with eye-catching font and font sizes.

   • Enter appropriate business text in the footer, such as `Invoice due and payable on receipt` and `Thank you for your order!`.

3. Make worksheet entries as shown in Figure 30.3.

- The entries in the upper-left corner of the worksheet are placeholders, to remind you to enter the customer's name and address. I placed a border around this group of cells so that the customer information would be visually set apart in the printed page (the worksheet gridlines won't be printed).

- In cell G1, enter =today() so that the current date is always shown when you fill out and print the invoice.

- Enter an items list in the middle range, and include columns for Item, Qty, Price, and Total.

  A short list of mock data is enough to get the invoice set up; you can add lots of items and prices after the invoice is finished and functional.

  You move this list around later to make it look good on the printed page, but cell B7 is a good starting point for the upper-left corner of your list.

Be creative

Remember, I'm showing you how I created my invoice solution; feel free to alter these steps to make your project unique and personal.

FIGURE 30.3

Rows 1 through 6 are formatted as Arial, 10-point font to distinguish them visually from the more important items and totals list. The items list is formatted Southern, 12-point font.

1 This is a Full Screen view

4. Enter the formulas for the item totals. I entered the formula `=IF(ISBLANK(Qty),"",Qty*Price)` in cell E8 and used AutoFill to copy it down the list.

- The item totals are calculated by multiplying the Price column label by the Qty column label in the `Qty*Price` portion of the formula.

- The item total is nested in an IF formula that reads "If the Qty value is blank, then show nothing, otherwise multiply the Qty value by the Price value". This prevents the invoice from displaying extra zeroes. It isn't necessary, but it's a nice touch.

5. Enter a total sum for the ordered items with the Sum function. Use AutoSum on the Standard toolbar to enter it quickly. Be sure the summed range includes all the cells in the Total column. (Figure 30.4 shows a sample item total formula and the list total formula.)

6. Add any other formulas you want, such as tax and shipping, below the list total.

7. Take a look at the invoice in Print Preview; it should look similar to the one shown in Figure 30.5. If yours looks unbalanced, show the margins, rearrange column widths and margin lines to fix it, and then return to Normal view.

SEE ALSO

➤ *To learn about using labels in formulas, see page 181.*

➤ *To learn more about the TODAY( ) function, see page 176.*

➤ *To learn more about nested IF functions, see page 174.*

Automate the Invoice with Macros

Now you can add the macros that turn this invoice into an efficient business solution, and if you have lots of orders waiting to be filled, these macros can save you considerable time.

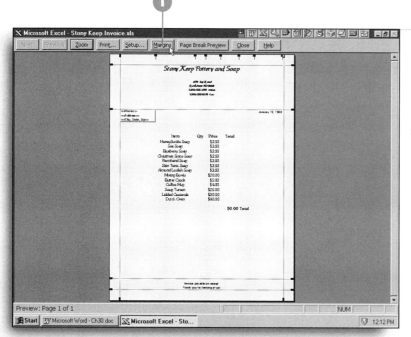

FIGURE 30.4

Leave a row between the list and the final total, or the final total may be hidden when the list is filtered.

FIGURE 30.5

Your invoice ought to look similar to this one thus far. Feel free to move margins and resize columns to make it look good.

1 Margins

Macro warning

When you open a workbook that contains macros, even your own, you're warned that macros can contain viruses—and it's quite possible, if your workbook has been in someone else's computer. These macros, however, are your own, and they're safe.

Oops, it's printing

After you click the Print button, Excel attempts to print the invoice page, but you don't need it printed. If your printer is on, it's printed. If you get a message complaining that your printer isn't on, click Cancel to stop the print process and get rid of the message. It doesn't matter whether you click Cancel before or after you stop recording because the macro records the Print command but not the Cancel command.

Create the macros that automate the invoice

1. Start the macro recorder (on the **Tools** menu, select **Macro**, and click **Record New Macro**).

2. Give the macro a name like FilterAndPrint.

3. Store the macro in **This Workbook**.

4. Click **OK**, and record the following steps.

5. Click the Item column label (cell B7 in my example).

   This step makes the macro start by selecting that cell so that AutoFilter can locate the list.

6. On the **Data** menu, select **Filter**, and click **AutoFilter**.

7. In the Qty column, click the filter arrow and click **(NonBlanks)**.

8. On the Standard toolbar, click Print. 🖨

9. On the Stop Recording toolbar, click Stop Recording. ■

   The macro recorder stops recording, and your worksheet is filtered (the list is hidden by the filter because there aren't any entries in the Qty column).

10. Start the macro recorder again (see step 1) to record the clean-up macro. Name it Finish, store it in **This Workbook**, and click **OK**.

11. Click the Item column label.

    You want the macro to start there, even if you've clicked elsewhere in the worksheet between macros.

12. Turn off the AutoFilter (on the **Data** menu, select **Filter**, and then click **AutoFilter**).

13. Select the cells in the Qty column, and press Delete.

    You can select as many cells below the column label as you want, but *don't* select the column label. If your list of items grows longer later, you can edit the macro to change the selected range.

    It doesn't matter that there's no data to be deleted right now because you're only recording steps for the macro.

14. Stop recording (on the Stop Recording toolbar, click Stop Recording).

Editing the Macro

The macro recorder recorded a default print setting of one copy, but I want to print two copies (one for the customer and one for my files). I edit the macro to change the number of copies it prints.

Inspect and edit your macros

1. On the **Tools** menu, select **Macro**, and click **Macros**.

The Macro dialog box appears (shown in Figure 30.6).

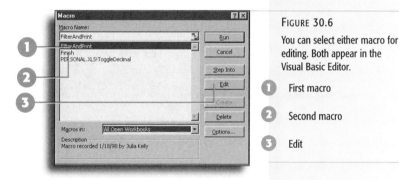

You always have another way

Another way to control the number of copies is to record the macro by opening **File**, selecting **Print**, and setting the **Number of Copies** to 2.

FIGURE 30.6

You can select either macro for editing. Both appear in the Visual Basic Editor.

❶ First macro

❷ Second macro

❸ Edit

2. Click either macro name and click **Edit**.

The Visual Basic Editor opens to your two macros (as shown in Figure 30.7).

3. In the last line of the FilterAndPrint macro (see Figure 30.7), where it reads Copies:=1, change the number 1 to 2 (it should read Copies:=2).

This change makes the macro print two copies instead of the default single copy.

4. Close the Visual Basic Editor (click its Close button).

5. Save your workbook.

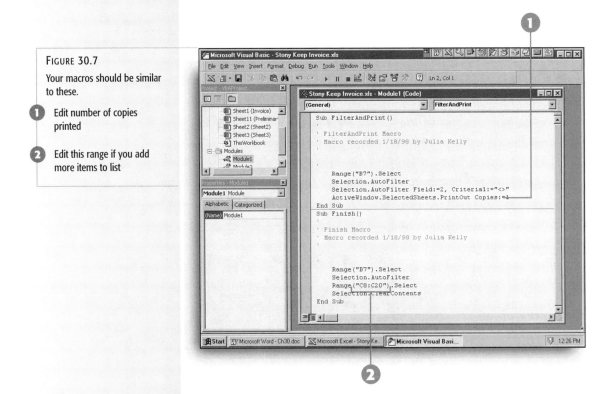

FIGURE 30.7

Your macros should be similar to these.

1 Edit number of copies printed

2 Edit this range if you add more items to list

Make the Macros Handy

Macros in a worksheet are timesavers only if they are easy for anyone who uses the worksheet to find and run them. Of course, you can add them to menus and toolbar buttons, but these macros are intended to be limited to this workbook, so it's not useful to have them taking up space on a menu or toolbar. Fortunately, you can run macros from graphical objects in a worksheet, which makes them constantly available, but only in the workbook where they're stored. If you assign your macros to text boxes, you can run and explain each macro with its own graphical object.

Add text boxes to run the macros

1. Display the Drawing toolbar.

2. On the invoice sheet, create two text boxes similar to the ones in Figure 30.8.

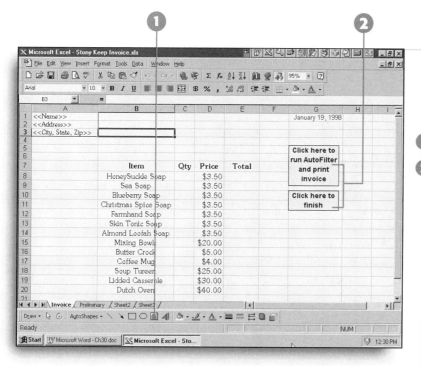

FIGURE 30.8

Text boxes are convenient because they can contain instructions, but you can use other graphic objects instead.

1 Text box

2 Formatted text boxes

3. Arrange the text boxes the way you want them on the worksheet.

4. Select both text boxes (press Shift and click both), and then double-click the border on one of them.

Double-clicking the border selects the object. Double-clicking inside the text box selects the text for editing.

The Format Object dialog box appears (shown in Figure 30.9).

5. On the **Properties** tab, click the **Don't move or size with cells** option, clear the **Print object** check box, and click **OK**.

Setting these properties prevents the text boxes from appearing on the printed invoice pages and from moving or stretching when the list is filtered.

6. Click the worksheet to deselect the text boxes.

7. Right-click the border on the top text box, and click **Assign Macro**.

I can't select any cells!

If you've been playing with graphic objects and you suddenly can't select any cells, click the Select Objects button on the Drawing toolbar to turn it off.

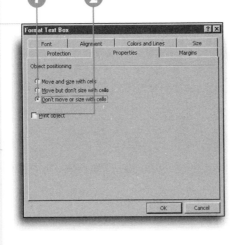

FIGURE 30.9

The Format Object dialog box applies your formatting choices to all selected objects.

 Click option

Clear check box

Okay, now how do I select it?

From here on out, if you need to select the text box to move it or edit it, either right-click it, or press Ctrl while you click it.

---

8. In the Assign Macro dialog box, click the **FilterAndPrint** macro name and click **OK**.

The macro is assigned to the text box. When you point to the text box, the mouse pointer becomes a small pointing hand, and if you click the text box, the macro runs.

9. Repeat steps 7 and 8 to assign the Finish macro to the lower text box.

That's it! To test your invoice and macros, type a few entries in the Qty column, click the first text box, and click the second text box to finish up the invoice process. (If your printer is turned on, two pages are printed.)

SEE ALSO

➤ *For more information on recording macros, see page 490.*

➤ *For more information on editing a macro after you've recorded it, see page 494.*

➤ *For more information on creating text boxes on a worksheet, see page 524.*

Theatre Seating

This project was a solution for a local community theatre that wanted to trade in their old plastic-and-grease-pencil reservations board for an electronic system. Not only are the entries more legible, but the reservations data can be tracked for other purposes by sending the Excel data to an Access database. The project consists of two different worksheets: a seating chart, with one copy for each show, and a single seat list that compiles all the names, phone numbers, and reserved seat numbers from all the seating charts in a neat list. (Figure 30.10 shows one of the seating charts.)

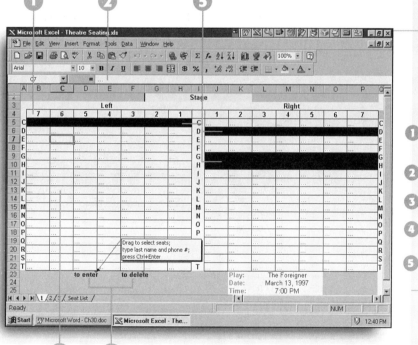

Oh, yeah, like I really need this.

I sincerely doubt that many of you will ever need this particular project, but I want to fire your imaginations about what kinds of unusual and creative approaches you can take with Excel in your own work. I'm sure many of you will get much more creative than this.

FIGURE 30.10

This seating chart is complex because of the way the theatre is laid out. I show you how to build a simpler example of this project.

1️⃣ Worksheet is formatted to resemble the specific theatre

2️⃣ Read full entry here

3️⃣ "..." keeps seat visually open

4️⃣ Comments with instructions

5️⃣ These seats are nonexistent in this theatre

How the Seating Chart Works

To use the seating chart, drag to select a group of seats for a patron, depending on how many seats they want and where they want to sit. Then type the patron's last name and phone number, and press Ctrl+Enter to enter the identical data in all the selected cells (which fills the seats). That's it; the Seat List worksheet automatically records your entries.

The entries in the Seating Chart aren't entirely legible unless you click a cell and read its entry in the Formula bar because each cell's entry is truncated by the entry in the cell to its right. You want to keep the entries truncated so that you can see at a glance which seats are still open. To keep a seat open, fill it with the entry .... To cancel seat reservations, replace the patron data with the ... entry in each seat. (Figure 30.11 shows the Seat List worksheet, where seats and patron information are automatically recorded in a more familiar format.)

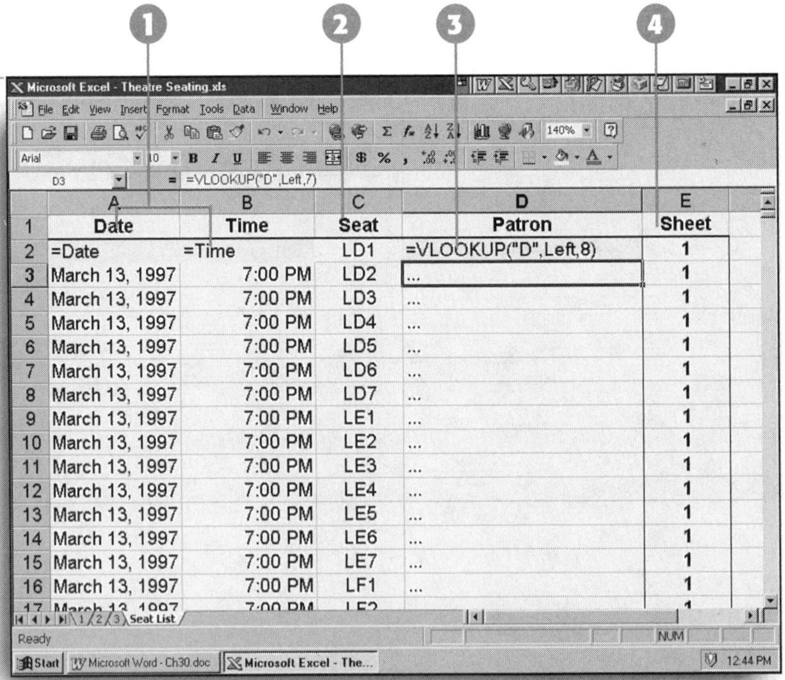

FIGURE 30.11

It's easier to read names and numbers in this list, in case the theatre needs to contact a patron. (I zoomed this worksheet to show you the formulas more clearly.)

 Show date/time

2 Seat number

3 Formula automatically looks up seat data in a named range

4 Quick reminder of the data source

Creating the Seating Chart Workbook

The fully functional seating chart I created for my local theatre (and showed you earlier) is a bit complex because most real-life projects are complex. I show you a simplified version, however, of how I combined Excel's features to make the project work. (The point of this demonstration is to show you how you can use Excel to do more than filter and subtotal lists of numbers.)

Create a simple version of this project

1. Create a worksheet that looks like the one in Figure 30.12.

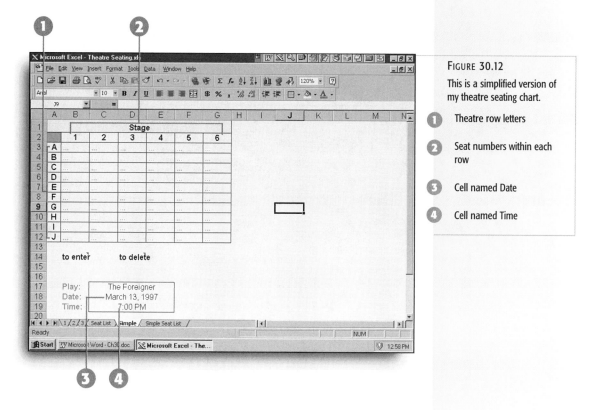

FIGURE 30.12

This is a simplified version of my theatre seating chart.

1 Theatre row letters

2 Seat numbers within each row

3 Cell named Date

4 Cell named Time

2. Select the range of seat cells and name them **Seats,** and then name the **Date** cell and the **Time** cell.

In this example, I've named the range A3:G12 "Seats". My lookup formula needs the row labels in column A, but doesn't need the column labels in row 2.

3. Add any helpful comments you might need (especially if someone else uses the workbook).

4. Save the workbook.

5. On a different worksheet, create the table shown in Figure 30.13.

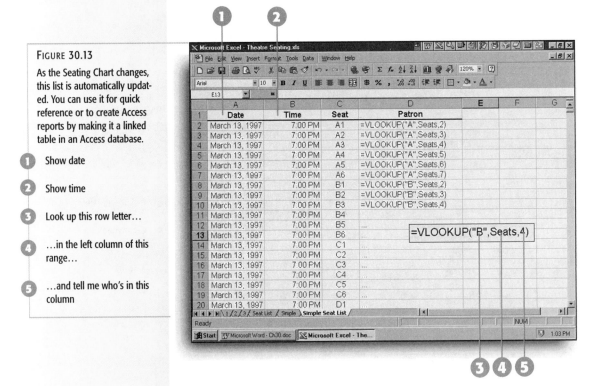

FIGURE 30.13

As the Seating Chart changes, this list is automatically updated. You can use it for quick reference or to create Access reports by making it a linked table in an Access database.

1 Show date

2 Show time

3 Look up this row letter…

4 …in the left column of this range…

5 …and tell me who's in this column

I've shown the formulas I used to build this list. They all use named cells and ranges on the Seating Chart worksheet.

6. Enter the formulas that look up data in the Seating Chart.

My VLOOKUP formula looks up a value (the row letter) in the leftmost column of a named range ("Seats") and returns the value from the column I specify (the seat number).

7. Enter some names in the Seating Chart to test your Seat List. Your VLOOKUP formulas may need some tweaking to be sure they all look up what you intend.

Figure 30.14 shows the completed Seating Chart and Seat List side by side in two windows so that I can test them easily.

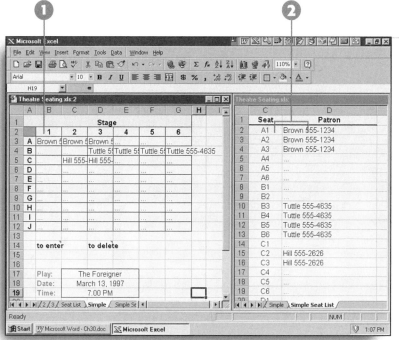

FIGURE 30.14

I can test the Seat List easily by using two windows to view my formulas and source data side by side.

1 Seat and patron

2 Seat and patron

That's it. To use the Seating Chart for several performances, create a copy of the finished worksheet for each performance. Change only the data that's different for each performance. (You need to check, and possibly change, the range names on each seating chart.) Add more VLOOKUP formulas to the Seat List to look up data from each Seating Chart.

SEE ALSO

➤ *For more information on writing a VLOOKUP formula, see page 170.*

➤ *For more information on naming cells and ranges, see page 182.*

➤ *For more information on using named cells and ranges in formulas, see page 186.*

➤ *For more information on copying worksheets, see page 76.*

Creative Charts

Create a bar chart that shows data with long labels

Create a stacked column chart that combines specific sets of data in each column

Creative Approaches to Charting

The ChartWizard is a highly capable charting engine, but occasionally you may need to display data that requires a little more creativity than you find in the ChartWizard alone. This chapter contains a couple of creative approaches to charting that might come in handy for you, but more than that, I want to get you thinking about how you can use the ChartWizard in combination with other Excel features to get exactly what you need.

I'm going to show you two real-life solutions to clients' data display questions: a chart display that combines a transparent chart and the worksheet underneath it and a stacked column chart that relies on a special data layout to compare information.

Giff's Chart

A client of mine (his name is Giff, and I named this chart after him) did a survey of company employees, averaged the responses, and wanted to chart them on a bar chart that showed the questions alongside the bars. The problem was that the ChartWizard had difficulty showing all the data just the way he wanted it displayed, so I tried combining an embedded chart with the worksheet beneath it. (The result is shown in Figure 31.1. These aren't real survey questions.)

Several ways could probably have been used to achieve the result my client wanted; however, the way I'm going to show you is meant to remove any perceived limitations on what you're able to do with a chart. But be warned: when you get creative like this, it takes more time and tweaking to get what you want.

Figure 31.2 shows the data with which I started. Next I show you how I created the finished chart. (My explanation isn't very detailed, because I want you to experiment to find out what you can do.)

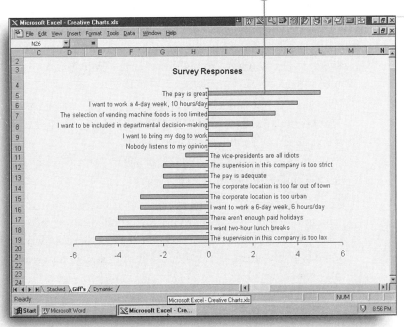

FIGURE 31.1

The data labels are actually entries in the worksheet beneath the chart, and the chart background is transparent.

1 Source data sorted to show bar lengths from high to low

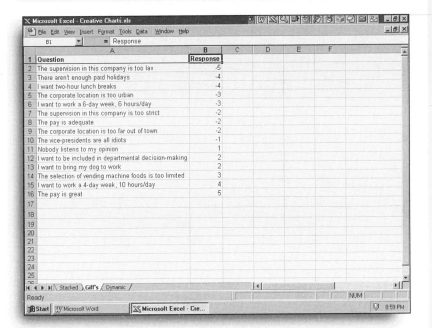

FIGURE 31.2

The data is simple, but I need to show the entire survey question, legibly, next to each marker in the chart.

To create Giff's chart

1. Sort the data so that the bar chart markers make a symmetrical picture, with marker values sorted from high to low.

2. Copy the data and paste it to another location in the worksheet, where you want to build the chart. (Copy the values, too, so you can re-sort them.)

   The chart is not connected to the values in the worksheet that become the data labels. This is a drawback, but it is worth it to get the finished chart I want.

3. Sort the pasted data in the opposite order and delete the values (as shown in Figure 31.3).

   You have to re-sort the data because a bar chart presents data in the opposite order from which it's laid out in the source table. (This is one of those little facts that isn't written down anywhere, but you figure it out when you start to play with charts.)

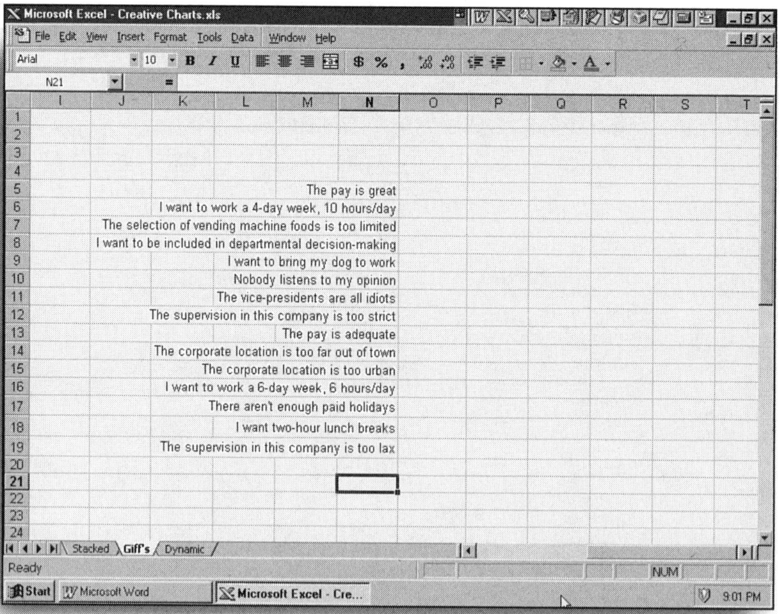

FIGURE 31.3

To use this technique, you need to sort the label data so that it matches up with the bar values in the chart.

4. Put the labels with positive values in one worksheet column, and right-align the cells.

5. Move the labels with negative values one column to the right, and left-align those cells (as shown in Figure 31.4).

6. Select all the label cells, and format them with a **Vertical** alignment of **Center** (on the Format Cells dialog box, **Alignment** tab).

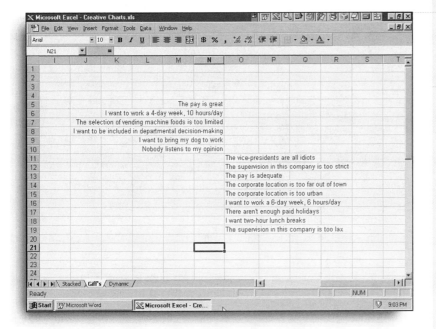

FIGURE 31.4
This label layout makes more sense after the chart is laid over it.

7. Create a bar chart from the source data.

- In step 2 of the ChartWizard, put the series in **Columns**.

- In step 3 of the ChartWizard, remove the legend and gridlines.

The finished chart looks like the one in Figure 31.5. Next I format it to make it work with the worksheet labels.

FIGURE 31.5

This chart still needs a lot of work to be what I want..

1 Remove axis labels

2 Leave tick marks

3 Make chart transparent

4 Line up markers with worksheet labels

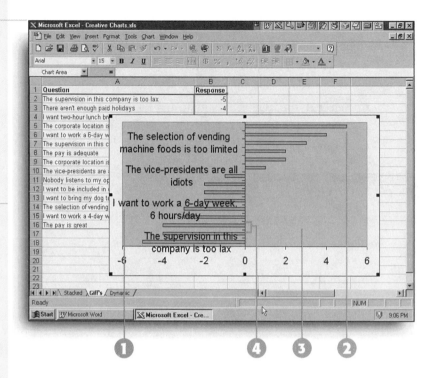

Draw attention to specific bars

You can make an individual bar stand out from the rest by changing its color or adding a striped pattern. Click the bar twice (not a double-click) to select it, double-click the selected bar, and change its color and pattern on the **Patterns** tab in the Format Data Point dialog box.

8. Double-click the central axis, and in the Format Axis dialog box, click the **Patterns** tab.

9. In the **Patterns** tab, under **Tick mark labels**, click **None**, and then click **OK**.

The axis labels are removed, but the tick marks remain.

10. Double-click the Chart Area. On the **Patterns** tab, under **Border**, select **None;** and under **Area**, select **None** and then click **OK**.

11. Double-click the Plot Area. On the Patterns tab, under **Border**, select **None;** and under **Area**, select **None** and then click **OK**.

This makes the Chart Area and Plot Area transparent and borderless, so the markers and axes float on the worksheet. You can't see through the chart yet because the chart object is still selected (see Figure 31.6). When you click the worksheet, however, you see the transparent chart overlaid.

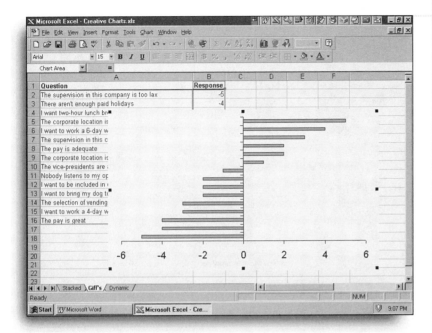

FIGURE 31.6

What remains is to line up the worksheet labels with the chart markers.

12. Right-click the Chart area and click **Fo̱rmat Chart Area**.

13. On the **Properties** tab, click the **Do̱n't move or size with cells** option and then click **OK**.

This keeps the chart from resizing when you resize the worksheet rows beneath it.

14. Resize the chart to be large on the worksheet and then click in a worksheet cell.

Because you can't see the worksheet cells beneath the chart when the chart is selected, you leave the chart in one place and move the column and row borders beneath it to line up the labels and markers.

15. Drag the column border nearest the central axis to line it up precisely under the center axis.

16. Select and drag each row border to line it up with a tick mark. This makes each vertically centered label line up with its marker.

17. When all the dragging is done, turn off the worksheet gridlines (on the **To̱ols** menu, click **O̱ptions**; and on the **View** tab, clear the **G̱ridlines** check box).

Try a rounded border

Another nice touch is a round-cornered border for an invisible chart. Instead of removing the Chart Area border, click the **Round corners** check box and change the border color and line weight to add more visual interest.

If your chart doesn't look like the one in Figure 31.7, keep tweaking it until you get what you want.

FIGURE **31.7**

Voilà! Now play with this and see what else you can do.

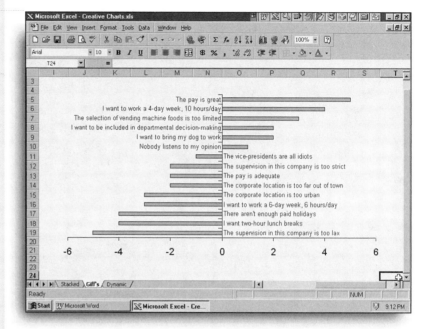

This chart is an example of the creative things you can do if you don't limit yourself to the built-in features in Excel.

SEE ALSO

➤ To learn more about creating a chart, see page 347.

➤ To learn more about sorting data, see page 247.

Stacked Columns

Another client had a quick question: How can I show income versus expenses in the same chart and in a stacked column format so that one column shows all the income and the other column shows all the expenses? The answer is shown in Figure 31.8.

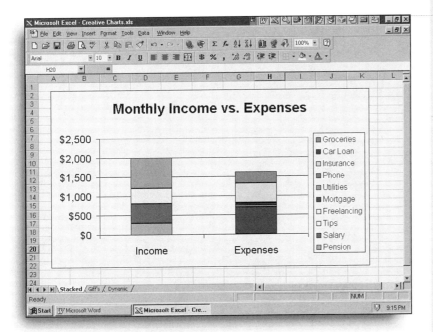

FIGURE 31.8

This is a neat, efficient way to compare income vs. expenses graphically. It would also work for comparing expenses in different corporate departments.

This is a pretty simple solution that relies on the layout of the chart's source data.

Figure 31.9 shows the data layout. The data for each stacked column is in its own category. It's not a complex solution; rather, it's one of those simple ideas that can be frustratingly elusive until someone points it out.

This short chapter is not meant to be a comprehensive treatise on creative charting, just enough to inspire you to try new approaches with your own data.

SEE ALSO
➤ *To learn more about creating a chart, see page 347.*

FIGURE 31.9

Changing the source data layout can change your chart rad-
ically. I charted the series in
rows in step 2 of the
ChartWizard.

1   Income stacked column

2   Expenses stacked column

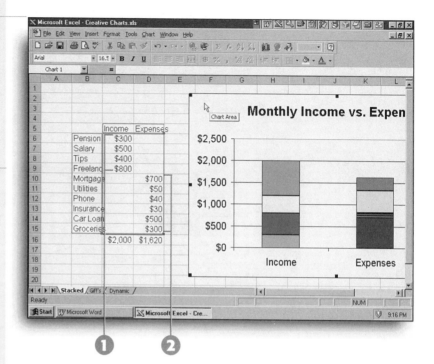

Glossary

absolute reference A cell reference that specifies the exact address of a cell. An absolute reference takes the form A1, B3, and so on.

activate (chart) Select a chart for editing or formatting. To activate a chart sheet, click the sheet tab. To activate a chart object on a worksheet, click the chart.

active cell The selected cell. You can enter or edit data in the active cell.

active sheet The sheet that you are currently working on. When a sheet is active, the name on the sheet tab is bold.

active window The window that you are currently using or that is currently selected. Only one window can be active at a time, and keystrokes and commands affect the active window.

add-in Files that can be installed to add commands and functions to Excel.

address The location of a cell on a sheet. The cell address consists of a column address and a row address, such as F12, in which F is the sixth column on the

sheet and 12 is the twelfth row on the sheet.

alignment The horizontal position of text within the width of a column.

argument Information you supply to a function for calculation. An argument can be a value, reference, name, formula, or another function.

arrow keys The up arrow, down arrow, left arrow, and right arrow keys (and diagonal keys on some keyboards) that are used to move the insertion point or to select from a menu or a list of options.

ascending A method of ordering a group of items from lowest to highest, such as from A to Z.

AutoFill A feature that enables you to create a series of incremental or fixed values on a worksheet by dragging the fill handle with the mouse.

AutoFormat (for charts) A combination of chart type, chart subtype, and other formatting characteristics, such as patterns and font, that you can quickly apply to a chart to change its appearance. In addition to Excel's built-in AutoFormats, you can create your own custom (user-defined) AutoFormats.

axes   Borders on the plot area that provide a frame of reference for measurement or comparison. On most charts, data values are plotted along the Y axis and categories are plotted along the X axis. On a typical column chart, the X axis is the horizontal axis and the Y axis is the vertical axis. Pie and doughnut charts have no axes, radar charts have a single central axis, and scatter charts have two value axes. Some 3-D charts have three axes (X, Y, and Z) for values, categories, and series.

border   A line that goes around text, cells, or tables. You can assign a variety of line styles and colors to a border.

cell   The intersection of a column and a row.

cell reference   Also known as the cell address. The set of column and row coordinates that identify a cell location on a worksheet.

chart   A graphical representation of worksheet data. A chart can be a chart object (located on a worksheet) or placed on a chart sheet (located on a separate sheet). Charts are linked to the data from which they were created and are automatically updated when worksheet changes are made.

chart area   The entire background in the chart, just outside the plot area. When the chart area is selected, uniform font characteristics can be applied to all text in the chart.

chart object   A chart located on a worksheet. A chart object behaves like other worksheet objects.

chart sheet   A sheet in a workbook containing a chart. When a chart sheet is active, the chart on the chart sheet is automatically activated.

chart type   A chart type is a specific kind of chart, such as area, bar, column, line, pie, doughnut, radar, XY (scatter), 3-D area, 3-D bar, 3-D column, 3-D line, 3-D pie, or 3-D surface. Each chart type has at least one subtype that's a variation of the original chart type.

ChartWizard   A series of dialog boxes that guides you through the steps required to create a new chart (or modify settings for an existing chart).

check box   A box that indicates with a check mark whether a feature is activated.

circular reference   A formula that refers to its own cell, either directly or indirectly.

Clipboard   A temporary holding area for data that is cut or copied. The data remains on the Clipboard until you cut or copy other data. You can paste, cut, or copy data from the Clipboard to another location, worksheet, workbook, or application.

collapse Click the small minus symbol next to a group heading to hide the items in that group.

column A vertical range of cells. Each column is identified by a unique letter or letter combination (for example, A, Z, CF, and so on).

column heading The label at the top of a column.

comment A note that explains, identifies, or comments on the information in a specific cell or range of cells.

comparison criteria A set of search conditions used to filter data. Comparison criteria can be a series of characters that you want matched, such as apple, or an expression, such as >300.

comparison operator A mathematical symbol used to compare two values (for example, =, >, <, =>, =<, <>).

constant A cell value that does not start with an equal sign. For example, the date, the value 345, and text are all constants.

copy To duplicate information from one location to another, either within a workbook, to another workbook, or to a file in another program.

cursor Also known as the insertion point. The flashing vertical line that shows where text is entered (for example, in a cell during in-cell editing).

custom sort order A non-alpha, non-numeric sort order, such as Low, Medium, High or Monday, Tuesday,

Wednesday. You can use one of the built-in custom sort orders, or create your own using the Tools, Options, Custom Lists dialog tab.

cut To remove selected information from one location so that you can paste it to another location within the workbook or to another workbook or to a file in another program.

data form A dialog box that you can use to see, change, add, and delete records from a list or database, or to find specific records based on criteria that you specify. You can display the data form for a list or database by clicking Data, Form.

data label A label that provides additional information about a data marker in a chart. Data labels can be applied to a single marker, an entire data series, or all data markers in a chart. They may be formatted and moved, but not sized.

data marker A column, bar, area, dot, slice, or other symbol in a chart that represents a single data point or value originating from a worksheet cell. Related data markers in a chart comprise a data series.

data point An individual value plotted in a chart that originates from a single cell in a worksheet. Data points are represented by data markers.

data region A range of cells containing data and bounded by empty cells.

data series A group of related data points in a chart that originates from a single worksheet row or column. Each data series in a chart is distinguished by a unique color or pattern. You can plot one or more data series in a chart (a pie chart is limited to one series).

database A range of cells containing data that is related to a particular subject or purpose. The first row in the database contains field names. Each additional row in the database is one record, and each column in the database is one field. In Excel, a database is also known as a list.

default A predefined setting that is built into a program and used when you do not specify an alternative setting. For example, a worksheet might have a default font setting of Arial, 10-point text.

delimiter A character, such as a tab, space, or comma, that separates fields of data in a text file.

dependents Cells containing formulas that refer to the active cell.

descending order Highest to lowest, such as Z to A or 10 to 1.

destination area The range of cells that you select to hold the summarized data when using the **Consolidate** command. The destination area can be on the same worksheet as the source data, or it can be on a different worksheet.

dialog box A box that appears when you choose a command that requires additional information. It may include areas in which you type text or numbers and view or change settings for options related to the command. If you don't understand an option, right-click it, and click the **What's This** button that appears.

drag-and-drop A mouse technique for directly moving or copying a block of information from one location to another. To drag an object, position the pointer over the object, hold down the mouse button while you move the mouse, and then release the mouse button when the object is positioned where you want it.

drop-down list box A single box with uneditable text and an arrow, paired with a drop-down list that appears when the user selects the arrow.

edit To add, delete, or change information, such as text or graphics.

embed To insert an object from a source program into a destination document. An embedded object maintains a connection to its original application so that you can open the original application and edit the embedded object by double-clicking it. *See also* **link**.

embedded object Data (such as text or graphics) that you can edit using the full resources of its source program while it is in a destination document. *See also* **embed**.

expand To click the plus symbol next to a group heading to display the items in the group.

export   The process of converting and saving a file to be used in a another program. *See also* **import**.

external reference   In a formula, a reference to a cell, range, or named area on a different worksheet.

field   In a list or database, a column of data that contains a particular type of information, such as Last Name, Phone Number, or Quantity.

file   A document that you create or save with a unique filename. In Excel, a file is a workbook.

file format   The format, such as text, Word, dBASE, FoxPro, and so on, of the file in which data is stored.

fill handle   The small black square in the lower-right corner of the selected cell or range (visible only if Allow cell drag and drop is activated). When you position the mouse pointer over the fill handle, the pointer changes to a black cross. Drag the fill handle to copy the contents to the adjacent cells or to create a series. Dragging the fill handle with the right mouse button displays a shortcut menu.

filter   A set of criteria that you can apply to records to show specific records. The records that match your criteria are listed, and all others are hidden.

floating palette   A palette that can be dragged away from its toolbar. *See also* **palette**.

floating toolbar   A toolbar that appears in a window with a title bar, stays on top of the other windows, and is not fixed in position.

folder   A container in which workbooks, other program files, and other folders are stored on your computer disks. Folders can help you organize your documents by grouping them into categories, as you would organize paper documents into file folders.

font   A collection of letters, numbers, and special characters that share a consistent and identifiable typeface, such as Courier or Times New Roman.

footer   Text that appears at the bottom of every printed page. *See also* **header**.

format   The way text and cells appear on a page. Types of formats include character, number, cell border, color, and more. Styles can contain any combination of these formats.

formula   An equation that produces a new value from existing values. A formula always begins with an equal sign (=).

Formula bar   A bar near the top of the Excel window that you can use to enter or edit values and formulas in cells or charts. Displays the formula or constant value from the active cell or object.

free-floating label   A label that's not linked to a chart object and can be moved anywhere on the chart.

function   A built-in formula that uses a series of values (arguments) to perform an operation and returns the result of the operation. You can use the Function Wizard to select a function and enter it into a cell.

goal seek   A tool for finding the input value that a formula requires to return a specific result. You can enter your goal value, select the variable that you want to change, and then let Excel find the value that returns your goal.

graphic object   A line or shape (button, text box, ellipse, rectangle, arc, picture) you draw using the tools on the toolbar, or a picture you paste into Excel.

gridlines   Lines that Excel displays on a worksheet to visually separate columns and rows into cells. By default, Excel doesn't print the worksheet gridlines, but you can choose to print them.

gridlines (chart)   Lines in a chart that extend from the tick marks on an axis across the plot area. Gridlines come in various forms: horizontal, vertical, major, minor, and various combinations. They make it easier to view and evaluate data in a chart.

group   In an outline or pivot table, detail rows or columns that are subordinate to a summary row or column.

handles   Small black squares located around the perimeter of selected graphic objects, chart items, or chart text. By dragging the handles, you can move, copy, or size the selected object, chart item, or chart text.

header   Text that appears at the top of every printed page. *See also* **footer**.

icon   A small graphic that represents an object, such as a program, a disk drive, or a document. When you double-click an icon, the item that the icon represents opens.

import   The process of converting and opening a file that was created in a another program. *See also* **export**.

insert   To enter text, data, or a graphic into a document, cell, or dialog box. You can also insert cells, rows, and columns into a worksheet. You insert information at the insertion point. *See also* **insertion point**.

insertion point   Also known as the cursor. A flashing vertical line that shows the text entry point. It appears in a cell or text box when you click the mouse pointer there.

installing an add-in   Copying the add-in program from the CD-ROM onto your hard drive so that it becomes available to a main program such as Excel. *See also* **loading an add-in**.

label   Text you provide to identify data.

landscape   The horizontal orientation of a page; opposite of *portrait*, or vertical, orientation.

legend   A box containing legend entries and keys that helps to identify the data series or categories in a chart. The legend keys, to the left of each legend entry, show the colors assigned to the data markers in the chart.

link   A data connection between a dependent worksheet (the worksheet that uses the data) and a source worksheet (the worksheet in which the original data resides). The dependent worksheet is updated whenever the data changes in the source worksheet. You can link graphics, text, and other types of information between a source file and a dependent file. *See also* **embed**.

list   A range of cells containing data that is related to a particular subject or purpose. In Excel, the terms *list* and *database* are used interchangeably.

loading an add-in   Activating an installed add-in so that a main program, such as Excel, can use the features provided by the add-in. *See also* **installing an add-in**.

macro   A sequence of VBA commands that you can record and then run to automate your work. A macro can be assigned to a shortcut key, button, or object for easy use.

marquee   *See* **moving border**.

mixed reference   In a formula, a combination of a relative reference and an absolute reference. A mixed reference takes the form $A1 or A$1, where A is the column cell address and 1 is the row cell address. For example, the mixed reference $A1 always refers to column A, regardless of the position of the cell containing the formula. The row address 1 refers to the row in relation to the cell containing the formula. If the cell containing the formula is copied down one row, the mixed reference $A1 changes to $A2.

move   To transfer information from one location to another, either within a workbook, to another workbook, or to a file in another program.

moving border   A moving dotted line that surrounds a cell or range of cells. For example, a moving border appears around a cell or range that has been cut or copied, or around a cell or range you are inserting into a formula.

name   A unique identifier you create to refer to a cell, a range, or a formula. When you use names in a formula, the formula is easier to read and maintain than a formula containing cell references.

nonadjacent selection   A selection of two or more cells or ranges that do not touch each other.

Normal style   The style applied to all cells on sheets until another style is applied.

Office Assistant   A truly annoying Help program that replaces the very useful Answer Wizard from Office 95. You might like it, and if you do, you can change its interface to any of several different characters. (If you don't like it, you can uninstall it.)

OLE (object linking and embedding)   A technology for exchanging data between different programs. Drag-and-drop and linking and embedding are examples of OLE features. *See also* **link** *and* **embed**.

open database connectivity (ODBC)   A Driver Manager and a set of ODBC drivers that enable applications to use Structured Query Language (SQL) as a standard language to access data created and stored in another format, such as FoxPro or Access.

option button   A button for selecting one of a group of mutually exclusive options.

options   The choices in a dialog box.

outline   A summary report of worksheet data that contains several nested levels of detail data, and summary data for each level of detail. Users can change the view of the outline to show or hide as much detail as they want.

palette   A dialog box containing choices for color and other special effects. A palette appears when you click a toolbar button, such as Border or Fill Color. *See also* **floating palette**.

pane   Panes enable you to view different areas of a large worksheet simultaneously. You can horizontally or vertically split a window into two panes, or you can split a window both vertically and horizontally to display four panes.

paste   To insert cut or copied text into a new location.

paste area   The destination for data that has been cut or copied.

path   The location of a file within a computer file system. The path indicates the filename preceded by the disk drive, folder, and subfolders in which the file is stored. If the file is on another computer on a network, the path also includes the computer name.

personal macro workbook   A hidden workbook that contains macros which are available every time you start Excel. When you record a macro, you can choose to record it into your personal macro workbook.

pivot table   An interactive worksheet table that enables you to summarize and analyze data from existing databases, lists, and tables. Use the PivotTable Wizard to specify the database, list, or table that you want to use and to define how you want to arrange the data in the pivot table. After you create a pivot table, you can reorganize the data by dragging fields and items.

pivot table column field   A field that is assigned a column orientation in a pivot table. Items associated with a column field are displayed as column labels.

pivot table data   In a pivot table, the summarized data calculated from the data fields of a source list or table.

pivot table data area   The part of a pivot table that contains summary data. Values in each cell of the data area represent a summary of data from the source records or rows.

pivot table detail item   An item associated with an inner row or column field in a pivot table.

pivot table field A category of data that is derived from a field in a source list or table. For example, the Year field in a source list or database becomes the Year field in a pivot table. Items from the source list or table, such as 1994, 1995, and so on, become subcategories in the pivot table.

pivot table item A subcategory of a pivot table field. Items in a pivot table are derived from unique items in a database field or from unique cells in a list column. In a pivot table, items appear as row, column, or page labels.

pivot table page field A field that is assigned to a page orientation in a pivot table. Items in a page field are displayed one at a time in a pivot table.

pivot table row field A field that is assigned a row orientation in a pivot table. Items associated with a row field are displayed as row labels.

plot area The area of a chart in which data is plotted. In 2-D charts, it is bounded by the axes and encompasses the data markers and gridlines. In 3-D charts, the plot area includes the chart's walls, axes, and tick-mark labels.

portrait A term used to refer to vertical page orientation. The opposite of *landscape*, or horizontal orientation.

precedents Cells that are referred to by the formula in the active cell.

precision The number of digits Excel uses when calculating values. By default, Excel calculates with a maximum of 15 digits of a value (full precision). If **Precision as displayed** is selected (on the **Tools**, **Options**, **Calculation** tab), Excel rounds values to the number of digits displayed on the worksheet before calculating. The **Precision as displayed** setting cannot be undone and applies to all worksheets in the workbook.

preview A view that displays your document as it appears when you print it. Items such as text and graphics appear in their actual positions.

print area An area of a worksheet that is specified to be printed.

print titles Rows or columns that you set to print at the top or left of every page. For example, if you select row 1 for a print title, row 1 is printed at the top of the data on every page. If you select column A for a print title, column A is printed at the left of the data on every page.

program A computer software package, such as a word processor, spreadsheet, presentation designer, or relational database.

query A means of finding exactly the data you want from a data source.

query definition Information that the Query Wizard uses to connect to and determine which data to retrieve from a data source. A query definition can include table names, field names, and criteria. A query definition is sent to a data source for execution in the form of a Structured Query Language (SQL) statement.

range   Two or more cells on a worksheet.

record   A single row in a list or database. The first row of a database usually contains field names, and each additional row in the database is a record. Each record in the database contains the same categories (fields) of data as every other record in the database.

reference   The location of a cell or range of cells on a worksheet, indicated by column letter and row number. For example, B2 and C3:D4 are references. *See also* **address**.

reference type   The type of reference: absolute, relative, or mixed. A relative reference (for example, A1) in a formula indicates the location of the referenced cell relative to the cell containing the formula. An absolute reference (for example, A1) always refers to the exact location of the referenced cell. A mixed reference (for example, $A1; A$1) is half relative and half absolute.

refresh data   Update a pivot table or a query.

relative reference   Specifies the location of a referenced cell in relation to the cell containing the reference. A relative reference takes the form A4, C12, and so on.

result cell   A cell on the worksheet that is recalculated when a new scenario is applied.

row   A horizontal set of cells. Each row is identified by a unique number.

R-squared value   A calculated value that indicates how valid the correlation in a trendline is.

scale   In a chart, the scale determines what values are displayed on an axis, at what intervals the values occur, and where one axis crosses another.

scenario   A named set of input values that you can substitute in a worksheet model to perform what-if analysis.

Scenario Manager   An add-in that enables you to create, view, and summarize scenarios.

scroll bars   The shaded bars along the right side and bottom of the Excel window. With the scroll bars, you can scroll from top to bottom in a long sheet, or from side to side in a wide sheet.

secondary axis   In a chart with more than one series, a secondary axis enables you to plot a series along a different value axis so that you can create two different value scales in the same chart.

select   To highlight a cell or a range of cells on a worksheet, or choose an object or a chart item. The selected cells, objects, or chart items are affected by the next command or action.

shortcut   An object that acts as a pointer to a document, folder, or program. If you double-click the shortcut, the object opens.

shortcut menu   A context-sensitive menu that shows a list of commands relative to a selected item. It appears when you right-click the item.

sort key   The field name or criteria by which you want to sort data.

sort order   A way to arrange data based on value or data type. An ascending sort order sorts text from A to Z, numbers from the smallest negative number to the largest positive number, and dates and times from the earliest to the latest. A descending sort order is the opposite of an ascending sort order, except for blanks, which are always sorted last. If you choose a custom sort order, an ascending sort order is the order in which the items appear in the Sort Options dialog box.

source   The document or program in which the data was originally created.

source data for pivot tables   The list, database, or table used to create a pivot table. Source data can be an Excel list or database, an external data source such as a dBASE or Microsoft Access file, Excel worksheet ranges with labeled rows and columns, or another pivot table.

source worksheet   The worksheet referred to by an external reference formula. The source worksheet contains the value used by the external reference formula.

split bar   The horizontal or vertical line dividing a split worksheet. You can change the position of the split bar by dragging it or remove it by double-clicking it.

status bar   The bar at the bottom of the screen that displays information about the selected command or tool, or an operation in progress.

Structured Query Language (SQL)   A language used for retrieving, updating, and managing data.

style   A named combination of formats that can be applied to a cell or range. If you redefine the style to be a different combination of formats, all cells to that the style was applied automatically change to reflect the new formats. A style can include (or exclude) formats for number, font, alignment, borders, patterns, and protection.

subtotal row   A row that displays one or more subtotals for columns in an Excel list. A list can contain multiple, nested subtotal rows.

summary data   For automatic subtotals and worksheet outlines, the total rows or columns that summarize detail data. Summary data is usually adjacent to and below the detail data.

summary function   The calculation you direct Excel to use when combining source data in a pivot table or a consolidation table or when inserting automatic subtotals in a list or database. Examples of summary functions include Sum, Count, and Average.

table   One or more rows of cells commonly used to display numbers and other items for quick reference and analysis. Items in a table are organized into rows (records) and columns (fields).

template   A workbook that you create and then use as the basis for other, similar workbooks. You can create templates for workbooks, worksheets, and chart sheets.

text box   A rectangular graphic object in which you can type text.

text file   A file that contains only unformatted text information, often as tab-delimited or comma-delimited lists.

tick marks   In a chart, small lines that intersect an axis like divisions on a ruler. Tick marks are part of and can be formatted with an axis.

title bar   The horizontal bar at the top of a window that displays the name of the document or program that appears in that window.

toolbar   A bar on which buttons for commands reside. You can change any toolbar or create new toolbars by adding, deleting, or rearranging buttons. Toolbars can be moved, or docked, at any edge of a program window. *See also* **floating toolbar**.

trendline   A graphical representation of a trend in a data series. Trendlines are used to study problems of prediction, also called regression analysis. Trendlines can be added to data series in 2-D area, bar, column, line, and XY (scatter) chart type groups, and can be formatted.

trendline label   Optional text for a trendline, including either the regression equation or the R-squared value, or both. A trendline label may be formatted and moved, but it cannot be sized.

VBA (Visual Basic for Applications)   A programming language used in Excel and other application programs.

Visual Basic editor   A small program included in Office 97 in which all Visual Basic editing operations take place. It replaces the old Excel Visual Basic module and is pretty much identical to the programming environment for Visual Basic 5.0.

wildcard character   A character (? or *) that stands for one or more other characters in search criteria. Used to find or filter data on a worksheet. An asterisk (*) represents any number of characters. A question mark (?) represents any single character in the same position as the question mark. To search for a literal question mark or asterisk, precede it with a tilde (~). For example, to search for an asterisk, type ~*.

workbook   An Excel file that contains at least one sheet.

worksheet   The primary document you use in Excel to store and manipulate data. A worksheet consists of cells organized into columns and rows, and is always part of a workbook. Several worksheets can appear in one workbook, and you can switch among them easily by clicking their tabs with the mouse.

X axis   On most charts, categories are plotted along the X axis. On a typical column chart, the X axis is the horizontal axis.

XY (scatter) chart   A 2-D chart that has numeric values plotted along both axes rather than values along one axis and categories along the other axis. This type of chart is typically used to analyze scientific data to see whether one set of values is related to another set of values.

Y axis   On most charts, data values are plotted along the Y axis. On a typical column chart, the Y axis is the vertical axis. When a secondary axis is added, it is a secondary Y axis.

Y-intercept   In a chart, the point at which a trendline meets the Y axis. Setting the Y-intercept enables you to change the way data appears in a chart without actually changing the scale of the axis.

Index

D

X-Y-Z